Dr. Bruce Maccabee has written an  intelligent overview
of the UFO phenomenon, which includ... his own
to CIA staff and others from the officia... world. ...
authority and insight by one of the lead... scholi...
field, *The FBI-CIA-UFO Connection* is meticulously research... and
reflects decades of involvement by the author.

Everything in this book is documented fact, presented in a
straightforward, no-nonsense style which is easy to read. Maccabee tells a
riveting story of an unfolding and building UFO reality in conflict with
now-transparent government attempts to explain them away and deny their
possible interplanetary origin. He dispenses with irrelevant and peripheral
material that clog so many other books on the topic, using once secret
official documents, investigated sightings and newspaper reports as the
basis for a crisp and fast-paced narrative. He knows how to focus on what
matters, and reveals a deep knowledge of the implications of key
developments within the current historical context.

The book is anything but dry—it is written as a page-turner, in short,
clear chapters punctuated with humor and a conversational style that makes
you want to keep reading. I trust Maccabee's expertise completely, and I
learned a great deal from this outstanding book, which concludes with the
best assessment I've ever read concerning the unending, unanswerable
question of a government cover-up. I recommend the book highly to
anyone interested in UFOs.

—Leslie Kean, author, *UFOs: Generals, Pilots, and Government*
Officials Go On the Record

Bruce Maccabee's new book is a sharp rebuke to die-hards and
ideologues on both ends of the UFO spectrum. It is a stinging, substantive
rebuttal to zealous debunkers who don't want the UFO subject to be taken
seriously because it proves, beyond any reasonable doubt, that officials at
the highest levels of our military and intelligence communities regarded the
UFO mystery as an issue of paramount importance. The documents which
Dr. Maccabbee helped to squeeze out of our government are amazingly
candid, precisely because they were never meant to be seen by the public.
Skeptics will not be able to dismiss this evidence by invoking swamp gas or
weather balloons.

The book is also a wake up call for those UFO faithful who breathlessly
await some sort of "Full Disclosure" by government officials. It's not going
to happen. The best glimpse we will ever get into the murky world of
official UFO files is by reading the materials that were plucked out of the
murky swamp before the spooks had time to react. This book delivers the
goods, and should be read by anyone who is a serious student of the subject.

—George Knapp, Investigative Reporter and author, *Hunt for the*
Skinwalker: Science Confronts the Unexplained at a Remote Ranch in
Utah

An astute researcher and analyst, Dr. Bruce Maccabee has produced a must-have compendium for every UFO aficionado. Based on his comprehensive notes and prodigious memory this book details the extensive post World War II history of these complex phenomena. Of note is his firsthand involvement with several of the government agencies that periodically over time have struggled to grasp the significance of this baffling enigma.

An accomplished optical physicist, his personal research includes analysis and authentication of some of the most important UFO photographs ever taken.

—John B. Alexander, Ph.D., author, *UFOs: Myths, Conspiracies, and Realities*

Bruce Maccabee has written the single-best volume documenting the strong interest in UFOs by two of America's leading (and most notorious) intelligence organizations: the FBI and the CIA. His emphasis is especially powerful when examining the decades of the Cold War, and he provides an overwhelming amount of officially released government documents to make the case that UFOs mattered a great deal to America's intelligence elite. And the reason wasn't simply because these groups were providing cover for other secret programs. Rather, UFOs themselves constituted an enormous problem, something that no one seemed to know how to discuss openly.

In addition, Dr. Maccabee gives an excellent insight into the attitudes that other key agencies had toward UFOs, notably the U.S. Air Force. He sheds light on how these various groups interacted with each other in handling this most difficult of problems: both from a public relations perspective, as well as from that of national security. This is a must-read, not only for students of UFOs, but for anyone interested in the history of the U.S. national security establishment.

—Richard M. Dolan, author, *UFOs and the National Security State, A.D., After Disclosure,* **and** *UFOs for the 21ˢᵗ Century Mind*

Dr. Bruce Maccabee has been in the forefront of scientific research related to UFOs for decades as will be obvious to all who read this stimulating and informative book. He brings to bear not only the intellectual discipline that accompanied his work for more than 35 years as an optical physicist for a United States Navy Research Lab, but also a willingness to get publicly involved in ufology. That takes courage. . . . There aren't many good books by scientists about UFOs. This is certainly one of the most informative.

—Stanton T. Friedman, nuclear physicist, author *Top Secret/Majic, Captured! The Betty and Barney Hill UFO Experience*

THE
FBI
CIA
UFO
Connection

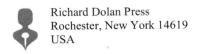

Richard Dolan Press
Rochester, New York 14619
USA

Richard Dolan Press and logo are
registered trademarks of Richard Dolan Press

Library of Congress Cataloging-in-Publication Data

Maccabee, Bruce
        The FBI-CIA-UFO Connection / by Bruce Maccabee, Ph.D.
    396 p. cm.
    Includes index.
    ISBN 978-1502317216
    1. Unidentified Flying Objects

    I. Maccabee, Bruce. Title

Cover art by Jeff Ritzmann

First published in the United States by Richard Dolan Press

THE FBI-CIA-UFO CONNECTION

THE HIDDEN UFO ACTIVITIES OF USA INTELLIGENCE AGENCIES

by Dr. Bruce Maccabee

Richard Dolan Press
2014

These are the *real* X-Files.

The truth is in here.

Contents

Dedication

This book is dedicated to my wife, Jan Pheneger Maccabee, to our children and grandchildren, and to my brother and sister-in-law, Bruce and Debra (Pheneger) Thomas. Bruce passed away February, 2013; he is greatly missed and will not be forgotten. This book is also dedicated to Floyd D. (Jake) Pheneger. Jake was a pioneer in the belief and studies of UFOs. A great man, indeed.

Acknowledgments

In order to compile this UFO history I have made use of the work of many investigators. In particular I thank the following people for their efforts in obtaining government documents other than the FBI documents (in alphabetical order): Jan Aldrich, Don Berliner, Stanton Friedman, Bill LaParl, Bill Moore, Jaime Shandera, Robert Todd and Barry Greenwood. I also thank the following people for their publications on the subject, publications which provided me with information and helped to clarify details of the history (in alphabetical order): Jan Aldrich, Don Berliner, Jerry Clark, Wendy Connors, Barry Greenwood, Mike Hall, Christopher Green, Loren Gross, Stanton Friedman, David Jacobs, Bill Moore, Ronald Pandolfi, Kevin Randle, Edward Ruppelt, Jaime Shandera, Don Schmidt, Brad Sparks and Michael Swords.

I also thank the early readers of this manuscript for their helpful comments, especially Elaine Douglass, Karl Pflock , Michael Swords and a certain astute person, formely in military intelligence, who wishes to remain unnamed.

Finally I thank the many government investigators, FBI, Air Force and CIA personnel, who generated these documents and thereby provided a paper trail that shows how the Air Force, FBI and CIA treated the UFO subject through the years.

Throughout this manuscript emphasized statements are italicized. However, italic statements which are contained within quotation marks or are contained in indented paragraphs are direct copies from original documents.

Foreword
by Stanton T. Friedman, Nuclear Physicist

D r. Bruce Maccabee has been in the forefront of scientific research related to UFOs for decades as will be obvious to all who read this stimulating and informative book. He brings to bear not only the intellectual discipline that accompanied his work for more than 35 years as an optical physicist for a United States Navy Research Lab, but also a willingness to get publicly involved in ufology. That takes courage. He is one of very few scientists who has actually published papers about UFOs in scientific journals. He lived and worked near Washington, D.C. which facilitated his involvement with the old National Investigations Committee on Aerial Phenomena based in Washington and made possible his decade and a half of interactions with certain CIA employees who were interested in the UFO subject. He also served for a number of years as the chairman of the Washington-based Fund for UFO research.

Dr. Maccabee provides inside information about his meetings with CIA personnel as well as details of a number of very interesting UFO cases which he investigated. They include the well known Japan Air lines (JAL 1628) case of November 17, 1986, the Gulf Breeze, Florida, UFO cases of November , 1987, the famous McMinnville, Oregon, UFO photos taken May 11, 1950, the New Zealand airborne sightings case of December, 1978, the Rogue River, Oregon, outstanding case of May 24, 1949, and a little-known case in which a large magnetic field was detected after a witness saw a UFO leave the area. Of the 5 witnesses in the Rogue River case, two had security clearances and reported their sighting to the Security Office at the Ames Research Laboratory where they worked.

For those who want comprehensive discussions, he also provides the false explanations put forth by the UFO debunkers and the internet locations at which one can find his detailed evaluations. He also relates that, when the Battelle Memorial Institute did the biggest study ever done, "Project Blue Book

Special Report 14," for the US Air Force, the unknowns comprised 21.5% of the 3201 cases studied. However, the Air Force did not publish that percentage but rather a much lower percentage, 3%. Furthermore, they claimed that these cases had insufficient information for identification. They did not tell the public that they had a separate classification for cases with insufficient information and that the unknowns did not fall into that classification. Nor did the Air Force report the fact, discovered by the Battelle study, that the better the case, with more credible witnesses and an abundance of information, the more likely it was to remain unknown after careful analysis, a discovery that was the complete opposite of what would be expected if all UFO sightings could be explained.

Bruce documents many examples of misinformation and disinformation from various Air Force Officers, the FBI, CIA etc. For those who think governments never lie, I recommend the discussion of the claim by a CIA historian that once the secret U-2 Spy plane started flying, it was responsible for about half of all UFO sightings reported to the Air Force. The CIA was pleased that people thought they were UFOs. Bruce obtained the figures for number of Blue Book sighting reports for a period before the U-2 started flying and the period after. There was no increase. Of course, it should be obvious that the U-2 flew very high and therefore was barely visible in daylight and couldn't be seen at night. Also, the U-2 did not have the characteristic common to flying saucers: no wings, no tail, able to hover or make right angle turns, or fly silently, or land and take off from a place not much larger than itself.

The CIA had claimed, at the beginning of a late 1970's Freedom of Information and Privacy Act (FOIPA) lawsuit, that all they had was a few documents written before the January, 1953, Robertson panel. They lied. Subsequently they released over 700 documents.

Bruce also discusses some of the strange claims from FBI Director, J. Edgar Hoover. In several memos, he claimed that the FBI was not and never had been investigating UFOs. However, under the FOIPA, Bruce requested any FBI UFO files and subsequently received over 1500 pages. He also notes the strange relationship between the USAF and the FBI and the importance of what the Air Force told the FBI in confidence. It was hard to separate foul-up from cover-up.

Of special importance is the insight he provides about how security works, for example, by calling attention to the fact that Top Secret information cannot be included in a memo rated only SECRET. There is a famous Sept. 23, 1947, SECRET memo "AMC Opinion Concerning Flying Saucers" from Air Force General Nathan Twining which some debunkers have tried to use as proof that there has never been a crash of a flying saucer because it talks about the absence of crash debris, when in fact it could not have included TOP SECRET information about such a crash. It should be noted that a Freedom of information suit against the National Security Agency forced the "release" of 156 TOP SECRET UMBRA pages of UFO documents Unfortunately, all but one sentence per page was redacted... whited out.

Bruce shows the importance of Air Force Chief of Staff, Hoyt Vandenberg's rejection of an "Estimate of the Situation," written during the late summer of 1948, which concluded that some UFOs were of extraterrestrial origin. Many Air Force officers took their cue from this rejection and subsequently avoided dealing seriously with that possibility.

An important point rarely discussed elsewhere is the CIA's concern that the Soviet Union might try to obtain classified information about secret US technology research projects by getting UFO researchers to dig into them in their efforts to dig out UFO secrets. This concern was heightened in the 1970's when, according to Bruce's CIA contact, the CIA received strong evidence that the Soviet Union intended to do exactly that. Bruce recounts an experience that confirms this Soviet intention.

Bruce gives the most detailed overview of the activities of Project Sign and Project Grudge, which had preceded the much better known Project Blue Book. He even quotes government officials agreeing about the poor quality of these projects. Of course, other writers have discussed these three projects and early (1950s) interest in UFOs by the CIA. Unique to this book are Bruce's descriptions of CIA interest in the UFO subject starting about ten years after the end (in 1969) of Project Blue Book.

There aren't many good books by scientists about UFOs. This is certainly one of the most informative. Bruce's sense of humor comes through as well. Enjoy.

Stanton T. Friedman
New Brunswick, June 2014

Introduction
The X Files Are Real!

This book would not exist if it weren't for the fact that Paul Trent took two pictures of a UFO in 1950.

This book would also not exist if Trent's photos had not been

Figure 1a: First Trent Photo

essentially endorsed by a scientist (Wm. Hartmann) involved with the Air Force sponsored UFO investigation that took place

Figure 1b: Second Trent Photo.

at the University of Colorado (the Condon Committee study) in 1968. If the photos had been rejected, I would not have decided to conduct my own investigation, and would not have learned that Trent claimed that he was visited by an FBI agent. And, if I had never learned about the claimed visit by the FBI, I would never have thought to write to the FBI to obtain any information they might have on UFOs. But I did write, in the fall of 1976, and I requested, based on the then-new Freedom of Information and Privacy Act, FOIPA), information they might have on Trent and any UFO documents that the FBI might have. I didn't really expect to get any documents, either on Trent or on UFOs in general, because the only information I had at that time indicated that the FBI had never investigated UFOs.

About two weeks after I sent my request, I received a letter saying that my request was number thirty-four thousand and then some, so I put the whole thing out of my mind, assuming that I might hear from the FBI in a decade or two.

To my great surprise, about 6 months later, I got a phone call from the equally surprised FBI agent who handled my request. He told me that there were over a thousand pages of "stuff" (actually 1,600 pages) related to UFOs in the FBI file at head-quarters in Washington, DC. So I got a pile of documents, and they form the basis for this book.

And Trent? The agent said it was against policy to discuss an investigation with a non-FBI agent. However, unofficially, they had nothing on Trent. (A brief discussion of the Trent photo case is in Appendix 1.)

What I learned from the FBI documents is that the FBI did interview witnesses of Unidentified Flying Objects when the modern era of UFO sightings began in the summer of 1947. The case files thus created are often called the X-Files, terminology that was popularized by a TV show of that name in the 1990s. The *X-Files* show was very entertaining because it was well written by people who were quite familiar with the phenomena they wrote about, but it does not accurately portray the fact that since the mid-1950s, the FBI has had little interest in UFOs. However, the show did get two things right, although probably by accident: (1) FBI agents did investigate saucer sightings in the early years and (2), UFO sightings were often filed under the title "SECURITY MATTER - X" as illustrated in Figure 2. These are the real X-Files.

SAC, San Francisco February 20, 1948

Director, FBI

FLYING DISCS
SECURITY MATTER - X

Reference is made to your letter in the captioned matter dated February 12, 1948.

Figure 2: Security Matter - X

Of more importance than the interviews is the fact that the FBI, for several years, collected and stored information provided by the Air Force. Some of the Air Force information in the FBI file cannot be found in the Air Force's version of the X-File, i.e., in the files of Project Blue Book, the publicly known UFO investigative activity of the Air Force.

Whereas the FBI interest in UFO investigation waned after several years, the interest of another government organization waxed greatly. That organization? The Central Intelligence Agency.

The FBI's approach to UFO investigation was to interview witnesses and pass the information to the Air Force. The CIA approach was different. The CIA bypassed the witnesses and, instead, investigated the Air Force! The CIA wanted to know whether or not the staff of Project Blue Book would be able to determine the underlying phenomena that caused the roughly 20% of the sightings that Blue Book claimed could not be explained as conventional phenomena (that is, as misidentifications, hoaxes and delusions). The CIA interest culminated in what became known as the Robertson Panel (to be described) where it was pointed out that real or not, UFO reports at a time of crisis could clog communication channels. This was, after all, the time of the Cold War with the Soviet Union. Therefore it was recommended that UFO reports be "debunked" in order to reduce the public interest in making such reports.

After this panel, in January, 1953, the CIA took little interest in the UFO subject until the 1970s, when certain paranormal investigations related to remote viewing became entangled with UFO sightings. In the latter 70s, I became directly involved with the UFO interests of some CIA employees, and I was told at one point that I had created a bunch of "spies" inside the agency, people who were searching for secret UFO evidence that the agency might have been withholding from the public.

From my studies of the Air Force, FBI, and CIA documents, I have concluded that there was enough information available in the "X-Files" to prove that "UFOs are real" and probably are "interplanetary" (to use their preferred parlance of the 1940s and 1950s). I have also concluded that top Air Force officials knew this but kept it secret.

But how can that be? It's all fiction, isn't it? After all, everybody knows that only "kooks and nuts" and people looking for publicity see UFOs, right?

Wrong. There are sightings by responsible citizens of the United States, by Air Force officers, by pilots, scientists, teachers, policemen, etc. In the FBI file, there is even a joint sighting by an employee of the National Security Agency and an employee of the FBI.

The records of these secret government UFO activities were not lost, they were merely unavailable to the American people until recent years. And now, thanks to the Freedom of Information and Privacy Act (FOIPA) and the efforts of many UFO investigators over the last forty years, you are able to read what the Air Force, FBI, and CIA knew more than half a century ago. The perpetrators of the UFO cover-up hope that you won't read this book and find out for yourself that some UFOs are evidence that Other Intelligences (OI) have been flying around in their Alien Flying Craft (AFC) which may be interplanetary.

The motto of the *X-Files* TV show was, "The Truth is Out There." And well it may be, but also . . . *the Truth Is in Here!*

Read on.

PART I
The UFO-FBI Connection

FBI Headquarters, Washington, DC.

Chapter 1
Hoover Lied!

"I would do it, but we first must have access to all discs recovered...."
—J. Edgar Hoover, July 11, 1947

A teletype machine at the headquarters of the Federal Bureau of Investigation (FBI) in Washington, D.C. suddenly sprang to life and began noisily typing out an urgent message from a Special Agent in Charge (SAC):

FBI ALBUQUERQUE
5:37 PM MST URGENT
TO: DIRECTOR, FBI
FROM SAC, ALBUQUERQUE 62 NEW MEXICO
UNIDENTIFIED FLYING OBJECT SOCORRO, NM
INFORMATION CONCERNING

The teletype message described the UFO sighting of Lonnie Zamora, a respected police officer in Socorro, New Mexico on April 24, 1964. Zamora had seen a strange, unidentified object and two human-like creatures on the ground near Socorro. The object then took off with a roaring noise and left indentations in the ground. He called on his radio for help and other officers arrived only minutes after it had disappeared in the distance, but in time to see Zamora looking as if he had seen a ghost.

Minutes later, the FBI arrived. Special Agent in Charge (SAC) Arthur Byrnes, acting in an unofficial capacity, interviewed Zamora and sent a teletype message to FBI headquarters the next day. Over the next few weeks, he sent several more messages to headquarters concerning the results of the Air Force investigation of this incident (described in Chapter 22) which, to this day, remains unexplained.

This is just one of the UFO sightings contained within FBI file 62-83894, the file on Flying Discs....the *real* X Files.

But, how can this be? Surely the FBI wouldn't get involved with anything as crazy as UFOs and flying saucers. Nowadays, the FBI does not investigate UFO sightings (so they say). But that

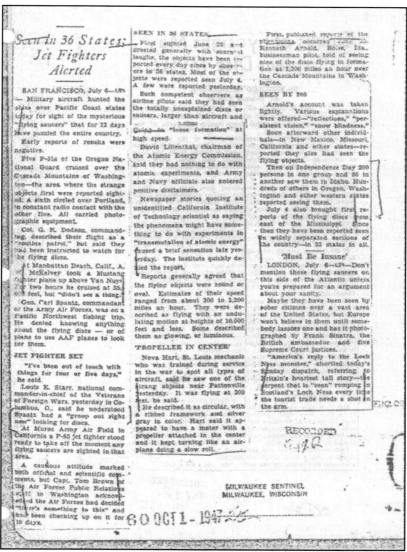

Figure 5: Example of Press Interest in Saucer Reports

made up the disc. If some of the parts did not originate in the USA, then there was the possibility that the disc was a form of sabotage or psychological warfare being waged against the USA by a foreign country.

The phrase "La. case" refers to a hoax device found in Shreveport, Louisiana on July 7. Someone had put together a model flying saucer and tossed it into someone else's back yard as a joke. Army intelligence agents had learned of it and had retrieved it for analysis before the local FBI agent had a chance to look at it. Nothing unusual was found. It included some electronic parts and mechanical parts with the words "Made in USA" written on it. The Shreveport case was not the only such hoax case in the FBI files from this period. Apparently some people thought the saucer sightings were a complete joke and decided to have fun at other people's expense. The files indicate a dozen or so hoaxes among the hundreds of honest reports.

Hoover officially approved Tolson's recommendation and thus began a two-month period of official investigation, followed by many years in which the FBI collected UFO related information from the Air Force and other sources. The FBI, with its penchant for collecting all sorts of information that might be of value to Hoover, did all this secretly. In 1976, when I requested any UFO information that the FBI might have, for release under the newly passed Freedom of Information and Privacy Act (FOIPA), I didn't expect to get anything. There had never been explicit evidence that the FBI was ever involved with UFO investigations. One person who should have known was Captain Edward J. Ruppelt, the first director of Project Blue Book, which was the publicly known UFO investigation project of the Air Force from 1952 to 1969. He wrote a history of the first eight years of Air Force flying saucer investigations, *The Report on Unidentified Flying Objects* (Doubleday, New York, 1956). According to Ruppelt, the FBI "was never officially interested" in UFO sightings. Therefore I was surprised to learn that there were well over a thousand pages of UFO related material in the FBI's "X-File".

I found that the FBI file provides a unique viewpoint on the early Air Force investigation because it contains comments by Air Force officers who were involved right at the beginning. The FBI file even contains some early records not in the files of P⋯ Blue Book, which the Air Force claimed was the com-
⋯ial Air Force collection of UFO sightings and docu-

Chapter 2
Security Matter X:
The Real X-File

Agents had been sending unofficial reports on saucers to headquarters for several weeks when, on July 30, 1947, a message went out to all the local offices:

> You should investigate each instance which is brought to your attention of a sighting of a flying disc in order to ascertain whether or not it is a bona fide sighting, an imaginary one or a prank. . . . The bureau should be notified immediately by teletype of all reported sightings and the results of your inquiries.

The directive also specified that FBI agents should provide copies of their reports to the Air Force investigators. According to the directive, the Air Force Intelligence had "some concern that the reported sightings might have been made by subversive individuals for the purpose of creating mass hysteria." However, the Air Force had also told the FBI that it was possible to drag several disc-shaped gliders behind a plane using a wire tow line. Upon release these discs "would obtain tremendous speed in their descent and would decend (sic) to the earth in an arc." The fact that the Air Force proposed this rather bizarre saucer hypothesis indicates that Air Force scientists believed the saucers were real flying objects and were attempting to determine how they could be explained as devices created by foreign countries. See Figure 6.

Over the next two months, the FBI interviewed more than a dozen witnesses and found no evidence of subversion. They did, however, find evidence of flying saucers.

Here are a few of the reports.

REPORTS OF FLYING DISCS September 17, 194
SECURITY MATTER - X

The above heading introduces the FBI inte

Johnson, a prospector. Johnson had written a letter to the Air Force in which he said he had seen the same objects that Kenneth Arnold had seen at about the same time during the afternoon of June 24.* The Air Force asked the FBI to interview Mr. Johnson.

According to the FBI report, during the afternoon of June 24,

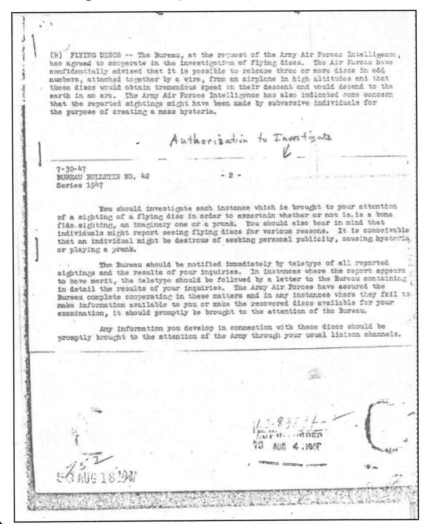

Figure 6: Authorization to Investigate

old reported seeing nine semicircular, flat shiny objects fly southward at high 1,700 mph—past Mt. Rainier in the State of Washington. These objects d right as they flew. They disappeared from his view near Mt. Adams, s south of Mt. Rainier.

Johnson was prospecting near Mount Adams. He saw the saucers fly overhead. He closely observed them through a telescope. (He is the first person known to have used a telescope to observe flying saucers.) He confirmed Arnold's description of the overall shape and high speed, and said that they appeared to him to be about 30 feet in diameter. He said they tilted back and forth as they flew and he last saw them "standing on edge" as they flew into a cloud. As these objects were passing overhead, the needle of his compass wobbled back and forth. (This is the first known report of electromagnetic effects of flying saucers.) Mr. Johnson told the FBI he had not learned of Arnold's sighting until several days later and he had written to the Air Force to "lend credence" to Arnold's report. The FBI agent noted that Johnson "appeared to be a very reliable individual" who been prospecting in the northwestern United States for forty years.

In the Project Blue Book records Fred Johnson's sighting occupies a unique position: it is the first of 701 UFO reports that the Air Force admitted it could not explain at the time Project Blue Book closed in 1969.[*]

Inasmuch as Arnold's sighting preceded Johnson's by a minute or so, the astute reader may ask why Arnold's sighting is not the first unexplained sighting (and Johnson's the second)? The answer is that the Air Force analysts claim to have explained Arnold's sighting as a mirage! Of course, it is illogical to imply that the objects seen by Arnold and Johnson could be both explained and unexplained. This is just one example of the illogical treatment of UFO sightings by the Air Force.[**]

* * *

TO: Director, FBI September 4, 1947
FROM: SAC Phoenix

---

[*] Project Blue Book (1952-1969), and its predecessors, Project Sign (1948-1949) and Project Grudge (1949-1952) are the only publicly known efforts of the Air Force to collect and categorize UFO sightings. The files of these projects were microfilmed and released to the National Archives in 1975.

[**] Note: the official Air Force explanation of Arnold's sighting and the several other explanations proposed by scientists and skeptics over the last 50 years have been proven wrong. See www.brumac.8k.com/KARNOLD/KARNOLD.html

SUBJECT: Reports of Flying Discs

Thus begins a letter to FBI headquarters concerning the interview of Mr. William Rhodes of Phoenix, Arizona, who had taken two pictures of a flying saucer near his home. The object in the pictures resembled the saucers reported by Mr. Arnold. Mr. Rhodes gave the negatives to the FBI with the understanding that they would be turned over to the Air Force Intelligence and that he probably wouldn't get them back. He never did. A year and a half later the pictures were published in an intelligence report, originally classified Top Secret, entitled "Analysis of Flying Object Incidents in the US," published jointly by the Directorate of Intelligence of the Air Force and the Office of Naval Intelligence. According to this document, "These photographs have been examined by experts who state they are true photographic images. . . " (This document, which is discussed in Chapter 5, was not declassified and released until 1985.)

* * *

URGENT. AUGUST 11, 1947
FLYING DISCS.
SECURITY MATTER DASH X

Thus begins a teletype message from Portland, Oregon, which reports that a former Navy pilot saw a mysterious flying object on two occasions the evening of August 6. The pilot was near the Tri City Airport at Myrtle Creek, Oregon, at an altitude of about 400 feet, when he first saw a glistening spherical object at an estimated altitude of 5,000 to 8,000 feet. It appeared to be metallic and traveling eastward while climbing at a speed of about 1,000 mph. He saw no vapor trails. After it disappeared, he landed the plane and then took off again as part of the instruction for his passenger, a flight student. Once again, he saw the spherical object, which again took off at high speed. He estimated the size at about 30 feet. To the flight student, the object appeared to be a 50 foot sphere. He said that the second object they saw departed straight upward at high speed and disappeared in about 45 seconds. The sky was clear and the sun low in the west at the time of the sighting.

* * *

URGENT SEPTEMBER 13, 1947
FLYING DISCS

This teletype message reads, in part:

(The) chief of Police, Portland (Oregon), states he observed at about 5:15 PM an object similar in size to a weather balloon, which appeared to be made of aluminum or some other bright metal, traveling rapidly northwest to southeast over Portland at an estimated 10,000 ft. Object veered to south and disappeared in the distance in approximately one minute. Also observed by Portland Police officers... investigation being conducted.

The follow-up report to the teletype message begins with the heading "FLYING DISCS, SECURITY MATTER - X." The report presents the testimony of several other policemen in the northeastern part of the city who first saw the object coming from the east. By radio, they asked officers further south to look for it. Chief Leon Jenkins then searched the sky and observed what "appeared to be a round silver object, about 10,000 feet high, traveling northeast to southwest." Initially, he thought it was a weather balloon, but then "further observation convinced him it could not be a weather balloon because of its speed which was extremely great." He watched the object gradually turn until it was traveling due south. "As it (turned southward) its shape seemed to change until it appeared to be egg-shaped. It disappeared in about 30 seconds."

* * *

FBI BUTTE 8-15-47 5:45 PM
DIRECTOR, FBI
URGENT

The flying disc "X-File" contains many sightings collected by the Air Force and provided to the FBI. These include numerous sightings by pilots, policemen, and others. The objects were always quite distant, except for one case. The closest encounter was that of Mr. A. C. Urie and his sons, who lived in the Snake River Canyon at Twin Falls, Idaho. At about 1:00 P.M., August 13, Mr. Urie "sent his boys to the (Salmon) river to get some rope from his boat. When he thought they were overdue he went outside his tool shed to look for them. He noticed them about 300 feet away looking in the sky and he glanced up to see what he called the flying disc."

This strange object was flying at high speed along the canyon, which is about 400 feet deep and 1,200 feet across at that point. It was about 75 feet above the floor of the canyon and moving up and down as it flew. It seemed to be following the contours of the hilly ground beneath it. Urie estimated it was about 20 feet long and 10 feet wide and 10 feet high, with what appeared to be exhaust ports on the sides. It was almost hat-shaped with a flat bottom and a dome on top. Its pale blue color made Urie think that it would be very difficult to see against the sky, although he had no trouble seeing it against the walls of the canyon. On each side there was a tubular-shaped fiery glow, like some sort of exhaust. He said that when it went over trees, they didn't sway back and forth, but rather the treetops twisted around, which suggests that the air under the object was being swirled into a vortex. He and his sons had an excellent view of the object for a few seconds before it disappeared over the trees about a mile away. He thought it was going 1,000 miles an hour. The sighting was given a humorous treatment by the local newspaper (see Figure 7-D).[*]

The FBI learned that Mr. Urie and his sons were not the only witnesses to a flying saucer on August 13. County Commissioner and former sheriff L. W. Hawkins and a companion were near the Salmon River Dam about 40 miles southwest of Twin Falls when they saw, high in the sky, two circular, reflective objects. Mr. Hawkins said a sound resembling an echo of a motor caused him to look upward and he saw these objects traveling at a great speed.

---

[*] In the documents relating to this case, and in many others in this book, there are blackouts of names. This is consistent with the "Privacy" part of the FOIPA: names of witnesses and non-government employees are crossed out. However, in most cases sighting witnesses are known from other sources. In the Urie case below he was named in newspaper stories. Also, in many cases the witnesses can be determined from the document because the censor overlooked the names!

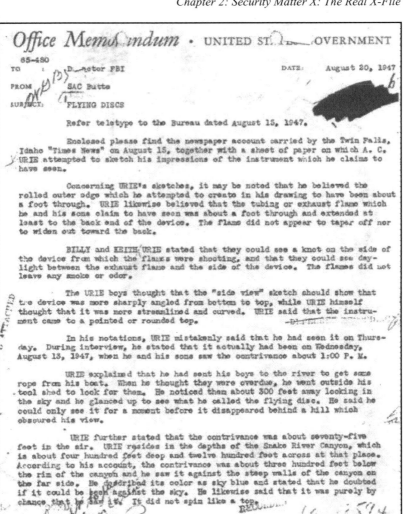

Figure 7a: Sighting by A. C. Urie

BT 65-460

As the machine went by the URIE place, the trees over which it almost directly passed (Mormon Poplars) did not just bend with the wind as if a plane had gone by, but, in URIE's words, "spun around on top as if they were in a vacuum."

KEITH URIE, eight years of age, said he first saw the machine coming down the canyon, heading from east to west and following the contours of the ground. BILLY, age ten, saw it almost immediately. Both watched it fly out of sight behind a tree in a matter of moments. They said they then ran to their Father and learned that he too had seen the machine.

URIE seemed completely sincere about the incident. He said his wife and daughter were in the house at the time and had not seen the machine. He questioned his brother, who also lives in the canyon, but his brother had been eating at the time and had seen nothing. URIE and his two boys maintained that they had never before seen one of the discs. URIE, when interviewed, appeared to be a sober, middle-aged man.

[redacted] who originally furnished Special Agents with information about the incident, likewise stated that URIE appeared completely sincere about the machine.

No further attempt was made to locate L. W. HAWKINS, inasmuch as [redacted] who was with HAWKINS at the time, was interviewed. [redacted] name was withheld from the newspaper because HAWKINS and [redacted] were fishing at Salmon dam while [redacted] was supposed to have been working in Twin Falls.

[redacted] said simply that he and HAWKINS could hear a roar. They looked up and could see two instruments flying at a great height, which [redacted] mentioned might have been between four thousand and six thousand feet. However, he said he had no idea how large the devices were and consequently, they may have been several miles away. He said that he and HAWKINS were satisfied they had seen something and they were very doubtful that they had seen two planes.

RJG:FO'S

Enc. (2)

Figure 7b: Sighting by A. C. Urie

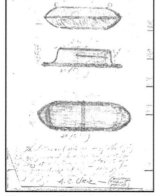

Figure 7c: Drawings by A.C. Urie

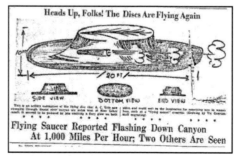

Figure 7D: Newspaper Report on Urie Sighting

Chapter 3
Secret Air Force Activities

". . . real and not imaginary or fictitious."
—Lt. General Nathan Twining, September, 1947

During July, August, and September of 1947, FBI headquarters received about two dozen sighting reports and some other documents from the Air Force. All of these reports and documents were supposed to have been contained within the records of Project Blue Book (which are on microfilm at the National Archives). However, some of these documents were found only in the FBI file. One of these provides an early Air Force assessment of the saucer situation. The document, reproduced below, is neither signed nor dated but the location of the document in the temporal sequence of the FBI file indicates that it was written in late July, after the Air Force had collected and analyzed about two dozen sightings.

> From (a) detailed study of reports selected for their impression of veracity and reliability, several conclusions have been formed:
> (a) This 'flying saucer' situation is not all imaginary or seeing too much in some natural phenomenon. Something is really flying around.
> (b) Lack of topside inquiries, when compared to the prompt and demanding inquiries that have originated topside upon former events, give more than ordinary weight to the possibility that this is a domestic project, about which the President, etc. know.
> (c) Whatever the objects are, this much can be said of their physical appearance:
> 1. The surface of these objects is metallic, indicating a metallic skin, at least.
> 2. When a trail is observed it is lightly colored, a Blue-Brown haze, that is similar to a rocket engine's exhaust. Contrary to a rocket of the solid type, one observation indicates that the fuel may be throttled which would indicate a liquid rocket engine.
> 3. As to shape, all observations state that the object is circular or at least elliptical, flat on the bottom and slightly domed on the top. The size estimates place it somewhere near the size of a C-54 or a Constellation.

4. Some reports describe two tabs, located at the rear and symmetrical about the axis of flight motion.

5. Flights have been reported from three to nine of them, flying good formation on each other, with speeds always above 300 knots.

6. The discs oscillate laterally while flying along, which could be snaking.

The above statement may well have been written by Lieutenant Colonel George D. Garrett of Air Force Intelligence at the Pentagon. It was Garrett who, on August 19, told the FBI liaison, Special Agent Reynolds, that whereas the "high brass" of the War Department had exerted "tremendous pressure" on Air Force intelligence to determine the cause of sightings of unidentified objects flying over Sweden in the summer of 1946, in this case (saucers over America) the "high brass appeared to be totally unconcerned." Garrett said that many of the witnesses were "trained observers . . . reliable members of the community" which, to him, meant that "these individuals saw something." Thus he had concluded that "there were objects seen which somebody in the Government knows all about."

Lt. Colonel Garrett's speculation caused the FBI to make further checks with the "high brass" of the Air Force to be sure that the FBI was not wasting its time investigating a secret project of the Armed Forces. Brigidier General Schulgen, who had initially contacted the FBI, assured the FBI that he would check into it. On September 5, 1947, General Schulgen wrote his response (see Figure 8):

> . . . a complete survey of research activities discloses that the Army Air Forces has no project with the characteristic similar to those which have been associated with the Flying Discs.

Although Garrett and the writer of the document discussed above (possibly Garrett) were wrong in guessing that saucers were a secret project of the Armed Forces, his speculation that they were something that the high brass knew about could have been valid. Specifically, if the material retrieved in early July at Roswell, New Mexico actually was wreckage of an alien spacecraft, then a few top government civilians and a few members of the "Top Brass" (the four star generals and their associates) who were in charge of the material would not have

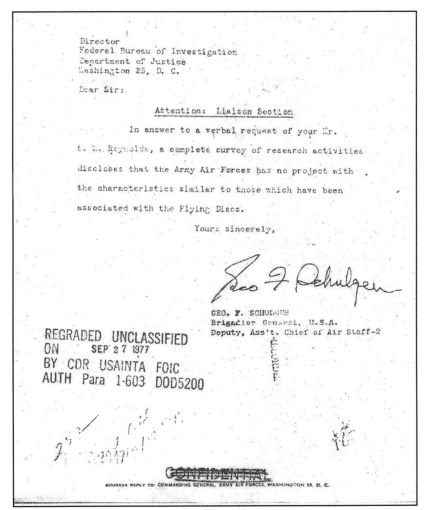

Director
Federal Bureau of Investigation
Department of Justice
Washington 25, D. C.

Dear Sir:

Attention: Liaison Section

In answer to a verbal request of your Mr.

S. L. Reynolds, a complete survey of research activities

discloses that the Army Air Forces has no project with

the characteristics similar to those which have been

associated with the Flying Discs.

Yours sincerely,

GEO. F. SCHULGEN
Brigadier General, U.S.A.
Deputy, Ass't. Chief of Air Staff-2

REGRADED UNCLASSIFIED
ON   SEP 27 1977
BY CDR USAINTA FOIC
AUTH Para 1-603 DOD5200

CONFIDENTIAL
ADDRESS REPLY TO: COMMANDING GENERAL, ARMY AIR FORCES, WASHINGTON 25, D. C.

Figure 8: Schulgen's Letter to the FBI

needed the visual sightings to prove that the saucers were real. They would have had the hard evidence as proof.

Then, after the "initial shock of discovery," the Top Brass would realize they needed the sighting reports in order to determine where the saucers were flying and what they were doing, i.e., the "tactics" of flying saucers. If they wanted the sighting reports but also wanted to keep the knowledge of the Roswell material restricted to very few people they would have to do two things simultaneously: (1) tell their employees (the "lower brass") to collect sighting information and (2) deny that there was proof the saucers were real.

The denial could come in two ways: (a) say that there was no convincing evidence and/or (b) act as if there were no hard evidence. In order to act as if there were no hard evidence, they would emphasize the importance of collecting sighting information in order to determine whether or not the saucers were real. Alternatively, if the lower brass (brigadier generals, colonels, captains, etc.) realized on their own, without prompting from above, that there was a potential threat posed by flying saucers, and began collecting and analyzing sighting information as part of their normal intelligence function, the Top Brass wouldn't even have to become involved.

Thus, if the Roswell material really was from a spacecraft, then the above document shows that by late July the cover-up had begun. The fix was in, and an iron curtain had descended over the hard evidence.

While the FBI agents were interviewing witnesses and collecting information, Army Air Force intelligence was hard at work trying to make sense out of the saucer sightings. At some time during the summer of 1947 (probably late July or early August) General Schulgen asked the Air Materiel Command (AMC) at Wright Field* to analyze sightings collected by Air Force Intelligence (AFI) and to provide an opinion on them.

Within the Air Materiel Command was a technical intelligence division designated T-2 and an engineering division called T-3. The members of these divisions were scientifically and technically trained Air Force employees whose job it was to analyze foreign aircraft to determine the level of technology and their warfighting capabilities. Several of the T-2 and T-3 personnel had already begun to pay attention to saucer reports, because they were actively involved in studying designs for saucer-like "low aspect ratio" aircraft that had been on the drawing boards of the German Air Force in WWII, such as designs by the Horton brothers. These designs, and even some of the scientists who had worked on them, had been brought to the United States for study

---

* Now Wright-Patterson Air Force Base [WPAFB] in Dayton, Ohio.

after the war. (Other scientists and design plans had been taken to the Soviet Union.) Hence they may well have thought that these designs had actually been built by a military organization in the USA. At the very least, they were probably more willing than most of the population—who believed an airplane needed wings in order to fly—to accept that the reports were reasonably accurate.

As requested, these employees analyzed the sightings and wrote a report, which was sent over the signature of Lieutenant General Nathan Twining, the Commanding General of the AMC, to General Schulgen. The letter, dated September 23, 1947, echoed the positive attitude, and even some of the wording, of the above report that was found only in the FBI file. According to the letter, the opinion of the AMC scientists and engineers was based on "interrogation report data" supplied by General Schulgen. (The letter does not mention any source of information other than sighting reports.)

In their opinion, "the phenomenon is something real and not visionary or fictitious" and "there are objects probably approximating the shape of a disc, of such appreciable size as to appear to be as big as man-made aircraft." The objects were described as metallic in appearance, circular or elliptical in shape, and with flat bottoms and domes on top. The objects were also characterized by their "extreme rates of climb," maneuverability, and general lack of noise. The letter stated that "It is possible within present U.S. knowledge—provided extensive development is undertaken—to construct a piloted aircraft" which would look roughly saucer shaped and "which would be capable of an approximate range of 7000 miles at subsonic speed."

In other words, in the opinion of the AMC scientists and engineers, saucers were probably based on known aerodynamic principles combined with advanced technological means for flight, i.e., not only possible, but probable! The letter suggested that the objects might be "of domestic origin—the product of some high security project not known to AC/AS-2 or this Command" or, a more disturbing possibility, that "some foreign nation has a form of propulsion, possibly nuclear, which is outside of our domestic knowledge." However, according to the letter, "a lack of physical evidence in the form of crash recovered exhibits" prevented AMC from conclusively identifying the craft.

The letter recommended that a special classified project be set up that would coordinate with the Army, Navy, Atomic Energy Commission, the Joint Research and Development Board, the Air Force Scientific Advisory Group and other advanced research agencies in order to study the saucer reports. Finally, the letter stated that AMC would "continue the investigation within its current resources in order to more closely define the nature of the phenomenon." He ended his letter by promising that Essential Elements of Information (EEI) would be "formulated immediately for transmission through channels." These EEI were needed in order to help military intelligence operatives throughout the world collect information about any flying saucers that were being made by foreign countries, particularly Russia and the Soviet Bloc countries.

The reference to a "lack of physical evidence" suggests either that the Roswell debris did not come from a flying saucer, or if it did that Twining didn't know about it. A third possibility is that Twining and the AMC analysts knew the Roswell material was hard evidence, but couldn't allow it to be mentioned in the letter.

Could it be that Twining had not been informed about the Roswell material? Yes, that is possible. Twining knew that he didn't know everything going on in U.S. military research. The letter suggests that the objects might be "of domestic origin... the product of some high security project not known to this command or to (General Schulgen)." Twining's suggestion that there might be something he didn't know about is a direct illustration of the way Top Secret information is protected. Top Secret information is often segmented or divided into "chunks" or "compartments."A person is allowed access only to the chunks of information that he needs to know in order to do his job. Only a few persons at the very top of the government and defense establishment know everything, or almost everything, about individual military research activities. They determine what their employees "need-to-know" in order to carry out their missions, and they authorize their employees special access only to the needed information.

This system of compartmentalization of information was developed during WWII in order to protect the knowledge about the atomic bomb and other secret technological advances (e.g., radar, bomb site, proximity fuse). Lt. General Twining, although head of the Air Materiel Command, was nevertheless an "employee" of the Top Brass (a four-star general such as Chief of Staff of the Army Air Force, General Carl Spaatz in 1947 and, in 1948, General Hoyt Vandenberg). Hence he knew that there could be projects, even projects carried out at AMC, which the Top Brass knew about but for which he had no "need to know" and therefore hadn't been told. Furthermore, it appears from the letter that he made the logical assumption that Brig. General Schulgen also did not know about any project that was creating flying saucers.

There is a fourth possibility: Twining knew the Roswell debris was extraterrestrial but the persons who actually formulated and typed the letter for Twining's signature did *not* know. The T-2 and T-3 personnel who wrote the letter based their conclusions on sighting information from Schulgen. They mentioned the lack of hard evidence and the possibility that the saucers were some secret project of which "this command" was unaware. When handed this letter, it is possible that Twining simply signed it as written, without correcting the statements about a lack of hard evidence and a high security project in order to maintain the tight security around the debris.

The most important aspect of Twining's letter is that by late September 1947, the AMC/T-2 investigators had concluded that flying saucers were real, unexplained objects. It is important to know of this early conclusion by Air Force intelligence, because a few years later, as the controversy over saucer sightings became popularized and politicized, the Air Force stated publicly that all sightings, including these early ones, could be explained. The claim was wrong, as I will show in this book.

Air Force intelligence was seriously worried about the possibility that the Soviet Union had gotten the jump on the United States by improving on innovative research of the German aeronautical engineers, Walter and Reimar Horton. They had designed an aircraft in which the main body was not a fuselage but rather a broad wing with the curved front, a "flying wing." The Air Force investigators wondered if the Soviets could actually have constructed such a craft and flown it over the United States. The Air Force initiated a search for the Horton brothers and for any information from foreign countries that might offer an explanation for the saucer sightings.

To aid in this search, the Essential Elements of Information (EEI) mentioned at the end of General Twining's letter were sent to the Army Counter Intelligence Corps (CIC). These EEI, not released by the Army Security Agency until 1994, show that the Air Force had determined that the saucers had some amazing capabilities. A formerly Secret cover letter for the EEI, found in the files of the Operations Branch of the 970th CIC and dated October 20, 1947 reads as follows:

"1. Attached hereto is an EEI written at Wright Field, Ohio, concerning the flying saucers recently sighted over the United States.
2. For your information, the Air Materiel Command at Wright Field is making a study of this subject and is constructing models to be tested in a wind tunnel. As a guide in constructing the models, descriptions from various persons who claimed to have sighted these objects were used. The Air Materiel Command is of the opinion that some sort of object, such as the flying saucer, did exist."

This document makes it clear that AMC considered the saucers to be real flying craft. Furthermore, this confirms rumors going back over sixty years that the Air Force made flying saucer models to test in wind tunnels.

In the EEI document, the AMC investigators discussed the work of the Horton brothers and suggested that perhaps the Soviets had pushed the development of flying wing aircraft and had thereby "leapfrogged" our own technological developments. This suggestion, although ultimately proven wrong, caused a considerable amount of confusion in later years, as the AMC and lower brass of the Air Force attempted to determine whether flying saucers were craft of another country, meaning Soviet, or craft of another world!

On October 28, 1947, the same day that the 970th CIC sent the EEI to its agents, General Schulgen's Intelligence Requirements Division of the AFI prepared an Intelligence Collection Memorandum and a list of Intelligence Requirements, both of which were based on the EEI document provided by AMC. The Collection Memorandum was written to justify the collection of information "in the field of Flying Saucer type aircraft." Most of the Collection Memorandum, presumably written by Lt. Colonel George Garrett, is simply a word-for-word copy of a similar portion of the AMC EEI document. Garrett's version of the (formerly secret) Collection Memorandum begins as follows, with italics to indicate words which Garrett added to the original AMC EEI document:

> An alleged 'Flying Saucer' type aircraft or object in flight, approximating the shape of a disc, has been reported by many observers from widely scattered places, such as the United States, Alaska, Canada, Hungary, the Island of Guam and Japan. The object has been reported by many competent observers, *including USAF rated officers*. Sightings have been made from the ground as well as the air.

In the summer of 1947, there were few newspaper reports of saucers seen in other countries. Since there were no widely publicized reports of foreign sightings, the skeptics, who lacked access to Air Force information, argued logically that flying saucers couldn't be vehicles from outer space—because if they were, they would have appeared in other countries as well. From the above paragraph, we now know what AFI (and the CIA, which obtained the reports from other countries) knew in 1947: saucers *were* sighted in other countries. The above paragraph also shows that the observers were not all untrained, "average" people who couldn't recognize normal things in the sky. Many of the observers were "rated USAF officers."

Colonel Garrett's draft Memorandum follows the EEI word-for-word through the list of "commonly reported features":

a. relatively flat bottom with extreme light reflecting ability
b. absence of sound except for an occasional roar when operating under super performance conditions
c. extreme maneuverability and apparent ability to almost hover
d. a plan form approximating that of an oval or disc with a dome shape on the top surface
e. the absence of an exhaust trail except in a few instances.....

f. the ability to quickly disappear by high speed or by complete disintegration

g. the ability to suddenly appear without warning as if from an extremely high altitude

h. the size most reported approximated that of a C-54 or Constellation type aircraft

i. the ability to group together very quickly in a tight formation when more than one aircraft are together

j. evasive action ability indicates possibility of being manually operated, or possibly by electronic or remote control devices

k. under certain conditions the craft seems to have the ability to cut a clear path through clouds--width of path estimated to be approximately one half mile. Only one incident indicated this phenomenon.

This list makes one thing abundantly clear, namely, that there had been enough credible saucer observations so that the Air Force could compile a list of specific, and rather startling, characteristics. These characteristics of flying saucers, which were not publicized (they appeared only in secret documents), have been reported by numerous witnesses throughout the years since this document was written.

Of particular interest are b, c, f, g and j, above. We had no silent aircraft at the time, and only helicopters could hover. Of course, they are not extremely maneuverable. Hence characteristics b and c could not be correlated with aircraft known at the time. Items f and g indicate that these objects are capable of extreme acceleration and can travel at such high speeds that they are effectively invisible to the observer. Over the years, many witnesses have reported sudden appearances, disappearances, or sudden changes in location of UFOs, but until recently the civilian community of ufologists (people who investigate sightings and study the phenomenon) had no optically recorded evidence, only personal testimony. However, there are now several video recordings of UFOs accelerating and moving at extreme speeds.[*] Objects which can achieve a large amount of acceleration and move through the sky at extremely high speeds would, for practical purposes, be "invisible" to anyone who wasn't looking in exactly the right place at exactly the right time

---

[*] Two of these videos are discussed in the book *UFOs Are Real and Here's the Proof* by Ed Walters and Bruce Maccabee, Avon Books, 1997.

to see a blur pass by.* Item j above indicates that saucers were intelligently controlled and not some unusual, previously unknown natural phenomenon.

Garrett's draft of the EEI continued by pointing out that the first sightings occurred around the middle of May 1947 (predating Kenneth Arnold's sighting), the peak activity was in early July, and the "last reported sightings took place in Toronto, Canada, 14 September." It goes on to state that "for purposes of analysis and evaluation" the objects were considered to be a "manned craft of Russian origin." (Note: the AMC analysts and Garrett had to assume the objects were under intelligent control because they seemed able to take evasive action.)

The AMC at Wright Field was not the only Air Force intelligence agency that took saucer sightings seriously. Documents which became available in the 1980s prove that the Air Force Office of Intelligence (AFOIN) in the Pentagon, here abbreviated AFI, was carrying out its own study of saucer sightings. The formerly secret AFI study, "Analysis of Flying Disc Reports," written in the late fall of 1947, was based on single and multiple witness visual sightings and several radar sightings. "Observers have indicated to be reliable and in some instances several observers have corroborated separate observations of the same phenomenon at the same time," according to the report. The characteristics of flying saucers listed by AFI are essentially the same as in the Intelligence Collection Memorandum discussed above, including the "ability to hover; to appear suddenly as if from a dive; to disintegrate or to disappear, perhaps by increasing speed; to group quickly in a tight formation, and to take evasive action."

According to this report, the AFI thoroughly investigated the saucer situation by (a) analyzing sightings (most remained unexplained), (b) checking with all known U.S. agencies that might have developed novel and highly secret circular aircraft (none did), (c) asking AMC to analyze sightings and form its own opinion (AMC responded in General Twining's September 23 letter), (d) asking the FBI to investigate the possibility of

---

* see "Acceleration" at
http://www.brumac.8k.com/Acceleration/ACCELERATION.htm

communist subversion (none was found), (e) asking the Air Weather Service to analyze the sightings to determine if any could be weather balloons (none were) and (g) analyzing the possibility that a foreign country (for example, Russia) could have leapfrogged the aeronautical technology of the USA.

The AFI could find no reason to believe any country had developed such a unique craft. Furthermore, the AFI analysts argued that even if another country had developed such a craft, that development would not explain the sightings over the USA, because the country wouldn't fly the craft in an area where the USA could learn its technological secrets if it crashed or was shot down. In spite of their inability to identify the nature or source of the flying discs, the AFI analysts concluded that "flying discs, as reported by widely scattered observers, probably represent something real and tangible, even though physical evidence, such as crash-recovered exhibits, is not available."* Whereas some reports might result from natural or manmade phenomena, "the likelihood that some observers actually saw disc-shaped objects sufficiently large to be compared in size with known aircraft cannot be dismissed."

In other words, AFI concluded that flying saucers are real, and probably not flying craft from a foreign country. The AFI study ends with the statement, "The Directorate of Intelligence, USAF, will continue to collect and analyze all reports of sightings of flying objects, lights, trails, etc. in an effort to develop an answer to the puzzling problem which they present."

On December 18, 1947, General McDonald, the Director of AFI, wrote a letter to Major General Craigie, the Director of Air Force Research and Development. The letter presented the overall AFI opinion on flying saucers (real and need investigation) and stated that General McDonald agreed with General Twining's recommendation to set up a special project for investigation and analysis of sightings.

---

* The inclusion of the statement that "crash-recovered exhibits are not available" indicates either that no flying disc had crashed (the Roswell material was not from a saucer), or that the existence of a crash was being withheld from AFI intelligence analysts, or that the writer of the AFI study was intentionally lying about the absence of crash debris.

On December 30, 1947, General Craigie responded by issuing a directive to the Commanding General of AMC (Twining) to set up a special project with the code name "Sign," at Wright Field. Craigie directed Project Sign to "collect, collate, evaluate and distribute to interested government agencies and contractors all information concerning sightings and phenomena in the atmosphere which can be construed to be of concern to national security."*

Although initial preparations for a special project had begun several months before in AMC, the final organization of Project Sign took place in early January, and the project officially began on January 22, 1948.

Sign immediately ran into problems. There was little financial support and the personnel of the project had to be borrowed from other projects. Nevertheless, within a few weeks, the Air Force and the Army issued their first offical requests for information on "Flying Discs." The Army's intelligence collection document was a shortened version of the AMC EEI document discussed above. The Air Force's intelligence collection request, issued in February, 1948, was not based on the EEI. Instead, it asked for basic sighting information such as location and date, time, weather, names of witnesses, number of objects, size, speed, etc.

Thus began the Air Force's 21 year foray into the realm of the impossible . . . *flying saucers.*

The Project Sign personnel were so impressed by the sightings that, about seven months later, they tried to convince the Chief of Staff of the Air Force, General Vandenberg, that flying saucers were interplanetary vehicles. However, Vandenberg rejected this idea and thereby removed interplanetary vehicles as an acceptable explanation for any of the sightings. His rejection had a negative impact on the AMC investigators. It forced them to use explanations (misidentification or misperception, delusion, hoax) which they really didn't think were correct for many sightings. Possible reasons for the rejection and its impact on the history of UFO research are discussed in Chapter 5.

---

* Note the non-specific wording of the last part of the sentence. Virtually any atmospheric phenomenon could be investigated if it could be construed to be of concern to national security. Where is the specific mention of flying saucers?

As for the FBI, by this time it was no longer in the saucer business. At least not officially.

Chapter 4
Ash Can Covers and Toilet Seats

F BI agents officially investigated saucer sightings for about a month and then abruptly ended the investigation as a result of a bit of a scandalous situation.

In August 1947, an FBI agent learned that the Air Force had not been totally honest when it asked for help. A letter from Lt. General Stratemeyer, Assistant Chief of Staff for Intelligence, to the Commanding Generals of the 1st, 2nd, 4th, 10th, 11th and 14th Air Forces, stated that the FBI had been brought into the investigation for the following reason: "to relieve the numbered Air Forces of the task of tracking down all the many instances which turned out to be ash can covers, toilet seats and whatnot." In other words, "whereas the Air Defense Command Air Forces would interview responsible observers," the FBI "would investigate incidents of discs being found by civilians on the ground," i.e., the hoax cases.

The letter, classified "Restricted" and dated September 3, 1947, was given to the FBI in San Francisco by Lt. Colonel Donald Springer. The agent sent a copy of the document to FBI headquarters along with the comment that "the Bureau might desire to discuss this matter further with the Army Air Forces both as to the types of investigations which we will conduct and also to object to the scurrilous wordage which, to say the least, is insulting to the Bureau."

On September 27, Director J. Edgar Hoover wrote a letter to Major General McDonald. In the letter he mentioned the comment about "ash can covers, toilet seats and whatnot," thereby demonstrating that the FBI had "penetrated" the Air Force secrecy about saucer investigation. He then pointed out that he couldn't "permit the personnel and time of this organization to be dissipated in this manner," and informed the General that the FBI would no longer investigate disc sightings. Instead, it would send

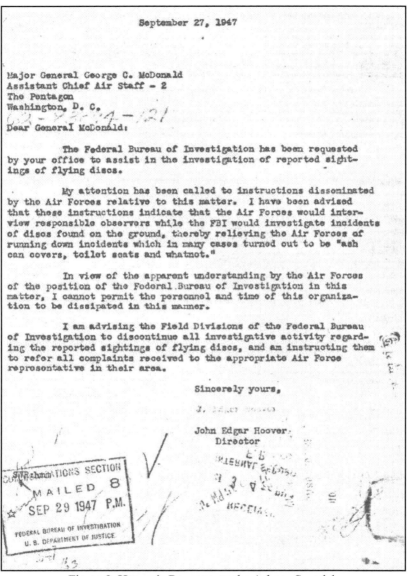

September 27, 1947

Major General George C. McDonald
Assistant Chief Air Staff - 2
The Pentagon
Washington, D. C.

Dear General McDonald:

The Federal Bureau of Investigation has been requested by your office to assist in the investigation of reported sightings of flying discs.

My attention has been called to instructions disseminated by the Air Forces relative to this matter. I have been advised that these instructions indicate that the Air Forces would interview responsible observers while the FBI would investigate incidents of discs found on the ground, thereby relieving the Air Forces of running down incidents which in many cases turned out to be "ash can covers, toilet seats and whatnot."

In view of the apparent understanding by the Air Forces of the position of the Federal Bureau of Investigation in this matter, I cannot permit the personnel and time of this organization to be dissipated in this manner.

I am advising the Field Divisions of the Federal Bureau of Investigation to discontinue all investigative activity regarding the reported sightings of flying discs, and am instructing them to refer all complaints received to the appropriate Air Force representative in their area.

Sincerely yours,

J.

John Edgar Hoover
Director

COMMUNICATIONS SECTION
MAILED 8
SEP 29 1947 P.M.
FEDERAL BUREAU OF INVESTIGATION
U. S. DEPARTMENT OF JUSTICE

Figure 9: Hoover's Response to the Ashcan Scandal.

all sighting investigation reports to the Air Force. See Figure 9.

On the first of October, FBI headquarters sent Bulletin #57 to all the FBI offices: "All future reports connected with flying discs should be referred to the Air Force and no investigative action should be taken by Bureau agents." Thus ended the period of official FBI investigation of flying saucer sightings. During this time, FBI agents had interviewed witnesses to about two dozen sightings. Roughly one quarter of the sightings they investigated involved hoax devices (model saucers).

However, Bulletin #57 did not end the saucer data collection activities of the FBI, nor did it close the "X file." In a letter to the Special Agent in Charge (SAC) at San Francisco, dated February 20, 1948, and entitled FLYING DISC, SECURITY MATTER - X, the FBI Director stated that in the future the FBI would collect information from witnesses who volunteered it and turn it over the Air Force. Furthermore, that the FBI would "receive any information which the Air Forces volunteer." It is this last phrase which makes the FBI file important for UFO research because, in the following years, Air Force representatives provided the FBI with information which was not provided to the American people. Most importantly, FBI headquarters stored this information.

Although the period of official investigation had ended, FBI agents interviewed a few more witnesses in the fall of 1947. In March 1948, the FBI received a letter from Senator Kenneth Wherry of Nebraska asking the FBI to comment on a disc observation described in a letter from one of Wherry's constituents, a resident of Benkelman, Nebraska.

According to the letter (published here for the first time), on March 13 at 2:30 p.m. Mountain Standard Time the man (whose name has been blacked out on the FOIPA-released document) heard a noise like a motor or a train at a very long distance on a quiet day. He looked into the sky. Then, he wrote:

At first glance (the object) looked like it might be a vapor trail left by a high flying plane. But the white streak that was in the sky never changed its shape or did it change in the direction of travel. It traveled much faster than any plane I have seen traveling in the sky high enough to leave a vapor trail. As near as I can describe this sight was that it might appear to be a streamlined train traveling at a very high altitude at a very high rate of speed. This rocket or whatever it might have been was high enough to disappear from sight while it was yet far above the horizon....The silver streak in the sky traveled as if it were a long connected streak. This did not resemble a line of smoke left by a train traveling along; it moved altogether as a unit.

The witness saw this object traveling east to west and thought it might have passed over Denver, Colorado. He ended his letter with the following statement:

> I am not writing this so that it might seem to be another disc fan or whatever you might call them. I just saw this and it has been on my mind and I thought if there was anything that I could be of help to solve this thing (sic) I would write this to you and you can forward this to the proper Dept. if it is necessary. If it is not against any regulation and if (it is) possible (I) would like to have (an) answer to this object (sic).

Hoover wrote to the witness that he had forwarded the letter to the "Secretary of the Army, National Defense Building, Washington, D.C." Presumably the letter would eventually have gotten to the Air Force and eventually to Project Sign at Wright-Patterson Air Force Base. However, a check of the master case file of Project Blue Book at the National Archives, which is supposed to list all the sightings received by the Air Force since early 1947, does not contain a listing for this sighting.

From April through July, 1948, the FBI had only a few communications with the Air Force regarding saucers. Then the FBI was called back into action by a postmaster. At noon on August 11 at Hamel, Minnesota, two boys, 8 and 10 years old, saw a silver, two foot diameter object like two plates lip-to-lip descend to the ground near them. It made a whistling noise and rotated as it contacted the ground with a crunching noise and then seemed to rebound upward. It hovered momentarily and sped off. The boys ran to their parents and appeared visibly frightened as they told what they had seen. Their parents covered the landing spot with a washtub and then reported the incident to the local postmaster. The postmaster knew of no reason to doubt the boys so he contacted the local FBI agent who interviewed the boys at their house. He saw a depression in the soil where the saucer had landed. The agent sent his report to the local Air Force intelligence representative. Since there was a depression, the Air Force decided it would be advisable to have the FBI laboratory analyze the soil. The FBI analyzed a sample for unusual metal particles, evidence of heat and evidence of radioactivity. Nothing unusual was found.

No one disputed the children's testimony at the time of the sighting, but a year later the Air Force sighting analysts, who were under pressure to explain every sighting in some way or other, concluded as follows: "This apparent bit of fantasy is hardly worth further consideration."

Chapter 5
Project Sign and the
Extraterrestrial Estimate

During 1948 the "X" file of the FBI was mostly dormant, not to awake again until January, 1949. The Air Force "X" file, on the other hand, was not dormant. It contained secret documents which showed it was very active, even approaching red hot. Although the FBI wasn't involved, it is important to learn what happened within the Air Force investigation in 1948 since that determined to a considerable extent what the FBI learned from the Air Force in later years.

As pointed out previously, there were two Air Force intelligence groups involved in saucer sighting analysis. One group, within AFI, was headquartered in the Pentagon. AFI would collect information related to foreign developments in aircraft for analysis by AFI experts. It would also send copies to AMC for an independent analysis by the experts at T-2 and T-3. With regard to the saucer sightings, the available records suggest that the AFI and T-2,3 personnel could be divided into two factions: those who believed that people were seeing real, significant objects and those who thought the sightings were mistakes, signifying nothing (after all, there was no "hard evidence"). Since it was the AFI which established the liaison with the FBI, the FBI file records show mainly the AFI opinion. (The AFI documents were not turned over to the National Archives when the Blue Book documents were in 1975. They were released ten or more years later.)

The intelligence group called T-2 or the "Analysis Division," was a part of AMC at Wright Field. In 1948, T-2 became the Technical Intelligence Division and then the Air Technical Intelligence Center (ATIC) while Wright Field, in Dayton, Ohio, was renamed Wright-Patterson Air Force Base (the base was referred to as Wright Field for many years after the name change). Sign and its successors, Grudge and Blue Book, were special projects within ATIC. Projects Sign and Grudge were poorly funded and the personnel involved were borrowed from other intelligence activities. This low level of support limited their data-gathering and analysis ability but did not limit their enthusiasm for the project. Several of the Sign investigators had already been studying saucer-like (low aspect ratio) flying craft for several years. They were involved with the analysis and exploitation of the German war research into wingless craft.* The AMC/ATIC personnel would analyze sightings and send copies of their work to AFI at the Pentagon. The records from AMC/ATIC and from the Air Force Office of Special Investigations, which handled most of the witness interrogations—the legwork of investigation—were turned over to the National Archives in 1975.

Fact: in a formerly Top Secret study written about 9 months after the start of Project Sign, but not released to the general public until 1985, AFI analysts reaffirmed the conclusion made in the fall of 1947 that flying saucers are real objects. Of more importance is the fact, according to Captain Edward Ruppelt in *The Report on Unidentified Flying Objects,* that in the summer of 1948, the ATIC/Sign investigators tried to convince General Hoyt Vandenberg, Chief of Staff of the Air Force, that flying saucers were interplanetary vehicles!

But, how could this be? Aren't all saucer sightings figments of the imagination or mistakes or hoaxes? That's what the Air Force told the public, and that's what the skeptics, the press, and most people believed. However that's not what AFI and ATIC believed in 1948, and here's the reason: there were dozens of sightings by credible witnesses, including Air Force and other military personnel, that could not be explained. Many of these sightings were obtained through official channels because of the information requests, such as the EEI discussed previously,

---

* It appears from the record that when saucers first began to be sighted these investigators took the sightings more seriously than most people because they already believed that craft shaped generally like saucers could fly. Of course, they would have assumed that the saucers were developments of another country, probably the Soviet Union, which had captured many German aeronautical researchers and documents.

which were sent to Air Force, Navy and Army units stationed throughout the world in early 1948.

In early 1948, Major General Charles P. Cabell replaced Major General McDonald as the Chief of the Air Intelligence Requirements Division of the Directorate of Intelligence in the Office of the Deputy Chief of Staff for Operations. On February 27, 1948, a month after Project Sign officially began, Lt. Colonel Garrett, acting for General Cabell, wrote a letter containing specific instructions that would apply to reporting flying disc sightings. The letter began:

> 1. It is Air Force policy not to ignore reports of sightings and phenomena in the atmosphere, but to recognize that part of its mission is to collect, collate, evaluate and act on information of this nature.
> 2. In implementing this policy the Air Materiel Command has been designated as the Air Force agency to collect, collate, evaluate and distribute to interested government agencies and contractors all information concerning sightings and phenomena in the atmosphere which can be construed to be of concern to the national security.

Unlike the previously discussed EEI with its list of intelligence requirements, the instructions included with this letter were to report the location, time, weather, names and occupations of observers, any photographs, the number of objects sighted, color, shape, speed, sound, altitude, maneuvers, etc. In other words, this letter requested specific information that would pertain only to visual sightings of objects in the atmosphere. This sort of information was used by AFI and ATIC analysts to determine saucer activities around the world. The letter specified that, rather than sending sighting reports to AFI headquarters at the Pentagon, the reports were to be sent directly to a special office, MCI, within ATIC at Wright-Patterson Air Force Base, Dayton, Ohio, thereby saving time by bypassing AFI. AMC would then send copies of the reports and analyses to AFI.

General Cabell's decision to speed up the AMC analysis process by having sightings sent directly to AMC meant that AFI had to rely on AMC for reports and analyses. This procedure allowed AMC effectively to control what AFI received. (Two and a half years later General Cabell would discover that this procedure had a negative impact on the Air Force saucer investigation. He would discover that skeptical ATIC analysts invented explanations for all the sightings, whether or not the explanations were reasonable, and sent these explanations to AFI. He further discovered that they had lied to him when they claimed they were carrying out unbiased investigations.)

By March 1948, Project Sign was well underway at ATIC. Reports from 1947 were being analyzed and new reports were being received. By this time, according to the Project Blue Book microfilm record at the National Archives, ATIC had collected approximately 130 reports. For years, civilian UFO investigators thought that these were the only sightings received by Project Sign up to that time. Then in early 1996, a document was released by the government which provides the first quantitative evidence that the Air Force may have withheld (or lost) sighting reports.

This information turned up in the transcript of the March 18, 1948 meeting of the Air Force Science Advisory Board (AFSAB). Although most of this Secret level meeting was devoted to presentations about various conventional Air Force advanced technology and technical intelligence projects, for a few minutes Colonel Howard McCoy, Director of Intelligence at AMC, discussed an unconventional intelligence project at ATIC:

> We have a new project - Project SIGN - which may surprise you as a development from the so-called mass hysteria of the past summer when we had all the unidentified flying objects or discs. This can't be laughed off. We have over 300 reports which haven't been publicized in the papers from very competent personnel, in many instances - men as capable as Dr. K.D. Wood, and practically all Air Force, Airline people with broad experience (sic). We are running down every report. I can't even tell you how much we would give to have one of those crash in an area so that we could recover whatever they are.

Since Colonel McCoy was the head of intelligence at AMC and therefore responsible for project Sign it is important to understand what he said . . . and what he did not say.

He approached this subject lightly, almost apologetically. I presume he took this approach because his audience consisted of scientists, most or all of whom were not involved in saucer investigations and knew only what had been reported in the press.

The scientific community was generally skeptical about the sightings, since the press had treated the subject lightly and the Air Force had not publicly reported the existence of any convincing evidence. Most, or perhaps all, of the members of Colonel McCoy's audience would not have known any more than was reported in the press and therefore would not have been inclined to treat the subject seriously.

Colonel McCoy, presumably to counter the anti-saucer bias of these scientists, began by telling them that the sightings were important and couldn't be simply "laughed off." He then stated that there were "over 300" unpublicized reports by "very competent personnel." The number he quoted is surprisingly large because the Project Blue Book microfilm lists only about 130 sightings as of March 1948, and many of these had been publicized. Perhaps he simply made an error in his recollection of how many sightings had been collected, but taken literally his statement suggests that there might be more than 160 sightings missing from the first 9 months of the Blue Book file—June 1947 to March 1948 inclusive.

To lend a weight of authority to his statement about the importance of the sightings, he mentioned Dr. Karl D. Wood, an eminent scientist and Head of the Aeronautical Engineering Department at the University of Colorado. Dr. Wood had reported a December, 1947, sighting of some sort of "strange aircraft" leaving a trail "not like a usual jet airplane trail." (Unfortunately the object was too high for Dr. Wood to see its shape.) McCoy indicated just how seriously ATIC was treating these sightings by saying that every one of them was being investigated.

His closing remark about wishing one would crash indicates his belief that they were solid objects, otherwise they couldn't crash, and also that the Air Force had to wait for one to crash because they couldn't shoot one down (had they been conventional enemy aircraft the Air Force could have shot one down). Of course the straightforward interpretation of his closing remark is that none had crashed. There are (at least) two other possible interpretations of his "wish:" (a) McCoy, being only a colonel, did not know about the Roswell debris (in other words, Twining or someone higher up had not told him) or (b) a more sinister aspect: he knew but had been ordered to mislead the audience in order to avoid any interest that would suddenly arise in the members of the scientifically trained audience if they thought that there were hard evidence of saucer reality.*

During the next seven months of 1948, the AMC collected about a hundred sightings, according to the tabulation presented in Project Blue Book Special Report #14 (published in 1955). They could not explain most of these sightings. Furthermore, some sightings seemed to indicate intelligent control of highly maneuverable craft. According to Captain Ruppelt in *The Report on Unidentified Flying Objects*, some of the reports were of average quality, puzzling but not totally convincing. However, a large proportion came from people whose reliability couldn't be questioned. Ruppelt cited the report by three scientists who, for 30 seconds, watched a "round object streak across the sky in a highly erratic flight path near the Army's secret White Sands Proving Ground." He mentioned the report by an Air Force C-47 crew of "three UFOs (that came rapidly) in from 'twelve o'clock high' to buzz their transport," and he also mentioned a "curious report from the Netherlands from several persons who had seen a rocket-shaped object with two rows of windows along the side." Ruppelt wrote that this latter report probably would have been ignored "except that four nights later a similar UFO almost collided with an Eastern Airlines DC-3." This is a reference to the famous Chiles-Whitted sighting of July 24, 1948. At 2:45 a.m., while flying at 5,000 feet near Montgomery, Alabama, Captain Clarence Chiles and copilot John Whitted saw a roughly rocket shaped, wingless object with what appeared to be windows and a blue glow of light. An FBI document dated January

---

* Note: he was speaking at a Secret level meeting to a sizeable audience of people, most or all of whom could do their Air Force work without knowing about crashed saucers, i.e., they had no "need-to-know" about such information. It is important to realize that because of military regulations to protect highly secret information, one cannot discuss Top Secret information at the Secret level. In some cases, one cannot even mention the existence of Top Secret information in a discussion at the Secret level (and sometimes not even during a discussion at the Top Secret level) without explicit authorization from the person(s) or agency in charge of the information.

31, 1949 (to be discussed later) provides a brief summary:

> In July 1948 an unidentified aircraft was 'seen' by an Eastern
> Airlines Pilot and Co-pilot and one or more passengers of the Eastern
> airline plane over Montgomery, Alabama. This aircraft was reported
> to be of an unconventional type without wings and resembled
> generally a 'rocket ship' of the type depicted in comic strips. It was
> reported to have had windows; to have been larger than the Eastern
> Airlines plane, and to have been traveling at an estimated speed of
> 2700 miles an hour. It appeared out of a thunderhead ahead of the
> Eastern Airlines plane and immediately disappeared in another cloud
> narrowly missing a collision with the Eastern Airlines plane. No
> sound or air disturbance was noted in connection with this appear-
> ance.

The pilots told the Air Force investigators that the object had
square windows, a cherry-red flame or wake from the back end
and that it seemed to be only a few hundred feet higher than the
plane. After it passed the plane it seemed to gain altitude and
then it disappeared above the broken clouds. Note that the
estimated speed was roughly 2,000 mph faster than our aircraft
could travel, but was much slower than the speed of a meteor.
And, of course, glowing meteors do not fly roughly horizontally
through clouds at 5,000 feet altitude.

There also seemed to be corroborating sightings. According to
Ruppelt, "a crew chief at Robbins Air Force Base at Macon,
Georgia, reported seeing an extremely bright light pass overhead,
traveling at a high speed. . . . A quick check on a map showed
that the UFO that nearly collided with the airliner would have
passed almost over Macon," which was about 200 miles away.
"The UFO had been turning toward Macon when last seen."
There was also a report from a pilot flying over northern North
Carolina who said he had seen a bright "shooting star" in the
direction of Montgomery at about the exact time of the Chiles-
Whitted sighting. Of course, a shooting star would not pass a few
hundred feet from a plane flying at 5,000 feet and then climb into
the clouds again; a meteor that low would crash. Hence whatever
they saw was not a meteor.

This sighting was the straw that broke the camel's back as far
as AFI and Project Sign were concerned. Something had to be
done to find out what these saucers were. According to the

official Blue Book records, by this time the AFI and ATIC investigators had collected over 200 sightings, most of which they couldn't explain. Major General Cabell wanted a definitive analysis of these sightings. On July 27, 1948 he directed the Air Estimates Branch of AFI at the Pentagon to prepare a study to determine the "tactics of flying objects" and the "probability of their existence." In response to this directive, the Air Estimates Branch wrote a document, to be discussed, that proposed a most likely explanation and contained recommendations on what to do next.

The ATIC/Sign investigators also reacted to the Chiles-Whitted sighting and began writing their own "Estimate of the Situation." Whether this was in direct response to General Cabell's July 27 letter to AFI or whether they did it on their own is not clear from the available record. The ATIC investigators used the same sighting information as the AFI investigators but carried out an independent analysis. Their written response to the Chiles-Whitted sighting was decidedly more daring than the AFI response. The ATIC version of the Estimate used technical information derived from various sightings to arrive at the conclusion that at least some UFOs were interplanetary craft.

Captain Ruppelt wrote about the Estimate in *The Report on Unidentified Flying Objects*. Ruppelt wrote that he personally read the Estimate, and that it presented the extraterrestrial conclusion based on sightings by scientists, pilots, and other credible observers. Ruppelt did not state in his book exactly when the Estimate was sent to General Vandenberg for approval, but he did say it was "a matter of days" before a sighting that occurred on October 1. Another clue to the date is available in the draft of the manuscript of his book, which has become available to researchers only in recent years. The draft lists 10 of the sightings discussed in the Estimate, only 3 of which were published in his book.

One of the unpublished sightings occurred at the atomic energy research facility known as Los Alamos in New Mexico (which would play an important role in sighting history in the months and years following the demise of the Estimate). According to Ruppelt's draft manuscript, "A group of people were waiting for an airplane at the landing strip in Los Alamos when one of them noticed something glint in the sun. It was a flat, circular object, high in the northern sky. The appearance and relative size was the same as a dime held edgewise and slightly tipped, about 50 feet away." This sighting occurred on September 23, 1948 (exactly a year after Twining's letter to Schulgen which said flying saucers are real!). Since the Estimate seen by Ruppelt included this sighting it must have been written and sent to Vandenberg after September 23 and several days before October 1.

According to Ruppelt, the Top Secret Estimate was passed, without comment, upward through the ranks, probably though the AMC chain of command, to General Vandenberg. General Vandenberg then rejected it for "lack of proof." Several of the Project Sign scientists and officers then went to the Pentagon to discuss the Estimate with Vandenberg. They tried to convince him that all their analyses logically pointed toward interplanetary vehicles but, according to Ruppelt, Vandenberg repeated his rejection.

Let's suppose there really was hard evidence known to Vandenberg but not to the aircraft and intelligence experts at Project Sign. At the same time, let us suppose that the experts logically and honestly arrived at the interplanetary conclusion even without hard evidence. Why wouldn't Vandenberg accept it? After all, they were the acknowledged experts in understanding foreign aircraft technology. They had found good reasons to say the saucers were interplanetary. Then, in a discussion which couldn't have lasted more than several hours, and may have lasted less than an hour, Vandenberg essentially told them, "Sorry, wrong answer." Why tell the experts that, in spite of a year of investigation and analysis, they were wrong? Was he truly unconvinced by their logic, or did he have a hidden agenda? Was he trying to cover something up? Methinks he did protest too much!

Since there are (at least as of the time of this writing) no documented answers to these questions, I can only speculate that he didn't want the ET conclusion to be accepted. Obviously, if it had been accepted, the reality of flying saucers would have become official Air Force policy. The conclusion might then have leaked out, and the Air Force would have had a big problem. It would have had to admit to the American people that alien craft were flying around and the Air Force could do nothing about it.

Vandenberg's rejection of the Estimate was a very important turning point—a watershed event in the history of the Air Force investigation. In rejecting the Estimate, Vandenberg effectively set forth a non-science based policy that UFOs or flying saucers could not be officially identified as extraterrestrial vehicles. One may imagine that the civilian scientists and military officials who worked on Project Sign were disappointed, perhaps even stunned, at the rejection. They knew that Vandenberg, because of his rank at the top of the military establishment, knew things they didn't. Perhaps they assumed that he rejected the ET conclusion because he knew the objects were something else, although they couldn't imagine what, since they had already considered and rejected the "secret US project" and the "advanced foreign aircraft" theories. Perhaps they assumed Vandenberg rejected it simply because he couldn't deal with the consequences of acceptance. Whatever the reasons, they were sent home, tails between their legs, with orders to find other explanations. Sometime later the order came to destroy all copies of the Estimate. (Evidently at least one survived for Ruppelt to read three years later, but then it, too, was destroyed.)

When a four star general speaks, lower ranks listen and act accordingly. The saucers appeared to be solid, mechanically engineered objects rather than natural phenomena or figments of the imagination. Therefore, if they couldn't be extraterrestrial vehicles they had to be man-made aircraft or missiles.

By early October 1948, the ATIC/Sign investigators were again seriously considering the possibility that saucers were super secret developments of the United States military or some civilian agency, developments which Vandenberg may have known about, but he wasn't willing to tell them. The problem then was to justify this explanation. During the previous nine months, Project Sign had sent requests for information on flying discs and aerial phenomena to numerous military and civilian intelligence agencies, including the Air Force, Navy, Army,

Counter Intelligence Corps, FBI, and more. Now they were going to try again. On October 7, 1948, Colonel McCoy wrote the following letter to the Navy, the Army and the CIA:

> This Headquarters is currently engaged in an intelligence investigation of all reported unidentified aerial phenomena. To date, no concrete evidence as to the exact identity of any of the reported objects has been received. Similarly, the origin of the so called 'flying discs' remains obscure. The possibility exists that some of the sighted objects are of domestic origin, i.e., unrecognized configurations of some of our latest aeronautical attainments, or that they are objects not readily recognized by the public - test vehicles in various stages of development, etc.
>
> Where security regulations will permit, it is requested that your office submit to....(a long mailing address)..any available evidence which might serve to indicate that these objects have a domestic origin.
>
> Your cooperation in so doing might greatly assist in identifying our own domestic developments from possible inimical foreign achievements.

Of course, they didn't receive any positive response.[*]

Since the saucers were not our missiles but appeared to be real objects, i.e., someone's missiles, they had to be of foreign origin. The only way the investigators could imagine the missiles to be of foreign origin was if the Soviets had pushed German WWII technology far beyond anything that we had imagined. And yet, they could not really accept that either. They were confident that the USA had the most advanced aircraft technology. Furthermore, they didn't believe that, even if the Soviets had such advanced aircraft, they would fly them over the United States where one might crash or be shot down. They were caught on the horns of a dilemma, and were being forced to reject the reality of the objects sighted. Thus began the decline in quality of the Air Force flying saucer investigation, one which would not be reversed, and then only temporarily, until late 1951.

---

[*] The fact that the Colonel McCoy would, once again, search for a domestic project to explain saucer sightings is certainly not consistent with the idea that he and those working for him knew of any hard evidence which would prove that saucers were real. If it is assumed that someone at Sign did know of hard evidence, then the appeal for help in the above letter must be considered to be a clever ploy to divert attention away from the hard evidence.

No documentation presently available indicates that the Estimate was a response to General Cabell's July 27 request for an evaluation. Nor is there any documentation which shows that General Cabell was even aware of the Estimate. Instead, the only available documentation indicates that General Cabell was not aware of the AMC opinion until after he asked for it in a November 3 letter (to be described) over a month after the Estimate had been rejected by Vandenberg. Perhaps General Cabell knew about the Estimate but didn't allow his knowledge to be documented. On the other hand, the ATIC/Sign investigators, being in a separate chain of command from AFI, may have acted entirely on their own in creating the Estimate of the Situation and then they may have simply bypassed AFI and sent the Estimate through AMC channels to Vandenberg. It may be that the ATIC/Sign personnel wrote and sent the Estimate simply to test the waters, that is, to find out if "interplanetary" was an explanation that the Top Brass would accept.

General Cabell did get a response to his July 27th request from AFI. On August 11, he was given an interim response on the methods of analysis "being utilized in the preparation of the required study and the methods suggested to Project 'Sign' personnel at Headquarters, Air Materiel Command, for pursuing flying object phenomena to the end that positive identifications might be achieved." The final response came as an attachment to an October 11 letter written by Colonel Brooke Allen, Chief of the Air Estimates Branch of AFI. It was not as bold as the Estimate, arguing only that the sightings were of real objects, and suggesting that they were of foreign (Soviet) origin. Although there is no direct evidence of this, the fact that the AFI and ATIC personnel worked quite closely on the sighting analysis suggests that the AFI intelligence personnel who wrote the response to Cabell were aware of the Estimate and its rejection at the very top and so wrote their response in a way which would not be rejected. Thus, in a sense, what follows might be considered the "cousin" of the Estimate. The report was sent along with the following Top Secret letter, which was not released to the public until the mid 1980s:

1. As directed by Cover Sheet, dated 27 July 1948, subject 'Pattern

of Flying Saucers,' a study was commenced to determine the tactics of flying objects and the probability of their existence.

2. The attached study, 'Analysis of Flying Object Incidents in the United States,' has been compiled in an attempt to answer the questions .

3. An exhaustive study was made of all information pertinent to the subject in this Division and the Intelligence Division of Air Materiel command. Opinions of both aeronautical engineers and well qualified intelligence specialists have been solicited in an endeavor to consider all possible aspects of the question.

4. Because the subject matter is of such an elusive nature, this study is presented as a preliminary report to be reconsidered when information at hand warrants it.

5. Tentative conclusions have been drawn and are as follows:

a. It must be accepted that some type of flying objects have been observed, although their identification and origin are not discernible. In the interest of national defense it would be unwise to overlook the possibility that some of these objects may be of foreign origin.

b. Assuming that the objects might eventually be identified as foreign or foreign-sponsored devices the possible reason for their appearance over the U.S. requires consideration. Several possible explanations appear noteworthy, viz:

1. To negate U.S. confidence in the atom bomb as the most advanced and decisive weapon in warfare.

2. to perform photographic reconnaissance missions.

3. To test U.S. air defenses.

4. To conduct familiarization flights over U.S. territory.

6. It is recommended that distribution of this study be limited to the Air Staff.

Here was an analysis of the situation that General Vandenberg could accept. Although the writers of this document concluded that flying saucers are real, there is no suggestion that they might be of extraterrestrial origin. Instead, this document confines the discussion to missiles which are (add qualifier of choice: probably, maybe, possibly, or "we hope") of foreign, i.e., Soviet, origin. The formerly Top Secret document attached to the above letter, entitled "Analysis of Flying Object Incidents in the U.S.," was jointly published in December, 1948 by the Directorate of Intelligence of the Air Force and by the Office of Navy Intelligence as "Air Intelligence Division Study No. 203" (declassified in 1985).

Following a standard format for such documents, it established that the sightings did, indeed, pose a problem by presenting a strong case for saucer reality. The main text states that about 210 sightings were analyzed and that:

> . . . among the observers reporting on such incidents are trained and experienced U.S. Weather Bureau personnel, USAF rated officers, experienced civilian pilots, technicians associated with various research projects and technicians employed by commercial airlines.

In other words, the witnesses were generally above average in credibility and accuracy of reporting, certainly not publicity seekers, dreamers, hoaxers, and town drunks. Two dozen unexplained sightings are summarized, including two that were investigated by the FBI: the William Rhodes sighting (his UFO photos were reprinted in the report) and the Portland Police officer sighting. Other summarized sightings were by meteorologists, scientists, private pilots (including Kenneth Arnold), commercial pilots, and military pilots.

Of particular interest are the following cases.

On November 12, 1947, the second officer of the Navy tanker *Ticonderoga*, 20 miles off the coast of Oregon, watched for 45 seconds as "two flying disks trailing jet-like streams of fire" traveled in a "long low arc" at a speed estimated at 700-900 mph.

On April 5, 1948, "three trained balloon observers of the Geophysics Laboratory Section of the Watson Laboratories, N.J. reported seeing a round, indistinct object in the vicinity of Holloman Air Force Base, New Mexico. It was very high and fast, and appeared to execute violent maneuvers at high speed. The object was under observation for approximately 30 seconds and disappeared suddenly."

Twenty five days later, on April 30, a Navy pilot flying near Anacostia, Maryland, saw "a yellow or light colored sphere, 25 to 40 feet in diameter" that was "moving at a speed of approximately 100 miles per hour at an altitude of about 4,500 feet."

On July 1, "twelve discs were reported over Rapid City Air Base by Major Hammer. These disks were oval shaped, about 100 feet long, flying at a speed estimated to be in excess of 500 mph. Descending from 10,000 feet, these disks made a 30-degree to 40-degree climbing turn accelerating very rapidly until out of sight." With sighting reports such as these, it is not surprising that Air Force intelligence was convinced that saucers were real and definitely not man made.

Not mentioned in this document are six of the ten sightings claimed by Ruppelt (in his draft manuscript) to be in the ATIC/Sign Estimate. The fact that some sightings attributed by Ruppelt to the ET Estimate are not found in this document can be considered to be evidence that it is not simply a modified version of the ET Estimate. Unfortunately, without a copy of the ET Estimate, we can never be certain just how dissimilar the two documents were.

According to this document, of the 210 sightings analyzed, only 18 could definitely be identified. Of the 18 explained sightings, "three were hoaxes and two were from unreliable witnesses." The other explained sightings were honest misidentifications or failures of the witnesses to recognize what they were seeing. Thus, the information in this report directly contradicted the public position of the Air Force that most sightings could be explained and that many sightings were from hoaxers and unreliable people. (Sounds a bit like a cover-up, perhaps?)

Meanwhile, we can imagine that back at ATIC, the Sign investigators were trying to recover from the Estimate debacle. Although the ET spacecraft explanation for saucers was disallowed by Vandenberg, his rejection did not apply to the possibility of spacecraft from another country on Earth! In an October 22 letter, Colonel William R. Clingerman, who was at this time the Acting Chief of the Intelligence Department and one of the Project Sign investigators, proposed a special study by the Rand Corporation to determine the technical requirements for creation of space-capable vehicles. According to the letter:

> The possibility that some of the unidentified aerial objects that have been reported in the United States and in foreign countries may have been experimental spaceships or test vehicles for the purpose of assisting in the development of spaceships has been given consideration by this Command. If such craft have actually been sighted it is believed more likely that they represent the effort of a foreign nation rather than a product from beyond the Earth.

Although Clingerman included the obligatory qualifier, "if

such craft have actually been sighted," it is clear that he was pushing the bounds of reason by suggesting that some country was advanced enough to experiment with vehicles capable of spaceflight. He probably did not believe that anyone on earth had created such vehicles. Nevertheless, he was sufficiently confident that some of the flying saucers were real that he was willing to spend government money to investigate the possibility that they were manmade spaceships or spaceship test vehicles. This document by Clingerman can be considered as further evidence that the spaceship hypothesis was seriously considered by the ATIC investigators.

On November 3, 1948, after reading the Top Secret AFI report, Cabell wrote to the Commanding General of AMC (now Lt. General Joseph McNarney) to point out that Project Sign had been set up under his command. Cabell went on to say:

> The conclusion appears inescapable that some type of object has been observed. Identification and the origin of the objects is not discernible to this Headquarters. It is imperative, therefore, that efforts to determine whether these objects are of domestic or foreign origin must be increased until conclusive evidence is obtained. The needs of national defense require such evidence in order that appropriate countermeasures may be taken.

During the previous months, members of the press had been nosing around trying to find out what the Air Force had learned about saucers after a year of study. One particularly insistent reporter was Sidney Shallett, a well-known writer for the very popular *Saturday Evening Post* magazine. Cabell reacted to Shallet's persistence and the general press interest by recommending, in the November 3 letter to General McNarney, that the Air Force should be "informing the public as to the status of the problem." He wrote: "To date there has been too little data to present to the public. The press, however, is about to take it into its own hands and demand to be told what we do or do not know about the situation. Silence on our part will not long be acceptable."

Cabell closed his letter by asking AMC for its "conclusions to date and recommendations as to the information to be given to the press. Your recommendation is requested also as to whether that information should be offered to the press or withheld until it is actively sought by the press." (The fact that Cabell asked for the AMC "conclusions to date" suggests that Cabell was not aware of the Estimate of the Situation.)

On November 8, Colonel McCoy responded in detail to Cabell's request for the AMC opinion. As you read this keep in mind that McCoy probably was aware of the ET Estimate and probably was aware of Vandenberg's rejection. If so, he was sensitive to the fact that ET had been removed from the list of acceptable explanations, leaving foreign missiles, misidentifications or misperceptions of natural phenomena or of manmade objects, hallucinations (psychological problems) and hoaxes as the only acceptable types of explanation.

> 1. In attempting to arrive at conclusions as to the nature of unidentified flying object incidents in the United States, this Command has made a study of approximately 180 incidents. Data derived from initial reports have been supplemented by further information obtained from check lists submitted by mail, from interrogations of other field agencies, and by personal investigation by personnel of this Command in the case of incidents that seem to indicate the possibility of obtaining particularly significant information.
> 2. The objects described fall into the following general classification groups, according to shape or physical configuration:
> a. Flat disc of circular or approximately circular shape
> b. Torpedo or cigar shaped aircraft, with no wings or fins visible in flight
> c. Spherical or balloon shaped objects
> d. Balls of light with no apparent form attached.

This formerly Secret letter (declassified in 1986) says that the ATIC/Sign personnel analyzed about 180 sightings (about 30 less than the 210 analyzed by the Air Estimates Branch in the Pentagon). According to this letter some of the round or balloon shaped objects had been identified as upper air balloons, some of the objects had been identified as "astrophysical" in nature, some may have had a psychological origin, some might have been hallucinations and some might have been deliberate hoaxes. (By not specifying the exact numbers this letter makes it sound as if a sizeable percentage had been explained, in contradiction to the "Analysis..." document which says that less than 10 percent (18 out of 210) had been positively explained.)

McCoy's letter then says that ATIC was in the process of hiring a prominent astrophysicist who would study the sightings to determine which could be stars, meteors, planets, etc.* ATIC was also coordinating "a study of psychological problems.... in coordination with the Aero-Medical Laboratory at this Headquarters." This study was intended to identify the sightings which could be reasonably explained as resulting from mental aberrations or the inability of people to accurately perceive and report unexpected phenomena. McCoy's letter continues:

> 6. Although explanation (sic) of many of the incidents can be obtained from the investigations described above there remains a certain number of reports for which no reasonable every day explanation is available. So far no physical evidence of the existence of the unidentified sightings has been obtained.

Here we find, once again, that they concluded, even in the absence of "hard evidence," that at least some of the sightings are of real, unexplainable flying objects. His statement that there is no physical evidence suggests that either he did not know of the Roswell material, that he knew but was intentionally covering it up in this letter, or else the Roswell material was not related to the saucer sightings. If the first possibility were true, then the above statement is further evidence of a cover-up at a very, very high level.

In the next paragraph, McCoy says that the various types of observed phenomena were not related to projects "of domestic origin" and that, although disc shaped aircraft could be made to fly, they would have "poor climb, altitude and range characteristics" with the available propulsion systems (propellor, jet). Colonel McCoy then says that a more awesome possibility had been considered:

> 8. The possibility that the reported objects are vehicles from another planet has not been ignored. However, tangible evidence to support conclusions about such a possibility are completely lacking
> The occurrence of incidents in relation to the approach to the

---

* This would be Dr. J. Allen Hynek, who was the Air Force consultant in astronomy from 1948 through 1969.

Earth of the planets Mercury, Venus and Mars have been plotted. A periodic variation in the frequency of incidents, which appears to have some relation to the planet approach curves, is noted, but it may be purely coincidence.

Evidently the ATIC analysts seriously considered the ET hypothesis, because they took the time to test the idea that the saucers might be coming from Venus or Mars in spite of the strong belief by astronomers that neither Mars nor Venus were populated with intelligent life. McCoy noted a periodicity in the sightings which seemed similar to the periodicity of planet approaches to the Earth, but this seeming correlation in the 1947-1948 sightings did not persist through the following years.

In this statement, we may be seeing a "Ghost of the Estimate." McCoy does not say that the ET hypothesis was proven false, but simply that the available evidence, being non-tangible, was not sufficiently convincing for it to be accepted. The implication of this statement is that, regardless of how good the sighting evidence might be, the ET hypothesis could be accepted only if hard evidence—crash debris and perhaps alien bodies—were available.

Colonel McCoy's letter presents the following conclusions:

a) In the majority of cases reported, observers have actually sighted some type of flying object which they cannot classify as an aircraft within the limits of their personal experience.

b) There is as yet no conclusive proof that unidentified flying objects, other than those which are known to be balloons, are real aircraft.

c) Although it is obvious that some types of flying objects have been sighted, the exact nature of those objects cannot be established until physical evidence, such as that which would result from a crash has been obtained.

These three paragraphs illustrate the confusion which set in when Vandenberg rejected the Estimate. In paragraphs (a) and (c) we find McCoy saying that observers actually sighted some types of flying objects, yet, in paragraph (b), he says there is no proof that these objects, other than balloons, are "real aircraft." Does this mean that the witnesses saw unreal aircraft which appeared real? Or does this mean that witnesses saw real objects which were not aircraft (i.e., not airplanes)?

Finally, Colonel McCoy answered General Cabell's question regarding what, if anything, should be said to the press:

> 11. It is not considered advisable to present to the press information on those objects which we cannot yet identify or about which we cannot present any reasonable conclusions. In the event that they insist on some kind of statement, it is suggested that they be informed that many of the objects sighted have been identified as weather balloons or astral bodies, and that investigation is being pursued to determine reasonable explanations for the others.

Evidently Colonel McCoy did not think it advisable to tell the American people the truth about the results of the saucer investigations. By advising General Cabell to tell the American people what amounts to an untruth, McCoy was recommending that the Air Force avoid (some might say "chicken out" from) facing up to the difficult issues that would be raised if the Air Force admitted that many of the sightings simply could not be explained as known objects or phenomena.

Instead, McCoy recommended a format for information release that became the basis of Air Force saucer information policy for most of the next twenty one years: (a) discuss openly the explained sightings, (b) formulate statements which make it appear to the American people that most sightings can be explained, (c) suggest that continued investigations will uncover explanations for those sightings not yet explained and (d), do not discuss the unexplained sightings. In later years, one more element would be added to this information release format: (e) state that the sightings which could not be explained simply had insufficient information for an explanation.*

On November 30, 1948 Major General Cabell again addressed the problem of the press in a letter to Brigadier General E. "Dinty" Moore, Assistant for Production of the Directorate of Intelligence. The letter, entitled "Publicity on Flying Saucer Incidents" referred to the AFI conclusion "that some type of

---

* A very comprehensive study of about 3,000 sightings, carried out in 1952-1953 and presented in Project Blue Book Special Report #14, showed that (e) was untrue: many of the unexplained sightings had more than enough information to confirm a conventional explanation if such were possible. The Air Force continued to use (e) in public statements anyway.

flying objects have been observed although their identification and origin are not yet discernible," and went on to say that "insufficient data is available to date to warrant any further action except continuing attempts to determine the nature and origin of these objects." Noting the "increasing pressure on the part of the U.S. Press to publicize 'flying saucer' incidents," Cabell said that he "has attempted to dissuade the Press from publishing articles of this nature" because the articles would be "speculative in nature and would probably result in a flood of reports, making the problem of analysis and evaluation ... increasingly difficult... ." He closed the letter by recommending that "inquiring agencies be informed that the Air Force is investigating carefully all valid reports..." and by requesting that the Secretary of Defense, James Forrestal, be asked to grant authority for the Air Force "to assist the press, upon request, in the preparation of such articles..."

Assist the press in writing articles? Does this mean that Cabell had a change of heart and would provide the press with honest-to-goodness flying saucer data? Or does it mean that by assisting the press Cabell could exert some control over what the press reported?

Sidney Shallett's persistence prevailed. He got approval for his flying saucer article from the Secretary of Defense, the Secretary of the Air Force and The Chief of Staff of the Air Force (General Vandenberg) who directed Air Force intelligence to assist Shallett. On January 5, 1949, Captain Burton English, Chief of the Review and Policy Section of the Directorate of Public Relations wrote a memo for Stephen Leo, the Director of Public Relations, regarding "Sid Shallett's 'Flying Saucers' article." Captain English placed certain restrictions on Shallett's "use of classified documents and intelligence files":

1. No documents classified Top Secret should be made available to him.

2. He should not be permitted to copy any documents emanating from a foreign source regardless of the classification.

3. The copies made of domestic documents should be classified, as indicated on the original documents, and should not be removed from the building.

The Air Force aggregate conclusions on various reports should not be made available to Mr. Shallett. In the event any foreign documents or information contained therefrom are used, I do not think that they should specify the area over which they were sighted, but rather that they be loosely identified as Europe or Asia, whichever the case may be.

Captain English also stated that his Directorate would review Mr. Shallett's article before publication.

About a week later, on January 13, 1949, Stephen Leo wrote to Lt. General Benjamin Chidlaw, who was the Deputy Commander of the Air Materiel Command, to alert him to the arrival of Mr. Shallett, whom he referred to as "our friend Sid Shallett." (Evidently Mr. Shallett had a close relationship with the Air Force.) Mr. Leo told Chidlaw that Shallett "had the approval of the Secretary of the Air Force, Chief of Staff of the Air Force and the Secretary of Defense," and that he had spent several days talking to officials at the Pentagon before traveling to AMC. Leo wanted Chidlaw to be sure that Shallett met Colonel McCoy and that "General Vandenberg wants him to be sure and talk to the staff involved on this project."

Mr. Leo continued:

Shallett has already gone through the two volumes of condensed incident summaries available here, including incidents 1 through 177, and he would like to go through the third volume which I understand your people have prepared. We would also like to have him accompany a field investigative unit if one happens to be sent out while he is there. He has indicated that he might like to contact some of the civilians who had provided information on this project and we have advised him that such contacts should be cleared through Colonel McCoy's shop.

Our intelligence people have had a telecon with McCoy's office, advising them of Sid's impending visit and, also, what material was provided here. The only restriction we have on the project is that no final, overall Air Force conclusions be revealed.

Mr. Shallett was provided the needed assistance by the Air Force, and by the end of January 1949 he had seen most or all of the sighting data. This assistance was, no doubt, very helpful to Mr. Shallett. However a cynic might make the following observation: Air Force intelligence really wanted no publicity because they feared that the publication of saucer stories would cause, quoting General Cabell writing in April, 1949, a "flurry of 'crank' reports and a consequent flooding of our investigative resources." Hence, Air Force intelligence may have decided to assist Mr. Shallett in order to influence or exert some control over Mr. Shallett's conclusions and thereby to damp down the public interest in making sighting reports. Whatever the reason for providing assistance, the fact is that the article, which was published in May 1949 (discussed in chapter 9), was almost 100% against saucer reality.

* * *

Project Sign formally ended in the middle of January 1949, but the saucer intelligence collection and analysis project continued under a new name, *Grudge*. During the following months, many of the senior Sign investigators, those individuals who had prepared the ET Estimate, were transferred to other projects. The remaining lower level Sign employees did little more than collect and file sightings while working on a final report that would summarize the findings of Project Sign. The quality of saucer investigations declined rapidly during Project Grudge as a strong skepticism set in at AMC. This was a reaction to Vandenberg's rejection of the logical conclusions presented in the Estimate. If the saucers weren't our projects, and if they couldn't be Russian devices and if they couldn't be ET craft, then, as illogical as it might seem, they had to be misidentifications, errors in reporting, delusions, anything but what they really appeared to be.

Although the investigative activity at Project Sign was winding down in late 1948 and early 1949, AFI in the Pentagon was maintaining its interest in saucer activity. On February 4, 1949, Major General Cabell issued "Air Intelligence Requirements Memorandum Number 4," entitled "Unconventional Aircraft," with the purpose "to enunciate continuing Air Force requirements for information pertaining to sightings of unconventional aircraft and unidentified flying objects, including the so-called "'Flying Discs,'" and "to establish procedures for reporting such information." This multi-page document specified the methods of reporting and the exact types of information desired relative to the observation (time, date, location, weather, etc.), relative to the observed object or objects (size, shape, distance, speed, color, etc.) and relative to the observer or observers (employment, hobbies, reliability, police or FBI records, etc.). The depth of the information requested in this memorandum made it clear that AFI was very serious about investigating saucer sightings..

It is a good thing AFI was still seriously interested, because a new version of the unidentified flying object phenomenon was about to begin. On October 14, 1948 Lt. Colonel W. Earle, Jr. of the Air Intelligence Requirements Division wrote a letter to the Plans and Collection Branch of Army Intelligence. The letter says: "Research which has been conducted by the Air Materiel Command reveals that groups of sightings of flying discs and/or other unidentified aerial objects occur at periodic intervals and that the beginning of a new interval is imminent." The letter then goes on to request help from the Army in reporting "sightings of unidentified aerial objects" directly to AMC "by the fastest means." The letter also asks that Army installations "initiate investigative action with special emphasis placed on the accumulation of photographic evidence of reported sightings."

On November 7, 1948, Colonel R. F. Ennis, acting for the Director of Army Intelligence, wrote the following memorandum to the commanding generals of the armies stationed in the continental U.S.:

> The Department of the Air Force has advised that sightings of 'Flying Discs' and/or other unidentified aerial objects occur periodically and that the beginning of a new period is imminent. It is requested that your command be particularly alerted to report sightings of any unidentified aerial objects to include, if possible, photographic evidence.

Only a month later, this AMC prediction was confirmed in an unexpected way when strange green lights were observed flying over sensitive military installations in the southwest, and these new sightings began just as the FBI was being dragged back into the saucer business.

Chapter 6
Protection of Vital Installations

F BI Director J. Edgar Hoover wanted to get out of the flying
saucer business and he succeeded for about a year, during
which time the Air Force grappled with the saucer mystery and
tried to make it go away. But saucers and unidentified aerial
phenomena didn't go away. Instead, they were seen in areas of
strategic importance to the United States, including areas where
atomic bombs were designed, tested, built, and stored.

Oak Ridge, Tennessee was one of those areas. During World
War Two, the War Department had established at Oak Ridge a
59,000 acre restricted area in which secret experiments were
carried out to obtain the material necessary for an atomic bomb.
Classified nuclear experiments and bomb fuel production were
still being done there in 1949. Naturally, the government wanted
Oak Ridge to be protected from Communist subversion and
spying, and the FBI was responsible for that protection. Hence a
close watch was maintained for anything out of the ordinary.

TO: DIRECTOR FBI January 10, 1949
FROM: SAC , KNOXVILLE
SUBJECT: "FLYING SAUCERS" OBSERVED OVER OAK
RIDGE AREA
INTERNAL SECURITY - X

Thus begins a letter sent to FBI headquarters which dragged
Hoover and his agents back into the saucer fray.

The Knoxville, Tennessee, FBI agent, C. C. McSwain, sent this
letter along with two photographs, which appeared to show a
flying saucer over Oak Ridge in July, 1947. The agent had been
given the photos by George Rathman, Chief Investigator of the
Security Division of the Atomic Energy Commission (predecessor of the Department of Energy) at Oak Ridge.

According to the letter, Mr. Rathman had gone to the trouble of locating and retrieving about two dozen copies of the pictures that the photographer had given to his friends. He had collected the photos at the request of Colonel C. D. Gasser, the Resident Engineer of the Nuclear Energy for the Propulsion of Aircraft (NEPA) Research Center at Oak Ridge because Gasser had become concerned about publicity regarding the photos. Colonel Gasser had also asked Rathman to advise persons who had the photos "to say nothing to anyone concerning them." (Gasser did not explain why this happened 1 1/2 years after the photos were taken.)

Rathman had then contacted the FBI to ask for an evaluation of the photos. Agent McSwain pointed out that, "In accordance with Bureau instructions, no active investigation of this matter was made." Nevertheless, Agent McSwain felt it was "advisable to interview Col. Gasser prior to submitting the photographs to the Bureau." The importance of this letter lies not in the fact that photos were submitted but rather in what Colonel Gasser told the FBI about the Air Force investigation.

In his September 1947 letter recommending a special project to study flying saucers, General Twining said that several special military research projects should be kept informed about the results of saucer investigations. Project NEPA was one of these special projects and so Colonel Gasser, who himself was an employee of AMC, was aware of some of the results of saucer research, but not all of it.

Gasser told Agent McSwain that "he knew nothing of an official nature concerning (saucers) other than the fact that they were believed by air force officials to be man-made missiles, rather than some natural phenomena." Gasser believed that "a great deal of information had been compiled concerning these missiles by air force intelligence and that research on the matter was being extensively done at Wright Field." He also said the Air Force was treating the matter seriously and that "the matter was being given absolutely no dissemination by the air force or other military personnel and that they had not deemed it advisable to advise him of all information pertaining to the missile." So far as he knew there were no pieces of a flying saucer available for analysis. It was his opinion that the best evidence available to the

Air Force at that time was "telephoto photographs which are now in the possession of the engineers at Wright Field," but he did not know how clear these photos were. Although he had not been told of any crashed flying saucer, he had heard of a report of a collision in early 1947 of a Czechoslovakian airliner with an unidentified missile, which he thought might have been a flying saucer.

Colonel Gasser said that these flying saucer "missiles" could travel "at a certain altitude above the contour of the ground" indicating some sort of "radio altimeter or radio control."* He was also aware of several sightings of vapor trails created by "aircraft" at extremely high altitude which left trails across the sky. He had observed one himself which was "completely unlike any vapor trail he had ever observed before in all of his experience with the air force. It was his judgement that whatever created the vapor trail was traveling at an unbelievably tremendous speed."

The most disturbing information provided by Colonel Gasser was his conjecture that these were Soviet atomic energy missiles. He based his conjecture on conversations with investigators at WPAFB and on reports written by intelligence agents in other countries. He pointed out that it was known . . .

> . . . as early as four years ago that some kind of flying disc was being experimented with by the Russians. In addition . . . he stated that more recent reports . . . from representatives of the Central Intelligence Agency in Southern Europe and Southern Asia (indicated that) the Russians were experimenting with some kind of radical aircraft or guided missile which could be dispatched for great distances out over the sea, made to turn in flight and return to the base.

In comparison, the USA experiments had only gone so far as "delivering a missile to the required point of impact and no consideration has been given to (giving) the missile the ability to return." He also claimed that "all appearances ..have usually approached the United States from a northerly direction and have been reported as returning in a northerly direction," as if they

---

* Recall the August 13, 1947 sighting by A. C. Urie, discussed in Chapter 2, who saw a saucer following the contours of the ground as it flew through the Snake River Canyon.

came to the USA over the North Pole and returned over the North Pole.*

Colonel Gasser also told the FBI that the presence of these "missiles" (saucers) had "given impetus to the research being done by the air force in their own program of nuclear energy for the propulsion of aircraft to develop guided missiles" and that "great efforts have been expended by the service to determine just what the nature of these missiles might be and . . . to decide whether or not an adequate defense can be established."

These latter statements of Colonel Gasser to the FBI show that the sightings of flying saucers had actually affected the direction of Air Force research into advanced forms of propulsion and defense (see Figures 10a and 10b). This is decidedly different from the "ho-hum" attitude the Air Force portrayed to the American people when it publicly emphasized that most sightings could be explained, that no evidence of advanced technology had been found and that saucer sightings were unimportant.

On January 24, 1949 an Assistant Director for Security, D. M. Ladd, summarized Gasser's remarks in a two page memorandum for J. Edgar Hoover. The memorandum made it clear that the matter of flying saucers was serious business, that AFI had compiled a lot of information on the subject, and that "research on the matter was being extensively done at Wright Field." The memorandum also discussed the Air Force opinion that saucers were "man-made missiles" operated by nuclear power and emphasized Gasser's conjecture that they were missiles flown from Russia which had the ability to turn around and return to their point of origin. The memorandum made it clear that the exact nature and origin of the missiles was not known and that much of what was reported was based on Gasser's own conclusions having read many intelligence reports on the sightings.

Although there is nothing in the available record to indicate Hoover's immediate reaction to this information, it must have made some impression on him. After all, the thought that a major enemy country could fly bomb-carrying missiles over our country

---

* This was incorrect information since saucers or "missiles" had been seen traveling in all sorts of directions. However, Gasser apparently believed it to be correct and the FBI took him at his word.

without hindrance is frightening. The fact that the Air Force seemed to be covering this up may have been disconcerting to Hoover. Perhaps the information from Gasser combined with the sudden appearance of strange lights over secure areas (next chapter) convinced Hoover that the American people should know more about these sightings than the Air Force was telling them. Perhaps Hoover became convinced it was necessary to break security to tell the American public that the Air Force thought Soviet missiles were overflying our country. I can't prove it, but there is evidence to suggest that Hoover did exactly this several months later.

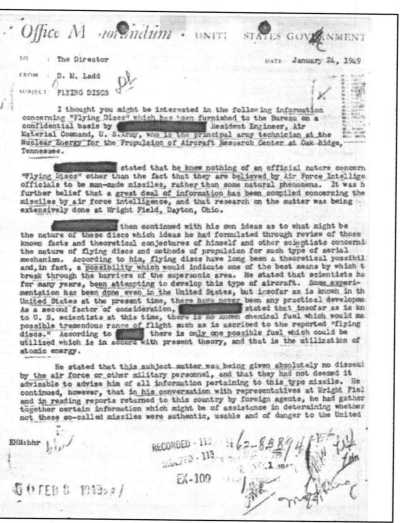

Office Memorandum • UNITED STATES GOVERNMENT

TO : The Director   DATE: January 24, 1949

FROM : D. M. Ladd

SUBJECT: FLYING DISCS

    I thought you might be interested in the following information concerning "Flying Discs" which has been furnished to the Bureau on a confidential basis by ███████ Resident Engineer, Air Material Command, U. S. Army, who is the principal army technician at the Nuclear Energy for the Propulsion of Aircraft Research Center at Oak Ridge, Tennessee.

    ███████ stated that he knew nothing of an official nature concern "Flying Discs" other than the fact that they are believed by Air Force Intellige officials to be man-made missiles, rather than some natural phenomena. It was h further belief that a great deal of information has been compiled concerning the missiles by air force intelligence, and that research on the matter was being extensively done at Wright Field, Dayton, Ohio.

    ███████ then continued with his own ideas as to what might be the nature of these discs which ideas he had formulated through review of those known facts and theoretical conjectures of himself and other scientists concerni the nature of flying discs and methods of propulsion for such type of aerial mechanism. According to him, flying discs have long been a theoretical possibil and, in fact, a possibility which would indicate one of the best means by which t break through the barriers of the supersonic area. He stated that scientists ha for many years, been attempting to develop this type of aircraft. Some experi- mentation has been done even in the United States, but insofar as is known in th United States at the present time, there have never been any practical developme As a second factor of consideration, ███████ stated that insofar as is kn to U. S. scientists at this time, there is no known chemical fuel which would ma possible tremendous range of flight such as is ascribed to the reported "flying discs." According to ████ there is only one possible fuel which could be utilized which is in accord with present theory, and that is the utilization of atomic energy.

    He stated that this subject matter was being given absolutely no dissemi by the air force or other military personnel, and that they had not deemed it advisable to advise him of all information pertaining to this type missile. He continued, however, that in his conversation with representatives at Wright Fiel and in reading reports returned to this country by foreign agents, he had gather together certain information which might be of assistance in determining whether not these so-called missiles were authentic, usable and of danger to the United

EHM:bhr

RECORDED - 11░ ░ 62-83894
INDEXED - 113
EX-109

50 FEB 8 1949 ⁄

Figure 10a: Colonel Gasser - Saucers Are Soviet Missiles

He pointed out that knowledge of such a possible aircraft is not by any means new and that it was known as early as four years ago that some type of flying disc was being experimented with by the Russians. In addition he said that more recent reports have been received from representatives of the Central Intelligence Agency in Southern Europe and Southern Asia to the effect that the Russians were experimenting with some type of radical aircraft or guided missile which could be dispatched for great distances out over the sea, made to turn in flight and return to the base from which it was launched. He related that this information was extremely worthy of notice as experiments in this country have so far only develope to the point where we are concerned with delivering a missile to the required point of impact, and no consideration has been given to imparting to that missile the ability to return. He also advised that it is a known fact that the Russians are attempting to develop some type of nuclear energy, that they received a wealth of information concerning nuclear energy at the time of their occupation in Germany, and that they have at their disposal a limited supply of fissionable materials. He pointed out that the Russians have some very capable scientists in the field of atomic energy and that, in addition thereto, they took into their custody some of the most advanced and capable scientists of the German Nation.

████████████ stated that a peculiar fact concerning these missiles is found in reports he has received, that from all appearances the missiles usually approach the United States from a northerly direction and have been reported as returning in a northerly direction. He advised that none have ever been known to crash, collide or disintegrate over American soil, but it would appear that they come to the United States, cruise around, and go back over the North Pole. He stated that insofar as is known to him there has never been any part of a missile of this type recovered from any source whatever in order that an analytical study of its nature could be made. He stated that one report has been received concerning a collision of these missiles with another type of aircraft. This report, according to him, emanated from Czechoslovakia and took place a short time under to the report of numerous discs over the United States. According to ████████████ a Czechoslova transport had reportedly collided with some unidentified missile while in mid-air over the ocean, and that the missile and transport were completely disintegrated without recovery of parts or survivors from either.

████████████ concluded that this matter, while still purely a matter of guesswork, is nevertheless a source of great concern to the military establishmen of this country. He advised that great efforts have been expended by the military service to determine the nature of these missiles and upon so determining, decide whether or not an adequate defense can be established. He stated that it has given impetus to the research being done by the air force in their own program of nuclear energy for the propulsion of aircraft to develop guided missiles.

ACTION:

None. The above is for your information.

Figure 10b: Col. Gasser - Saucers Are Soviet Missiles

Chapter 7
Great Balls of Fire

"After the practice period LaPaz assumed that the missiles would be loaded with an atomic warhead."
—from an FBI memorandum, February 10, 1949

A month before the FBI interview with Colonel Gasser, agencies responsible for security at atomic defense installations in the southwest were suddenly confronted with a puzzling and frightening nighttime phenomenon: the repeated appearance of greenish lights moving at high speed through the sky near these installations.

These lights began appearing at the end of November 1948, as if to satisfy Lt. Colonel Earle, Jr's prediction of an imminent increase in sightings (see the end of Chapter 5). They were very bright green-yellow lights, somewhat like large meteors which generally are called "fireballs."* The greenish lights appearing near the sensitive installations would have been identified as fireball meteors if it weren't for three peculiar and disturbing characteristics: their colors were unusual, they were seen many times per month in the vicinity of the atomic defense installations in New Mexico, and they were hardly seen anywhere else. Even though it soon became apparent that they weren't fireballs in any ordinary sense of the word, these lights were given the name "green fireballs."

The first ones to appear in the skies over New Mexico were thought by the observers to be green military flares and were ignored. However, a series of sightings on December 5 made the flare idea seem impossible. A dozen (!) green fireballs were seen traveling generally north to south between 7:30 p.m. and 11:30 p.m. by security guards at military installations in the vicinity of Albuquerque and Las Vegas in New Mexico (Las Vegas is east

---

* Fireball meteors are much larger, brighter and longer lasting than the typical meteor, which is small piece of material that makes a fleeting streak in the sky. Fireballs can be startling in their brilliance and duration, lasting sometimes up to 10 or more seconds. They appear randomly all over the world but are rarely seen more than once a year from any one location.

of Santa Fe). Some of the witnesses were guards at Sandia Base where atomic bombs were being assembled.* These sightings really caught the attention of the security forces and the next day Lt. Colonel Doyle Rees, Commander of the 17th district of the Air Force Office of Special Investigations (AFOSI) at Kirtland Air Force Base in Albuquerque, launched an intense investigation into the possibility that the fireballs were related to conspiracy and sabotage.

No sooner had the AFOSI investigation begun than there was another sighting: December 6, at 10:55 p.m., a security guard at Sandia Base saw a green fireball traveling north to south. The next night a security guard at Los Alamos, NM, saw a fireball traveling on a north-south trajectory! (Los Alamos is a laboratory west of Santa Fe and north of Albuquerque that had been constructed during WWII as a secure area where atomic bombs were designed.) AFOSI investigators Melvin Neef and John Stahl checked with every agency in the area that could have been launching green flares. None had. Neef and Stahl wanted to see one for themselves, so they boarded a small plane during the evening of December 8. At 6:35 p.m., while flying at an altitude of 5,000 feet near Las Vegas, New Mexico, they saw one burst into full brilliance seemingly instantaneously. It traveled almost parallel to the horizon for about 2 seconds, then dimmed while suddenly dropping downward, leaving a trail of reddish-orange sparks that lasted another second. It was decidedly un-fireball-like.

The next day Agent Neef contacted Dr. Lincoln LaPaz, the Director of the Institute of Meteoritics at the University of New Mexico. Dr. LaPaz had a Top Secret clearance and had worked with the Air Force during WWII at the White Sands Proving Grounds. The sighting descriptions reported by Neef interested him and he began a nightly watch for Geminid meteors which were being seen at the time.** In Dr. LaPaz's opinion, based on

---

* Now the Sandia National Laboratory, which is at the east side of Kirtland Air Force Base near Albuquerque.

** At several times during the year the Earth passes through regions of space where there are numerous small chunks of matter, leftovers from the "tails" of long-gone comets. The Geminid meteor shower, with meteors seeming to come from the years of experience observing meteors, the Geminid meteors were neither extremely bright nor green. In a letter to Doyle Rees, written on Dec. 13, he stated that observations made between the evening of the 9th and the morning of the 12th confirmed his opinion. He further stated that:

> ... all meteors both Geminid and non-Geminid that I have observed during periods of Geminid activity since December 1, 1926...a total of 414 (for which) color was reported. . . (of these) none . . . were (described) as green or greenish.

On the night of December 12, 1948 LaPaz became a witness. While riding westward from Las Vegas, New Mexico in a car with two Air Force officers, he saw a bright green light suddenly appear and travel in a horizontal trajectory north to south for about two seconds. It turned out that the same fireball was observed from Los Alamos. This allowed LaPaz to locate the path of the object by triangulation. His analysis showed it traveled a distance of about 25 miles at an altitude of about 10 miles and at a speed of 8 to 12 miles per second (typical meteors and fireballs burn up at altitudes around 50 miles). There was no noise, yet there should have been, according to LaPaz, if it were a normal meteor. At the end of his December 13 letter to Colonel Rees he wrote, "I am now convinced the various 'green flare' incidents reported to the AFOSI are <u>not</u> meteoric in nature." [underlined in the original]

The intelligence agencies responsible for protection of the atomic installations were not comforted by Dr. LaPaz' opinion that the green fireballs were not normal fireball meteors. Jerry Maxwell, the FBI Special Agent in Charge at Los Alamos, asked the FBI agent at El Paso to check with the White Sands Proving Grounds about the possibility that some rockets had been test fired during the periods of fireball observation. White Sands reported that no rockets had been fired.

Mr. Maxwell told Colonel Rees that "the FBI was carrying out any undeveloped leads relating to these phenomena that were brought to their attention."

---

direction of the constellation Gemini, occurs typically around December 10-12, with occasional meteors as early as December 3.

Agent Maxwell then became an active investigator. He accompanied LaPaz and several AFOSI agents to a nightwatch in the mountains west of Los Alamos on December 19. Unfortunately, they were one night too early. Had they been watching the next night, they would have seen something truly amazing: a green fireball that changed direction!

The time was 8:54 p.m. on December 20. The witnesses were security guards at two locations near the Los Alamos laboratory. Dr. LaPaz analyzed their sighting descriptions and on December 30 he wrote to Lt. Colonel Rees as follows:

> It is found that the fireball doubly observed by Wilson, Truett, Strang and Skipper appeared at a height of at least 10 miles and descended at an angle of about 45 degrees to the vertical (according to Truett's estimate) to .... an elevation of only 2.3 miles above the horizontal plane (illegible) the point from which Strang and Skipper observed. As the fireball approached... (the 2.3 mile altitude) its path leveled off and from (then) to its point of disappearance ..., the fireball followed a nearly horizontal path approximately 7.5 miles long, moving with a velocity of between 3.75 and 7.5 miles per second, depending upon the duration estimate adopted... The foreward extension of the fireball's trace on the earth as determined by the above projections, passes some six miles to the north of the town of Los Alamos. It should be noted that the descending branch of the path of the fireball was observed by Inspector Truett alone, but he was absolutely certain that his observation of this portion of the path was correct. It should also be noted that no sound was heard, although the distance from the observers to the fireball and from the fireball to the earth could only have been a few miles at most. I have no hesitancy in testifying that an object possessing the flight path and other peculiarities observed by Wilson, Truett, Strang and Skipper was not a falling meteorite.

The next sighting occurred December 28. Again, the flight path appeared to be horizontal from northeast to southwest but the color was different; it was blue-white. Just before the object disappeared it created a vapor trail which remained in the sky for several minutes. The witness could see this vapor trail being blown and dissipated by the wind. After reading about sightings such as these one can easily see why LaPaz was convinced these fireballs were not normal fireball meteors.

The intelligence agencies responsible for protecting the secret military installations had a jurisdictional dispute over which agency should take the lead in the investigation of these fireballs. By the end of December, the AFOSI had taken charge. From then on, the FBI merely sat in on the conferences where green fireballs were discussed. Incredibly, these conferences would occur over the next two years.

Were the intelligence agencies worried by these sightings near secure military installations? You bet they were, considering world events at this time, a time of spies and intrigue. In the years following WWII the Soviet Union had been exerting political and military pressure on neighboring countries to join with them in building what became a barrier of satellite states between the Soviet Union and Western Europe. The cold war had heated up and it was obvious that the Soviets were on the march. Czechoslovakia had been forced to join the Communist Block a year before. The Berlin Blockade had begun the previous April (1948) and was continuing. Who knew where the Soviets would strike next, and with what weapons? The Soviet scientists were known to be working feverishly to create an atomic bomb. It was also known that the Soviets had captured German rocket scientists and missiles when they took over the eastern part of Germany. Would the next Soviet weapons be missiles with atomic bombs?

At the same time, the USA was attempting to put some teeth into its undisguised threat to use atomic weapons if war broke out with the Soviets. Two years earlier, in December 1946, President Truman had established the Atomic Energy Commission (AEC) to manage the atomic weapons program. It was Truman's intent to use the threat of "The Bomb" to keep the Soviets under control. In order to make this threat realistic, however, it was necessary that the USA have a supply of atomic bombs. In 1945, there were only two atomic bombs in existence—and they were both used that summer. Bomb production resumed after the war and the production rate increased slightly, limited primarily by the availability of nuclear fissionable material. By the end of 1946 there were nine atomic bombs. By the end of 1947 there were 13 and by the end of 1948 there were 50.

These bombs were designed at Los Alamos. Fissionable material was made at the Hanford nuclear facility in state of

Washington and at the Savannah River nuclear plant in South Carolina. Bomb parts and the fissionable material were shipped to Sandia Base at Albuquerque (about 60 miles south of Los Alamos) for assembly. The assembled bombs were shipped to Fort Hood, Texas and stored in a special facility known as Killeen Base. These areas were prime targets for Soviet espionage and so any potentially threatening phenomenon had to be investigated.

First the appearance of flying saucers, and then the appearance of the green fireballs, threw a cold chill onto the warm complacency of our security agencies. Could it be that our arch enemies had really made a "quantum jump" beyond our own rocket technology? Could the green fireballs be Soviet missiles targeted against our defense installations? No one doubted that the fireballs were being seen. But, what were they? A memorandum to the Director of Intelligence of the Fourth Army at Fort Sam Houston, Texas, from Army Colonel Eustis Poland, dated January 13, 1949 demonstrated the level of concern and listed several theories:

> Agencies in New Mexico are greatly concerned over these phenomena. They are of the opinion that some foreign power is making 'sensing shots' with some super-stratosphere devise (sic) designed to be self-disentergrating. (sic) They also believe that when the devise is perfected for accuracy, the disentegrating (sic) factor will be eliminated in favor of a warhead.
>
> Another theory advanced as possibly acceptable lies in the belief that the phenomena are the result of radiological warfare experiments by a foreign power, further, that the rays may be lethal or might be attributed to the cause of some of the plane crashes that have occurred recently.
>
> Still another belief that is advanced is that, it is highly probable that the United States may be carrying on some top-secret experiments.

This memorandum ended by proposing that "a scientific board be sent to this locality to study the situation" because "these incidents are of such great importance, especially as they are occurring in the vicinity of sensitive installations."

Then the "big one" occurred: a green fireball was seen by over a hundred people in West Texas, New Mexico and Colorado during the night of January 30. According to a Confidential,

Priority message from the Commanding Officer at Kirtland Air Force Base to the Air Force Director of Special Investigations (copy to the FBI):

> Estimate at least 100 total sightings. AEC (Atomic Energy Commission), AFSWP [Air Force Special Weapons Project—in charge of nuclear weapons], 4th Army local commanders are purturbed by implications of phenomena.

Perturbed, indeed, because they could not prove that these were not Soviet missiles that were being tested for bombardment of the very installations where our atomic bombs were designed and built.

The next day, the Special FBI Agent in Charge at San Antonio., Texas, wrote a letter to inform FBI headquarters of what had been going on.

> TO: DIRECTOR , FBI
> Jan. 31, 1949
> FROM: SAC, San Antonio
> SUBJECT: PROTECTION OF VITAL INSTALLAT IONS
> At recent Weekly Intelligence Conferences of G-2 (Army Intelligence), ONI (Office of Naval Intelligence), OSI (Air Force Office of Special Investigations) and FBI in the Fourth Army Area, Officers of G-2, Fourth army have discussed the matter of 'Unidentified Aircraft' or 'Unidentified Aerial Phenomena' otherwise known as 'Flying Discs,' ' Flying Saucers,' and 'Balls of Fire.' This matter is considered Top Secret by Intelligence Officers of both the Army and Air Forces." [underlining in the original; see Figure 11a.]

Thus begins a two page letter, Figures 11a and 11b, to FBI headquarters describing the onset of the green fireball phenomenon which military intelligence considered to be Top Secret. The SAC briefly summarized the previous history:

> It is well known that there have been during the past two years reports from various parts of the country of the sighting of unidentified aerial objects which have been called in newspaper parlance 'flying discs' and 'flying saucers.' The first such sightings were reported from Sweden and it was thought that the objects, the nature of which was unknown, might have originated in Russia.

The reference to sightings in Sweden concerns objects termed

Office Memorandum · UNITED STATES GOVERNMENT

TO: DIRECTOR, FBI

DATE: January 31, 1949

FROM: SAC, SAN ANTONIO

SUBJECT: PROTECTION OF VITAL INSTALLATIONS
BUREAU FILE # 65-58300

At recent Weekly Intelligence Conferences of G-2, ONI, OSI, and F.B.I., in the Fourth Army Area, Officers of G-2, Fourth Army have discussed the matter of "Unidentified Aircraft" or "Unidentified Aerial Phenomena" otherwise known as "Flying Discs", "Flying Saucers", and "Balls of Fire". This matter is considered top secret by Intelligence Officers of both the Army and the Air Forces.

It is well known that there have been during the past two years reports from the various parts of the country of the sighting of unidentified aerial objects which have been called in newspaper parlance "flying discs" and "flying saucers". The first such sightings were reported from Sweden, and it was thought that the objects, the nature of which was unknown, might have originated in Russia.

In July 1948 an unidentified aircraft was "seen" by an Eastern Airlines Pilot and Co-Pilot and one or more passengers of the Eastern Airlines Plane over Montgomery, Alabama. This aircraft was reported to be of an unconventional type without wings and resembled generally a "rocket ship" of the type depicted in comic strips. It was reported to have had windows; to have been larger than the Eastern Airlines plane, and to have been traveling at an estimated speed of 2700 miles an hour. It appeared out of a thunderhead ahead of the Eastern Airlines plane and immediately disappeared in another cloud narrowly missing a collision with the Eastern Airlines plane. No sound or air disturbance was noted in connection with this appearance.

During the past two months various sightings of unexplained phenomena have been reported in the vicinity of the A.E.C. Installation at Los Alamos, New Mexico, where these phenomena now appear to be concentrated. During December 1948 on the 5th, 6th, 7th, 8th, 11th, 13th, 14th, 20th and 28th sightings of unexplained phenomena were made near Los Alamos by Special Agents of the Office of Special Investigation; Airline Pilots; Military Pilots, Los Alamos Security Inspectors, and private citizens. On January 6, 1949, another similar object was sighted in the same area.

███████████, a Meteorologist of some note, has been generally in charge of the observations near Los Alamos, attempting to learn characteristics of the unexplained phenomena.

Up to this time little concrete information has been obtained.

JEJ:md
SA-100-7545
El Paso (2)
Dallas (2)
Little Rock (2)
Oklahoma City (2)

Figure 11a: Fireballs - Top Secret

"ghost rockets," which were reported by numerous witnesses in 1946 and were thought by the Swedish military to be Soviet missiles. An investigation of these sightings by Swedish and U.S. military scientists failed to find hard evidence to prove that these "rockets" were Soviet devices. Nevertheless, some of the sightings were so well witnessed that the sightings could not be

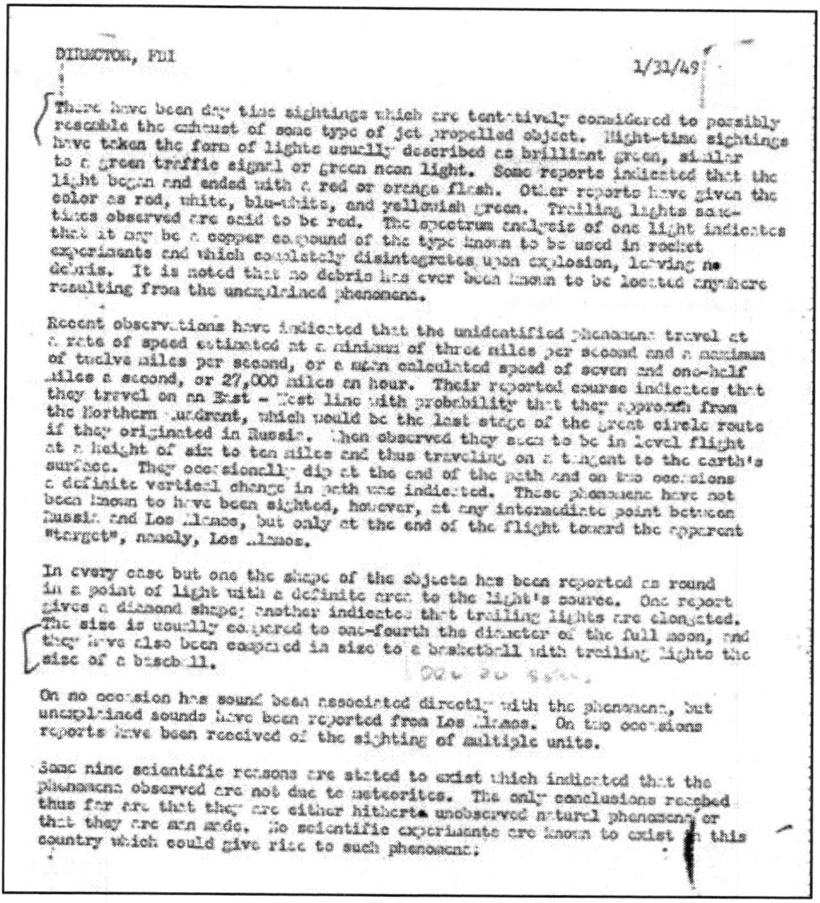

DIRECTOR, FBI

1/31/49

There have been day time sightings which are tentatively considered to possibly resemble the exhaust of some type of jet propelled object. Night-time sightings have taken the form of lights usually described as brilliant green, similar to a green traffic signal or green neon light. Some reports indicated that the light began and ended with a red or orange flash. Other reports have given the color as red, white, blue-white, and yellowish green. Trailing lights sometimes observed are said to be red. The spectrum analysis of one light indicates that it may be a copper compound of the type known to be used in rocket experiments and which completely disintegrates upon explosion, leaving no debris. It is noted that no debris has ever been known to be located anywhere resulting from the unexplained phenomena.

Recent observations have indicated that the unidentified phenomena travel at a rate of speed estimated at a minimum of three miles per second and a maximum of twelve miles per second, or a mean calculated speed of seven and one-half miles a second, or 27,000 miles an hour. Their reported course indicates that they travel on an East - West line with probability that they approach from the Northern quadrant, which would be the last stage of the great circle route if they originated in Russia. When observed they seem to be in level flight at a height of six to ten miles and thus traveling on a tangent to the earth's surface. They occasionally dip at the end of the path and on two occasions a definite vertical change in path was indicated. These phenomena have not been known to have been sighted, however, at any intermediate point between Russia and Los Alamos, but only at the end of the flight toward the apparent "target", namely, Los Alamos.

In every case but one the shape of the objects has been reported as round in a point of light with a definite area to the light's source. One report gives a diamond shape; another indicates that trailing lights are elongated. The size is usually compared to one-fourth the diameter of the full moon, and they have also been compared in size to a basketball with trailing lights the size of a baseball.

On no occasion has sound been associated directly with the phenomena, but unexplained sounds have been reported from Los Alamos. On two occasions reports have been received of the sighting of multiple units.

Some nine scientific reasons are stated to exist which indicated that the phenomena observed are not due to meteorites. The only conclusions reached thus far are that they are either hitherto unobserved natural phenomena or that they are man made. No scientific experiments are known to exist in this country which could give rise to such phenomena.

Figure 11b: Fireballs - Top Secret

attributed to war nerves or psychosis. Many of the sighted objects were lights of various colors, sometimes trailing sparks and trails as they flew through the sky. No final explanation was ever publicized, if indeed one was found.

The agent then described the Chiles-Whitted sighting of July 24, 1948 of a "rocket ship" that appeared "out of a thunderhead ahead of the Eastern Airlines plane and immediately disappeared in another cloud, narrowly missing a collision with the Eastern Airlines plane" (discussed in chapter 5) before getting on to the main subject of his letter:

During the past two months various sightings of unexplained phenomena have been reported in the vicinity of the AEC Installation at Los Alamos, New Mexico, where these phenomena now appear to be concentrated. During December, 1948 on the 5th, 6th, 7th, 8th, 11th, 13th, 14th, 20th, and 28th sightings of unexplained phenomena were made near Los Alamos by Special Agents of the Office of Special Investigation, airline pilots, military pilots, Los Alamos Security Inspectors and private citizens. On January 6, 1949 another similar object was sighted in the same area.

Dr. Lincoln LaPaz, a Meteorologist [*sic*, should be meteoricist] of some note, has been generally in charge of the observations near Los Alamos, attempting to learn characteristics of the unexplained phenomena. Up to this time little concrete information has been obtained.

There have been day time sightings which are tentatively considered to possibly resemble the exhaust of some type of jet propelled object. Night-time sightings have taken the form of lights usually described as brilliant green, similar to a green traffic signal or green neon light. Some reports indicated that the light began and ended with red or orange flash. Other reports have given the color as red, white, blue-white and yellowish green. Trailing lights sometimes observed are said to be red. The spectrum analysis of one light indicates that it may be a copper compound of the type known to be used in rocket experiments and which completely disintegrates upon explosion, leaving no debris. It is noted that no debris has ever been known to be located anywhere resulting from the unexplained phenomena.

The agent then described the travel paths and speeds of the fireballs and made a statement which may have shocked J. Edgar:

> Their reported course indicates that they travel on an east west line with probability that they approach from the Northern Quadrant, which would be the last stage of the great circle route if they originated in Russia.

As if this weren't scary enough, being consistent with Colonel Gasser's opinion that the saucers had been launched from Russia, the agent went on to say that Dr. LaPaz listed half a dozen reasons why "the phenomena observed are not due to meteorites" and that:

> . . . the only conclusions reached thus far are that they are either hitherto unobserved natural phenomena or that they are man made. No scientific experiments are known to exist in this country which could give rise to such phenomena.

Hoover's reaction to learning about the fireballs is not contained within the available FBI records. However, one might guess that, after comparing this information with what Colonel Gasser said, Hoover reached the logical conclusion that atomic powered missiles from Russia were being targeted at our atomic installations.

On February 7, 1949, Colonel Eustis Poland wrote again to the Director of Army Intelligence about the "'unusual lights' that have been observed for some time past in the vicinity of Los Alamos." The memorandum says that, "due to the inexplicability of this phenomena, it has become a matter of some concern to this Headquarters as well as the USAEC and the OSI." Therefore, the Security Division of Los Alamos had recommended that "representatives of the three interested services" (Army, AEC, AFOSI) "hold a joint conference to include eminent scientists appointed for the purpose." The conference was scheduled for February 16.

Apparently the Director of Army Intelligence was not worried, inasmuch as he responded by indicating that the "inexplicability" resulted only from a lack of data and that "it is not believed that any 'unnatural' or hostile basis exists for these occurrences or that they are due to 'unconventional aircraft.'"* Another Army memorandum from the office of the Director of Army Intelligence indicates that the AEC was not worried either:

> ... check with AEC discloses that they will not officially approve such a meeting, as they do not think the phenomena justifies such action.

On February 10, FBI headquarters received a letter from SAC, El Paso, Texas, which summarized Dr. LaPaz's frightening hypothesis (See Figure 12):

> Dr. LaPaz advanced the theory . . . that the objects were controlled missiles traveling around the earth at an altitude of approximately 25 miles and at a speed of approximately 15 miles per second. The missile was probably controlled by agents stationed at various intervals who are able to bring the missile down over a designated area and explode it. . . . Dr. LaPaz added that he believed the

---

* "Unconventional aircraft" in this context meant flying saucers.

Russians or some other country was practicing with these weapons which carried no war head and were being exploded at an altitude of approximately 10 miles. After the practice periods LaPaz assumed the weapons would be loaded with an atomic war head.

Dr. LaPaz, a top meteor expert, said these fireballs were not natural phenomena. However, Army intelligence couldn't accept LaPaz's alternative Russian missile theory, because the Army and Air Force were certain that the United States was at least even with, if not well ahead of, the Soviet Union in the development of nuclear energy and long range missiles. Furthermore, they did not believe that the Soviet Union would actually test their missiles over the USA.* Therefore, in spite of Dr. LaPaz' opinion, many intelligence officers believed these fireballs would turn out to be unusual but natural phenomena.

The fireball sightings attracted the interest of Theodore von Karman, a famous mathematician who was the chairman of the Air Force Science Advisory Board. (Recall that Colonel McCoy of AMC/ATIC, in March 1948, told the AFSAB about project Sign and the saucer investigation. See Chapter 5.) On February 11, 1949, he wrote a letter to General Cabell to indicate that, although he was extremely skeptical about flying discs and other unidentified flying objects, he was impressed by the quality of the fireball observations and by LaPaz's analysis. He therefore recommended that the Air Force take a scientific approach and attempt to obtain objective measurements of the fireballs. An aide to General Cabell, in responding to von Karman's letter, stated that AMC/ATIC had already contacted Dr. LaPaz and offered him the job of acting as an astrophysical consultant to Project Grudge. However, LaPaz, living in New Mexico, was too far away from Dayton, Ohio to be able to work closely with the AMC personnel, so he had recommended Dr. J. Allen Hynek, who was a professor of astronomy at Ohio State University. It was Hynek's job to supply astronomical explanations whenever possible for sightings of unconventional objects, including green

---

* By carrying out such tests they would risk losing their technological advantage because one of the missiles might malfunction and crash, thereby handing their secret technology over to the USA. Certainly, the Americans knew they would never do the reverse.

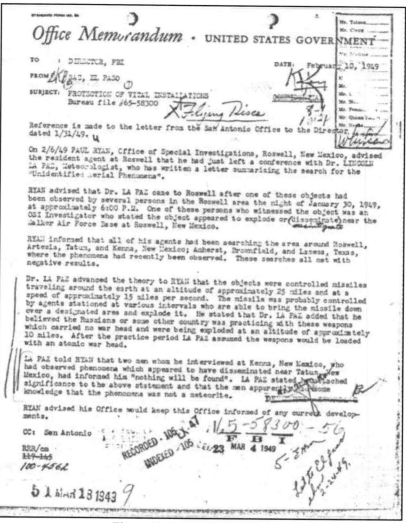

Figure 12: La Paz Fireball Theory

fireballs.* The aide to Cabell also wrote that 20 percent of the 210

* Hynek, who died in 1986, was the Air Force astronomy consultant from 1948 through the closing of Project Blue Book in 1969. Although initially very skeptical, by the 1960s he had begun to realize that saucers, or Unidentified Flying Objects, were real phenomena that deserved investigation. In 1973, he founded the Center for UFO Studies to collect and analyze UFO sightings and related phenomena.

incidents had been explained, mostly as weather balloons.* With regard to the remainder, there was no tangible evidence which proved the objects to be from a foreign nation, even for the sightings outside the USA. Furthermore:

> . . . the possibility of foreign devices becomes more remote in the case of domestic incidents, and would represent achievements which defy many well defined limits in aeronautical science.

Cabell's aide did not respond directly to Von Karman's recommendation for objective measurements. Instead the aide responded by saying that AMC/ATIC was analyzing the sightings and attempting to explain them.

On February 16, a meeting was held at Los Alamos to attempt to arrive at a conclusion regarding the fireballs. Present were representatives of the Fourth Army, the Air Force Special Weapons Project, the FBI (Agent Maxwell), the AEC and the University of California (which "ran" Los Alamos under contract to the Defense Department and the Atomic Energy Commission). The best known scientist at the meeting was Dr. Edward Teller. The director of Los Alamos laboratory, Dr. Norris Bradbury, was also there.

Dr. LaPaz, as the meteor expert, essentially ran the meeting. He began by discussing the characteristics of ordinary meteors and then described how these differed, listing half a dozen peculiarities, including the color and essentially horizontal path. The meeting went on for several hours and numerous related subjects were discussed. Perhaps one of the most puzzling facts was this: whereas meteor reports for most of the USA were average for the months of December, January, and February, no green fireballs had been reported in areas other than the Los Alamos, Las Vegas (NM) and West Texas areas. Another aspect which confounded the experts, including Dr. Teller, was that no noise had ever been reported, even though shock waves would have been expected for material objects moving through the atmosphere at speeds of

---

* That would mean roughly 40 sightings had been explained. The "Analysis of Flying Object Incidents in the U.S." discussed in Chapter 5 indicated that only 18 had been explained.

several miles per second.* Teller suggested the lights might be non-material, perhaps optical phenomena of some sort. The meeting concluded with more questions and no answers.

A further report on the green fireball mystery came to FBI headquarters on March 22 from SAC, San Antonio. (See Figures 13a and 13b). According to this report, at the weekly intelligence conferences there were discussions about the green fireballs which were "considered secret by Intelligence Officers of both the Army and Air Force." He learned from Army Intelligence that the:

> . . . above matter is now termed 'Unconventional Aircraft' and investigations concerning such matters have been given the name 'Project Grudge.'

This was a reference to the fact that Project Sign had been terminated in January, 1949. Recall that a new name, Grudge, had been given to the continuation of the Project Sign intelligence collection and analysis effort. The new project was intended to handle both flying disc and green fireball investigations.

In the March 22 letter, SAC San Antonio mentioned the February 16 conference at Los Alamos and then said he had been told by Army intelligence that:

> . . . as of November 1, 1948 information had been received from higher Military authorities that the Air Force had advised that such sightings occur periodically and that another period of sightings was then imminent. Further, on February 14, 1949, higher Military authorities advised that it was believed that ultimately it would be found that the phenomena in question would have a natural explanation.

There was no reason given as to why "higher Military authorities" believed the green fireballs would "have a natural explanation," in contradiction to Dr. LaPaz's opinion that they weren't meteors. Perhaps it was wishful thinking on the part of the higher authorities. Perhaps they stated this opinion in order to avoid the very difficult political situation which would ensue if they

---

* Lack of sound despite high speed has been a consistent characteristic of "flying saucers."

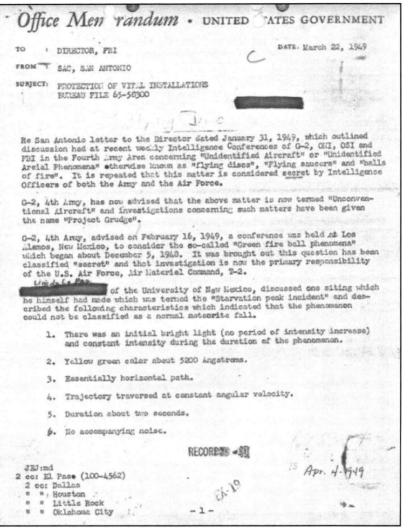

Office Memorandum • UNITED STATES GOVERNMENT

TO : DIRECTOR, FBI   DATE: March 22, 1949

FROM : SAC, SAN ANTONIO

SUBJECT: PROTECTION OF VITAL INSTALLATIONS
      BUREAU FILE 65-58300

Re San Antonio letter to the Director dated January 31, 1949, which outlined discussion had at recent weekly Intelligence Conferences of G-2, ONI, OSI and FBI in the Fourth Army Area concerning "Unidentified Aircraft" or "Unidentified Areial Phenomena" otherwise known as "flying discs", "Flying saucers" and "balls of fire". It is repeated that this matter is considered secret by Intelligence Officers of both the Army and the Air Force.

G-2, 4th Army, has now advised that the above matter is now termed "Unconventional Aircraft" and investigations concerning such matters have been given the name "Project Grudge".

G-2, 4th Army, advised on February 16, 1949, a conference was held at Los Alamos, New Mexico, to consider the so-called "Green fire ball phenomena" which began about December 5, 1948. It was brought out this question has been classified "secret" and that investigation is now the primary responsibility of the U.S. Air Force, Air Material Command, T-2.

_____ of the University of New Mexico, discussed one siting which he himself had made which was termed the "Starvation peak incident" and described the following characteristics which indicated that the phenomenon could not be classified as a normal meteorite fall.

     1. There was an initial bright light (no period of intensity increase) and constant intensity during the duration of the phenomenon.

     2. Yellow green color about 5200 Angstroms.

     3. Essentially horizontal path.

     4. Trajectory traversed at constant angular velocity.

     5. Duration about two seconds.

     6. No accompanying noise.

RECORDED

JEJ:md
2 cc: El Paso (100-4562)
2 cc: Dallas
 " " Houston
 " " Little Rock
 " " Oklahoma City   - 1 -

Apr. 4 1949

Figure 13a: Green Fireball Conference

admitted that the fireballs were not natural phenomena.

What the agent reported next in the same letter was not at all reassuring. In fact, it must have appeared to the security agencies that things were really getting out of hand, because there had been several incidents of "flares" seen:

... north of Killeen Base in the area of the Vital Installation at Camp Hood, Texas. ... It has been concluded that the flares seen near Killeen are probably similar to the phenomena previously noted in

DIRECTOR, FBI   March 22, 1949

It was brought out that since December 5, 1948 there have been more than
ten incidents analagous to the "green fireball" above described and some
twenty others with minor deviations from the above. It is also pointed out
that the only sitings which had occurred seemed to have been confined to the
Los Alamos, Las Vegas, and West Texas triangle.

G-2 also advised that as of November 1, 1948, information had been received
from higher Military authorities that the Air Force had advised that such
sitings occur periodically and that another period of sitings was then
imminent. Further, on February 14, 1949, higher Military authorities advised
that it was believed that ultimately it would be found that the phenomena
in question have a natural explanation.

It is further noted that about 7:30 p.m., March 6, 1949, what was at first
thought to be a flare was seen approximately one-half mile north of Killeen
Base in the area of the Vital Installation at Camp Hood, Texas, and a second
flare was noticed at 1:45 a.m., March 7, 1949, approximately three miles from
Killeen Base. It has since been concluded that the flares seen near Killeen
are probably similar to the phenomena previously noted in the Los Alamos,
Sandia Base Area although these are the first sitings of such phenomena near
Camp Hood.

There appears to be reason to believe that the above-mentioned phenomena may
be connected with secret experiments being conducted by some U.S. Government
Agency as it is believed that the United States is farther advanced in guided
missile development than any foreign power.

Although the primary responsibility for investigating such matters is now
with the U.S. A.F. Air Materiel Command, G-2, 4th Army is still interested
in being advised of any further sitings of such phenomena which might be
observed.

Figure 13b: Green Fireball Conference

the Los Alamos, Sandia base area.

In other words, the luminous nighttime phenomena which had first been seen around the areas where atomic bombs were designed (Los Alamos) and built (Sandia Base) were now being seen where the bombs were stored! Recall that these sightings were unique to the American southwest. There were no similar concentrations of fireball sightings anywhere else. It may have seemed to some of the intelligence agents that the green fireballs were following the atomic bombs.

According to the agent's letter:

There appears to be reason to believe that the above-mentioned phenomena may be connected with secret experiments being conducted by some U.S. Government Agency as it is believed that the United States is farther advanced in guided missile development than any foreign power.

The SAC letter of March 22 illustrates just how confused the security officers and intelligence agents were by the green fireball sightings. They accepted the fact that the fireballs were real objects or phenomena and were trying to determine the most likely, or the least unlikely, explanation for the sightings. They rejected the Soviet missile theory in spite of LaPaz's analysis. The suggestion by "higher Military authorities" that the fireballs were natural phenomena did not convince them, because Dr. LaPaz had rejected the "natural" theory. Furthermore, they were fully aware that, in spite of having Top Secret clearances, they didn't know about every Top Secret test program of the United States military. Therefore, the only remaining possible explanation, since the ET explanation had been ruled out by the Air Force (Vandenberg), was that these objects were secret test devices of the U.S.

It was at about this time, while Hoover's FBI was digesting Colonel Gasser's Soviet missile theory and learning of the green fireballs over the nuclear weapon areas in the southwest, that the FBI received 50 copies of General Cabell's Air Intelligence Requirements Memorandum #4, titled "Unconventional Aircraft" and dated February 15, 1949 (mentioned near the end of the Chapter 5). The stated purpose of the document was to "enunciate continuing Air Force requirements for information pertaining to sightings of unconventional aircraft and unidentified flying objects, including the so-called Flying Discs."

This memorandum contained a sighting report form many pages long and very detailed. It must have appeared to the FBI that the "high brass" of the Air Force was desperate for information about "unconventional aircraft" and green fireballs.

This veritable deluge of unsettling information caused the FBI to modify its policy on saucer sightings. An assistant to D. M. Ladd wrote a memorandum recommending that the FBI issue a new directive to the FBI agents throughout the country. The memorandum includes the following paragraph, which emphasizes the source of concern for the FBI:

> (Col. Gasser) . . . has recently and confidentially advised the Bureau that flying discs are believed by the Air Force to be man-made missiles rather than some natural phenomenon and that as much as four years go it was learned that some type of flying discs were being experimented upon by the Russians. It was further determined from Colonel Gasser that most all of the flying discs seen by persons in the

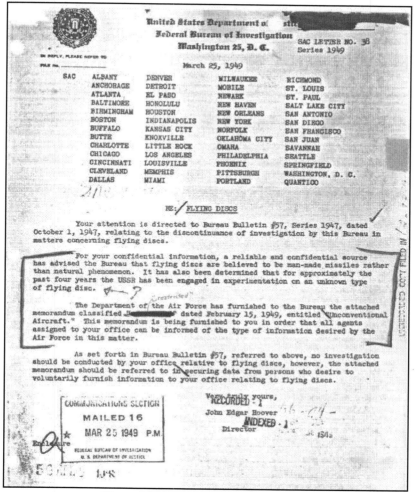

United States Department of Justice
Federal Bureau of Investigation
Washington 25, D. C.

SAC LETTER NO. 38
Series 1949

March 25, 1949

SAC
ALBANY   DENVER   MILWAUKEE   RICHMOND
ANCHORAGE   DETROIT   MOBILE   ST. LOUIS
ATLANTA   EL PASO   NEWARK   ST. PAUL
BALTIMORE   HONOLULU   NEW HAVEN   SALT LAKE CITY
BIRMINGHAM   HOUSTON   NEW ORLEANS   SAN ANTONIO
BOSTON   INDIANAPOLIS NEW YORK   SAN DIEGO
BUFFALO   KANSAS CITY   NORFOLK   SAN FRANCISCO
BUTTE   KNOXVILLE   OKLAHOMA CITY SAN JUAN
CHARLOTTE   LITTLE ROCK   OMAHA   SAVANNAH
CHICAGO   LOS ANGELES   PHILADELPHIA   SEATTLE
CINCINNATI   LOUISVILLE   PHOENIX   SPRINGFIELD
CLEVELAND   MEMPHIS   PITTSBURGH   WASHINGTON, D. C.
DALLAS   MIAMI   PORTLAND   QUANTICO

RE: FLYING DISCS

Your attention is directed to Bureau Bulletin #57, Series 1947, dated October 1, 1947, relating to the discontinuance of investigation by this Bureau in matters concerning flying discs.

For your confidential information, a reliable and confidential source has advised the Bureau that flying discs are believed to be man-made missiles rather than natural phenomenon. It has also been determined that for approximately the past four years the USSR has been engaged in experimentation on an unknown type of flying disc.

The Department of the Air Force has furnished to the Bureau the attached memorandum classified _____ dated February 15, 1949, entitled "Unconventional Aircraft." This memorandum is being furnished to you in order that all agents assigned to your office can be informed of the type of information desired by the Air Force in this matter.

As set forth in Bureau Bulletin #57, referred to above, no investigation should be conducted by your office relative to flying discs, however, the attached memorandum should be referred to in securing data from persons who desire to voluntarily furnish information to your office relating to flying discs.

Very truly yours,

John Edgar Hoover
Director

RECORDED
INDEXED

COMMUNICATIONS SECTION
MAILED 16
MAR 25 1949 P.M.
FEDERAL BUREAU OF INVESTIGATION
U. S. DEPARTMENT OF JUSTICE
Enclosure

Figure 14: Sac Letter of March 25, 1949

United States approached this country from a northerly direction and returned in the same direction, indicating the strong possibility that they are coming from Russia.

The memorandum referred to the recent receipt of "a sufficient number of copies of a memorandum dated February 15, 1949, captioned 'Unconventional Aircraft' which can be furnished to our field offices." (The FBI knew that AFI was serious because the AFI had taken the time to type all 50 copies rather than forcing the FBI to use its own secretaries to make copies.) The memorandum ended by pointing out that the matter of flying discs was "of sufficient importance to the internal security of the country that our field offices should secure as much information as possible from complainants in order to assist the Department of Air Force."* On March 25, the FBI issued "SAC letter No. 38, series 1949," which reads as follows (see Figure 14):

> Your attention is directed to Bureau Bulletin #57, Series 1947, dated October 1, 1947, relating to the discontinuance of investigation by this Bureau in matters concerning flying discs.
>
> For your confidential information, a reliable and confidential source has advised the Bureau that flying discs are believed to be man-made missiles rather than natural phenomenon. It has also been determined that for approximately the past four years the USSR has been engaged in experimentation on an unknown type of flying disc.
>
> The Department of the Air Force has furnished to the Bureau the attached memorandum classified "restricted" dated February 15, 1949, entitled "Unconventional Aircraft." This memorandum is being furnished to you in order that all agents assigned to your office can be informed of the type of information desired by the Air Force in this matter.
>
> As set forth in Bureau Bulletin #57, referred to above, no investigation should be conducted by your office relative to flying discs, however the attached memorandum should be referred to in securing data from persons who desire to voluntarily furnish information to your office relating to flying discs.

This situation regarding fireballs and flying discs must have appeared to the FBI to be quite confusing. On the one hand, the AFI desired information on sightings of unconventional aircraft (flying saucers) and green fireballs. The AFI clearly considered these to be real objects. Some elements of the Air Force believed they were Soviet missiles being tested over the USA. At the same time, other elements of the Air Force couldn't believe that the Soviets would be stupid enough to test missiles over the USA, so they suggested that these were secret U.S. devices. But why would the Air Force want sighting information on America's own secret projects? And if that weren't confusing enough, "higher military authorities" were saying the green fireballs would turn out to be natural phenomena, presumably meteors, in contradic-

---

* Here "complainants" means persons who voluntarily submit flying disc information to the FBI.

tion to Dr. LaPaz's claim that they couldn't be meteoric in origin.

With all this contradictory information, what was a poor FBI agent to think?

Chapter 8
An Unimpeachable Source

On April 4 the agent in San Antonio further updated the situation in a letter to headquarters:

> Lights of unknown origin were observed on March 6, 7, 8 and 17, 1949, by military personnel of the alert force stationed approximately 1,000 yards east of the fences which surround the Killeen Base.

Many months later, Project Grudge personnel—who tried to explain all saucer and fireball sightings—decided that the March 6, 7, and 8 lights must have been meteors. However, the March 17 sighting at 7:52 p.m. was too much for them. It remains unidentified. The witnesses were guards at the Second Armored Division, who for an hour watched eight large red, green, and white flare-like objects fly around, generally in straight lines.

In the April 4 letter, SAC San Antonio reported that on March 31, at 11:50 p.m., another witness saw a lighted object which was described as being different from what had been seen before. It was so unusual the FBI agent described it:

> . . . (the) lighted object about the size of a basketball, reddish white in color, followed by a fire trail, was observed southwest of Killeen Base adjacent to Camp Hood, Texas. The observation was made by Lt. Frederick Davis who was in charge of a platoon, Company C, 12 armored Infantry Battalion, which is assigned as part of an alert force (called force Abel) from Camp Hood, whose function is to protect the installation at Killeen Base.
>
> Davis advised that the object was at an altitude estimated at 6,000 ft., was traveling parallel to the ground and passed directly over him at a rapid rate of speed. It was in view 10 to 15 seconds and suddenly disappeared high in the sky without having ascended. No sound or odor was detected. The night was clear and visibility good. The object passed almost directly over the air strip at Killeen Base.
>
> When Davis attempted to advise his headquarters by telephone immediately after the sighting, he heard static or electrical interference on the telephone line which he stated might be possible radio

interference.

This is case number 326 in the master list of about 13,000 sightings collected by Projects Sign, Grudge, and Blue Book. Recall that after Vandenberg rejected the ET explanation, there were only two other explanations available to the investigators at ATIC/Grudge: natural phenomena or man-made missiles, where man-made meant "of foreign origin," i.e., Soviet missiles. However, in this case they couldn't believe a Soviet missile was flying over Killeen Base. Therefore it had to be a natural phenomenon. They identified it as a meteor in spite of the low altitude and lack of sound.

In the same letter SAC San Antonio called the attention of FBI headquarters to a radio broadcast by respected newsman Walter Winchell:

> It is noted that Mr. Walter Winchell, on his Sunday evening broadcast, April 3, 1949, stated that 'flying discs' seen in this country definitely emanated from Russia.

Evidently this caught the attention of the agencies that were aware of the green fireball threat to vital installations because an intelligence officer of the Fourth Army contacted the FBI at San Antonio for more information:

> On April 4, 1949, G-2, 4th Army, contacted this office, inquiring as to whether we had any information that would substantiate or discredit the statements made by Walter Winchell.
>
> In view of the interest and concern of the 4th Army military authorities who have the duty of protecting the vital installations at Los Alamos, N.M., Sandia Base, N.M. in the El Paso division, and the Camp Hood area in the San Antonio Division, it is suggested that the Bureau may desire to arrange to have Mr. Winchell interviewed concerning the source of his information that 'flying discs' emanated from Russia.

Hoover's response to the agent's suggestion came on April 26 (see Figure 15):

SAC - San Antonio
Director - FBI
FLYING DISKS
INTERNAL SECURITY - R
In regard to your request for information that would substantiate or

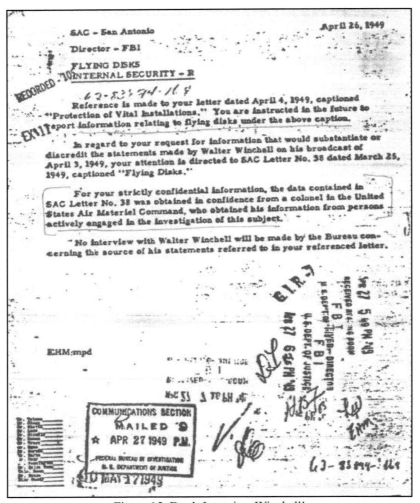

Figure 15: Don't Interview Winchell!

discredit the statements made by Walter Winchell on his broadcast of April 3, 1949, your attention is directed to SAC Letter No. 38 dated March 25, 1949, captioned 'Flying Discs.'

For your strictly confidential information, the data contained in SAC Letter No. 38 was obtained in confidence from a colonel in the United States Air Materiel Command, who obtained his information from persons actively engaged in the investigation of this subject.

No interview with Walter Winchell will be made by the Bureau concerning the source of his statements referred to in your letter.

Why didn't Hoover want to find out the source of Winchell's information? After all, Winchell was perhaps the most influential news commentator of his day. He wouldn't be expected to make such an important statement without some supporting evidence or at least an unimpeachable source. And certainly any evidence Winchell had that proved the Russians were sending missiles over the USA would be valuable to the FBI, as it would have important political ramifications, affecting everyone up to the President. One can imagine the furor if the FBI had presented President Truman with undeniable evidence that the Russians were testing missiles over the USA and the Air Force couldn't do anything about it.

Now, years later, we can guess why Hoover didn't want Winchell interviewed: *Hoover* was Winchell's unimpeachable source!

Preposterous? Consider this.

Winchell and Hoover had been very well acquainted for many years. Winchell had closely followed Hoover's exploits in the 1930s, when Hoover was chasing the mobsters of that era. Consider also the information that Winchell conveyed: saucers are missiles from the Soviet Union. That is not what the Air Force was saying publicly but it is what Colonel Gasser had confidentially told the FBI several months before. Hoover, of course, knew this. He also knew of Dr. LaPaz's theory that the green fireballs were Soviet missiles. Hence Hoover had the information which Winchell reported.

It is, of course, possible that Winchell had gotten the information from an Air Force official. However, I think this unlikely. If Winchell had learned this from an Air Force source, Hoover wouldn't have known who had leaked the information and so he might have wanted to have Winchell interviewed. On the other hand, if Hoover had told Winchell he obviously would have known the source. Furthermore, Hoover wouldn't want some FBI agent to find out that he had leaked this important, classified information to Winchell.

Why would Hoover tell Winchell? Perhaps he was disturbed by the failure of the top generals and the President to react seriously to what was clearly perceived by the people closest to the problem as a continuing real threat to our most "vital installations." Perhaps Hoover decided to use the press to try to create pressure on the government to react—to do something.

However, the government did not react to Winchell's announcement. Why not? Weren't the President, *et.al.* worried about the Soviet threat? Of course they were. And one can imagine that if verified Soviet missiles had been spotted flying toward the USA, there would have been harsh words, if not all-out war.

Of course, if the top brass and the President knew that the strange lights were something else, perhaps something that couldn't be defended against, perhaps something related to extraterrestrial intelligence, they wouldn't have been worried about a Russian threat. Instead they would have tried to downplay the importance of the sightings by publicly claiming that they all could be explained as natural events.

Oh, and by the way, that's what exactly what they did!

There was heightened press activity for a few days after Winchell's announcement, as the news media attempted to confirm his statement. Of course, the Air Force and government officials denied that saucers were Russian missiles and assured everyone there was nothing to worry about. Then, three weeks later, two very convenient events happened (convenient for the Air Force in its attempt to decrease public interest in saucers): the report of Project Sign was released and three days later Sydney Shallet's article on the Air Force's saucer investigation was published. Neither of these publications was favorable toward saucers as extraterrestrial. Once again public pressure on the Air Force ended. But the saucer sightings didn't.

Chapter 9
Air Force: No Such Thing
UFOs: We're Baaack

I t was at this time, when the security agencies were getting an extreme case of the jitters over saucers and fireballs and the Air Force was disparaging Winchell's statement, that a highly credible, yet unexplainable, daytime sighting occurred near one of the restricted military test areas.

The sighting by Charles Moore and four Navy enlisted men at Arrey, New Mexico, not far from the White Sands Proving Grounds and Alamagordo, New Mexico, convinced many people that, not only were flying saucers real, they were highly advanced technological devices, advanced beyond anything human beings could create.

On April 24, at about 10:30 a.m. Mr. Moore, a graduate engineer, aerologist and member of the Navy's high altitude balloon project team, and the Navy men were tracking a balloon that had been launched ten minutes earlier, when Mr. Moore and the others noticed another object moving through the sky nearly in the direction of the balloon. This object was large and bright enough so that it could be seen with the naked eye. He tracked it with the theodolite (a type of telescope) they had been using to follow the balloon. Through the telescope it appeared to have an elliptical shape with about a 2.5 to 1 ratio of the maximum to minimum dimensions. The object traveled in a large arc through the sky, appearing first in the southwest at about 210 degrees azimuth and 45 degrees elevation. It then traveled rapidly eastward passing through 127 degrees azimuth and 60 degrees elevation (the approximate location of the sun) and then turned northward. It traveled to the north-northeast at about 20 degrees azimuth and stayed at that azimuth while it climbed from a 25 degrees elevation to about 29 degrees. Evidently it traveled almost directly away from the observers at a high speed. It had been visible for about a minute.

During the first portion of observation, Moore estimated that it traveled at an angular rate of about 5 degrees per second, and he estimated its angular size at 0.02 degrees. Moore thought that the altitude was as high as 300,000 feet (60 miles), which would make its length about 100 feet and its speed about 18,000 mph, but it may have been lower, in which case the speed and size would be smaller.* For example, if it had been at 100,000 feet it would have been about 30 feet in size and traveling about 6,000 mph. Moore launched another balloon which, after about an hour and a half, burst at an altitude of about 93,000 feet, having traveled only about 13 miles horizontal distance from the launch site. Hence there were no high speed winds at any altitude to 93,000 feet. Moore filed a report with the Navy Special Devices Center, where it attracted a great deal of interest. The report also turned up in the flying saucer file of the CIA as well as in the Project Blue Book file, where it is officially unexplained. It is not in the FBI file.

Moore's sighting was known to only a few people when, three days later, on April 27, 1949, the director of AFI briefed the Deputy Chief of Air Force Operations on the status of the UFO project. The Director of AFI also sent to the Joint Intelligence Committee (JIC) a formal report "On Unidentified Aerial Objects." (The JIC was composed of representatives from the several armed services, plus the State Department, CIA and FBI. There is no mention of this report in the FBI record, however.) This report essentially summarized the results of Project Sign with an interpretation or slant that was biased by the new policy of skepticism toward UFO reports. The important summary of results was in the Appendix, which states as follows:

> 1. As of March 10, 1949, a total of 256 incidents involving unidentified aerial objects had been recorded under Project Sign. The majority of these were domestic observations but there were many reports from foreign sources. In each incident the observers have been interrogated by investigators and the results have been analyzed by technical personnel.

---

* Since only the angular size and angular speed were measured, the calculated size and speed are proportional to the assumed distance.

2. Condensed summaries have been prepared on each incident to provide basic information to individuals and agencies having a responsibility or interest in the project.

3. The extreme lack of accurate observed details and unpredictable occurrence of incidents have made positive identification extremely difficult. Data on unidentified aerial objects has grouped the incidents as follows: 13.3% discs; 43% spherical or elliptical (sic) shape (including balls of fire); 6% cylindrical shape; 2.5% winged objects; 32.2% shapes other than those above.

According to the report, graphical methods were used to relate sightings to shape, location, direction of flight, missile test areas, airfields and airports, radio beacons, radar stations, meteorological stations, balloon releases, celestial phenomena, and flight paths of birds. A preliminary psychological analysis of reports by the Aero-Medical Laboratory of AMC indicated that "a considerable number of incidents can be explained as ordinary occurrences that have been misinterpreted, as a result of human errors."

The Air Weather Service had studied the first 172 sightings, and reported that 24 of them could be correlated with releases of weather balloons. The report stated that:

Professor Hynek, Ohio State University Astrophysicist and head of the University Observatory . . . indicates that 30 percent of the first 200 reports are positively attributable to astronomical phenomena, and 45 percent could be explained on the basis of such phenomena or the sighting or weather balloons or other objects.

Even though this indicated that at least 75% of the sightings could be explained, the possibility that some sightings might be "space ships or satellite vehicles" caused them hire the Rand Corporation to carry out "a special study . . . to provide analysis from this standpoint" and also to "provide fundamental information, pertaining to the basic design and performance characteristics that might distinguish a possible 'space ship.'"

However, the scientists at Rand, after analyzing all the reports, concluded "there is nothing in any reported incidents which would go against a rational explanation." The ATIC report to the JIC briefly discussed the possibility that "ball lightning" might account for some sightings, but "it appears that the subject of 'ball lightning' occupies an undetermined status and authorities are not at all convinced that such a phenomenon actually exists." The report also mentioned the green fireball sightings and the belief of Dr. von Karman that this problem "is more properly in the field of upper atmosphere research than the field of intelligence." The report also stated that:

Credible unexplained incidents which might involve the use of atomic powered craft of (un)usual design should be considered jointly by the Atomic Energy Commission and highly competent aerodynamicists to determine the necessity for further consideration of such incidents by the National Defense Intelligence Agencies.

The report concluded as follows:

17. The majority of reported incidents are reliable to the extent that they have involved the sighting of some object or light phenomenon.

18. In spite of the lack of accurate data provided by witnesses, the majority of reported incidents have been caused by mis-identifications of weather balloons, high altitude balloons with lights and/or electronic equipment, meteors, bolides , and the planet Venus.

19. There are numerous reports from reliable and competent observers for which a conclusive explanation has not been made. Some of these involve descriptions which would place them in the category of new manifestations of probable natural phenomena but others involve configurations and described performance which might conceivably represent an advanced aerodynamical development. A few unexplained incidents surpass these limits of credibility.

20. It is unlikely that a foreign power would expose a superior aerial weapon by a prolonged ineffectual penetration of the United States.

The last comment indicates that the writers of this report rejected the Soviet saucer hypothesis, as had the ATIC analysts in the past. They did admit that there were numerous unsolved sightings, some of which "surpass these limits of credibility" by which they meant that the descriptions were so accurate and the objects were so unlike man-made craft as to be incredible.

Two days later, the Air Force publicly announced the results of its first saucer investigation. The Office of Public Relations of the National Military Establishment issued a Memorandum, for immediate release to the press which was described as "a digest of preliminary studies made by the Air Materiel Command, Wright Field, Dayton, Ohio on 'Flying Saucers." The title of the

Memorandum was *Project Saucer*. It was a sanitized version of the final report of Project Sign, which had been completed in February after Project Grudge had formally taken over the saucer and fireball investigations.

Because the project names Sign and Grudge were classified, the public version was called *Project Saucer*. The Project Saucer report, like the JIC report discussed above, pointed out that there were unsolved sightings and left the door open for the possibility that some UFO sightings might represent something new. It therefore may be considered as the last gasp of the investigators who ran Project Sign in the heady days of September 1948, when they tried to convince General Vandenberg that saucers were interplanetary craft. On the other hand, the report also tried to make it appear as if the unsolved sightings would eventually be solved.

Hence the National Military Establishment may have thought that it would provide a sort of technical backup to the previously mentioned article that was being prepared by Sidney Shallett. Perhaps by coincidence—or perhaps not—Shallet's article appeared in the *Saturday Evening Post* only three days later. In a letter dated April 25, 1949 from General Cabell to the Director of Public Relations, Cabell pointed out that although Shallett was "urged not to attempt his article" he wrote it anyway and "presumably others also will be so inclined." Shallett had been given access to AMC/ATIC material on saucers and Cabell could "see no grounds for denial of a similar (access) to other correspondents." He went on to say:

> Since the attached article includes essentially the same material made available to Mr. Shallett, there do not appear to be any grounds for denying this material to others, similarly interested and equally responsible. On the other hand, it is certain that the release of this article on any broad basis would result in a flurry of 'crank' reports and a consequent flooding of our investigative resources. The end result would be a disservice to our effectiveness in eliminating the presently remaining question marks. Our efforts must be based upon reports by other than 'cranks' who will make their reports without the spur of widespread press speculation.

General Cabell concluded his letter by saying he did not object to the release of the Project Saucer report, but that he thought, in order to "reduce its use on a broad scale," it should be made available at the public relations office rather than distributed widely as a press release. Evidently the National Military Establishment thought otherwise. The memorandum was widely distributed.

According to the "Saucer" report, since the "birthday" of Project Saucer on January 22, 1948, the Air Force had studied more than 240 domestic and 30 foreign sightings. After spending a year studying these sightings:

> . . . with the assistance from several other government and private agencies, and with the entire facilities of the Wright Field laboratories at their disposal, Project 'Saucer' personnel have already come up with identification of about 30 percent of the sightings studied thus far as conventional aerial objects. It is expected that further probing of incidents in relation to weather balloon locations, etc., will provide commonplace answers to at least an equal number of the sky riddles.
>
> Answers have been—and will be—drawn from factors such as guided missile research activities, weather and other atmospheric sounding balloons, astronomical phenomena, commercial and military aircraft flights, flights of migratory birds, shots from flare guns, practical jokers, victims of optical illusion, the phenomena of mass hallucination, etc.

However, the Air Force admitted that "there are still question marks in the 'Saucer Story." The Air Force considered it "highly improbable" that any foreign country had created flying saucers, and "visitations from Mars, Venus, or other distant planets attached to other star systems is looked upon as an almost complete impossibility."

So what were the unidentifiable saucers?

> (Whereas) . . . no definite and conclusive evidence is yet available to either prove or disprove the existence of at least some of the remaining unidentified objects as real aircraft of unknown and unconventional configuration, exhaustive investigations have turned up no alarming probabilities.

The 22-page report described several sightings, discussed the methods of investigation and the potential explanations and then concluded:

The 'saucers' are not a joke. Neither are they cause for alarm to the population. Many of the incidents already have answers, meteors, balloons, falling stars, birds in flight, testing devices, etc. Some of them still have question marks. It is the mission of the AMC Technical Intelligence Division's Project 'Saucer' to supply the periods.

In other words, there was no real conclusion. Instead, the Air Force said this about the unexplained sightings: don't worry, we're working on it! The answers will come soon. The Air Force wanted the public to believe that everything was under control.

However, if the National Military Establishment thought that the Saucer report, when combined with Shallett's article, would put a damper on saucer interest, it was wrong. By admitting that a large fraction of the sightings were unexplained and by not positively ruling out interplanetary vehicles, the Air Force left open the door for the unworldly to enter the public discussion. Astute investigative reporters realized this and one reporter, in particular, made it the cornerstone of his proof that saucers were extraterrestrial visitors. This particular reporter would become the most vocal critic of Air Force saucer policy in years to come.

The release of the Project Saucer report may have made the press and the general public feel good, but it didn't impress security guards around Fort Hood and Killeen Base. On the same day as the release of the Project Saucer report, they saw unexplained phenomena four times between 9:20 to 9:40 p.m., and then nine times the next day between 8:30 and 9:30 p.m.. These guards may have thought that the saucers and fireballs had decided to retaliate against the writers of the Saucer report. The sightings are summarized below to illustrate the varying types of phenomena reported.

APRIL 27

#1: 9:20 PM; small; dull violet; first seen stationary, 6-7 feet above ground and 10-12 feet from 2 witnesses; then departed to the west; seen for 60 seconds; no sound, no odor; passed through branches of a tree, thereby establishing conclusively its location and approximate size; level flight.

#2: 9:25 PM; size of baseball; bright white; round; no glare; first seen 6-7 feet above ground, 200 yards away; level flight in a semicircular path around witnesses; light was round but "had a point shaped apparatus extending two to four inches behind it; the point of the cone was to the rear."

#3: 9:37 PM; size of a silver dollar; "rustless white" in color no glare; first seen 100 feet from 4 observers; 6 - 8 feet above the ground; approached 4 observers in a zig-zag path going on and off; no sound; no odor; no trail.

#4: (time not given); similar to #3.

APRIL 28

#1: 8:30 - 8:50 PM; 1 observer; 4 objects seen individually at 5 minute intervals; each in sight 3 - 5 minutes; moving slowly, rising slightly, then falling; size of a tennis ball at arm's length (roughly 10 ft in diameter if 100 ft away; proportionally larger or smaller if the distance were larger or smaller); white turning to red and then to green.

#2: 8:30 PM; 1 observer; 1 object seen intermittently at 5 minute intervals over 1 1/2 hours; horizontal flight toward the south at 3 mph; appeared to be about 10" in diameter; white, then turned red.

#3: 8:37 PM; 4 observers; 8 or 10 lights occurring at intervals of 5 minutes; each in sight for about 5 minutes; moved in southerly direction at low speed; constant elevation; made a turn; size of softball at arm's length (about 10 ft if 100 ft away); one appeared to have a cone shaped rear end tapering to a point; white, turned to red, and then to green.

#4: 8:40 PM; 1 observer; one light; just above treetops; about the size of a baseball at arm's length; slow speed; white light with red blinking light.

#5: 9:00 PM; 1 observer; four lights, no pattern; size of tennis ball at arm's length; 5 mph toward the south; first light was white, then red and then green; the other three lights were white only.

#6: 9:10 PM; 1 observer; one object; about the size of a baseball at arm's length; about 300 yards away (corresponding to roughly 90 feet in diameter if 900 feet away); observed for 8 - 10 minutes; stationary (color not reported).

#7: 9:10 PM: 1 observer; one object; size of baseball at arm's length; white; moved northward; in sight for about 2 seconds; estimated speed, 75 mph; described as being like a 75 watt bulb at 50 - 75 ft.

#8: 9:30 PM; 2 observers; one light; 10-15 inches long; observed for 5 -6 minutes; moved in southerly direction; speed estimated at 10 - 15 mph; color changed from white to red to green.

#9: 9:30 PM; 1 observer; one light appeared three times for 3, 2 and then 1 minute (approximately) durations; moving toward the west; speed about 5 mph; round; about the size of a baseball at arm's length; bright white, then turned to red.

The Project Saucer press release implied that the Air Force would eventually discover explanations for all the sightings. This put the Project Grudge personnel under pressure to explain all the sightings. Hence, for each sighting, they tried to find a few descriptive details which, when considered alone while ignoring other details if necessary, might suggest plausible explanations. The sightings by the security guards were assumed not to be hallucinations so the explanations had to involve real objects or phenomena. The Grudge personnel therefore claimed the April 27 lights were birds and the April 28 lights were flares or fireworks.

Another sighting on the day following the release of the Project Saucer report was a real challenge to the Grudge investigators. It did not appear near a military installation, but it was important because it was a daytime sighting. It occurred at Tucson, Arizona at 5:45 p.m. Several witnesses saw a sausage or cigar shaped object travel from the northeast to the southwest over a time period of 12 minutes or so. The object was shiny metallic and it reflected the sun. It appeared to be revolving as it moved like the "slow roll of an airplane." There was no noise, nor was there exhaust or a vapor trail. There were no wings or engines or "protuberances of any sort." It appeared to be traveling at 300-600 mph. The Project Grudge personnel had to leave this one unexplained.

The Project Saucer press release was written in a way which implied that all the unexplained sightings could be simply unusual natural phenomena. The Air Force hoped that this would allay any fears the public might have that the Air Force had lost control of the saucer situation and would dampen public interest in the subject. However, as pointed out previously, the report did not absolutely rule out the possibility that some sightings might be truly "revolutionary" in nature. A couple of days later, Sidney Shallett's flying saucer article in the *Saturday Evening Post* magazine seemed to squash that possibility.

The first part of the article was published on April 30, three days after the release of the Saucer report. The second part was published a week later. In the first article, entitled "What You Can Believe About Flying Saucers," Shallett was very critical of saucer sightings, which he referred to as the "great Flying Saucer Scare." He used phrases such as "fearsome freaks" and "full blown screwiness." He said that the Air Force had reluctantly been dragged into investigation of saucer sightings because of the public furor in the summer of 1947.* Shallet also said that, based on what he had been shown by the Air Force, there was not a "scrap of bona fide evidence" that saucers represented either a technological development of the human race or visitors from another planet. In other words, according to Shalett, all saucer sighting reports belonged to the following three general categories: (a) misidentifications and failures to identify natural and manmade phenomena, (b) delusions and mental aberrations, or (c) publicity seekers and hoaxers. Shallet's second article supported the viewpoint in his first article by demonstrating how experienced observers such as pilots could be fooled. The bottom line: saucer sightings are basically mistakes, they are certainly nothing to worry about and the Air Force has everything under control so don't worry, be happy!

The Project Saucer report stated that saucer sightings were "no joke" and indicated that the ATIC investigators believed, but could not prove, that all the unexplained sightings were natural phenomena. This left the door open a crack for the possibility that some unexplained sightings might not be natural phenomena. The Shallett articles, on the other hand, presented a more positive attitude toward explanation, an attitude that more accurately portrayed the beliefs of the Grudge personnel (Colonels and below) at the time. They were quite certain that, because saucers couldn't be ours and couldn't be theirs (Soviet's) and couldn't be ETs, then they must be natural phenomena, hoaxes, or delusions and therefore of little importance to the Air Force. As will be seen, this was not the belief of General Cabell and other High Brass.

After this article was published, the Grudge investigative activities steadily declined, with the project virtually shutting down in August, 1949. However, the analysis of the previously received unexplained sightings referred to in the Project Saucer

---

* This was wrong. The available Air Force records clearly show it was sightings by Air Force pilots and not public furor that attracted the interest of the Air Force.

report continued because the Grudge personnel knew that sooner or later they would have to supply explanations for all of them.

To the skeptical world, the decreased Air Force interest in saucers probably appeared logical because saucer sightings were nothing to worry about—so why investigate? However, to the FBI, with its connection to the insiders at the Air Force and its knowledge of the green fireball reports, this may have looked like a cover up.

Chapter 10
Observers of Unquestioned Reliability

T he "unimportant" yet unexplained phenomena seen in the southwest had established quite a track record by this time, and they were still being seen. According to a summary of observations written by Lt. Colonel Doyle Rees in May 1950, by the end of April 1949 the total number of sightings in the vicinity of the previously mentioned areas in New Mexico and at Camp Hood was about 50. Of these, a dozen were labeled as "'Disk' or variation," indicating that there were flying saucer or "flying machine" aspects to some of the sightings. According to Rees, the witnesses in these sightings were:

> . . . scientists, Special Agents of the Office of Special Investigations (IG) USAF, airline pilots, military pilots, Los Alamos Security Inspectors, military personnel and many other persons of various occupations whose reliability is not questioned.

Rees' list included Charles Moore's sighting, which was rated as very reliable. It did not, however, include an even more important sighting that occurred a month later, because it did not occur within the area of Rees' investigative jurisdiction. Instead, it occurred many hundreds of miles away at the mouth of the Rogue River in Oregon. This sighting is important because of the quality of the observations by the several observers, and because of the fact that the witnesses reported the sighting only to their local security agency and to the AFOSI.

During the afternoon of May 24, five people, three men and two women, were in a boat, fishing near the mouth of the Rogue River in Oregon. At about 5 p.m., they were looking eastward, scanning the river with 8-power Navy binoculars looking for signs of fish jumping, when they first noticed a strange circular object approaching from the northeast. They watched it for about two and a half minutes as it stopped and hovered east of them before it departed at high speed in a southward direction. The sky was clear and the afternoon sun was at their backs. To the naked eye it appeared shiny and shaped like a coin with the flat surface parallel to the ground. At its closest, it seemed to be only a couple of miles away and about a mile high. They heard no noise.

Two of the witnesses, a draftsman and a wind tunnel mechanic, were employees of the Ames Research Laboratory at Moffett Field, south of San Francisco.* These two men shared the 8-power binoculars. Each had about a minute to look at the object through the binoculars. They observed that the object was circular and thin relative to its diameter, with a shape similar to that of a pancake, and with some sort of a vertical fin on the upper surface at the trailing edge. They could see no wings, no antenna, no lights, no propellors and no jet engines. According to the AFOSI report:

> (The) object appeared round and shiny, something like a fifty-cent piece, viewed from below and to one side. Object's color was silvery and it appeared round in plan view. . . Just before Mr. Gilbert Rivera handed the glasses to Mr. Donald Heaphy the object made a turn on its vertical axis with no tilting or banking. . . The trailing edge of the object as it traveled appeared somewhat wrinkled and dirty looking.

The trailing edge looked "wrinkled and dirty," but there were no exhaust ports. Then they saw it speed off in a southeasterly direction, "accelerating to the approximate speed of a jet plane" in a few seconds without making any noise. About three weeks, later the Ames employees reported their sighting to the security office at Moffett Field. The security office then requested that AFOSI agents investigate the sighting.

In 1952, Project Blue Book hired the Battelle Memorial Institute in Columbus, Ohio, to carry out a statistical study of flying saucer reports that occurred between 1947 and the end of 1952. The main intent of the study, called Project Stork, was to determine whether or not there were consistent differences between sighting reports that were explained and those which could not be explained as mundane phenomena. To carry out this

---

* The Ames Research Laboratory carries out research on jet engines, among other things. Employees have Secret or Top Secret security clearances.

study, the Battelle scientists, working along with the Air Force personnel at ATIC, first analyzed each sighting to determine whether or not it could be identified. The scientists were able to do much better in explaining sightings than the Air Force had done in 1948 and 1949: they were able to explain about 70% of the 3,201 sightings they studied. About 10% of the sightings had too little information for a positive identification. However, about 20% had sufficient information for identification, yet resisted explanation. Of these they found a dozen which they considered to be the most descriptive of the sighted phenomena.

The sighting described here is the best of that dozen. The two main witnesses were technically trained and, as nearly as can be determined from the case file, thoroughly reliable. In the final report of the study, called Project Blue Book Special Report Number 14, the scientists included two rough sketches made by the witnesses, showing two views of a circular object with a thickness much less than its diameter, no wings, no tail and no engine, but a "wrinkled" outer edge. See Figure 16.

The description of the object by the witnesses is very clear: it was neither an ordinary aircraft nor a hallucination. It either was a hoax or the real thing—a flying saucer. Could it have been a hoax? I would say unequivocally no, because the two Ames employees reported their sighting to the security officer at Moffett Field. A hoaxer might report a sighting to the press, radio or TV, but no person of reasonable intelligence whose job depended upon holding a security clearance would try to hoax the security officer where he worked. Furthermore, there is no evidence that this sighting was ever mentioned in a news story or in the popular literature. Apparently, these witnesses reported the sighting to no one but the Ames security officer. The security officer then requested an investigation by the AFOSI. The AFOSI investigators interviewed all of the witnesses once and interviewed the Ames employees a second time. The interviews established the high degree of credibility of this sighting.

The Project Blue Book microfim file at the National Archives is supposed to contain all the records collected by the Air Force. In that file there are two sightings listed for May 24, 1949. One sighting, case number 402, is explained as "aircraft." The second

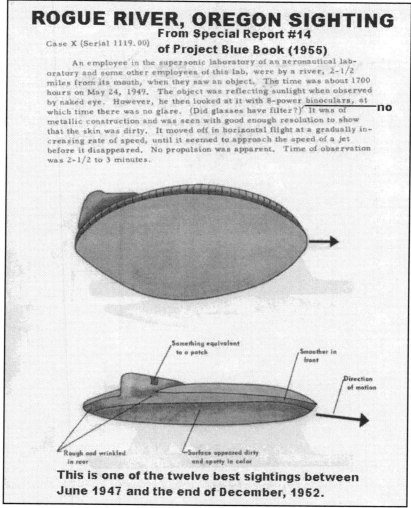

ROGUE RIVER, OREGON SIGHTING

From Special Report #14

Case X (Serial 1119.00)

of Project Blue Book (1955)

An employee in the supersonic laboratory of an aeronautical laboratory and some other employees of this lab, were by a river, 2-1/2 miles from its mouth, when they saw an object. The time was about 1700 hours on May 24, 1949. The object was reflecting sunlight when observed by naked eye. However, he then looked at it with 8-power binoculars, at which time there was no glare. (Did glasses have filter?) It was of metallic construction and was seen with good enough resolution to show that the skin was dirty. It moved off in horizontal flight at a gradually increasing rate of speed, until it seemed to approach the speed of a jet before it disappeared. No propulsion was apparent. Time of observation was 2-1/2 to 3 minutes.

no

Something equivalent to a patch

Smoother in front

Direction of motion

Rough and wrinkled in rear

Surface appeared dirty and spotty in color

This is one of the twelve best sightings between June 1947 and the end of December, 1952.

Figure 16: Rogue River Sighting

sighting, not numbered, is explained as "kites." The second sighting is not numbered because, according to a handwritten note, the "cards" are missing. This means that the copy of the AFOSI investigation report, which originally was sent to Project Grudge, had been removed from the sighting file by someone many years before the file was released in 1975. Fortunately, the original AFOSI investigation report was not kept at Blue Book headquarters but rather at the headquarters of AFOSI, so when the Air Force released the combined AFOSI and Blue Book records to the National Archives, I was able to find the record of this case investigation in the AFOSI section of the microfilm.

So, how did Project Grudge personnel explain this multiple witness sighting, you may ask? First, accidently (or intentionally?) they divided it into two parts and treated each separately. The sighting numbered 402 in the master case list contains the interview of one of the two women. According to the AFOSI report this lady was interviewed on August 8 (the last of the witnesses to be interviewed) and said that:

> . . . at approximately 1700 hours, 24 May 1949, she and four other persons, while fishing on the Rogue River near Elephant Rock, approximately 1 1/2 miles above the highway bridge near Gold Beach, Oregon, sighted an object described as being round in shape, silver in color, and about the size of a C-47 aircraft. When first brought to Mrs. McBeth's attention by one of the other witnesses, the object appeared to be three or four miles away. It was coming from the east but later turned to the southwest. It appeared to be traveling at the same rate as a C-47. It made no noise, left no exhaust trail, and made no maneuvers. The interviewee stated that she was not familiar with aircraft; therefore she could not estimate with any accuracy the speed or altitude at which the object was traveling. Mrs. McBeth made the comparison between the object and a C-47 because she is familiar with that type of aircraft. Her son has pointed out C-47s to her as they flew over the Gold Beach.

Based on this verbal evidence the Grudge personnel identified the object as an "aircraft" because "No data (were) presented to indicate object could NOT have been an aircraft" [capitalization in the original]. The Grudge personnel were able to offer that explanation only because they (1) ignored her claim that the object was circular and (2) treated her description separately from the descriptions by the other witnesses.

In order to explain the sighting by the other four witnesses the Grudge personnel used information provided by the AFOSI investigator. This man checked airport records for air traffic or anything else that could conceivably have been in the area at that time. There were no known aircraft in the area. However, the agent learned that radar kites, which are balloons supporting thin metallic radar reflectors, were launched twice a day from military radar installations near San Francisco. He wrote in his report that:

These devices are of aluminum sheet, approximately 5 feet on a side, roughly diamond shaped and containing a double set of triangular fins on the top side. These are carried aloft by gas filled balloons approximately 2 feet in diameter when they leave the earth. When these devices reach high enough altitude, the expanding gases cause the balloon to burst and the devices known as 'kites' fold and drift earthward. It is possible that one of these devices from one of these radar installations may have been blown as far North as Gold Beach, Oregon, on 24 May 1949.

A typical radar kite is shown in Figure 17.

This is where the official "kites" explanation comes from. (I don't know why the explanation is plural.) Based on this information, it is immediately obvious to the most casual observer that what they saw was a radar kite, right?

Not! The description given above is sufficient to make it clear that a radar kite is not pancake shaped. Furthermore, such a kite, if traveling through the air, would be supported by one or more

balloons which would have been obvious to the witnesses, since the balloons are about the same size as the kite, and it could have moved no faster than the wind. If the kite were falling because the balloons had deflated, the witnesses would have seen it fall rather than accelerate to a high speed and disappear in the distance.

As illogical as it may seem, the Project Grudge and Blue Book analysts, acting on the behalf of the U.S. Air Force officially accepted "kites" as the explanation for the sighting.

However, the Battelle scientists knew better: they did not accept the Air Force explanation. Neither do I.

I have found another reason to reject the Air Force explanation. An errant radar kite launched from the San Francisco area would have had to be carried north-northwestward a distance of about

Figure 17: Radar Kite

300 miles. About 30 years after the AFOSI closed their investigation of this case, I reopened it and completed it by obtaining the weather records for the coast of northern California and Oregon. These records show that the winds at all altitudes for the day of the sighting and the day preceding were blowing from the west to the east, and could not have carried a balloon from San Francisco northward to the Rogue River. The AFOSI agent who conducted the investigation of this case could have discovered that for himself in 1949. Apparently he decided to end the investigation once he had found a possible explanation.

The fact that this explanation was accepted as official is clear evidence that the Grudge personnel applied the policy of explaining sightings any way possible, following the Vandenberg rejection of the Estimate.

More recently, there has been the suggestion that the object was a blimp traveling generally southward but making a turn toward the witnesses before heading south again. This suggestion spurred a search for all possible blimps along the west coast and where they may have been at the time. The actual flight record of the only possible blimp was found in an archive and it showed the blimp to have been hundreds of miles away.[*]

---

[*] For further information and a detailed analysis of this sighting see http://www.brumac.8k.com/Rogue/RogueRiver2.htm.

Chapter 11
Don't Worry Be Happy

On May 5, 1949, only five days after the Project Saucer report told everyone that flying saucers and related phenomena were nothing to worry about (so be happy!), and about two and a half weeks before the sighting described in the previous chapter, there was a secret meeting at Camp Hood, Texas. The meeting was a discussion of the continuing phenomenon of "unusual lights."

Why? Because by this time there had been so many sightings, that the people responsible for security of Killeen Base were not happy—they were in fact very worried. According to an AFOSI report, at the previous weekly intelligence conferences in April the AFOSI, FBI, ONI, the Army Special Weapons Project (ASWP at the Killeen Base) and the Fourth Army representatives had disputed over which agency had the investigative jurisdiction over these sightings (recall that there had been a similar dispute in December, 1948, over the Los Alamos area sightings). The dispute was resolved by having the AFOSI, the ASWP, and Fourth Army investigate sightings within the various areas of Camp Hood where they were in control. The FBI had no part in this inasmuch as the FBI was authorized only to investigate civilian sabotage or subversion.

Of greater importance than the dispute is the fact that the main subject of discussion was the repeated sightings of strange lights. According to the AFOSI report, the participants discussed the possibility that the observers might have failed to identify fireflies or other natural causes because of a lack of training. The participants agreed that a "more exact and comprehensive system of observing was necessary." The representatives of the Fourth Army and the ONI:

> . . . expressed great concern about the unknown phenomena as they
> believed some of the sightings to be valid, and even after all

questionable sightings were discounted, that there remained a sufficient number of unknown manifestations to cause grave concern.

On the other hand, the Special Weapons Project representatives were not worried because they believed that they had adequate security measures. They believed that "a logical natural explanation could be found for the strange lights." The FBI representatives were non-committal. The Fourth Army, in order to resolve the questions, proposed that a special observation team made up of "trained Artillery observers" should be stationed around the base every night.

Over the next two weeks, the special observing plan was put in force by the Fourth Army. It was a very meticulous plan which began with the reason for its existence:

TO: All members of the Artillery Training Force

1. You are familiar with the fact that there have been numerous reports within the past year of a phenomena (sic) appearing in several parts of the United States commonly called 'flying discs' or 'flying saucers.' Sufficiently authentic reports of this condition have been received by the Department of the Army to justify a detailed study.

2. In the past several weeks, this condition has been reported as occurring, intermittently, over the southern portion of the Camp Hood Military reservation. You have been designated as part of a force to determine accurately the following information.

a) Does this condition exist and, if so, to what extent?

b) A description of the phenomenon

c) Its location, altitude and duration

d) If it is produced by any individual or machine on the ground, to apprehend such individuals.

3. This entire project has been classified as 'Confidential' and, as such, you will not discuss any phase of the operation, or your work in connection with it, with anyone except as is required by your work.

The plan was to have observers at several locations in communication with a command post at all times. Whenever a "phenomenon" would appear, the first to see it would alert the others and then they would all watch while recording exact directions and angular elevations. The resulting data would allow for triangulation and size estimates.

During the weekly meeting on May 19, the Fourth Army announced the preliminary results. All the attendees agreed that the "new observation system instituted by the Fourth Army provided precise results and definitely indicated that the unknown phenomena in the Camp Hood area could not be attributed to natural causes."

Project Grudge personnel were not involved in these observations.* The conclusion of Projects Sign and Grudge that the unexplained sightings could be explained as natural phenomena, and certainly were nothing to worry about, had already been publicized in the Project Saucer report. They assumed they didn't need any more sighting data. Now, only a few weeks later, an explicit investigation by the Army had shown that the strange lights were not natural phenomena. Did this result bother the AMC/ATIC personnel? Not a bit, as the FBI was to find out in the latter part of May.

For the FBI, these Army experiments may have once again cleared up the controversy: the objects were Soviet missiles! Perhaps Hoover felt justified if, in fact, he had broken security over a month earlier in order to alert the USA, through Walter Winchell, that we were virtually under attack from the Russians.

Then Winchell returned into the picture in a way which muddied the waters once again.

According to a May 26 office memorandum written by one of the FBI agents, Mr. Hoover received a telegram from Winchell. This was a telegram which had been sent to Winchell in early May by none other than Robert Ripley of 'Believe It Or Not" fame. Apparently Ripley believed that he had located "the only authentic Japanese flying saucer in this country." Winchell wanted the FBI to confirm or deny that there could be such a thing. One of the FBI agents contacted someone in the Intelligence Division of the Army (G-2) and was told that they had "no information concerning any Japanese flying saucer ever having been recovered in the United States."

The FBI file does not indicate what ultimately became of Ripley's Japanese "saucer."** However, the file does report what

---

* They may not even have been aware of the army's efforts to do what Dr. von Karman had recommended to the Air Force: get more precise observational data.

** It subsequently turned out to be one of the "fire balloons" that was launched by the Japanese during WWII in an attempt to bomb the west coast of the USA.

the FBI's information source was told by the AMC/ATIC personnel about the continued saucer sightings:

This matter was discussed with Colonel (name censored) OSI-USAF, who advised on April 27, 1949 that he had interested himself in the flying saucers and related subjects and that in so far as could be determined by him through his sources in the Air Force, which are excellent, there is no authentic information available concerning the phenomenon of flying saucers. He advised he would check with the authorities at Wright Field to determined if any information is available concerning the recovery of a Japanese flying saucer.

Colonel (...) has now (the latter part of May) advised that there is no information available in any arm of the Air Force to the effect that any flying saucers of any kind have been recovered in the United States. Colonel (...) stated delay had been encountered in determining this fact inasmuch as inquiries had been directed through individuals known to him and trusted by him and not through the usual channels from which he possibly would receive a stock answer.

Well, now, this is a "Don't Worry, Be Happy" answer if ever there was one.

"No flying saucers of any kind have been recovered . . . ."

So, what did you expect? The documentary record indicates that AMC/ATIC personnel (Colonels and below) didn't know about any crashed saucer debris or, if they did, they certainly weren't going to tell someone who didn't have clearance for that sort of information.

What about the Colonel's statement that there was no authentic information available? On the face of it, this implies that Air Force had no proof that flying saucers were real, unexplainable objects. This statement must have puzzled the FBI, because only about four months earlier, in January, Colonel Gasser had said that there was authentic information which suggested the disc objects were Russian missiles. Then there were all the indisputable reports of strange "green fireball" phenomena in the vicinity of "vital installations" for which Dr. LaPaz proposed the Russian missile theory. And finally there were the recent Army observations which proved that the phenomena did not have a natural origin. With all this observational evidence, how could the AMC/ATIC personnel say that there was no "authentic information"?

The FBI must have been utterly confused. J. Edgar's head was spinning . . . *real* . . . *not real.* Real on Monday, Wednesday and Friday . . . etc.

The AMC/ATIC personnel were able to say with a straight face that there was no authentic information because they didn't believe the sightings were valid. At this time, in the late spring of 1949, Project Grudge was operating on the assumption that all sightings could be explained as mistakes, natural phenomena, delusions, and hoaxes because they didn't believe the objects or phenomena were our secret experimental devices, they didn't believe the objects or phenomena were Russian (or other foreign) devices, and they couldn't, because of General Vandenberg's rejection of the Estimate, seriously consider the ET possibility.

One person who believed the green fireballs, at least, were natural phenomena was Dr. Joseph Kaplan, a professor of physics at the Institute of Geophysics at the University of California, a member of the Air Force Scientific Advisory Board and formerly of the Operational analysis Branch of AMC. At this time he was acting as a consultant to AMC. Kaplan first heard of the green fireballs in February 1949. He then alerted Dr. von Karman to the fireball sightings and the work of Dr. LaPaz. Von Karman then sent a letter to General Cabell recommending that the Air Force investigate these sightings more fully (see Chapter 7). Cabell then asked Kaplan to continue to study the problem.

In early July 1949, Cabell wrote to Kaplan to ask about the status of the fireball investigation. Kaplan responded that he had been very impressed with the sightings by the security guards and that he was particularly interested in their descriptions of the unusual green color. Kaplan pointed out that green is the color of aurora afterglow.[*] He therefore suggested that perhaps the green fireballs were actually some new form of aurora occurring at low altitude and low latitudes. He admitted, however, that this proposal could neither explain the observed trajectories nor the geographical localization over New Mexico and western Texas.

---

[*] The aurora is a greenish glow in the upper atmosphere that is created when electrons and ionized atoms ejected by the sun hit oxygen atoms. It is often seen near the poles of the Earth where magnetic lines of force "funnel" electrons downward into the thin upper atmosphere.

Kaplan mentioned that Dr. Norris Bradbury, the director of the laboratory at Los Alamos, proposed to hold a conference in September to discuss the sightings, and said that he planned to attend the conference to present his aurora hypothesis as a potential explanation for the fireballs.

On August 16, 1949, the FBI agent in San Antonio again mentioned the sightings around the military installations:

> I am attaching hereto a number of copies of reports being received in great numbers in this office concerning the so-called flying disks or unnatural phenomena being frequently observed around Camp Hood, Texas. This is, of course, a primary concern of the Air Corps. Consequently, this office is following the practice of reviewing the data and destroying them in the event there appears to be nothing of FBI interest therein. It is pointed out that the filing of these would result in the rapid accumulation of very bulky files. Unless the Bureau believes this is unwise this practice will continue.

The FBI file does not contain a response to the above letter, nor does it contain the reports sent by SAC San Antonio.

Fortunately, the AFOSI file does contain the reports. The sighting catalogue by Lt. Colonel Doyle Rees, mentioned before, lists Camp Hood/Killeen Base (CH/KB) sightings on May 6, 7, 8, July 11, 28 (3 sightings), 30 (2), August 10 (8), 11, 12 (2), 14 and 20. Thus there were files on 22 sightings just in those months. No wonder that SAC San Antonio was worried about the accumulation of paper. Previously there had been about 10 sightings in March but none in April.

It is a matter of interest that there are no further listings of sightings at Fort Hood in Colonel Rees' catalogue, which runs to May, 1950. Had the "fireballers" completed their surveillance of Fort Hood? The same catalogue shows that sightings in the Los Alamos-Sandia Base area continued into August 1949. In May 1949, there were 5 sightings, in June there were 5, there were none in July and in August there were 10. Furthermore, sightings in the Los Alamos-Sandia Base area continued at a rate of several per month through the next year and caused the Air Force to set up an observing project which provided photographic proof of the existence of flying saucers. Proof that was suppressed.

Chapter 12
Twinkle Twinkle Little Fireball

B etween May 1, 1949 and the end of that year, the FBI had very little UFO action. FBI headquarters received a copy of a sighting by a Navy pilot and a couple of reports from civilian witnesses. During the same time period, according to the Project Blue Book master list file at the National Archives, Project Grudge (like it or not!) received about 250 reports, a few of which are discussed below.

One of the reports received by the FBI is published here for the first time because it illustrates a class of unidentified objects which has been reported many times over the years, but which receives very little media interest because these objects are small. The witness's name was removed from the FBI document when it was released to the public. He wrote:

> An incident happened this afternoon which after consideration I felt I should report. I most certainly do not want this incident disclosed, as I do not want any publicity concerning it. If you regard it of no special interest to the FBI please disregard this correspondence.
>
> I was flying from Clark Field to Parkersburg, W. Va. this afternoon and about four miles airline, southwest of Parkersburg I suddenly noticed a bright yellow object coming directly toward me. It came at me with such speed, added to my 100 mph forward speed, that it startled me and had passed by in a matter of a couple of seconds. But it passed by about 100 feet under my ship and about 50 feet to my right, and because of the dark green background of forests below I was able to get very clear outline of the object and what I believe is a very accurate description.
>
> Color - bright canary yellow
> Length - 15 to 18 inches
> Diameter - about 4 inches at the largest part
> It resembled a rocket, in fact was about the same shape and proportions as the fuselage of a Lockheed Air Force X-90.
> No wings but vertical and horizontal fins on rear 1/3 of the rocket.

No visible means of propulsion such as a propeller, vapor trail, smoke or exhaust.

The front of the rocket was very sharp with a needle nose, the needle looked about 6" long and was the size of a lead pencil.

The rear end was blunt similar to the rear end of a jet fuselage.

It appeared to have spent its force and seemed to be dropping slightly as it passed by, or had been fired or launched from a higher altitude than I was flying.

It happened at 2:45 on September 25, 1949.

I was flying at an altitude of 3450 ft above sea level.

I was flying a course of 60 degrees (E. NE.) and the rocket was traveling almost west at 240 degrees.

The visibility was exceptionally good (30 miles).

The letter also described the type of aircraft the witness was flying in (a Luscombe 8A, NC 1440K) and the exact location of the sighting. The FBI retyped the letter and sent it to the Director, Office of Special Investigations of the Inspector General of the Air Force at the Pentagon. However, it does not appear in the file of reports collected by Project Grudge.

Meanwhile, back at the "vital installations," Army intelligence and the AFI continued to monitor sightings. ATIC/Grudge was not investigating sightings and, in spite of the Army's request, never did send a trained observer team to Camp Hood. Moreover, the new director of ATIC intelligence, Colonel Harold Watson, who took over in July 1949, was strongly anti-UFO. Under his direction Project Grudge only analyzed previous sightings. His goal was to be able to explain each one in order to justify the public statements released in the Project Saucer report. These efforts were to prove valuable in December 1949 when the first major challenge to the Air Force was published.

Because ATIC/Grudge did not participate in the Army observation experiments, no ATIC observer was present to witness the success of these experiments during the nights of May 4, 6, 7, 8 and 23. Nor did Grudge personnel participate in the triangulation (localization) of a UFO.

This occurred on the night of June 6, when observers at two locations at Camp Hood saw a hovering orange light. They determined that it was about 3 miles away from one of the observation posts, 4½ miles from the other, and about a mile high. The estimated size, based on the distance and measured angular size of the light, was 30 to 70 feet. After hovering it started to move in level flight and then burst into small particles. It had been visible for almost three minutes, a significant amount of time. Months later, Project Grudge personnel, in their attempts to explain everything, identified this as a "balloon."

Dr. LaPaz continued to monitor sightings of the so-called fireballs. On August 17, 1949 he wrote another report to Lt. Colonel Rees. He went into great detail about attempts to detect copper dust in the atmosphere after two green fireball sightings. He pointed out that such dust had, in fact, been detected but that there was no conclusive evidence that the dust was not from some earthly source. He emphasized that a greater measurement effort was needed because if it could be proven that green fireballs created copper dust, then this would be strong confirming evidence that the fireballs were not meteors. He also summarized the results of investigations into sightings in June, July, and early August and pointed out that in most reports the fireballs were described as falling vertically downward rather than traveling horizontally as in previous months. He pointed out that perfectly vertical falls were as extraordinary as perfectly horizontal trajectories. He also suggested that the Institute of Meteoritics should publicize its interest in receiving reports of meteors and sky phenomena in order to collect more reports.

The Army and Air Force had tried to keep a lid on the sightings around the New Mexico area but news leaked out anyway. The August 30 issue of the *Los Angeles Times* carried a story about saucers seen at the White Sands Proving Grounds, where advanced rockets were tested. According to the story, technicians in the area had seen strange objects flying over during normal operations. In one case an object seemed to be traveling along with a rocket. The story even summarized the sighting by Charles Moore discussed previously (Chapter 9). The appearance of the *Los Angeles Times* article caused Army intelligence, responsible for security around White Sands, to try to determine the source of the leaked information. The source turned out to a Navy rocket scientist, Commander Robert McLaughlin. Although Army Captain Edward Detchmendy, the Army Public Information Officer, was angry at the leak, Commander McLaughlin was not reprimanded for a breach of security. In fact, about six months later, he wrote a magazine article about these events!

In early September 1949, a new discovery seemed to confirm the suggestion that fireballs and saucers could be Soviet atomic powered missiles: specially instrumented aircraft flying over the northern Pacific detected a cloud of radioactive dust. Over the next few days the cloud was tracked and analyzed. The conclusion: the Russians now had atomic bombs. No one knew just how advanced the Soviet delivery systems might be. Could they really fly an atomic bomb over the southwestern USA?

A month later, the theory that flying saucers used nuclear fuel received a further boost from sightings around Mt. Palomar. During October, high speed objects were seen flying past the observatory where the Office of Naval Research had placed a cosmic ray monitoring station with Geiger counters and chart recorders. On the 14th, at 1:14 p.m., a witness saw a dozen and a half objects fly past. The silvery objects had no wings or tails, they seemed to be about mile up and they emitted a strange noise. A technician happened to check the Geiger counters a few hours later and found that at the time of the sighting the recorder pen had gone wild. Several days later, at 7:20 a.m. on the 17th, a member of the staff of Palomar Observatory, while checking on the Geiger counters, saw a small black dot zip by beneath the 7,000 feet cloud ceiling. At the same time the recorder pen went off scale. The Navy and Air Force were immediately informed. A third sighting near Palomar, of a single, high speed object with no wings or tail on October 21, did not affect the Geiger counters.

There was a dispute over whether or not there had been electrical malfunctions during the October 14 and 17 sightings. The technicians who designed the equipment were sure that the high scale readings were not electrical malfunctions. The Navy took an interest in these sightings and went so far as to carry out a test in which they had Navy aircraft fly past Mt. Palomar to find out whether or not the passage of ordinary aircraft would affect the Geiger counters. As expected, there was no effect. Some more people now believed in atomic powered saucers. Several months later, the equipment was removed from Mt. Palomar for a detailed study and it was found that there was a loose fuse clip. When jiggled it caused the pen to move erratically. The technicians were not able to determine whether or not this explained the coincidence of anomalous readings with the saucer sightings.

The continued sightings of unusual phenomena in the New Mexico skies were the subject of a joint intelligence meeting during the afternoon of October 14 at the Los Alamos National Laboratory. This was the meeting, originally planned for September, which Dr. Kaplan had mentioned in his July letter to General Cabell (Chapter 11). The meeting was held at the request of Dr. Norris Bradbury, the Director of the laboratory. A month before, Kaplan had met with personnel from the Geophysical Sciences Branch of Air Force Research and Development and convinced them of the seriousness of the matter. With their help, Kaplan succeeded in getting some action. A month before the meeting, on September 14, under the authority of General Hoyt Vandenberg (the man who had rejected the Estimate the year before!), the Geophysical Sciences Branch of Air Force Research and Development ordered the new AMC commander, Lt. General Benjamin Chidlaw, to begin an investigation of the unusual phenomena. The investigation would be carried out at the AMC's Air Force Cambridge Research Laboratory (AFCRL) in Boston. Furthermore, AFCRL was directed to send representatives to the Los Alamos meeting.

Several of the attendees were the illuminati of the military science community: Dr. Edward Teller, "Father of the H-Bomb" (recall that he had attended the first green fireball conference in February, 1949), Stanislaw Ulam (worked with Teller on the H-Bomb), and George Gamow, astrophysicist (famous for his "Big Bang" theory and nucleosynthesis of elements). Dr. Lincoln LaPaz (who had analyzed dozens of green fireball sightings by this time), and of course Dr. Bradbury were also present. In addition, two other physicists from Los Alamos and the intelligence contingent were there: Lt. Colonel Doyle Rees and Captain Melvin Neef of the 17th District, AFOSI. Others in attendance were Major L. C. Hill of the Fourth Army, Major Frederic Oder, Director of the Geophysical Research Division of the USAF (the Cambridge representative), Major K. Kolster, AFSWP, Sandia

Base, Sidney Newberger, Chief of Security at Los Alamos and, of course, the ever-present FBI, represented by SAC Albuquerque (Phil Claridge) and SAC Los Alamos (Jerry Maxwell).

It was Dr. Kaplan's intention to have LaPaz outline the fireball problem for these people and to enlist their support for setting up a research project. As is usual for a classified meeting, the security instructions were outlined, and it was pointed out that the subject matter was classified Secret under the "code name Grudge" even though Grudge personnel were not present.* Then LaPaz reviewed previous observations in the Sandia-Los Alamos area and the main elements of his presentation at the February meeting. His discussion contrasted two possibilities: natural vs. man-made. The scientists did not reject Dr. LaPaz's man-made hypothesis, but they did reject Dr. Kaplan's auroral hypothesis for the very reasons listed by Kaplan in his letter to Cabell: auroras are not localized, they are generally seen much farther north, and auroras do not travel along horizontal paths.

Although Dr. Kaplan was not successful in convincing the attendees that fireballs were some new form of aurora, he was successful in enlisting their support for obtaining better observational data. The attendees recommended "that a project be set up at the earliest date in order to make photographic, sound, and mathematical observations on a continuing basis."

So, finally, after ten months of continual green fireball reports, some important people were pushing for an investigation. Dr. von Karman asked Dr. Kaplan to make a special report on fireballs during the AFSAB meeting on November 3, 1949. At that meeting, Kaplan presented a brief history of the fireball sightings and summarized the analytical work by LaPaz. He made a strong case that the fireballs were real objects, as opposed to misidentified meteors or psychological aberrations. He further stated that he had written a report on the fireballs. This report had been sent to General Cabell who, in turn, had sent it to the Geophysical Directorate at AFCRL where they were "setting up the necessary observational program to obtain pictures and spectra." Kaplan did not present his auroral hypothesis at the

---

* Recall that the investigative activities of Project Grudge had ended several months before.

AFSAB meeting. Instead, he merely said that he believed the fireballs to be some new type of natural phenomenon.

On November 7 Major Oder, Director of AFCRL, wrote his report on the Los Alamos meeting to the Commanding General (CG), AMC (Chidlaw). Here is a shortened version of the report (Note: the Chief of Staff, USAF was General Vandenberg):

> In accordance with instructions in classified letter from Chief of Staff, USAF, to CG, AMC, subject 'Light Phenomena,' .... the undersigned attended a conference at Los Alamos on the subject of a phenomena (sic) observed in the northern New Mexico area. The phenomena has the appearance of a green fireball and because of the fact that it had been observed only (as far as can be determined) in the northern New Mexico area and only since the year 1947, has caused a high degree of apprehension among security agencies in the area. .... In view of the fact that the phenomena has been observed by independent and trained observers there is little doubt that something was actually observed.
>
> The first part of the conference was devoted to a summary presentation of all collected and organized observational information regarding green fireballs....
>
> The second part of the conference was a discussion by the scientists present of various possible explanations and hypotheses concerning the phenomena. Little success was had.
>
> It was the conclusion of the group present at the meeting that the present information on the phenomena was not sufficiently quantitative and objective to allow any profitable scientific consideration. Instrumental observations (especially photographs, triangulation and spectroscopic) were considered essential.
>
> Dr. Joseph Kaplan... (will recommend to the next meeting of the Scientific Advisory Board) that the USAF provide a suitable investigation of the phenomena using the Geophysical Research Directorate, AFCRL, AMC as the agency for the project.
>
> It is the opinion of this office that...AFCRL is capable of performing the required investigation...provided that necessary funds, personnel authorizations and equipment are provided. Inasmuch as the phenomena appears to be atmospheric in nature, such an assignment is considered appropriate.[*]

The combined actions of Dr. Kaplan and Major Oder were

---

[*] By the time Major Oder got around to writing this letter, Dr. Kaplan had already presented his fireball report to the Science Advisory Board.

successful. On December 9, a deputy to Lt. General Chidlaw wrote a letter of recommendation for continued research under the Air Force Geophysical Research program and requested that the Research and Development Board approve the necessary funds. On December 20, 1949, Colonel Benjamin Holzman, in the office of Major General Donald Putt, the Air Force Director of Research and Development (who was also the Military Director of the AFSAB), wrote a letter of concurrence which pointed out that "prior to approval of the Research and Development Board . . . it will be necessary for you to prepare a project plan" and a budget.

Everything was go for the first instrumented search for unidentified phenomena (fireballs and saucers). Unfortunately things proceeded slowly and there was a budget crunch. Nevertheless, according to a May, 1950 letter to General Putt, AMC stated that it had been able to "initiate subject project on a limited basis utilizing personnel and equipment which have become available at Holloman Air Force Base." The letter mentions in particular the use of "Askania phototheodolites in order to provide trajectory data and photo records," spectrographic cameras and radio spectrum analyzers.

This was the beginning of project with the delightful name of Twinkle. It was during the time of this project that one of these Askania phototheodolites got the proof of the existence of "flying saucers." It was also during this project that the proof was ignored or covered up.

Chapter 13
Project Grudge vs. The ETH

Six days after General Putt approved Project Twinkle, a very important event in UFO history occurred: a magazine article claimed that information collected by the Air Force proved that flying saucers were extraterrestrial craft. This astounding statement, published in the January issue of *True Magazine*, was given credibility by the fact that it had been written by a retired Marine Corps aviator, Major Donald Keyhoe, an independent reporter who was to become the most consistent critic of the Air Force policy toward UFO sightings. In the article, "The Flying Saucers Are Real," Keyhoe claimed he had reached that conclusion after studying the Project Saucer report, the available sighting reports and after talking with witnesses and Air Force representatives. He further claimed that saucers were spaceships of several types that had been visiting the earth for over a hundred years, at least.

This magazine hit the stands a day after Christmas 1949 and immediately the news media were on a roll. The story made front page news throughout the United States.* The very next day, the press fury increased as the Air Force exercised its preplanned retaliation.

The release of Project Saucer in April 1949 and the publication of Sydney Shallet's articles had not quieted down the public interest in saucer reports. A few reporters knew that the Air Force had not been dragged reluctantly into saucer investigation by civilian saucer sightings, as claimed by Shallet, but rather had become interested because Air Force personnel were also witnesses. These reporters thought the Saucer report was really intended to divert attention from the real story, whatever that

---

* *True Magazine* later stated that that particular issue of *True* contained the most widely read and discussed magazine article ever up to that time.

was. Because the Project Saucer report had not flatly said all sightings had been explained, and because it said the investigation was continuing, it had left open the door for three possibilities, the latter two of which were potentially quite frightening: (a) the U.S. government had developed a technology so secret that the Air Force could not refer to it publicly and, in fact, had to deny its existence to cover it up (shades of Stealth in more recent times); (b) the Russians had developed a totally new and superior weapon system with potentially disastrous consequences for the free world; and (c) intelligent beings from outer space were visiting earth.

Because of these possibilities, reporters began to pester AFI and ATIC to learn about the latest on the Air Force investigation. They realized that the story behind any one of these possibilities would be the news scoop of the year. The only response they got from the Air Force was that the investigation was ongoing. The late August 1949 article about saucers being seen at White Sands increased the press interest. Some reporters, including Keyhoe, began to do their own investigations. They traveled around the country and talked to witnesses who, they discovered, were generally credible people who had seen and reported incredible objects.

Of course, the Air Force was aware of all these press activities and expected a big story to come out eventually. The only questions were who would write it and when would it be published.

During the spring of 1949, ATIC personnel had stopped the careful study of new sightings. Instead, they concentrated their activities on analyzing old sightings so that they could prepare the final "Grudge Report." This report would be needed to close out the project in a manner consistent with the official Air Force policy, as implied in the Project Saucer report, that all sightings could be explained. The ATIC personnel pushed to get the Grudge report finished as soon as possible so it would be ready when needed. It turned out that the timing was perfect. Shortly before Keyhoe's article was published, the final report was ready and, according to Ruppelt in *The Report on Unidentified Flying Objects*, ATIC formulated a plan for a response to whatever would be the first article to hit the newsstands. When the *True Magazine* article appeared, the Air Force was ready.

On December, 27, 1949, the day after Keyhoe's article, the Air Force rained on his parade by executing the first part of the plan: the Air Force held a press conference which featured a general saying everything was hoaxes, hallucinations, and misidentifications of known objects. The General also made the following announcement:

> The Air Force has discontinued its special project investigating and evaluating reported flying saucers on the basis that there is no evidence the reports are not the result of natural phenomena. Discontinuance of the project, which was carried out by the Air Force, was concurred in by the Department of the Army and Navy.
>
> The Air Force Materiel Command has been working very closely with intelligence on the whole matter of flying saucers.
>
> We probably have the most complete file on the saucers anywhere, but there is nothing new or startling to indicate that the saucers are interplanetary visitors.
>
> Continuance of the project is unwarranted since additional incidents now are simply confirming findings already reached.

The Air Force then carried out the second part of the plan: the Air Force announced that the final Grudge report would be declassified and made available in a few days. Apparently the top Air Force officials believed that the release of the Grudge report would be enough to kill the saucer stories forever. They were wrong.

Whereas Keyhoe's work was impressive, the 600-page Grudge Report was unconvincing. There were too many poor or just plain wrong explanations. Instead, of making the saucer problem go away it merely increased the confusion over what really was going on.

According to the report, Project Grudge had carefully studied 237 sightings, which was 33 fewer than Project Saucer (Project Sign), which had studied 240 domestic and 30 foreign sightings for a total of 270). From this, the press may have concluded that Project Grudge had received no new reports from early spring of 1949 through December 1949. Of course, this conclusion was false. The Project Blue Book master list shows that Grudge received 250 sighting reports between May 1 and December 31 and 446 for the whole year. The reason that analyses of these sightings did not appear in the final report is simply that the Grudge personnel felt it to be a waste of time, because the newer reports were similar to the older ones. The press reporters did not know about all of these new sightings, since this information was not released until years later.

The Air Force had told the press that all sightings could be explained and proclaimed that the Grudge report would prove it. Although on the face of it, the final report did seem to support this claim, astute reporters were not convinced. The report showed that, with the help of Dr. Hynek, the consultant in astronomy, they had been able identify 32% as astronomical.* With the help of experts at the Air Force Weather Service and Air Force Cambridge Research Laboratory, the Grudge personnel identified 12% as sightings of weather balloons or high altitude Skyhook balloons. The Grudge personnel and the expert consultants further concluded that about 33% were hoaxes or had insufficient information for evaluation. That meant that the expert consultants could not offer explanations for 23% of the sightings (55 out of the 237). This did not stop the Grudge analysts, however. The last of several appendices to the Grudge report included the official explanations for the unexplained sightings!

This Appendix created a big problem for the Air Force because members of the press who read it were not convinced. The explanations seemed at the very least, strained, and in some cases simply wrong. Ruppelt, in *The Report on Unidentified Flying Objects*, cited one good example of the approach to explaining these reports. In a 1948 report, which was analyzed by Dr. Hynek and the Air Weather Service, an Air Force pilot had reported seeing a glowing white light over Andrews AFB. He chased it for ten minutes as it went through some turning maneuvers before it finally "headed for the coast." He did manage to get a glimpse of a dark oval object smaller than his airplane. "I couldn't tell if the light was on the object or if the whole object had been glowing," he reported. Witnesses on the ground concurred with the pilot's

---

* Many of the green fireball reports were claimed to be meteors, despite Dr. LaPaz's arguments against that identification.

report: they had seen the light and the airplane chasing it. Hynek reported it was not astronomical and the Air Weather service reported that it was not a balloon. This didn't stop the Grudge personnel: the official explanation was . . . *balloon!*

Ruppelt illustrated the press reaction to the Grudge explanations by referring to a conversation he had several years later with one of the reporters who had gotten a copy of the report:

> He said the report had been quite impressive, but only in its ambiguousness, illogical reasoning and very apparent effort to write off all UFO reports at any cost. He personally thought that it was a poor attempt to put out a 'fake' report full of misleading information, to cover up the real story.

Because the Grudge report included an explanation (correct or not) for each sighting, it was able to present the following conclusion:

1) . . . unidentified flying objects constitute no direct threat to the national security of the United States.
2) Reports of unidentified flying objects are the result of:
    (a) A mild form of mass hysteria or 'war nerves.'
    (b) Individuals who fabricate such reports to perpetuate a hoax or seek publicity.
    (c) psychopathological persons.
    (d) misidentification of various conventional objects.

So, there you have it. After two and a half years of investigating, starting in the summer of 1947, the Air Force publicly concluded that there was nothing to flying saucers and related unusual phenomena. The sightings were of such little importance that the analysis project was being closed. (The Air Force did not tell the public that the project had virtually died six months before.) So the outside world, along with most of the people who worked for the Armed Forces, ATIC, AFI, AFOSI, and the FBI, may have wondered whether the Air Force had really lost interest in UFOs, or whether it had taken its interest underground.

Fact: AMC claimed that the closing of Grudge was the end of Air Force saucer investigations.

Fact: AMC lied.

Fact: A year and a half later, Major General Cabell admitted that the Grudge Report was "unscientific worthless tripe."

Fact: Only about two weeks later, government investigative organizations were asked to be on the alert for saucer sighting reports.

On January 12, 1950, Major General Cabell circulated to intelligence agencies a new memorandum regarding the reporting of "Unconventional Aircraft." According to the memorandum:

In the future any information obtained on this subject should be accorded the same consideration as that given to intelligence information on other subjects.

Saucer investigations did not end, and the most convincing were yet to come.

Chapter 14
A Knight in Grudging Armor

In spite of protestations by the Air Force, reports of flying saucers and related phenomena would not go away. In spite of the continued sightings, Grudge presented the party line as stated in December 1949, at each opportunity: flying saucers/UFOs are not ET craft because Project Grudge proved that all sightings have been explained. Of course, Grudge had proved no such thing. Nevertheless, even the FBI was not immune to this party line.

In late March 1950, FBI headquarters received from Guy Hottel, the SAC for Washington state, a memorandum which stated that "an investigator for the Air Forces" had told Mr. Hottel that three crashed saucers had been recovered in New Mexico, along with 9 bodies of 3 foot tall aliens. See Figure 18.

The credibility of this report (to be discussed) is questionable but the importance of this report is what it caused J. Edgar to do. He directed Special Assistant D.M. Ladd to ask the Air Force "just what are the facts re 'flying saucers?'" Hoover wanted "A short memo as to whether it is true or just what the Air Force, etc. think of them." In other words, it appears that Hoover was completely, and justifiably, confused by the conflicting pronouncements by the Air Force.

The FBI-Air Force liaison, Agent S. W. Reynolds, who had been contacted by General Schulgen almost three years before at the very beginning of the saucer controversy, met with AFI representatives, Major Boggs and Lt. Colonel J.V. Hearn. Reynolds reported on the meeting as follows:

> The Air Force discontinued their intelligence project to determine what flying saucers are the latter part of last year. They publicly announced to the press in December, 1949, that the project had been discontinued. They advised that the press release had been concurred in by the Army and Navy. The reason for the discontinuance,

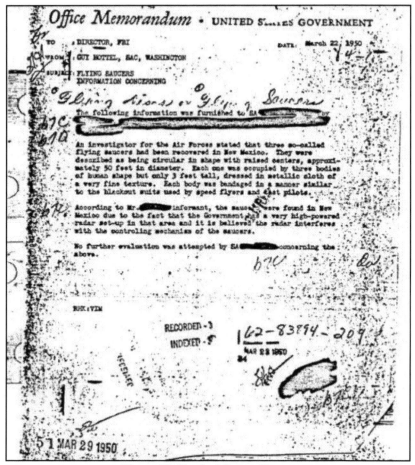

Figure 18: Crashed Saucer Report

according to Major Boggs and Lieutenant Colonel Hearn, was that after two years of investigating over three fourths of the incidents regarding flying saucers proved to be misidentifications of a wide variety of conventional items such as lighted weather balloons and other air-borne objects.

Colonel Hearn pointed out that the Commanders of the various areas are charged with the security of those areas. Reports concerning flying saucers received at this time will be investigated by the Area Commander and his report submitted to the Air Force Intelligence Division as an intelligence item.

Major Boggs and Lieutenant Colonel Hearn made the observation that many of the reported sightings of flying saucers at this time appear to be an outgrowth of recent magazine articles. They reiterated that the Air Force is conducting no active investigation to determine whether flying saucers exist or what they might be.

This waffling answer was clearly intended to imply that the Air Force didn't think much of flying saucers. They admitted that reports were still coming in, but they weren't being analyzed by any central group because most of the previous sightings had been explained and Project Grudge had been closed. Any sighting analysis had to be done at the location of the sighting and information forwarded as ordinary intelligence. Hearn and Boggs did not give the FBI any impression of what ATIC might be doing with the collected sighting reports. Whether or not this non-answer satisfied Hoover is not reflected in the flying disc file.

Another article in *True Magazine* provided a direct contradiction to the official Air Force policy as stated by Boggs and Hearn. The March 1950 issue contained an article by Commander Robert McLaughlin, who had been the Chief of the Navy missile test activities at the super secret White Sands Proving Ground test and development area. Recall that he had been the source of information about White Sands sightings that had leaked to the press during the previous summer (Chapter 12). In the *True* article, entitled "How Scientists Tracked Flying Saucers," he discussed the tracking of a saucer during a missile test. He reported that several times during 1948 and 1949, his crew at White Sands had observed UFOs. One of the sightings he mentioned was that of Charles Moore, which has already been described. By referring to calculations based on measurements by the White Sands instruments, he concluded that the saucers were not a natural phenomenon and voiced his opinion that saucers were "space ships" operated by "intelligent beings." When queried about McLaughlin's ET conclusion, the Air Force referred to the Grudge report, stating that there was no evidence that saucers were other than hallucinations, hoaxes, and errors in identification. So, had McLaughlin's scientists hallucinated?

The controversy over saucer reality again became a hot press item in early April in response to a surge in sightings the previous month (the Air Force received over three dozen reports in March). The *New York Times* of April 4, 1950 carried an article saying that saucers were real and were secret U.S.

warplanes. The controversy over whether or not the saucers were secret weapons elicited a response directly from the White House. According to the *New York Times* of April 5, White House Press Secretary, Charles Ross, "seemed to demolish the element of reality that had been creeping into current reports of flying saucers" when he stated that "no one . . . knows anything about them, including the President." Ross admitted that the Navy had experimented with a disc shaped craft,[*] but that this aircraft could not be the source of saucer reports. Ross also indicated that no other country was operating flying saucers over the USA.

Four days later, the *New York Times* carried another story about the President's reaction: "The President said he was just as puzzled as the next fellow by the latest flurry of reports about weird and wonderful sights in the sky." According to this article:

> . . . if the Air Force thought that its official report [the Grudge Report] would put an end to speculation, it was underestimating the public curiosity and imagination. If anything the theories have multiplied.

According to this article the publicly discussed theories were (a) U.S. secret weapons, (b) foreign (Russian) secret weapons, (c) weather balloons, (d) planets and meteors, (e) optical illusions and (f) interplanetary visitors. The Air Force vehemently denied that saucer sightings were (a), (b) or (f), but obviously the press and the general public were not convinced by the denials.

Two weeks later, on May 22, the FBI received a Confidential document which was a clear statement of the official Project Grudge opinion of flying saucers. It was written as an "insider's" response to public comments in the press by Captain Eddie Rickenbacker, a famous pilot. He was quoted in the press as saying "There must be something to them for too many reliable persons have made reports about them. . . . However, if they are real you can rest assured that they are ours."

The insider's response shows just how cynical the ATIC personnel were about the flying saucer reports. It begins with a

---

[*] The Navy's XF-5-U circular, propeller driven "flying pancake" that never got more than several feet above the ground.

brief discussion of ancient sightings of strange aerial phenomena and mentions the Swedish "ghost rocket" sightings in 1946. It then discussed the present sightings and the Air Force response to them:

The USAF for a long time conducted a thorough investigation of each of the hundreds of incidents involved. It found that approximately 75% of the reports could be related to known causes such as meteorological balloons, aircraft, meteors and other common phenomena. A public statement was issued debunking the entire existence of flying disks or saucers. This did little to cut down the flood of reports. It only resulted in convincing a large number of people that the National Military Establishment was trying to cover up our own experiments with new weapons.

Many theories have been advanced to explain these reports of aerial phenomena over the U.S. These include space ships, Soviet guided missiles or aircraft, probably atomic powered, U.S. experiments with new weapons, natural phenomena and mass hysteria or other psychological causes. While it is not possible to categorically rule out the space ship theory it is very easy to do so on reasonable grounds. The existence of any form of life on other planets is extremely tenuous and debatable. The level of technical achievement required to launch piloted or pilotless missiles from one planet to another and return is several orders of magnitude beyond that existing on Earth today and probably would have resulted in some firm contact prior to this, either through deliberate landings or unscheduled crashes. (Even these have been reported in the press - complete with descriptions of men only 18 inches tall! Such reports are sheer fabrication.)

The document then rejects the Soviet missile hypothesis and the secret U.S. missile hypothesis. ("There is absolutely no evidence ...")

The document concludes as follows:

The continued reporting of aerial phenomena must then be attributed to a mass hysteria caused by the present tenseness in the international situation; the public belief in the ability of science to accomplish miracles; and to statements by 'name' individuals hinting at the existence of a new weapon. Such statements, of the type attributed to Rickenbacker, often solicited in the most sensational form by news reporters in order to make a good story, make people watch the sky and any object they cannot immediately recognize is called a 'flying saucer.' This helps to maintain the 'chain reaction' of such reports.

Since this document accurately expressed the opinion of some (many?) of the personnel at ATIC, it is not surprising that investigative activity had virtually ended.

During the spring and summer of 1950 the FBI received only a few reports. Then, in late August, FBI agent A. M. Belmont provided a summary of the fireball situation which showed—surprise—that the Air Force had not stopped investigating the sightings:

Information Concerning Phenomena in New Mexico
Aug. 23, 1950

(1) The OSI has expressed concern in connection with the continued appearance of unexplained phenomena described as green fireballs, discs and meteors in the vicinity of sensitive installations in New Mexico.

(2) Dr. LaPaz, meteor expert of the University of New Mexico, reported that the phenomena does not appear to be of meteoric origin,

(3) OSI has contracted with Land-Air, Inc., Alamagordo, New Mexico, to make scientific study of the unexplained phenomena.

Observations of aerial phenomena occurring within the vicinity of sensitive installations have been recorded by the Air Force since December, 1948. The phenomena have been classified into 3 general types which are identified as follows:

(1) Green fireballs, objects moving at high speed in shapes resembling half moons, circles and discs emitting green light.

(2) Discs, round flat shaped objects or phenomena moving at fast velocity and emitting a brilliant white light or reflected light.

(3) Meteors, aerial phenomena resembling meteoric material moving at high velocity and varying in color.

The above phenomena have been reported to vary in color from brilliant white to amber, red and green.

Since 1948 approximately 150 observations of aerial phenomena referred to above have been recorded in the vicinity of installations in New Mexico. A number of observations have been reported by different reliable individuals at approximately the same time.

Dr. Lincoln LaPaz, Institute of Meteoritics, University of New Mexico, submitted an analysis of the various observations on May 23, 1950. He concluded, as a result of his investigation, that approximately half of the phenomena recorded were of meteoric origin. The other phenomena commonly referred to as green fireballs or discs he believed to be U.S. guided missiles being tested in the neighborhood of the installations. Dr. LaPaz pointed out that if he were wrong in interpreting the phenomena as originating with U.S. guided missiles that a systematic investigation of the observations should be made immediately. Dr. LaPaz pointed out that missiles moving with the velocities of the order of those found for the green fireballs and discs could travel from the Ural region of the USSR to New Mexico in less than 15 minutes. He suggested that the observations might be of guided missiles launched from bases in the Urals.

On the basis of the investigations made by Dr. LaPaz and the Air Force it was concluded that the occurrence of the unexplained phenomena in the vicinity of sensitive installations was a cause for concern. The Air Force entered into a contract with Land-Air, Incorporated, Alamagordo, New Mexico, for the purpose of making scientific studies of the green fireballs and discs. It was pointed out in the summary furnished by OSI on July 19, 1950, that the unexplained green fireballs and discs are still observed in the vicinity of sensitive military installations.

The Air Force together with Land-Air, Incorporated, have established a number of observation posts in the vicinity of Vaughn, New Mexico, for the purpose of photographing and determining the speed, height and nature of the unusual phenomena referred to as green fireballs and discs. On May 24, 1950, personnel of Land-Air, Incorporated, sighted 8 to 10 objects of aerial phenomena. A 24-hour day watch is being maintained and has been designated as 'Project Twinkle.'

The Albuquerque Office, in a letter dated August 10, 1950, advised that there have been no new developments in connection with the efforts to ascertain the identity of the strange aerial phenomena referred to as green fireballs and discs. The Albuquerque Office advised that (name removed from FOIA document)..., Project Engineer, had been informed of the Bureau's jurisdiction relative to espionage and sabotage and arrangements have been made so that the Bureau will be promptly advised in the event additional information relative to this project indicates any jurisdiction on the part of the Bureau.

One can imagine that this news came as a surprise to J. Edgar and the FBI after being told officially, only 5 months earlier, by Major Boggs and Lieutenant Colonel Hearn of ATIC that the Air Force was out of it, no longer investigating the saucers, which were "believed to be natural phenomena."

What the FBI hadn't been told by Boggs and Hearn, perhaps because they didn't know, was that the continued sightings had kept AFI and AFOSI interest alive during the latter half of 1949 and the first half of 1950, even though ATIC was officially no longer interested in sightings. However, ATIC interest in saucers was regenerated three months after Boggs and Hearn spoke to the FBI by a memorandum from Brig. General Ernest Moore of Air Force intelligence, which was supported by an official directive from Major General Cabell. General Moore's memorandum reads as follows:

1 July 1950
MEMORANDUM FOR: CHIEF, Evaluation Division
CHIEF, Air Targets Division
CHIEF, Air Estimates Division
SUBJECT UNIDENTIFIED OBJECTS
The continued reports of sightings of unidentified aerial objects require that cognizance of the activity be a continuing function. When Project 'Grudge' was abolished, it was not intended that this function should be ignored as a possibility of foreign activity. Consequently, the Evaluation Division should continue to monitor these reports and handle each incident in accordance with the evaluation of the relative importance in each case.

General Moore's memorandum indicates that although Grudge was abolished, just as the press release in December 1949, stated, it was the intent of AFI that ATIC personnel should continue to analyze sightings in the event that a saucer or UFO should turn out to be some foreign, i .e., Soviet, aircraft. Six days later, Major General Cabell sent a directive to Colonel Watson who was in charge at ATIC:

July 7, 1950
I am sending this by Major Pianitza hoping to save the bother of an officially coordinated directive. General Cabell's views regarding the 'Flying Saucer' project are in substance as follows:
(a) He feels that it probably was a mistake to abandon the (Grudge) project and to publicly announce that we are no longer interested. However, the decision having been made, he feels that it was incumbant upon him not to overrule, at least for the time being.
(b) Our instructions, which rescinded a long list of letters to numerous agencies, were published in an unnumbered HQS, USAF letter, File AFOIR-CO 7 dated 12 January 1950, Subject : 'Reporting of Information on Unconventional Aircraft.' The last paragraph of this letter requested all recipients to continue to treat information and observations received as intelligence information and to continue the processing in a normal manner. We have continued to receive from

many USAF sources a number of reports of this nature.

(c) General Cabell's views are that we should reinstate, if it has been abandoned, a continuing analysis of reports received and he expects AMC to do this as part of their obligation to produce air technical intelligence. He specifically desires that the project, as it existed before, be not fully re-implemented with special technical teams traveling around the country interviewing observers etc., and he is particularly desirous that there be no fanfare or publicity over the fact that the USAF is still interested in 'flying saucers.' (under-lines in the original)

(d) General Cabell desires that we place ourselves in a position that, if circumstances require an all-out effort in this regard at some future time, we will be able to announce that we have continued quietly our analysis of reports without interruption.

(e) Under this philosophy, then, we will continue to receive from USAF sources reports of 'flying saucers' and we will immediately transmit these reports to AMC. You will be at liberty to query, through AFOIC-CC normal channels the USAF source for more information. We will also be scanning State, CIA, Army and Navy incoming reports for pertinent information which will be relayed to AMC...

(f) Ordinary newspaper reports should be analyzed without initiating specific inquiry. Information received direct from non-USAF individuals may be acknowledged and interrogated through correspondence. Where geographically convenient, specific sightings may be investigated quietly at your discretion, by AMC depot personnel and requests for investigation may be filed with your local OSI office.

(g) Queries from news agencies as to whether USAF is still interested in 'flying saucers' may be given a general answer to the effect that AMC is interested in any information that will enable it to produce air technical intelligence - and just as much interested in 'flying saucer' information as it would be in any other significant information. Work in the 'flying saucer' field is not receiving 'special' emphasis because emphasis is being placed on all technical intelligence fields.

The foregoing is probably in more detail than is necessary. If, after reading this you are still uncertain as to what to do, give me a call. If this clarifies your questions, go ahead under AMC's general directive to produce air technical intelligence.

Wow! No mincing of words here. The top AFI guy was not happy with the way AMC was handling the saucer situation. One may imagine that the colonels and captains jumped out of their chairs and saluted briskly as they received their direct orders to do something.

Two months later, in September 1950, General Cabell requested a slight modification to this directive. Referring to (c) above, he indicated that he did want to have investigative teams available and that "it will be AMC responsibility to send such teams as they consider necessary."

Not only did General Cabell order AMC to revitilize Grudge, he also issued yet another intelligence collection memorandum. On September 25 this was received by the Director of the FBI as well as by numerous Air Force and Army Commanding Generals, Navy Intelligence, the State Department and the CIA. The memorandum asked for the usual details about any sighting, asked for the information to be sent as quickly as possible by electronic means with a follow-up written report, and made one further request: "It is desired that no publicity be given this reporting or analysis activity." In other words, this is important stuff and we are interested, but let's not tell anybody who doesn't need to know, such as the American people.

So, General Cabell was a Knight in Shining Armor, come to rescue flying saucer sightings from the dungeon of Project Grudge. Unfortunately, he was not entirely successful, as he found out a year later. Colonel Watson and the Grudge staff were basically anti-ufo. They did not carefully study the sighting reports which AFI sent to them. All they did was invent plausible explanations for the sightings and send these explanations to AFI. The reports were seldom filed. A year later, when Captain Edward Ruppelt took over the project, he found that many reports had been packed into boxes and others were simply lost.

Cabell's displeasure at the lack of ATIC activity is not surprising, considering the number and quality of sighting reports being received by AFI and passed on to ATIC for analysis. Reports in 1950 began on January 2. There were about a dozen sightings in January and again in February, and over three dozen in March. After that, they continued at a rate of one to two dozen every month for a total of about 240 sightings for the year. By far the largest proportion were from the USA, but there were some from other countries as far away as Japan, Cyprus, and Chile. In fact, in retrospect it appears that a world wide flap of sightings occurred.

The reader can probably imagine the confusion in the press that resulted from the contrast between the large number of reports by scientists and pilots who believed they had seen something truly unusual and the publicly expressed Air Force attitude that there was no evidence of something unusual. To add to the confusion, there were also fake crashed saucer reports.

How to separate the wheat from the chaff? That was the problem, and it could only be solved by good investigation, good data, and good analysis.

Good data. That was what Project Twinkle was intended to supply. And it did.

Too bad the data were ignored or suppressed.

Chapter 15
Twinkle Twinkle Little Craft

"No information was gained"
—Dr. L. Elterman

"Objects are sighted in some number."
—from a report to Dr. Mirarchi

The efforts of Dr. Kaplan and Major Oder to start a fireball research project came to fruition in the spring of 1950. A $20,000 half-year contract was signed with the Land-Air Corporation, which operated the phototheodolites at White Sands. Land-Air was to set up a 24-hour watch at a location in New Mexico to be specified by the Air Force, and the phototheodolite operators at White Sands were to film any unusual objects which happened to fly past.

The investigation began on March 24, 1950. By this time there had been many sightings in the southwest according to the sighting catalogue compiled by Lt. Colonel Rees of the 17th District OSI at Kirtland, AFB, many of them around Holloman AFB.

His catalogue shows the following data for New Mexico in 1949: the area of Sandia Base in Albuquerque (17 sightings, mostly in the latter half of the year); Los Alamos area (26 sightings spread throughout the year); Vaughn area (none); Holloman AFB/Alamogordo/White Sands area (12); other areas in southwest New Mexico (20). The total number of sightings in 1949 was 75. For the same areas in the first three months of 1950 there were: Sandia (6, all in February); Los Alamos (7); Vaughn (1); Holloman AFB/Alamogordo/White Sands (6); others (6). For the first three months of 1950, the total number of sightings had already reached 26.

With all these sightings, the scientists were quite confident that they could "catch" a fireball or a saucer.

On February 21, an observation post, manned by two people, was set up at Holloman with a theodolite, telescope and camera. The post was manned only from sunrise to sunset. The observers saw nothing unusual during a month of operation. Then the scientists decided to begin a constant 24-hour watch on the first of April that would last for six months, with Land-Air personnel operating cinetheodolites* and with Holloman AFB personnel manning spectrographic cameras and radio frequency receivers. Thus began Project Twinkle with the high hopes of solving the fireball/saucer mystery.

A year and a half later, in November, 1951, Dr. Louis Elterman, the Director of Project Twinkle, who worked at the Atmospheric Physics Laboratory (APL) of the Geophysical Research Division (GRD) of the Air Force Cambridge Research Laboratory (AFCRL), wrote the final report. According to Dr. Elterman's report, Project Twinkle was a dismal failure: "no information was gained." He recommended it be discontinued. His recommendation was accepted. See Figures 19A and 19B.

But was it a failure? Was there really no information gained? Recall the FBI report presented in the last chapter which stated that on May 24, 1950, personnel of Land Air saw 8 to 10 unidentified objects. Isn't this "information?" Let us look more carefully at Project Twinkle.

According to Dr. Elterman, before Twinkle began there had been "an abnormal number of reports" from Vaughn, New Mexico, so it was decided to place a lookout post there. Why this place was chosen is a mystery to me. It is about 120 air miles from Los Alamos, about 90 from Sandia Base and nearly 150 from Alamogordo/Holloman AFB. I have listed above the sighting statistics for the various New Mexico areas, being careful to list the sightings around Vaughn separately. Note that Vaughn had only 1 sighting in the whole previous year. So why did they "waste" a lookout post at Vaughn? Why didn't they put one at Los Alamos or at White Sands? Did they think that they could triangulate over a very large baseline distance with the lookout post at Holloman AFB, or were they actually trying to avoid sightings? These are questions which must forever remain unanswered.

Anyway, it was a mistake. After Project Twinkle began, the sighting rate dropped precipitously. The Blue Book sighting list

---

* Theodolites with movie cameras that continually record what the telescope "sees," as well as the pointing direction, azimuth, and angular elevation.

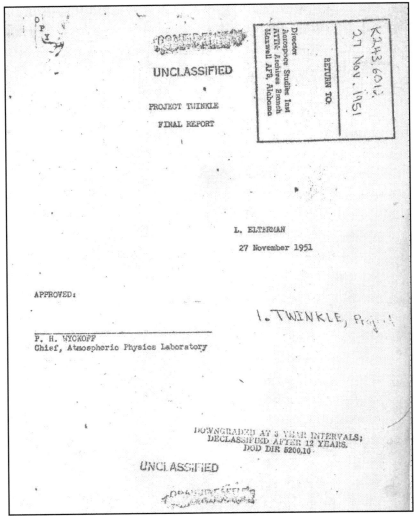

Figure 19A: Project Twinkle Report

shows one sighting in April, one in May and one in August in the Holloman area. There were also fewer sightings in the other areas. In fact, for the period from April 1 to October 1, covered by the first Land Air contract, there were only about eight sightings in the whole of New Mexico as compared with the roughly 30 sightings during the previous six months.

The effect of this sudden decrease in sighting rate is reflected in the Twinkle Final Report, which stated there were very few observations. However, of more importance is what is not

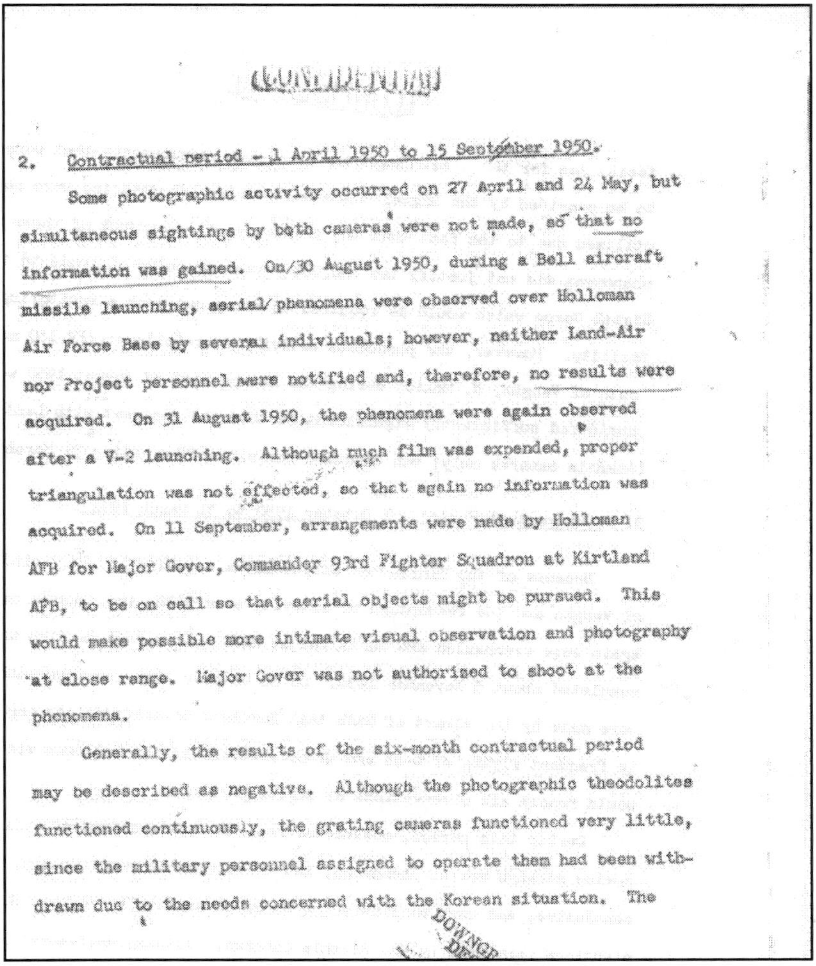

CONFIDENTIAL

2. Contractual period – 1 April 1950 to 15 September 1950.

Some photographic activity occurred on 27 April and 24 May, but simultaneous sightings by both cameras were not made, so that no information was gained. On 30 August 1950, during a Bell aircraft missile launching, aerial phenomena were observed over Holloman Air Force Base by several individuals; however, neither Land-Air nor Project personnel were notified and, therefore, no results were acquired. On 31 August 1950, the phenomena were again observed after a V-2 launching. Although much film was expended, proper triangulation was not effected, so that again no information was acquired. On 11 September, arrangements were made by Holloman AFB for Major Gover, Commander 93rd Fighter Squadron at Kirtland AFB, to be on call so that aerial objects might be pursued. This would make possible more intimate visual observation and photography at close range. Major Gover was not authorized to shoot at the phenomena.

Generally, the results of the six-month contractual period may be described as negative. Although the photographic theodolites functioned continuously, the grating cameras functioned very little, since the military personnel assigned to operate them had been withdrawn due to the needs concerned with the Korean situation. The

Figure 19B: Page 4 of the Project Twinkle Report

reflected in the report, what the report ignored or covered up: the fact that Twinkle was successful.

So that you can understand where the writer of the Project Twinkle report was dishonest, here is one part of it, verbatim. Commenting on the "first contractual period, 1 April 1950 to 15 September 1950," Dr. Elterman wrote:

> Some photographic activity occurred on 27 April and 24 May, but simultaneous sightings by both cameras were not made, so that no information was gained. On 30 August 1950, during a Bell aircraft missile launching, aerial phenomena were observed over Holloman Air Force Base by several individuals; however, neither Land-Air nor

Project personnel were notified and, therefore, no results were acquired. On 31 August 1950, the phenomena were again observed after a V-2 launching. Although much film was expended, proper triangulation was not effected, so that *again no information was acquired*. [emphasis added]

During the second contractual period, 1 October 1950 to 31 March 1951 there were no sightings. It was as if the phenomenon had reacted to the setting up of observation posts by ending or moving elsewhere. There were continuing sightings in other parts of the country, and even a few in the other parts of New Mexico, but none near Holloman AFB. The lack of sightings was enough to end the contract. After the contract ended, there were discussions about what to do with the data and whether or not to continue observations at some low level of effort. It was decided in the late spring of 1951 not to continue the special effort. Elterman, writing in November, 1951, recommended "no further expenditure" of time and effort, and there was none.

But what about the sightings during the first half of the contract, the sightings at Holloman Air Force Base in April and May, 1950? According to Elterman, no information was gained. Was Elterman justified in making such a comment?

No! Certainly information "is gained" when a number of qualified observers simultaneously view unidentified objects from various locations. And more information is gained if some of these observers film these objects through cinetheodolite telescopes. There is useful information even if a "proper triangulation" is not accomplished. And there is even more information gained if a proper triangulation is accomplished.

And one *was* accomplished, only Elterman didn't mention it.

Further on in the report, Dr. Elterman indicated a serious deficiency in the operational plan for Project Twinkle. The project scientists knew that they might have some film to analyze, but according Elterman there were insufficient funds built into the contract to analyze the film. After a discussion with Mr. Warren Kott, who was in charge of the Land-Air operations, Elterman estimated that it would take 30 man-days to analyze the film and do a time correlation study which "would assure that these records did not contain significant material." According to Elterman, "no provisions are contained in the contract" for this analysis.

One reads this previous statement with some astonishment. They set up a photographically instrumented search for unknown objects and then failed to provide for the film analysis if they were lucky enough to get film. What sort of a scientific project is that? Did they want to succeed or did they want to fail?

Furthermore, Elterman's statement that a time correlation study should be done to assure that the records contained no significant material sounds as if he had already concluded that there was no worthwhile evidence in the film. Does this sound like an unbiased investigation?

Near the end of the report, Elterman supported his statement that "no information was gained" by offering explanations for the sightings: "Many of the sightings are attributable to natural phenomena such as flights of birds, planets, meteors and possibly cloudiness."

The average scientist reading the Project Twinkle Final Report would probably accept Dr. Elterman's opinion as the final word on the subject. Only the perceptive scientist would realize that Dr. Elterman had not actually proven his statement to be true, even though he presumably had access to the photographic evidence which would prove it, if it were true.

Dr. Anthony Mirarchi was not the average scientist. He was skeptical, all right, but he was skeptical of the glib explanations. In 1950 he was the Chief of the Air Composition Branch at GRD/AFCRL. Project Twinkle began as Dr. Mirachi's project. However, he retired from AFCRL in October, 1950, so he was not involved with Twinkle when Dr. Elterman wrote the final report a year later. (Dr. Mirarchi may never have seen that report.)

Dr. Mirarchi visited Holloman Air Force Base in late May 1950, and requested a brief report on the April 27 and May 24 sightings which Elterman mentioned (see above). Fortunately, the brief report to Mirarchi survived in the National Archives microfilm record where it was found in the late 1970s, long after the Twinkle report had had its (evidently intended) debunking effect on the green fireball sightings. This document completely refutes Elterman:

1. Per request of Dr. A. O. Mirarchi, during a recent visit to this

base, the following information is submitted.

2. Sightings were made on 27 April and 24 May 1950 of aerial phenomena during morning daylight hours at this station. The sightings were made by Land-Air, Inc., personnel while engaged in tracking regular projects with Askania Phototheodolites. It has been reported that objects are sighted in some number; as many as eight have been visible at one time. The individuals making these sightings are professional observers. Therefore I would rate their reliability superior. In both cases photos were taken with Askanias.

3. The Holloman AF Base Data Reduction Unit analyzed the 27 April pictures and made a report, a copy of which I am enclosing with the film for your information. It was believed that triangulation could be effected from pictures taken on 24 May because pictures were taken from two stations. The films were rapidly processed and examined by Data Reduction. However, it was determined that sightings were made on two different objects and triangulation could not be effected. A report from Data Reduction and the films from the sighting are enclosed.

4. There is nothing further to report at this time.

The writer of this letter is not known (no signature). The Data Reduction report attached to the letter reads as follows:

Objects observed following MX776A test of 27 April 1950
2nd Lt. (name censored) EHOSIR 15 May 50

1. According to conversation between Colonel Baynes and Captain Bryant, the following information is submitted directly to Lt. Albert.

2. Film from station P10 was read, resulting in azimuth and elevation angles being recorded on four objects. In addition, size of image on film was recorded.

3. From this information, together with a single azimuth angle from station M7, the following conclusions were drawn:

a). The objects were at an altitude of approximately 150,000 ft.

b). The objects were over the Holloman range between the base and Tularosa Peak.

c). The objects were approximately 30 feet in diameter

d). The objects were traveling at an undeterminable, yet high speed.

(signed)
Wilbur L. Mitchell
Mathematician
Data Reduction Unit

So, there you have it, four unidentified objects—UFOs—were flying at 150,000 feet near the Top Secret White Sands Proving

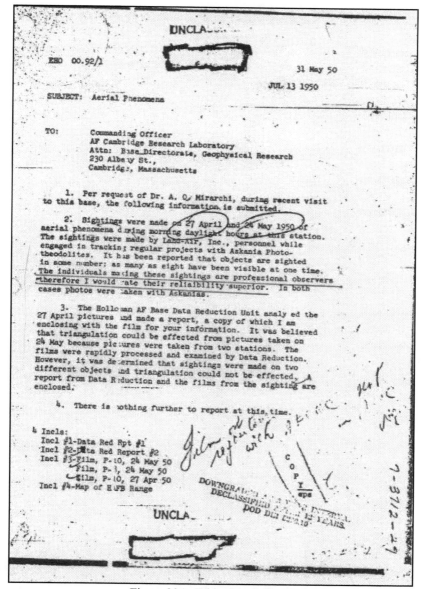

Figure 20A: White Sands Proof

Ground. Each was roughly 30 feet in size. The sighting was similar to that of Charles Moore a year earlier.

Could Mr. Mitchell and the Askania operators have made a mistake? Not likely. Their business was tracking fast moving objects (rockets) and calculating the trajectories of the rockets.

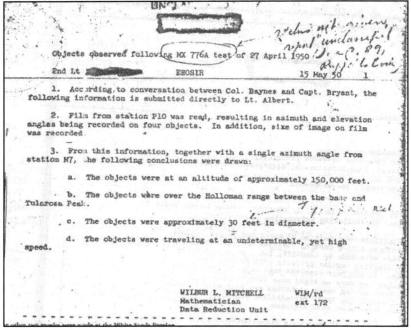

Figure 20B: White Sands Proof

As the writer of the above letter stated, "The individuals making these sightings are professional observers. Therefore I would rate their reliability superior."

Human beings had made no objects that could fly at 150,000 feet in the spring of 1950. So, *what* were they? *Whose* were they?

Compare the above letter with the first paragraph of Elterman's statement where he says ". . . simultaneous sightings by both cameras were not made so that no information was gained." It seems that Elterman got his information on these sightings from this report to Dr. Mirarchi. Yet he did not even give a hint of the existence of the most important result of Project Twinkle, the April 27 triangulation which yielded information on altitude and size. Could it be that he didn't know about the Data Reduction Unit report? Or did he know and choose to purposely ignore or withhold the information?

Ruppelt, in *The Report on Unidentified Flying Objects*, described the April, 27 event in more detail. A guided missile had just been tracked and the cinethodolite crews were starting to unload their cameras when someone spotted objects moving through the sky. The camera stations were linked by a telephone network, so that crew alerted the others. Unfortunately, all but one camera had been unloaded and the UFOs had departed before the other cameras could be reloaded. According to Ruppelt, "the photos from the one station showed only a smudgy dark object. About all the film proved was that something was in the air and, whatever it was, it was moving." Evidently Ruppelt didn't know that a triangulation had been accomplished

Ruppelt also discussed the May 24 event and its failure at triangulation due to the fact that the two cameras were looking at different objects. Ruppelt wrote that in February 1951, when he first learned of these sightings (this was about 9 months before he became the director of Project Grudge and over a year before the name was changed to Blue Book):

> The records at AMC didn't contain the analysis of these films but they did mention the Data Reduction Group at White Sands. So, when I later took over the UFO investigation I made several calls in an effort to run down the actual film and analysis.

Unfortunately, he was not successful, even though he did manage to contact, through a "Major who was very cooperative," two men who had analyzed what was either the film from May 24 or August 31 (see Elterman's statement above regarding the August 31 sighting). Ruppelt wrote as follows:

> [The Major's] report . . . was what I had expected—nothing concrete except that the UFOs were unknowns. He did say that by putting a correction factor in the data gathered by the two cameras they were able to arrive at a rough estimate of speed, altitude and size. The UFO was 'higher than 40,000 feet, traveling over 2,000 miles per hour, and it was over 300 feet in diameter.' He cautioned me that these figures were only estimates, based on the possibly erroneous correction factor; therefore they weren't proof of anything—except that something was in the air.

Obviously Ruppelt underplayed the importance of this report by suggesting that the films didn't prove anything. So what, if the size, distance and speed estimates might be wrong. Maybe the speed was only 1,000 mph or maybe the height was only 30,000 feet. The point is, something was there, obviously large, fast and unusual or the camera crews wouldn't have bothered to film it! Since Ruppelt apparently was not aware that a triangulation had been accomplished for the April 27, sighting one wonders if he would have tried to downplay that film, also, as not "proof of anything."

At the bottom of the report to Dr. Mirachi is a list of enclosures which shows that two reports (Data Red Report #1 and Data Red Report #2) and three films (P-10 and P-8 of May 24 and P-10 of April 27) were sent to Mirarchi along with a map of the Holloman range showing, I presume, the locations of the cameras. There is a hand written note "Film on repository with AFCRL" and a few other undecipherable scribbles. Recent attempts to locate these films have failed.*

Incidently, the Project Blue Book master sighting list indicates that all four of the sightings listed by Elterman had "insufficient information" for evaluation.**

The sighting rate in New Mexico dropped nearly to zero in the latter part of 1950, and remained low in 1951. During 1951, there were about a dozen sightings in New Mexico, most of which occurred away from Holloman AFB. The most important of these took place on January 16 at Artesia, while Project Twinkle was still going on, but Project Twinkle personnel were not involved. During the early morning, two Navy balloon project engineers launched a giant Skyhook balloon near Artesia. Near the end of the day, it caused a rash of sightings over western Texas. But the important events occurred in the morning while the balloon was still near the Artesia airport.

At about 9:30 a.m., the project engineers were observing the balloon which, by this time, was at its maximum altitude of about 110,000 feet and its maximum diameter of about 110 feet. As they watched it drift in an easterly direction at about 5 mph, they noted another round object which appeared in the clear sky not far from the balloon, seemingly above it. This unidentified object appeared to be dull white in color and considerably larger than the balloon. This object went out of sight in the distance.

The engineers then traveled several miles westward to the

---

* Mirarchi died in the 1960s before this information became available to UFO investigators.

** For a more complete discussion of the White Sands Proof see http://www.brumac.8k.com/WhiteSandsProof/WhiteSandsProof.html.

Artesia airport to view the balloon from another location. Again, while watching the balloon high overhead, this time in the company of the airport manager and several other individuals, they and the others saw two dull grey objects at a very high altitude. These two objects came from the northeast toward the balloon, made an arc (a turn) of about 300 degrees around the balloon, and then departed in a northerly direction. The objects seemed to be the same size, relative to the balloon, as the object seen earlier. They were separated by a distance about seven times the diameter of either one and, when they made the sharp turn, seemingly around the balloon, they appeared to tilt on edge and could not be seen until they apparently leveled out again. The objects traveled at high speed and, after passing around the balloon, disappeared in the distance in several seconds. In the Blue Book master list, this case is listed as having insufficient information, apparently because Project Grudge did not learn of this sighting until over a year later.

Although Dr. Mirarchi retired in October 1950 and had no part in writing the final Twinkle report that was completed over a year later, his involvement with the green fireballs and saucers did not end when he retired. Four months later, he returned to action in a public way and his actions nearly got him into serious trouble three years afterward.

In the middle of February, 1951 *Time* magazine published an article that featured a well known scientist, Dr. Urner Liddel of the Naval Research Laboratory near Washington, DC. In the article, Dr. Liddel stated that he had studied around 2,000 saucer reports, and in his opinion the only credible saucer sightings were actually sightings of misidentified Skyhook balloons, balloons which had been kept secret by the armed services. Apparently Dr. Liddel wasn't aware of the several sightings by balloon project scientists. That is, the men who launched and tracked the balloons also saw UFOs!

Evidently, Dr. Mirarchi felt it was his civic duty to repudiate Liddel's claims, because two weeks later he responded publicly. According to a United Press story filed on February 26, 1951 Mirarchi said that, after investigating 300 reports of flying saucers, he believed that the saucers were missiles from Russia which had photographed our atomic bomb test sites. According to the United Press article the 40 year old scientist who "for more than a year conducted a top secret investigation into the weird phenomena said that he had worked with balloons and balloons did not leave an exhaust trail." Another reason given against the balloon explanation was that balloons could not be seen at night. Mirarchi explained how:

> . . . scientists had picked up dust particles containing copper which could have come from no other source than the saucer motive plants [the engines]." *

The article continued:

> "flying saucers or 'fireballs' as [Mirarchi] terms them, were regularly observed near Los Alamos until he set up a system of phototheodolites to measure their speed, size and distance away. . . . but the fireballs mysteriously ceased appearing before the theodolites could go to work. Dr. Mirarchi concludes that spies must have tipped off the saucers' home base.

Mirarchi referred to two sightings for which there was photographic evidence: a single photo of a round glowing object and a motion picture which "showed one streaking across the sky for one and a half minutes." Mirarchi went on to say that he was aware that some sightings were actually sightings of balloons, but that "there was too much evidence in favor of saucers to say they could have all been balloons. 'I was conducting the main investigation. The government had to depend on me or my branch for information.' He said he did not see how the Navy (i.e., Dr. Liddel) could say that there had been no concrete evidence on the existence of the phenomena."

Mirachi concluded by accusing the government of committing "suicide by secrecy" for not admitting that the saucers were real and probably missiles from Russia.

Strong words. So strong they nearly got Mirarchi in trouble

---

* This was a reference to efforts by Dr. LaPaz to have air samples taken after a green fireball sighting to see if there were any small particles of copper or copper compounds in the air. Such compounds "burn green" or give off a characteristic green color when heated, so LaPaz had conjectured that the green color could be attributed to burning copper compounds associated with the fireballs. In one case there was success in detecting such particles, although LaPaz was not completely convinced that the particles were from the fireball.

more than two years later. According to an Air Force document (released in 1991!), in 1953, during a time of espionage and spy hunting* the FBI queried the Air Force as to whether or not Mirarchi should be investigated for breaking security. Lt. Colonel Frederick Oder, who had been instrumental in getting Project Twinkle started (see Chapter 12), responded by writing that, because Mirarchi had released to the newspaper some information that was classified Confidential or Secret it:

> . . . could cause serious harm to the internal security of the country
> . . . if it were to fall into unfriendly hands . . . both from the point of
> view of the prestige of our Government and the point of view of
> revealing our interest in certain classified projects.

Brigadier General W. M. Garland, who was in charge of ATIC in 1953, decided not to pursue Dr. Mirarchi because, in his opinion, the information was not that important. Furthermore, in General Garlands' opinion, the facts about saucers being missiles, as stated in the newspaper article, had been "disproved or are, at best, personal opinions, and are not considered classified data." In other words, General Garland apparently believed that the green fireball and saucer sightings were not Russian missiles, although he did not say what he thought they were.

Perhaps General Garland let Mirarchi off the hook because he recalled that there had been a recommendation to declassify and release the results of Project Twinkle in December 1951, a month after the final report was written. However, he could find no record of declassification in the files of AMC. Evidently he was not aware of the recommendation against declassification contained in a February 1952 letter to the Directorate of Intelligence from the Directorate of Research and Development which states:

> The Scientific Advisory Board Secretariat has suggested that this
> project not be declassified for a variety of reasons, chief among
> which is that no scientific explanation for any of the 'fireballs' and
> other phenomena was revealed by the (Project Twinkle) report and
> that some reputable scientists still believe that the observed phenom-
> ena are man-made.

---

* The Rosenbergs, atomic spies, were executed in 1953.

Another letter, this time from the Directorate of Intelligence to the Research Division of the Directorate of Research and Development, dated March 11, 1952, adds another reason for withholding the information from the public:

It is believed that a release of the information to the public in its present condition would cause undue speculation and give rise to unwarranted fears among the populace such as occurred in previous releases on unidentified flying objects. This results from releases when there has been no real solution.

In other words, Air Force Intelligence had realized that the public could see through the smokescreen of previous explanations and wanted real answers. So, if they couldn't come up with real answers it was better to say nothing.

Over a year after Mirarchi responded to Liddel, *LIFE Magazine* published an article on flying saucers (discussed in Chapter 19). In that article, the authors described some of the sightings which caused the Air Force to start Project Twinkle. One of the hundreds of letters which the magazine received in response to that article was from Captain Daniel McGovern who wrote:

I was very closely associated with Projects 'Twinkle' and 'Grudge' at Alamogordo, N. Mexico where I was chief of the technical photographic facility at Holloman Air Force Base. I have seen several of these objects myself and they are everything you say they are as to shape, size and speed." *

The green fireballs, or something like them, have been seen occasionally in various places in the years since Project Twinkle, but not in anything like the southwestern concentration of the 1948-1950 sightings. No one at the time could determine what they were, and we still don't know.

---

* *LIFE*, April 28, 1952.

Chapter 16
Saucers at Oak Ridge

T he summer and fall of 1950 was an important time in the history of UFO phenomena. The first book devoted to flying saucers, *Flying Saucers are Real,* written by Donald Keyhoe (Fawcett, New York, 1950) was published in June. This book expanded on his *True* magazine article of six months before. Keyhoe argued that the Air Force was covering up evidence that proved saucers were ET craft because the Air Force was worried about an Orson Wells "War of the Worlds" type of panic if the information became public. Nevertheless, there had been some leakage of information, such as the article by Commander McLaughlin about sightings at White Sands. Keyhoe suspected that such leaks were intended to prepare humanity for the eventual news. Furthermore, he suspected that the arrival of the saucers was related to our detonations of atomic (fission) bombs, which were first tested at White Sands. He suggested that perhaps the aliens wanted to prevent us from destroying the Earth with the much more powerful hydrogen (fusion) bombs.

During the time between the publication of Keyhoe's magazine article and the publication of his book, there were important national and international political and military developments which affected the FBI perception of the flying saucer problem. The Cold War was hot. The Berlin Blockade had been overcome by the Berlin airlift, but the Russians had taken over the satellite countries of East Germany, Poland, Czechoslovakia, Hungary, and Yugoslavia. Then, on June 25 North Korea marched about 60,000 men into South Korea and began the Korean War. Both the Soviet Union and China were aiding North Korea. The South Korean Army, not fully prepared, collapsed under the weight of the attack, and two days later President Truman ordered U.S. troops to South Korea. The next day Seoul fell to the North and General MacArthur reported that the South Korean army was too demoralized to mount an effective resistance. Two days after that, Truman ordered U.S. ground forces to Korea. The first post-WWII war was on.

Meanwhile, at the end of January 1950, President Truman announced that work would begin on the hydrogen bomb. The race for the Super Bomb was on.* Suddenly spies were being caught everywhere. In February, Klaus Fuchs was arrested for giving secrets of the atomic bomb to the Soviets.** FBI Director Hoover made a personal report to President Truman on Fuchs' capture and subsequent confession in Britain. A few days later, Senator Joe McCarthy announced that there were over two hundred Communist Party members working for the Department of State. Five months later, about the time that the Korean War began, Harry Gold and David Greenglass were caught and provided information about a spy ring directed by the Rosenbergs, which had provided atomic secrets to the Soviets during WWII.

All of this espionage activity may have affected the FBI view of the UFO phenomenon, because the Air Force was clearly worried about the green fireball and disc phenomena seen near the nuclear installations. The question was, could they be related to Communist subversion? After all, Colonel Gasser had indicated that the saucers were man-made missiles, but not made by the USA.

Soon after the publication of Keyhoe's book, and at a time when the Air Force was publicly disparaging the subject, the first highly credible motion picture of saucers was taken at Great Falls, Montana, on August 5, 1950. The Air Force wanted to look at it but didn't want to give the owner, Nicolas Mariana, any hint of particular interest in the subject. According to an AFOSI document, the agent contacting Mariana was to:

> . . . exercise every caution so as not to unduly excite his curiosity or interest or in anywise conclude that the Air Force may have reversed its policy from that previously announced with regard to the exis-

---

* America won with the first test in November 1952.

** Fuch's spy activities were in large part the cause of the Soviet Union's successful detonation of a fission bomb in August 1949.

tence or non-existence of such unconventional objects.

In later years, this film would cause a great controversy as the Air Force claimed that the two objects in the film were Air Force jets. However the objects certainly didn't look like jets to Mariana and his secretary. When first sighted, the objects were quite close and appeared to be round and rotating. Unfortunately by the time Mr. Mariana had got his camera they were considerably farther away so the film images appear as small, bright oval dots.

The images certainly do not look like jets, and a scientific test performed years later indicated that jets filmed under similar circumstances would have been identified as such. The Air Force nevertheless claimed the objects were jets, even though the investigation turned up evidence that the only pair of jets which passed through the area of the sighting did so ten days after the film was shot.

All this time, the FBI was quietly monitoring the fireball and saucer situation. Recall that in late August 1950 (see Chapter 14) Agent A. H. Belmont had written a memorandum to Special Assistant D. M. Ladd summarizing recent developments regarding green fireballs and saucers. On October 9, Mr. Ladd wrote a memorandum for Mr. Hoover providing an update on Project Twinkle. The memorandum stated that, "To date the Air Force has not advised U.S. of any new developments in connection with this project." Evidently the Air Force had not told the FBI about the multiple witness sightings and filming of multiple objects on August 30 and 31. Mr. Ladd also made an explicit comparison between saucer sighting reports (referred to as "complaints") and the war in Korea, which to this point had been going reasonably well, since the North Korean army had not (yet) succeeded in pushing the United Nations and United States forces into the sea:

> According to Bureau files, an average of approximately three or four complaints have been received per month from June through September. These complaints were brought to the attention of OSI. A review of Bureau files does not indicate that there has been any increase in sightings of these phenomena during or as a result of the war in Korea.

Mr. Hoover was probably glad to see that there were so few complaints and that there was no apparent connection with the war. However, there still was the major question of the origin of the phenomena seen near the vital installations and the secondary question of just what the Air Force was doing about it. Mr. Ladd provided the following comments on these subjects:

> The Bureau has been advised in the past by OSI that many of the sightings reported to them were determined by investigation to have been of weather balloons, falling stars, meteorological phenomena and other air-borne objects.
>
> Bureau liaison determined on the morning of October 9, 1950 from OSI headquarters that the investigation of these aerial phenomena are being handled by OSI, Wright Field, Ohio. Their investigation of these phenomena fails to indicate that the sightings involved spaceships or missiles from any other planet or country.
>
> According to OSI, the complaints received by them have failed to indicate any definite pattern of activity. OSI further advised they are closely following the investigation of the captioned matters and they will advise this Bureau of any matters of interest.

Once again the FBI was told that the Air Force was sufficiently worried about these phenomena to continue secretly investigating, even though many sightings could be explained. Since the Air Force was once again ruling out the interplanetary and "foreign country" explanations the FBI could only presume that all saucer sightings resulted from misidentifications, delusions, and hoaxes.

Then the saucer controversy suddenly heated up again with the publication of the second flying saucer book, *Behind the Flying Saucers* by Frank Scully (Henry Holt, New York, 1950), in early September. Whereas Keyhoe had based his book on official sources and sightings, Scully based his book on a crashed saucer report! According to Scully, a total of three flying saucers had crashed and had been analyzed by government scientists.* The analysis of the saucers showed that they were fantastic devices and were piloted by little man-like creatures. Scully's book claimed that the story was first told during a lecture by oilman

---

* There was no connection between Scully's crash story and the Roswell crash story.

Silas Newton at the University of Denver on March 8, 1950 and that he had researched the story.* It turned out later that the source for Scully's story was a wealthy oilman by the name of Silas Newton who claimed he had gotten the details from another man who, in turn, claimed to be one of the government scientists who analyzed the saucers. Scully apparently did not realize the story was highly questionable (it was claimed to be a hoax several years later, although recent research places the hoax explanation itself into question).**

Scully's book made quite a splash and regenerated the public saucer controversy, claiming that a mysterious government scientist had verified the facts of the crash. Furthermore, Scully severely criticized the Air Force and all government authority, arguing that there had been extreme incompetence, a "double standard of morality" and official censorship. Scully's story was so fantastic that it was almost uniformly panned by the media. On the other hand, Keyhoe's more rational approach was not as flashy, but it convinced more people.

Keeping in mind that these books were coming at a time of "atomic paranoia," it is not surprising to see that Hoover took a particular interest in Scully's book. Ever on the alert for Communist subversion, on October 13 he sent an urgent teletype message to SAC Los Angeles:

> FLYING SAUCERS. YOU ARE INSTRUCTED TO DISCREETLY DETERMINE THROUGH APPROPRIATE SOURCES OF YOUR OFFICE WHETHER FRANK SCULLY AUTHOR OF THE BOOK QUOTE BEHIND THE FLYING SAUCERS UNQUOTE IS IDENTICAL TO THE FRANK SCULLY WHO HAS BEEN ACTIVELY ENGAGED IN COMMUNIST ACTIVITIES SINCE THE LATE NINETEEN THIRTIES IN THE TERRITORY OF YOUR OFFICE.

Evidently SAC Los Angeles didn't respond immediately because Hoover sent another request on October 17 and yet

---

* Recall it was on March 22, 1950 that Guy Hottel, SAC Washington, wrote to Hoover about three crashed saucers, a message that prompted Hoover to ask "what are the facts re flying saucers." See Chapter 14 and Figure 18.

** See *The Aztec Incident/Recovery at Hart Canyon*, Scott and Suzanne Ramsey, Aztec.48 Productions, Mooresville, N.C.

another on October 18. There is no document in the Flying Disc file which indicates whether or not SAC Los Angeles answered Hoover, or whether Frank Scully, the author, was a Communist sympathizer.

On the same day that Hoover initiated the investigation of Frank Scully, the FBI received the first information on strange happenings at yet another "vital installation." This was the Oak Ridge National Laboratory in Tennessee.

William Gray, SAC Knoxville, reported that radar had detected unidentified objects over Oak Ridge, the home of Project NEPA, the project to develop atomic powered aircraft. Colonel Gasser's project!

On the 19th of October, before the FBI was fully aware of what was taking place at Oak Ridge, Hoover received from Mr. Ladd more information about Air Force activities:

> The matter of flying saucers was discussed by Special Agent [name censored] with Major General Joseph F. Carroll of OSI on October 16, 1950, at which time General Carroll advised that insofar as he has been able to determine the Air Force is not working on any type of 'flying saucer' or 'flying disc.' General Carroll stated that the Air Force is working on high altitude rockets and jet aircraft. He stated these experiments may account for some of the reports concerning flying saucers but that the Air Force is not apparently working on anything which is the cause of the many flying saucers reports. He stated that the Air Force program for investigating reports concerning flying saucers, etc., has been reinstituted at Wright Field and that any pertinent information of interest coming to his attention will be furnished to the Bureau.

Recall that Major General Cabell, Director of AFI, had requested that AMC reinstate the investigation and analysis at ATIC. On September 25, 1950, the Bureau received from Cabell a copy of an intelligence collection memorandum entitled "Reporting of Information on Unconventional Aircraft." This was yet another request to provide sighting information with the added request that "no publicity be given this reporting or analysis activity." The memorandum to Mr. Ladd, quoted above, reflected this new activity at ATIC. Once again, the Air Force was privately contradicting its public stance that saucer sightings were not worthy of attention. In private, the Air Force and the

FBI found out that sightings which were about to occur at Oak Ridge were worthy of attention—a lot of attention.

Recall that, in January 1949, Colonel Gasser had reported to the FBI that two photos of a UFO had been taken near Oak Ridge in the summer of 1947. That was the first Oak Ridge sighting. The second occurred at about noon on May 25, 1949. It was a multiple witness sighting of a strange flat metallic object passing over the area while making a cracking noise. The third occurred at 7:00 p.m., June 20, 1949. Several people observed three objects, two rectangular in shape and one circular, flying over Oak Ridge.

After that there were no unusual observations until March 1, 1950. At 11:15 p.m. that night, a Knoxville radio amateur with experience in radar technology, Stuart Adcock, called the local FBI agent, Mr. Robey, to report that he had detected an object circling at an altitude of about 40,000 feet over Oak Ridge. He was using a surplus military radar set. Adcock reported another detection the next day at 11:15 a.m.. This time the object was about 100,000 feet up. The Army Counter Intelligence Corps (CIC) and the AFOSI sent representatives to Adcock's house on the night of March 2 and they saw radar returns indicating an object at high altitude at about midnight. Over the next several days Adcock's radar occasionally indicated the presence of an object.

The local CIC and OSI agents were not radar experts, but it appeared to them that the radar set was not particularly reliable. To help in the investigation a radar expert was requested, but he didn't arrive until March 8, two days after Adcock had left town. The local Navy Training Center radar equipment did not detect anything in the area where Adcock reported a radar target, but it was not adapted to the detection of objects at such a high altitude. A joint experiment was carried out using both Adcock's and the Navy's radar sets. They both detected two aircraft that were flying at 2,000 feet, indicating that Adcock's radar was working correctly. Adcock's last high altitude radar detection occurred during the morning of March 6, after which he left town (reason unknown). The local OSI agent attempted to contact Adcock, but was not able to and the investigation was ended on March 8.

There was no conclusion as to what, if anything, Adcock had detected. SAC Robey reported to FBI headquarters that the most impressive thing to him had been the "lack of any agency actually taking responsibility for the situation and taking any action to verify or disprove the threat." He also pointed out that it was many hours after the initial detection or "threat" was reported that any action at all was taken. Evidently Oak Ridge was not as well protected against a threat of sabotage as the security agencies had hoped.

Seven months later, at 11:25 p.m. on October 12, a military radar unit at Knoxville Airport suddenly detected 11, "and possibly more," unidentified targets moving over the restricted flight zone at Oak Ridge. This time action was taken. At 11:30, the radar station commander scrambled an F-82 fighter. It was in the air nine minutes later. The fighter was vectored toward two targets and, according to the radar, closed with the targets, but the pilot saw nothing. Ground observations also failed to detect anything in the sky. No unusual objects were seen visually or on radar for the next two days. Then the "dam broke."

On October 15, at 3:25 p.m., three Oak Ridge security guards and a caretaker saw an exceedingly strange object, described as looking like a rectangular playing card with a long thin tail, moving through the atmosphere in the vicinity of the restricted zone. It appeared to be carrying out controlled maneuvers. The Knoxville radar showed on its screen some strange targets at the same time as the visual sightings. Again an aircraft was scrambled and saw nothing. The Project Blue Book master list shows that ATIC could not explain the visual sighting.

The next day at about 1:30 p.m., John Isabell, a security guard of the Oak Ridge Patrol Force, saw a silver-white spherical object traveling from the southwest to the northeast and passing over the K-25 restricted area at high altitude. It was white or silvery and round like a ball. The second sighting on that day occurred at "exactly 2:55 p.m." Mr. Isabell and two other members of the patrol force saw the same round object approaching from the northeast at a lower altitude and speed. The object, while spinning about an axis, traveled in a wide circle toward the southwest and disappeared. In a couple of minutes it reappeared in the southwest at a very high altitude and headed northeast at a high rate of speed. The guard phoned the information on the sighting immediately to headquarters where radar was picking up an indistinct target every third or fourth sweep over the K-25 area. An F-82 was scrambled. The ground witnesses reported that the fighter plane arrived about 15 minutes after the object had disappeared.* Later on, during the evening, some of the security guards heard strange, loud noises.

That same day, October 16, the local Army Counter Intelligence Corp (CIC) agent decided it was time to review the situation. He wrote a report mentioning the 1947 and 1949 sightings and discussed the recent sightings. The CIC took these sightings very seriously and thoroughly checked the backgrounds of the witnesses by using employment records and FBI reports in order "to ascertain their reliability, integrity and loyalty to the United States Government." There was no reason found to discredit these witnesses, many of whom were professional security guards.

The CIC and the other security agencies discussed the situation and attempted to arrive at some conclusions. The CIC report of these discussions makes amusing reading in view of the concerted attempt later on by ATIC to explain the sightings any way possible. One gets the impression from the following document that, when it came to explaining UFO sightings as mundane phenomena, the security officials who were involved in the investigations had "been there, done that" and now they were looking for something new and convincing to explain these sightings:

> The opinions of the officials of the Security Division, AEC, Oak Ridge; Security Branch, NEPA Division, Oak Ridge; AEC Security Patrol, Oak Ridge; FBI Knoxville; Air Force Radar and Fighter Squadrons, Knoxville; and the OSI, Knoxville, Tennessee, fail to evolve an adequate explanation for OBJECTS SIGHTED OVER OAK RIDGE, however the possibilities of practical jokers, mass hysteria, balloons of any description, flights of birds (with or without cobwebs or other objects attached), falling leaves, insect swarms,

---

* The ATIC sighting analysts subsequently decided that this object was a balloon in spite of the description of spinning and in spite of the odd flight path.

peculiar weather conditions, reflections, flying kites, objects thrown from the ground, windblown objects, insanity, and many other natural happenings have been rejected because of the simultaneous witnessing of the objects with the reported radar sightings; because of the reliability of the witnesses; because of the detailed, similar description of the objects seen by different persons; and because of impossibility.

"Because of impossibility"? What was that supposed to mean? It meant that all the suggested explanations had been rejected because, in view of the high quality of the witnesses and the descriptive details, these explanations were impossible. So, having rejected mundane explanations, what were these objects? The CIC agent continued:

> The trend of opinions seem to follow three patterns of thought. The first is that the objects are a physical phenomenon which have a scientific explanation; the second is that the objects are experimental objects (from an undetermined source) guided by electronics and the third is similar to the second except that an intended demoralization or harrassment is involved. The fantastic is generally rejected.
>
> These objects have apparently followed only two patterns. The first is that they were sighted at the same hour on two consecutive days and the second is that the time of flight is either to or from the Northeast and Southwest, which directions (are) parallel the terrain ridges in the locality.

The fantastic is generally rejected?

It is not too surprising that "the fantastic" would not be in an official report. However, the fact that it was rejected means that they at least thought about "the fantastic." They also showed a healthy degree of skepticism regarding the ATIC treatment of such sightings because they questioned the ATIC "identification" of the image in the 1947 photographs as a photographic flaw:

> Attention is invited to the 1947 photograph of a flying object. Atomic Energy Commission officials advise that the Air Force Laboratory at Wright Field, Ohio, indicate that the object is a water spot on the photograph. Because this object does not resemble other water spots of the photograph and because the object in the second photograph is following the dim trail left by the first object, some officials at (the) Atomic Energy Commission question the veracity of this statement. They also believe it is significant that the Air Force did not return the negative of this print.

These security agencies were quite correct to be skeptical of the ATIC treatment of these sightings. The Project Blue Book record shows that the radar sightings were identified as "radar peculiarities," the first October 16 sighting was identified as an aircraft and the second as a balloon (even though the description of the object was the same for both sightings). Only the October 15 sighting of a "card with a tail," discussed above, was listed as Unidentified.

Copies of the reports by the CIC agents were made available to the FBI. When he saw them Hoover may have wondered if the saucers had now transferred their activities from the west, where atomic bombs were designed, built and stored, to Oak Ridge where nuclear energy was being studied as a possible source for propulsive power.

Strange noises were also part of the phenomena reported. Major Ronniger, a Senior Instructor at Oak Ridge, reported that at 3 p.m. on October 15 he heard a sound like the blast of a jet engine. He and another person searched the sky for such an aircraft but could find none. The next day several security guards reported that around 8 p.m. they heard what sounded like the blast of a jet several times. Each time the noise lasted about 3½ seconds. "The sounds seemed to leave the vicinity making an ascent almost vertical. None of the guards could see an object in the sky."

By October 16 things were already hot at Oak Ridge, but that was only the beginning. Four days later, at 4:55 p.m. on October 20, Larry Riordan, the Superintendent of Security for the X-10 control zone became a witness. While driving to a residential area he saw an object which he thought at first was a balloon which had lost its "basket." It was generally round, appeared to "come together at the bottom in wrinkles (rather indistinct) and something was hanging below." It appeared to be 8 to 10 feet long and lead or gunmetal colored. It didn't seem to be moving but, since he was traveling and only saw it for a number of seconds, he couldn't be sure. He was sure it wasn't a weather balloon, although he thought it might have been a gas bag balloon launched by the nearby University of Tennessee Agricultural Research Farm. On the same day at 3:27 p.m. the radar unit at the Knoxville airport detected radar targets near the area of Mr. Riordan's sighting and scrambled a fighter plane. The pilot searched the area for about an hour and a half, which included the time of Mr. Riordan's sighting, and found nothing.

Three days later, October 23, at 4:30 p.m., Francis Miller, an Oak Ridge laboratory employee, while driving along a road in Oak Ridge saw an object that appeared to be less than half a mile away and between 1,000 and 2,000 feet up. It appeared as an "aluminum flash" that was traveling in a south-southeast direction. He only saw it for a few seconds. Subsequently it was discovered that a nuclear radiation detection station (a Geiger counter) in the vicinity of the sighting registered a burst of alpha and beta radiation. The purpose of this station was to detect any leaks of radiation from the Oak Ridge Laboratory. There was no leakage of radiation, however. An expert from the Health and Research Division analyzed the readings from the Geiger counter and pronounced them unexplained. This association between radiation detection and a UFO sighting was similar to that at Mt. Palomar mentioned in Chapter 13. Whether the reading of the Geiger counter was actually a result of nuclear radiations or whether the presence of the UFO induced a transient electrical fault in the counter or whether there was some other explanation is not known. This case does not appear in the Project Blue Book file.

During the evening of the next day, there was a "light in the sky" sighting by two witnesses who were at widely separated locations. The first to see it was Mr. William Fry, the Assistant Chief of Security for Project NEPA. He was at a drive-in theater with his family at about 6:45 p.m. waiting for the movie to begin when he saw the lighted object in the southwest while casually looking around the sky. He reported to the CIC investigator:

> I observed what I at first thought to be an unusually bright star. The exceptional brilliance caused me to continue to observe it when it suddenly seemed to change color rapidly from a reddish hue to a bright orange and again to a brilliant light blue. [His wife and son also saw it.] . . . A few moments later I heard a plane directly overhead making passes over the Oak Ridge area, which was later identified as one of the F-82 fighter planes from the Air Force unit stationed at McGhee-Tyson Airport.. [At this point Mr. Fry went to

a phone and called someone to look, but the person could not see it because of the hills and trees.]

While returning to my car I met a friend . . . who stated he had been observing the object. I continued to observe the object with my wife but it seemed to be in a more northerly position which caused me to select a fixed point to determine whether or not the object was changing in either direction or altitude. There seemed to be a deviation from north to south for approximately five to ten degrees. The changing colors were still very evident but the object seemed to be continually getting smaller and smaller as though it was becoming more distant. At approximately 7:18 by my watch it disappeared from view entirely. During these observations my wife continued to report to me the identical things that I was observing. During the entire time the F-82 airplane continued to make passes over the area until approximately 7:15. The weather conditions were excellent; the air was calm; and the sky was cloudless with the exception of a very slight haze over the distant horizon.

The following morning, upon reporting to work I confided my story to [name censored] stationed at Oak Ridge with the NEPA project, but I hesitated to go on record as having observed such an unidentified object.

Mr. Fry did go on record because he learned that he was not the only witness. Air Force Major Lawrence Ballweg also saw the light. He reported as follows:

On the evening of 24 October 1950 at approximately 1855 (6:55 p.m.) I heard a plane fly over my home in the Woodland area. Being a curious individual I went outdoors to watch it with my binoculars. While looking for the plane I saw an object in the western sky which appeared at first to be a star but upon closer observation I noticed that it was rapidly changing colors from red to blue to white. When first seen it appeared to be moving very slowly in a northwest direction. It was moving relative to the other stars. The object was too small to be able to see any details even with the glasses. It disappeared from sight about 1920 (7:20 p.m.). During this period of time my wife also observed the object.

Mr. Fry then learned that the radar unit had also detected something. He was told that an unidentified object appeared at 6:30 p.m. at an altitude of approximately 5,000 feet in the same general vicinity as the object he saw. The radar target disappeared at 7:20 p.m.. The complete radar report to the CIC investigator says that targets appeared at 6:23 p.m. moving over the restricted flight zone, and at 6:26 p.m. a fighter was scrambled to the area but failed to see anything.

Considering that the atmosphere can make a star or planet which is within a few degrees of the horizon appear to change color and move very slightly or twinkle, one might be tempted to identify the light as the bright planet Venus or a very bright star seen in the west an hour after sunset, which was at about 6 p.m. local daylight savings time. However, two elements of the description reject that sort of explanation. First, the light was described by Major Ballweg as moving relative to the stars. Since Major Ballweg used binoculars to view the light it is likely that his description of motion is accurate. Furthermore, it must have been quite large because Mr. Fry, not using binoculars, also detected motion. Second, Major Ballweg said that the light appeared over a telephone pole that was about 100 yards away. That would make the angular elevation greater than 5 degrees. According to the CIC investigator, Mr. Fry indicated that the elevation from his location was 30 to 40 degrees above horizontal. Hence it was so high in angular elevation that atmospheric effects would not make it appear to change color, and there would be no noticeable effects other than the normal twinkling which affects stars at any angular elevation. The final reason for rejecting Venus or a bright star is that Venus was below the horizon at the time and there were no excessively bright stars in that sector of the sky at the time.

The disappearance of the radar target at the same time as the light suggests that the UFO was some kind of metallic unknown object hovering in the vicinity of Oak Ridge. This is another Oak Ridge sighting that is not in the Blue Book file, nor are the following October events.

About six hours later, between 2 a.m. and 3 a.m., October 25, the radar unit reported several slowly moving objects such as had been seen previously. On October 26 at 5 a.m., Colonel Edwin Thompson heard an intermittent noise like the blast of a jet, similar to what had been reported on the 15th and 16th. He saw no aircraft associated with the noise. Three days later, seven people waiting at the Knoxville Airport:

> . . . saw an object traveling to the Southwest at a great rate of speed.

[name censored], who has considerable flying experience, was extremely excited and stated that this object was not an aircraft. He described it as a circular object, leaving a trail of smoke.

There were two reported sightings on November 5. At 9:29 a.m., an object was detected on radar traveling over the restricted area at a speed of 80 mph. A fighter aircraft attempted an intercept and then trailed the object for 20 miles. The pilot reported no visual contact. Two and a half hours later, at 11:55 a.m., Don Patrick of the NEPA Division saw a very strangely shaped object travel by, apparently just above the mountain range. It seemed to change rapidly from a pear shape to a bean shape, and then other sausage-like shapes as it traveled. Although the shape changed, the overall size was roughly constant. It appeared translucent, but had well-defined edges as seen against the sky and background clouds. There was no particular color and there were no bright highlights. Mr. Patrick at first thought it was a balloon, but then realized that the shape changes and rapid motions meant it was something else. He told the CIC investigator that:

> . . . the core (dark triangular portion) remained constant and the apex of the core varied only a few degrees while the body of the object seemed to change shapes rapidly and would become elongated during a quick movement of the object.

Project Blue Book files list this sighting as unidentified.

As part of the CIC agent's attempts to explain these sightings, he asked Mr. J. Holland, chief of the Weather Section of the AEC at Oak Ridge, to provide information on balloon launches at the times of the sightings. There was no correlation. The only sighting that could have been a balloon was the October 20 sighting, and even that was not correlated with the Weather Section data. With regard to the radar detections during the previous month, Mr. Holland said radar could be reflected from patches of ionized air and, if a large quantity of radioactive material were released, it might provide sufficient ionaization of the air. However, he didn't believe any such release had occurred. According to the CIC agent's report, the Weather Section would carry out research to determine whether or not "radioactive energy ejections" could cause radar returns. There is no report on

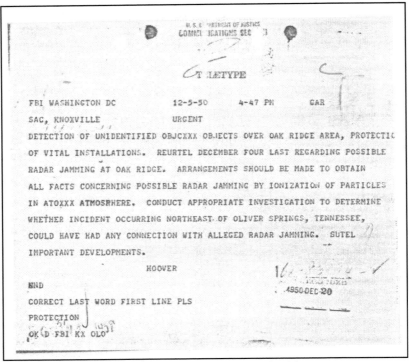

Figure 21: Radar Jamming at Oak Ridge

the results of the radar research.

Between 5 and 11 p.m. on November 29, radar targets returned to the Oak Ridge area. Fighters were scrambled. Pilots saw nothing. However, at 7 p.m., during this period of radar sightings, graphic records of Geiger counter detections in the restricted area of Oak Ridge indicated an abnormal increase in alpha and gamma radiation that could not be attributed to a known source. Apparently, this was too much for the officials in charge of Oak Ridge security. They held a two day meeting to discuss the "operational difficulties" of the early warning radar of the Air Defense Command at Knoxville. AFI was asked to investigate the situation and to set up a separate radar set for comparison.

The suggestion that some radar targets might be the result of ionization of the air by nuclear radiation must have been on the mind of Mr. Gray, SAC Knoxville, because on December 4 he called FBI headquarters and discussed the speculation that releases of radioactive material could have caused the anomalous radar targets observed. The next day, Hoover sent an urgent teletype to SAC Knoxville:

> Arrangements should be made to obtain all facts concerning possible radar jamming by ionization of particles in the atmosphere. Conduct appropriate investigation to determine whether incident occurring northeast of Oliver Springs, Tennessee, could have had any connection with alleged radar jamming." [See Figure 21]

Unfortunately, any information that might have been available on the Oliver Springs case has not been released. Nor is there any available response to Hoover's teletype message.

On December 5 and 6, there was a discussion of the technical aspects of the radar sightings with ATIC and intelligence officials. They concluded that the targets were probably "radar angels." These are reflections of objects on the ground which are observed only because of a temperature inversion—which bends the radar radiation downward.

On the other hand, that did not mean that there were no flying saucers around. At about 12:50 p.m., December 5, the wife of one of the security officers saw an unusual object north of her position, flying apparently over the Post Office building in Oak Ridge. It appeared to be a couple of miles away and 500 feet above the ground. It seemed to be made of highly polished aluminum or metal that reflected the sun. Its shape was round and flat like a disk. She saw the object for about a minute as it flew in a direct course eastward. Ten minutes later, another woman at a different location observed the same or a similar object heading westward. The OSI agent who investigated this case learned that there was an east wind at 6 mph and a clear sky. No balloons had been launched near that time. He also learned that there were two airborne aircraft at the time, but both were about fourteen miles south of the witnesses.

Despite the lack of evidence, ATIC subsequently claimed that the witnesses saw an aircraft. Indeed, ATIC would eventually claim that most of these events were mundane (radar anomalies, balloons, aircraft). Only two of the Oak Ridge sightings were left officially unidentified by ATIC.

Even so, the local military officials and scientists were not so certain of such easy identifications. They planned to begin their own scientific investigation. Lt. Colonel John Hood, the AMC Field Engineering Officer, outlined the plan in a December 5 memorandum entitled "Technical Approaches to the Problems of UFOs." He proposed placing radiation counters over a wide area. After there had been sufficient anomalous object reports to establish a pattern, the data recorded by these counters would then be compared for time and location with the sightings "to see if any change in the background (radiation) occurs with the presence of sighted objects." He also proposed that portable counters be made available which could be taken to the area of a sighting. Along with the counters, he proposed that an aircraft with Geiger counters and also a magnetometer be made available. The magnetometer would indicate any fluctuations in the local magnetic field associated with sightings. In addition, he proposed more accurate radars capable of measuring height as well as range and azimuth. This plan was to begin operating near the end of December.

Meanwhile, the next anomalous event in the Oak Ridge area was yet another appearance of radar targets which "blanketed the radar scopes in the area directly over the government Atomic energy Commission projects. . . these objects could not be identified from the radar image and a perfect fighter interception met with negative results."

The last Oak Ridge sighting of any consequence occurred on December 18 at about 8:30 a.m. Groups of people in separate cars traveling to work saw an unusual object fly over the area. To the Air Force officers in one of the cars, it appeared as a bright reflection from a very distant aircraft. It was southwest of them and they only saw it for a few seconds. At the same time, several other NEPA project employees were in another car at a different location. They saw this object for about 30 seconds before it was obscured by the nearby hills. They described it as a bright circular light with an intensity greater than that of the full moon. It was between 15 and 30 degrees above the horizon as it moved in a northwesterly direction. They observed a strange effect on the circular light: it seemed to:

> . . . darken, starting at approximately 7:00 to 9:00 o'clock along the perimeter and continuing to darken along the perimeter and inner

area until the light was concentrated in approximately 1:00 to 3:00 o'clock position of a very small diameter, at which point it appeared somewhat similar to a large star.

About the time that Colonel Hood's research plan was to be put into effect, the last two Oak Ridge sightings occurred. These were on December 20 and January 16. The December 20 case was another radar-only event (no visual contact) and the January 16 sighting involved sightings of stars. The Oak Ridge flap was over. There were no more sightings until a single one in the late fall of 1951. By that time the research project had effectively died. Thus, as happened with Project Twinkle in New Mexico, just as the local scientists and security agencies were about to carry out precise research that could prove the UFOs were real anomalous objects, the UFOs disappeared!

In retrospect, although it might be possible that some of the radar detections were weather anomalies caused by temperature inversions in the atmosphere (the "radar angels"), the visual sightings cannot be so easily dismissed.

Chapter 17
Immediate High Alert!
For Flying Saucers

One of the most important documents about secret activities of the Air Force in the early years was written in November, 1950. It did not involve the FBI, but it is important because it provides further support for the idea that the government has been covering up conclusive evidence of ET reality.

It should be apparent from what I have written that the Air Force appeared to be taking a split personality approach to the UFO problem. Sometimes an Air Force representative would tell the FBI or the general public that there was nothing to UFO sightings and there was no research going on. At some other times Air Force representative would tell the FBI, but not the general public, that investigations were ongoing because the sightings around "vital installations" and military bases were important enough to require continual attention.

During this period, roughly 20 percent of the sightings were unidentified, according to Project Blue Book Special Report #14, written in 1953.* After ruling out natural phenomena, there were only three classes of phenomena which could explain the unidentified sightings: ET craft, man made missiles (Soviet), or "mass hysteria." The staff at ATIC rejected the ET possibility in spite of any positive proof they might have because they had been told by Vandenberg that ET was not an acceptable explanation. The ATIC staff did not believe that Soviet missiles could be responsible for the unexplained sightings. The only remaining phenomenon was "mass hysteria" caused by the societal tensions of the time. This was the conclusion stated in the May 1950 ATIC document that responded to Captain Rickenbacker's public statement (see Chapter 14). On the other hand, the "mass hyste-

---

* Of course the Air Force didn't tell anyone that fact.

ria" explanation was not particularly tasteful either, because it implied that Air Force and commercial pilots were in a "hysterical" state whenever they reported unidentified flying objects.

Rejection of the mass hysteria hypothesis threw the explanation back to the previous two—or to a fourth possibility, which was that the unexplained sightings *could* have been explained if there had been more information. Accepting this fourth possibility was equivalent to saying that even the 20 percent unidentified could be explained, but without having to specify exactly how.

The FBI heard this non-explanation, as well as the "man made missile" explanation, for saucer sightings from the lower brass (colonels and below) at the Pentagon. But at the Top Secret, Special Access level, the story was different.

Enter one Wilbert B. Smith, a scientist working for the Canadian Department of Transport. He had a Master of Science degree in electrical engineering and set up a network of stations in Canada to measure changes in the ionosphere, which is important for long range radio transmission. When he first heard of flying saucers, which were reported in Canada as well as the United States (and most other countries), he began to toy with the idea that these were craft which made use of the Earth's magnetic field for propulsion. By the fall of 1950, he had concluded that the saucers were probably small ET craft which were flying to Earth from a large mothership in orbit at some great distance.

Smith had a Top Secret clearance. In September, he attended an electronics conference in Washington, D.C., just after reading the books by Donald Keyhoe and Frank Scully. During his visit there, according to his own records, he made contact, through the Canadian Embassy, with an American missile control expert, Dr. Robert Sarbacher. Smith wanted to know what the USA was doing with respect to the flying saucer mystery.

Sarbacher had done military research during WWII, but by 1950 he no longer worked for the government. However, as a "dollar a year man" who still had his clearance for classified material, he was an unpaid consultant to researchers at Wright Patterson Air Force Base. The WPAFB researchers had told him about some of the developments in flying saucer research.

In handwritten notes dated September 15, 1950, Smith recalled that Sarbacher told him: (a) flying saucers exist and the facts regarding crashed saucers in Scully's book are substantially correct; (b) they did not originate on Earth; and (c) the subject of saucers was classified higher than the hydrogen bomb, which was the most highly classified publicly known research program at that time.

Two months later, on November 21, Smith wrote a Top Secret Memorandum for the Canadian Department of Transport in which he suggested doing research into the possibility of obtaining power from the Earth's magnetic field and also suggested the possibility that "our work in geomagnetics might well be the linkage between our technology and the technology by which the saucers are designed and operated." Smith then summarized his conversation with Sarbacher as follows: (1) the matter is classified more highly than the H Bomb; (2) saucers exist; (3) their "modus operandi" is unknown but a small group "headed by Dr. Vannevar Bush" is attempting to determine how they work; and (4) the matter of flying saucers is considered to be of great significance.

Considering that this information from Mr. Smith is found in a formerly Top Secret document released in the late 1970s by the Canadian government, it must be taken seriously. Several UFO investigators interviewed Dr. Sarbacher in the early 1980s before he died. I was one of those investigators. He told me that, although he had never seen a saucer himself, he did know some engineers who worked at WPAFB in the late 1940s—they told him there was wreckage and bodies! Furthermore, he told me he had gained the impression from their descriptions that these creatures were lightweight and constructed somewhat like insects. He said that he did not know why the subject was still secret in the 1980s. He also recalled that Dr. Vannevar Bush, Dr. John von Neumann and Dr. Robert Oppenheimer were among the scientists working on the saucer problem. These men were, of course, top scientists of the day, with Bush being "the top of the top" as far as political connections were concerned, having organized virtually all of the U.S. military research carried out during WWII.

According to Mr. Smith and Dr. Sarbacher, at the Top Secret

level flying saucers were considered to be *very* important.

A teletype message found in the FBI file further indicates the level of importance that the intelligence community sometimes attached to saucer sightings. Recall that on December 5, Hoover sent a teletype message in which he asked SAC Knoxville to investigate "radar jamming" at Oak Ridge (see the previous chapter). Then, three days later, FBI headquarters received the following message from SAC Richmond, Virginia (see Figure 22):

URGENT. DECEMBER 8. RE: FLYING SAUCERS. This office very confidentially advised by Army Intelligence, Richmond, that they have been put on immediate high alert for any data whatsoever concerning flying saucers. CIC here states background of instructions not available from Air Force Intelligence, who are not aware of reason for alert locally, but any information whatsoever must be telephoned by them immediately to Air Force Intelligence. CIC advises data strictly confidential and should not be disseminated.

How very strange for the Counter Intelligence Corps to be put on immediate high alert for any data regarding objects/phenomena/craft which ATIC claimed could all be explained and were no threat to the security of the United States! Are we to presume the CIC had nothing better to do than to run around chasing will o' the wisps and similar ethereal things of no consequence to national defense? *Clearly not.* This teletype message proves—not hints, nor suggests, but proves—that Air Force Intelligence at the Pentagon, which requested the immediate high alert, considered the subject of flying saucers to be important—very important—contrary to the publicized ATIC opinion.

And well they might, because saucers and other unexplained phenomena had been reported many times near vital installations. This teletype also shows that AFI treated its interest in utmost confidence. The existence of an alert was strictly confidential and not for dissemination. One gets the impression that merely by telling the FBI of the alert, the local CIC agent was breaking security. Further evidence of the level of secrecy is the fact that AFI had not informed the CIC agent of the reason for the alert. Even the local AFI agent, who told the CIC agent, didn't know

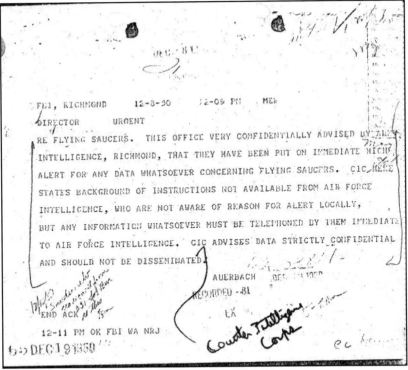

Figure 22: Immediate High Alert

the reason.

Apparently, the reason for the alert was only known to the Top Brass with Top Secret/Special Access/Need-to-Know level of clearance for classified information.[*]

The existence of this teletype message raises (at least) two related questions: why an immediate high alert, and why on December 8?

Neither of these questions can be definitely answered at the present time, because the CIC and AFI records relating to this simply have not been found, even after a search at my (FOIA) request of CIC records by the Army Security agency. However, there were UFO sightings on December 6 which are in the Blue Book file: one at Westover Air Force Base in Massachusetts and

---

[*] In order to do their jobs the local agents, who also had Top Secret clearances, didn't need to know why AFI Headquarters wanted information; they only needed to know that AFI wanted information.

one at Fort Myers, Florida. The latter case is listed as unidentified. Perhaps the alert was caused by one of these. Maybe the alert was related to the "radar jamming" reported at Oak Ridge three days earlier.

Or perhaps it was related to an odd event that occurred the morning of December 6, an event which caused the U.S. government to go on alert.

The story behind this incident is not completely known. However, the available information is intriguing. While reading what follows, keep in mind that the global political situation was very unsettled. Russia and China were becoming potent adversaries with the stated purpose of overthrowing the capitalist democracies. The war in Korea was viewed as the first real military contest between communism and capitalism, and it was not going well for the USA. Ever since the beginning of the war six months earlier, the U.S. government had been worried about the Chinese response to the United Nations attempts to preserve the independence of South Korea. These worries increased after General MacArthur landed at Inchon in September and succeeded in driving the North Korean army back across the 38th parallel (the agreed-upon northern boundary of South Korea). In October and November, U. N. troops pushed into North Korea under MacArthur's orders to destroy the North Korean army.

Finally, on November 25, the Chinese counterattacked with about 200,000 men, a number which doubled over the next month. The U.N. forces had about half the Chinese number, and once again were in danger of complete defeat. In the USA, such a situation caused near panic. President Truman was worried about the possibility that the war would widen, even bringing on World War III, which could necessitate a nuclear response. The Joint Chiefs of Staff had sent a warning to U.S. forces commanders throughout the world of a heightened possibility for world war. It was during these perilous times that a large group of unidentified aircraft were detected approaching the USA from the north, and they appeared to be headed toward Washington, D.C.

There are three published versions of what happened during the morning of December 6. The first version comes from the autobiography of Secretary of State, Dean Acheson.* The second version is based in an interview with Mr. Acheson.** It differs slightly from Mr. Acheson's own version. The third is in *Memoirs of Harry S. Truman: Years of Trial and Hope 1946-1952.**** Looking first at Secretary Acheson's autobiography we find that on the morning of December 6:

> ... soon after my arrival at the (State) Department, Deputy Secretary of Defense Lovett telephoned a report and an instruction from the President. Our early warning radar system in Canada had picked up formations of unidentified objects, presumably aircraft, headed southeast on a course that could bring them over Washington in two or three hours. All interception and defense forces were alerted. I was to inform but not advise the Prime Minister (Clement Atlee of Britain). The Pentagon telephones would be closed for all but emergency defense purposes and he could not talk again. Before he hung up, I asked whether he believed that the objects that were picked up were Russian bombers. He said that he did not. Getting Oliver Franks on the telephone I repeated the message. He asked whether the President had canceled the eleven-thirty meeting with Atlee, and was told that he had not. We agreed to meet there. Before ending the talk, he wondered about the purpose of my message. I suggested fair warning and an opportunity for prayer. As we finished, one of our senior officials burst into the room. How he had picked up the rumor I do not know, perhaps from the Pentagon. He wanted to telephone his wife to get out of town, and to have important files moved to the basement. I refused to permit him to do either and gave him the choice of a word-of-honor commitment not to mention the matter to anyone or being put under security detention. He wisely cooled off and chose the former. When we reached the White House, Lovett told us that the unidentified objects had disappeared. His guess was that they had been geese.

There are several important points to keep in mind as you read the following versions of what happened. Acheson said that "early warning radar in Canada" had detected "formations" (plural) of "unidentified objects, presumably aircraft" which were

---

* Acheson, Dean, *Present at the Creation* (W.W. Norton, NY, 1969), pages 479-480.

** Published in *The Wise Men* by Walter Isaacson and Evan Thomas (Simon and Shuster, NY, 1986), pages 544-545.

*** (Doubleday, NY, 1956, Vol. 2), page 405.

headed "southeast" in a direction that could put them over Washington, D.C. in 2 to 3 hours. Using an estimated top speed of 300 mph for Soviet bombers, this would put them a mere 600 - 900 miles from Washington at the time of first detection. Acheson ended his story by saying that, after he arrived at the White House, that is, at about 11:30 a.m., Defense Undersecretary Lovett told him he thought that the objects had turned out to be geese.

The next version of the story, told in *The Wise Men,* is based on an interview with Mr. Acheson:

> For a moment on the morning of December 6, he thought his nightmare (of world war) had come true. At 10:30 a.m. Bob Lovett called him from the Pentagon and abruptly informed him in his laconic voice: 'When I finish talking to you, you cannot reach me again. All incoming calls will be stopped. A national emergency is about to be proclaimed. We are informed that there is flying over Alaska at the present moment a formation of Russian planes heading southeast. The President wishes the British ambassador to be informed of this and be told that Mr. Attlee should take whatever measures are proper for Mr. Attlee's safety. I've now finished my message and I'm going to ring off.' Acheson cut in, 'Now wait a minute, Bob, do you believe this?' 'No,' Lovett replied, and hung up. Acheson sat in his office and waited. The Air Force scrambled. A senior official burst in asking permission to telephone his wife to get out of town and wondering if he should begin moving files to the basement. Acheson tried to sooth him. A few minutes later Lovett calmly called back. The radar blips were not Soviet bombers after all. They were flocks of geese.

This version makes it seem that the alert period was very short, only a few minutes. However, by combining the information in this version about the beginning time, 10:30 a.m., with the information in Acheson's biography about the ending time (after Acheson arrived at the White House), about 11:30 a.m., we find that the alert lasted about an hour. This version is more specific as to where the objects were: they were detected over Alaska, which is over 3,000 miles from Washington, D. C. If that were true it would have taken much more than 10 hours for the planes to arrive over Washington.

President Truman wrote about the same episode:

Shortly before we went into that morning meeting, Under Secretary Lovett called from the Pentagon, reporting that the radar screens of some air defense installations in the far north were reporting large formations of unidentified planes approaching. Fighter planes were sent up to reconnoiter and alerts were flashed to air centers in New England and beyond. But about an hour later—while I was meeting with (Clement) Attlee—Lovett notified me that the report had been in error. Some unusual disturbance in the Arctic atmosphere had thrown the radar off.

President Truman's version of the event suggests that the objects may have been detected north of the eastern United States rather than over Alaska. The fact that fighter aircraft were scrambled indicates that this alert was treated as a serious event by the Continental Air Command. Truman's explanation is somewhat different from Acheson's. Here we learn that the radar detections were caused by some sort of atmospheric disturbance.

An unpublished version of this event is found in the official transcript of the meeting between Truman and Atlee which is preserved at the Truman library:

At this point (in the meeting) Mr. Connelly entered the room and handed the President a report from Deputy Secretary of Defense Lovett. Mr. Lovett was reporting that the 'alert' that had reached the President an hour earlier when it was thought that a large number of unidentified airplanes were approaching the northeast coast of the United States, had now been due to erroneous interpretation of atmospheric conditions. The President informed the Prime Minister that the report of the planes was in error. The Prime Minister expressed relief and gratification.

This version, based on notes made at the time rather than upon memories years afterward, says the unidentified objects were approaching the northeast coast of the United States, clearly contradicting Acheson's assertion that they were detected over Alaska. Unless, of course, there were two groups of objects. Furthermore, this version indicates Lovett was the source of the "atmospheric effects" explanation mentioned by President Truman. But Lovett was also the source of the "geese" explanation reported by Acheson. So, which explanation was right? Or was neither correct?

A report carried by the International News Service reported yet another explanation:

> Washington D.C., 6 December 1950 (INS): A warning of an impending air attack resulted in a false alarm in this capitol city today. No air raid alarms were sounded, but functionaries charged with the Civil Air Defense of Washington were alerted that an unidentified aircraft had been detected off the coast of the State of Maine at mid-day. Later, a spokesman for the Air Force stated that interceptor aircraft had been dispatched, and that the object in question had been identified shortly thereafter as a North American C-47 aircraft which was approaching the continent from Goose Bay, Labrador. The warning was said to have been useful in verifying the efficiency of the Washington Civil Defense System. Civil Defense officials declined to comment on the incident.

This report, supposedly based on an Air Force statement, says the radar target was from a single aircraft approaching from a location near Goose Bay, Labrador. It says nothing about Alaska.

It appears that this supposed attack did have repercussions in Alaska. The *New York Times* published a story with a December 7, Anchorage Alaska, dateline which said that:

> All military personnel in Alaska were called on 'alert' tonight, but Air Force officials said that the order was purely a 'precautionary measure.' Military police rounded up soldiers and theatres and radio stations made special announcements that troops were to return to their posts. Within a few hours there were no military personnel to be seen on Anchorage streets. Officials at Elmendorf Air Force Base said the alert had been in effect since the outbreak of the fighting in Korea. But they added that the air force had increased its vigilance here in recent days."

Further evidence of the official jitters is in the statement in the *Washington Post* on December 10 that "President Truman is 'seriously considering declaration of national emergency' which could lead to an 'immediate all-out mobilization.'"

Flocks of Geese? Arctic atmospheric effects? A single C-47 aircraft? Or something else? Not until 1987 was further information on this event found during a random search of documents that had recently been released by the Air Force, and sparse information at that. On December 6, Air Force Colonel Charles Winkle, Assistant Executive in the Directorate for Plans, wrote a memorandum for Secretary of Defense George Marshall about this event. It confirms the alert:

SUBJECT: Air Alert - 1030 Hours , 6 December 1950

1. The ConAC (Continental Air Command) Air Defense Controller notified the Headquarters USAF Command Post that at 1030 hours a number of unidentified aircraft were approaching the northeast area of the United States and that there was no reason to believe the aircraft were friendly.

2. This information was further amplified at 1040 hours as follows. By radar contact it was determined that approximately 40 aircraft were in flight, at 32,000 feet, on a course of 200 degrees in the vicinity of Limestone, Maine.

3. The emergency alert procedure went into effect immediately.

4. The Office of the President was notified. Brigadier General Landry returned the call and stated that the President had been notified and that:

a. All information in this matter was to be released by the Department of the Air Force.

b. Office of the President would release no information.

c. The substance of a and b above was to be passed to the Office of the Secretary of Defense.

5. At 1104 hours the ConAC Air Defense Controller state that the original track had faded out and it appeared that the flight as originally identified is a friendly flight.

6. ConAC took immediate action to dispatch interceptors on the initial contact.

The technical information in this document is sparse but sufficient to allow us to make some deductions. There are details which call into question all of the previous explanations. By combining the information from these various sources I estimate that these objects were first detected in the direction of Goose Bay, Labrador (which is about 500 miles north-northeast of Limestone, Maine). Their distance when first detected was probably close to the 200 mile limit of the capability of the search radar in Maine. The radar operators then tracked these objects continuously for ten minutes and determined that they were traveling south-southwestward (a course of 200 degrees). This course would take them over the eastern USA including the Washington, D.C. area. They must have appeared or "painted" as 40, convincingly solid, moving targets on the radar screen. If they were detected 200 miles from Limestone and ten minutes later reached "the vicinity" of Limestone their speed would have been nearly 1200 mph. If they had not been detected until they were 100 miles away their speed would have been nearly 600 mph. Even this lower speed would be much too fast for the Soviet bombers of those days.[*]

The statement that there was "no reason to believe the aircraft were friendly" means that the Continental Air Command officials were not able to identify the aircraft from a known flight plan, nor were they able to communicate with the aircraft by radio. Ten minutes after the initial detection the radar operators had determined that there were 40 objects at an altitude of about 32,000 feet. Evidently the radar images were so good that the operators were certain that these objects were unidentifiable yet solid targets, presumably aircraft, flying at a high altitude. This is decidedly different from what the operators would have concluded had the radar showed relatively slow moving geese or atmospheric effects or a single C-47. Geese, C-47s, and atmospheric effects don't travel at 600 mph or 1,200 mph at 32,000 feet.

According to Winkle's document, the radar track "faded out" at 11:04 a.m., or about 20 minutes after the objects were near Limestone. If the objects had continued on the 200 degree course at the same speed, for example at 600 mph, in 20 minutes they would have been beyond the range of the of Limestone radar, which would explain the fading of the track.

The strangest statement in the document is: "it appears that the flight as originally identified is a friendly flight." What does that mean? Didn't they know for certain? Didn't they track the "friendly aircraft" until they were positive? Are we to believe that they scrambled aircraft and put the USA into a state of immediate high alert and then weren't able positively to identify the aircraft?

One would expect if there had been upwards of forty friendly aircraft coming from the north toward the USA border, someone would have been aware of it. There would have been a flight plan. At the very least these aircraft would have acknowledged the attempts to contact them by radio, attempts which must have

---

[*] Tu-4A atomic bomb carrying copy of the B-29; top speed about 350 mph at 33,000 feet altitude; range about 3,300 miles if operated at 10,000 feet altitude.

been made numerous times starting with the first detection by radar. Either the flight plan or the radio identification would have been passed to the local commanders of the Continental Air Command aircraft to prevent needless scrambling of aircraft.

If they were friendly aircraft, why did Undersecretary of Defense Robert Lovett tell Dean Acheson that flocks of geese flying over Alaska caused the radar targets? Why did Undersecretary Lovett tell the President that artic atmospheric conditions caused the radar targets? Why did the Air Force tell the press that a single C-47 caused the whole alert?

Presumably these were the explanations offered by the Top Brass after being told the details by the people who were directly involved with the radar detections and the scramble. Was the Top Brass embarrassed by the initial misidentification of a "friendly flight" and afraid to admit it? (I doubt that.) Or did Top Brass tell the President and the Undersecretary of Defense what these targets really were but the these gentlemen, for some reason, when writing about it years later still could not reveal the exact nature of these objects to anyone else?

There must be other Air Force documents not yet released which clarify this situation. However, based on the information available in this document combined with the fact that CIC was put on immediate high alert for flying saucer information only two days later, I can suggest another explanation: the radar targets were flying saucers.

One ominous implication of these events is that we, or the Soviets, might fail to immediately identify groups of flying saucers and, thinking an attack was imminent, scramble atomic bomb-carrying aircraft—thereby accidently starting a war. I suspect that this possibility was not overlooked by the highest government officials.

The failure of the Air Force to immediately identify unknown aircraft in other incidents played an important role in the involvement of the Central Intelligence Agency with saucer sightings a year and a half later.

Chapter 18
I've Been Lied To!

The FBI's "X-file" has few entries for the year 1951, probably because this was a down year for UFO sightings. The Blue Book master list has 240 sightings in 1950 but only 171 in 1951.

In January 1951, the FBI added to its file a copy of a *LOOK* magazine article based on interviews with ATIC director, Colonel Harold Watson. Recall that Colonel Watson was the person who had virtually shut down Project Grudge in 1949. He did this in spite of orders from General Cabell to carry out a good investigation. Perhaps he downplayed Project Grudge because it was poorly funded. Perhaps he just thought that saucer investigation was a waste of time. For whatever reason, during the interviews Colonel Watson followed the party line: all sightings were explainable and saucer investigation was a waste of time. The magazine article, written by Robert Considine, didn't give the witnesses an even break. Entitled "The Disgraceful Flying Saucer Hoax," the article characterized UFO witnesses as "true believers," "members of the lunatic fringe," "gagsters," and "screwballs," and claimed that the sighting reports were a result of "cold war jitters," "mass hysteria," hallucinations" and "mirages." This was like a recycling of Shallett's article almost two years before.

The FBI memorandum which mentions this article indicates that it was filed "for information purposes." One can only imagine what the FBI officials thought about this article after what they had been through in the previous two years, with the frightening information from Colonel Gasser, the many unexplained sightings near "vital installations" in New Mexico and the sightings over Oak Ridge. To add to the confusion, during the month after Considine's article, *Time* magazine carried an article by Navy scientist Dr. Urner Liddel in which he claimed that all credible sightings were Skyhook balloons. This was followed by several newspaper articles in which Dr. Anthony Mirarchi rebutted Liddel and said the saucers were Russian missiles (see Chapter 15).

The only FBI teletype message about a sighting in 1951 was received at FBI headquarters on September 20. It discussed an important series of radar sightings at Fort Monmouth, New Jersey. These sightings, which occurred on September 10 and 11, involved detections of objects which could alternately hover or move at high speed. Not mentioned in the FBI teletype is the report of a pilot in a training aircraft who saw a UFO moving in the area at the same time. There is no evidence that the FBI responded in any way to these events. However, the Air Force certainly did respond and in a big way. In fact, as a result of immediate top level interest, these sightings played an important role in the history of the Air Force UFO project.

Major General Cabell, the Director of Air Force Intelligence, learned of the sightings soon after they occurred and asked ATIC/Project Grudge for a special briefing. Following the lead of Colonel Harold Watson, whose opinion had been expressed in the January *LOOK* magazine, the few staff people still working on Project Grudge did not take the sighting seriously. They assumed that General Cabell wanted an explanation so they tried to think of a good one to get the pressure from Washington "off our backs." From the teletype messages they learned that the sightings had taken place at a radar school. They assumed the radar operators were unskilled and the pilot was inexperienced. Based on these assumptions the Grudge staff concluded that the sightings were errors caused by lack of experience. This explanation satisfied Colonel Watson and he was about to send it to the General when a message came to ATIC saying the General expected them to carry out an on-the-spot investigation. This was something they never did, but to pacify the General they tried to make it look as if they had planned an investigation all along ("Yes, General. Of course we were planning to go there, General."). Two members of the ATIC staff immediately flew to Fort Monmouth. While there they learned that General Cabell expected a briefing immediately after they completed their investigation. The pressure was on.

They interviewed the radar operators and the pilot and passenger in the aircraft. The evidence seemed strong that a real UFO was involved rather then atmospheric effects or inexperience. They also learned that the press had picked up on the story, which disturbed them because (a) many people thought UFOs were from outer space and ATIC didn't want the fact of project interest in the sightings to cause any alarm, (b) Colonel Watson wanted to keep a low profile in the hopes that if "you stick your head deep enough into the sand" the problem would go away, and (c) Colonel Watson had told the press that the Project had been closed in the hope that the press would lose interest and "go away." (General Cabell knew Watson had told the press that the Project was closed, but Cabell assumed that Watson was lying in order to cover up the real investigative activity. It was OK with Cabell if Watson lied to the press, as long as he told the truth to Cabell. However, Cabell would soon find out that Watson had been telling the truth to the press and lying to Cabell!)

The two ATIC officers flew to Washington and reported what they found to General Cabell during a special meeting at the Pentagon. After hearing the Monmouth report General Cabell asked about Project Grudge itself, how well was it going? With Colonel Watson absent (he had not been part of the investigating team and he had not flown from ATIC to attend the meeting), one of the ATIC officers felt it safe to "spill the beans." He told the General that Project Grudge was essentially dead. There was no real sighting analysis. Each sighting was explained in any way that seemed feasible and the explanation was sent on to Washington. The sighting files were scattered and many sighting reports had been boxed up and put away.

General Cabell now realized what had happened: the lower brass had taken to heart the official Air Force dogma that flying saucers didn't exist and saucer reports were mistakes or just plain garbage. They had stopped taking the Project work seriously, even after he had ordered a revitalization in the summer of 1950. Even worse, to cover up their inactivity they had lied to him during the previous months and years when they reported that the Project was alive and well and analyzing sightings.

Cabell was angry. "I've been lied to," he said several times to his staff of Colonels. He wanted the lying to stop and the Project once again revitalized. "I want an answer to the saucers and I want a good answer." It was General Cabell's feeling that as long as there was any question as to whether or not all sightings could be explained, the Project should continue. General Cabell criticized the December, 1949 Grudge report saying it was the "most poorly written, unconclusive piece of unscientific tripe" he had ever read.* In contrast to the official Grudge conclusion (everything is explainable), General Cabell said "Anyone can see that we do not have a satisfactory answer to the question."**

So, here was the man sitting at the top of Air Force Intelligence telling his "employees" that they had screwed up because they had taken the public Air Force statements to be the gospel truth and hadn't obeyed direct orders, which were to provide good analyses of sightings. When the General speaks, the Colonels and the rest listen. Project Grudge was reorganized. The person brought in to carry out the reorganization was Captain Edward Ruppelt.

Ruppelt took over Project Grudge in late September 1951. He immediately began planning for the future. He was the first director since the early Project Sign days to proceed in a straightforward scientific manner with a minimum of bias and prejudgement. He wanted as his staff only those people who could approach the subject seriously and with an open mind. Part of his reorganization plan was to have ATIC hire scientific consultants. This was approved and ATIC hired the Battelle Memorial Institutute in Columbus, Ohio, to analyze sightings using what were then advanced computer-based methods and to develop a standard sighting form. In early 1952, the reorganization was formalized as the project name was changed to the name which dominated the press reporting on saucer sightings for the next 17 years, Project Blue Book. Moreover, plans were devel-

---

* He did not say why he had kept his mouth shut about this feeling for over a year and a half.

** Writing many years later in a personal memorandum which included much of the information related in the above paragraphs, Edward Ruppelt characterized Cabell as a "believer."

oped to get proof of saucer reality by obtaining photos of radarscope traces of UFOS and photos of the UFOs themselves.

This was a decided improvement in the approach to solving the saucer mystery. However, if the Air Force had known what was going to happen six months later, it would have done more than change the project name and buy a few cameras. It would have begun preparation for a nationwide saucer "attack."

Chapter 19
The Year of the UFO

A whole UFO book could be written about this one year, during which ATIC received over a thousand sighting reports. The title would be *1952*, and the subtitle would be *The Year of the UFO*. What I present here will only scratch the surface of that amazing year.

During the latter half of 1951, there were important changes in the UFO project at ATIC and also in Air Force Intelligence at the Pentagon. General John A. Samford replaced General Cabell as Director of Intelligence.* The new Director soon learned that that the subject of UFOs received top level attention. On January 3, 1952, Brigadier General William M. Garland, Assistant for the Production of Intelligence, wrote a memorandum for General Samford with the title "(SECRET) Contemplated Action to Determine the Nature and Origin of the Phenomena Connected with the Reports of Unusual Flying Objects." This memorandum begins as follows:

> 1. The continued reports of unusual flying objects requires positive action to determine the nature and origin of the phenomena. The action taken thus far has been designed to track down and evaluate reports from casual observers throughout the country. Thus far, this action has produced results of doubtful value and the inconsistencies inherent in the nature of the reports has given neither positive nor negative proof of the claims.

Here we find a general in Air Force intelligence admitting that there was no negative proof of the claims. Yet the Air Force had been saying publicly for several years that there *was* negative proof, that all sightings had been explained. Clearly the men on the inside were more honest with each other than with the

---

* Cabell subsequently retired from the Air Force and became an assistant director of the CIA.

American people about the fact they had not been able to prove flying saucers were only mistakes or figments of the imagination.

By this time it had become a standard procedure to appeal to the Soviet Menace in order to legitimize requests for action and the expenditure of funds. General Garland, too, justified the added effort he would propose by referring to the potential Soviet threat:

> 2. It is logical to relate the reported sightings to the known development of aircraft, jet propulsion, rockets and range extension capabilities in Germany and the U.S.S.R. In this connection, it is to be noted that certain developments by the Germans, particularly the Horton wing, jet propulsion, and refueling, combined with their extensive employment of V-1 and V-2 weapons during World War II, lend credence to the possibility that the flying objects may be of German and Russian origin. The developments mentioned above were contemplated and operational between 1941 and 1944 and subsequently fell into the hands of the Soviets at the end of the war. There is evidence that the Germans were working on these projects as far back as 1931 to 1938. Therefore, it may be assumed that the Germans had at least a 7 to 10 year lead over the United States in the development of rockets, jet engines and aircraft of the Horton-wing design. The Air Corps developed refueling experimentally as early as 1928, but did not develop operational capability until 1948.

Notice how cleverly the general has described the possible threat from Russian developments based on German war research and has concluded that the Russians might have a 7 to 10 year lead on the United States in producing advanced aircraft. Nowhere did he mention that the same argument had been rejected in previous years because (a) the ATIC and AFI investigators in 1947 and again in 1948 could not accept the idea that the Soviets were that far ahead of us and (b) even if they were that far ahead they would never fly their advanced aircraft over the United States (we wouldn't do the reverse). Could it be that he didn't know about the previous rejection of the "Soviet Hypothesis?" Could it be that he was not sufficiently intelligent to deduce for himself that the idea of the Soviets testing their advanced aircraft over the United States was ridiculous? Or could it be that he actually doubted the Soviet Hypothesis but used it anyway to justify spending money on saucer investigation?*

Having established a "credible" threat General Garland continued:

3. In view of the above facts and the persistent reports of unusual flying objects over parts of the United States, particularly the east and west coast and in the vicinity of the atomic energy production and testing facilities it is apparent that positive action must be taken to determine the nature of the objects and, if possible, their origin. Since it is a known fact that the Soviets did not detonate an atomic bomb prior to 1949, it is believed possible that the Soviets may have developed the German aircraft designs at an accelerated rate in order to have a suitable carrier for the delivery of weapons of mass destruction. In other words, the Soviets may have a carrier without the weapons required while we have relatively superior weapons with relatively inferior carriers available. If the Soviets should get the carrier and the weapon, combined with adequate defensive aircraft, they might surpass us technologically for a sufficient period of time to permit them to execute a decisive air campaign against the United States and her allies. The basic philosophy of the Soviets has been to surpass the western powers technologically and the Germans may have given them the opportunity.

In the preceding paragraph the general pressed two hot buttons. One was the reference to sightings of UFOs/saucers over the atomic installations (green fireballs, etc.). These installations were considered the keystone to our development of so-called "defensive" atomic weapons (ie. weapons of mass destruction). Although the Air Force publicly played down the importance of these sightings, it is clear that they had had an impact at the top of the command structure. The other hot button was the fact that the Soviets, now with a known nuclear capability, might have a delivery system superior to the bombers of the United States and her allies.

The general concluded:

4. In view of the facts outlined above it is considered mandatory that the Air Force take positive action at once to definitely determine the nature and, if possible, the origin of the reported unusual flying objects. The following action is now contemplated:

---

* We will shortly see how this same ploy was used by a scientist to get money for a trip to Europe.

a) require ATIC to provide at least three teams to be matched up with an equal number of teams from ADC (Air Defense Command) for the purpose of taking radar scope photographs and visual photographs of the phenomena
b) select sites for these teams based on concentrations of already reported sightings over the United States (these areas are, generally, the Seattle area, the Albuquerque area and the New York-Philadelphia area) and
c) take the initial steps in this project during early January, 1952.

It is obvious that the general wanted action, ostensibly to protect the United States from the possible Soviet advancements in aeronautical research. However, information contained in a memorandum written by Captain Ruppelt suggests that Garland may have had an ulterior motive. According to Ruppelt (from his personal papers):

General Garland was my boss at ATIC from the Fall of 1952 until I left. He was a moderately confirmed believer. He had seen a UFO while he was stationed in Sacramento, California. He was General Samford's assistant in the Pentagon before he came to ATIC.

Since he had seen a UFO it is possible that he already knew it wasn't a Soviet device and he was really using the Soviet ploy to justify an investigation of interplanetary vehicles. This possibility gains further support from what he did only a month or so after this document was written: he suggested the interplanetary hypothesis to writers of a *LIFE* magazine article (to be described).

Ruppelt began the process of carrying out Garland's recommendations, but it was slow going. By the time things were starting to move in the late spring Project Blue Book was swamped with sightings. The investigation teams proposed by the general were never formed, but a plan for instrumentally recording sighting information was carried out, according to a Project Blue Book staff Study written in July, just one month before the ADC issued a requirement that radar scope cameras be available to radar operators. During the spring and summer of 1952, the Collection Division of ATIC developed a stereo camera with a diffraction grating for color analysis of photographed objects. ATIC ordered 100 of these special cameras to be delivered in September. Blue Book planned to give these cameras to military and civilian control tower operators and to the Ground Observer Corps. Too bad these cameras arrived too late for the big flap!

As of March 1952, it had been more than three years since Colonel Gasser had told the FBI that saucers were Soviet missiles and more than two years since the green fireballs had caused a minor panic among security agencies. It was over a year since the UFO scare at Oak Ridge, and over a year since the public controversy sparked by the Considine article and the Liddel-Mirarchi debate. There had been scattered news stories about flying saucers during 1951 and there had been many sightings, but the FBI was not involved with any of them. If Mr. Hoover thought about saucers at all, he probably assumed they had all been explained by the Air Force and that saucer sightings had simply faded away.

If that is what he believed, then he was in for a shock. The first inkling that something was still going on saucer-wise came on March 25 when Headquarters received a report from an artist living in Chicago. The local Chicago agent reported that an artist (name censored in the released document) contacted the FBI and described the following sighting:

> ... he saw a flying disc at 9:00 a.m. on March 6, 1952. (name) stated that he was looking out of a window at his home which faces south when he saw a flying disc at approximately 7,000 feet above Fullerton Avenue. The angle of elevation of the disc above the horizon was 45 degrees. The disc came out of a cloud in the east, stopped and hung motionless in mid air for a split second, then flew south at great speed. He described the disc as approximately six feet in diameter, circular, white in color with a bluish tinge. The disc, he said, appeared to have been constructed out of a metal similar to aluminum. He also stated that he saw no exhaust, lights, or heard no sound connected with its movements. . . . He said it disappeared out of sight in approximately three seconds. . . . He said it went so fast it appeared to flutter.

SAC Chicago reported that he sent a copy of the sighting report to AFOSI. However, this is yet another sighting that did not get into the Blue Book file.

On the seventh of April, FBI Headquarters received another report, this time from Nashville, Tennessee. A Naval serviceman (name censored) reported to the FBI that on March 13, at 10:20

p.m.:

> . . . while standing in the back yard . . . and looking toward the moon, which was in the southwest section of the sky, he observed an object which was approximately 20 degrees above the horizon. (He) described this object as being circular in shape, approximately one-half the (angular) size of the moon, deep bright blue in color, very vivid blue. He stated the object had a slight reddish fringe on the aft end. The object appeared to be moving from the northwest to the southeast. He stated that the object was not in his vision more than three seconds. It made no sound. (He) stated that at the time he observed this there were no clouds in the sky, the stars were out, and the moon was full.

This is one more sighting which did not get to the Blue Book sighting collection.

Ten days after this sighting, one of the assistant directors at FBI headquarters added to the file a copy of an article which appeared in the April 7 issue of *LIFE* Magazine—an issue that would not soon be forgotten (see Figure 23).

The cover of this issue was an irresistible combination of sultry sex and saucers. It shows a dreamy Marilyn, with her eyes half closed and her luxuriously loose dress slid well down below her shoulders. She was the "talk of Hollywood," the cover asserted. For those who could remove their eyes from her provocative appearance there was, in the upper right hand corner of the cover, a statement which must have come as a shock to most everyone, including the Air Force: "There is a case for interplanetary saucers." I don't know how many copies of this issue were sold, but I bet they sold a bunch!*

The case for interplanetary saucers was made in an article written by H. B. Darrach, Jr. and Robert Ginna and entitled "Have We Visitors from Space?" Next to the title was the attention-grabbing answer to this question: "The Air Force is now ready to concede that many saucer and fireball sightings still defy explanation; here *Life* offers some scientific evidence that there

---

* The issue cost only 20 cents!

Figure 23: LIFE Magazine, April 7, 1952

is a real case for interplanetary flying saucers."

The article, based on a year-long investigation by Ginna, included information directly from the Air Force file. Ginna had visited ATIC on March 3 and, with the complete cooperation of Captain Ruppelt and the Project Blue Book staff, he had reviewed sighting reports and analyses, some of which were declassified at his request. The authors also interviewed high level Air Force officials at the Pentagon. They were told that the Air Force was carrying on a "constant intelligence investigation" and would attempt to get radar and photographic data and that "attempts will be made to recover such unidentified objects." They were also told that the Air Force was, for the first time, since December 1949, inviting "all citizens to report their sightings to the nearest Air Force installation."

The authors discussed ten previously unpublished sightings (several of which have been presented) and concluded that Russian weapons, atmospheric phenomena, Skyhook balloons, secret weapons, hallucinations and psychological aberrations could not explain these cases. According to the authors, "These disclosures, sharply amending past Air Force policy, climaxed a review by *LIFE* with Air Force officials of all facts known. . ."

and "The Air Force is now ready to concede that many saucer and fireball sightings still defy explanation." Furthermore, they quoted Dr. Walther Reidel, a German rocket scientist, as saying that, in his opinion, these objects "have an out-of-this world basis." To top it off, the authors quoted an intelligence officer as saying that "The higher you go in the Air Force the more seriously they take the flying saucers." A reader of the article might well have gotten the idea that top Air Force officers were thinking *interplanetary.** The article ended with a series of questions which pointed toward the interplanetary answer:

> What power urges them at such terrible speeds through the sky? Who, or what, is aboard? Where do they come from? Why are they here? What are the intentions of the beings who control them? . . . Somewhere in the dark skies there may be those who know!

Although they did not so much as mention Major Donald Keyhoe and the startling conclusion he had published in *True* magazine two and a half years before, you can bet that he was cheering for Darrach and Ginna!

The *LIFE* magazine statement that the Air Force was taking saucers seriously was diametrically opposed to many previous public statements but, of course, the Air Force had not stated that the saucers might actually be extraterrestrial vehicles. Even in private at ATIC there was no endorsement of the interplanetary hypothesis. In a Secret monthly Status Report on the activities of Project Blue Book, dated April 30, 1952, Captain Ruppelt wrote "It should be noted here that the conclusions reached by *LIFE* are not those of the Air Force. No proof exists that these objects are from outer space."

Actually Ruppelt should have been more specific in saying that the ATIC/Project Blue Book staff did not endorse the *LIFE* conclusion because, as he admitted in *The Report on Unidentified Flying Objects*, other Air Force officials did endorse that conclusion. According to Ruppelt, some "high ranking officers

---

* This idea would be conveyed to the FBI as fact several months and many hundreds of sightings later!

in the Pentagon—so high that their personal opinion was almost policy" did believe the saucers were extraterrestrial and expressed that opinion to Mr. Ginna. At least one of these high ranking officers was none other than General Garland! Recall that Ruppelt, in his personal papers, noted that Garland had seen a UFO while he was stationed in Sacramento. Ruppelt also wrote that "(Garland) was the inspiration behind the *LIFE* article by Ginna. He gave Ginna his ideas and prompted *LIFE* to stick their necks out."

According to Project Blue Book records the *LIFE* article was mentioned in more than 350 newspapers across the United States and ATIC received 110 letters concerning the article. *LIFE* itself received more than 700 letters. The letters discussed old sightings and theories about sightings. Blue Book braced for an onslaught of new sightings that didn't come . . . at least not right away. On the day after the magazine hit the stands Blue Book received nine sightings, but then only a couple on the next day.

In the following days other publications disputed the *LIFE* article. The *New York Times* criticizing Darrach and Ginna for being "uncritical." The *New York Times* author claimed that the Project Grudge report of two years proved that all sightings could be explained. Of course he did not know that General Cabell had described the Grudge report as so much "tripe."

Ruppelt's claim that high level officers actually believed saucers were interplanetary is confirmed in an indirect way in a memorandum written on April 29, 1952. This document was written to justify a trip to Europe by Dr. Stephen Possony and Lt. Colonel Sterling, both members of a "special study group" that had been organized to study "advanced delivery systems," i.e., advanced aircraft. Possony, an Air Intelligence Specialist with high-level connections in the Pentagon, and Sterling, Chief of the Special Study Group, wanted a five-week trip to visit various military headquarters in Europe. They began their memorandum by stating that the Air Force can remain effective only by anticipating future developments of enemy weapon systems. However, they wrote, "there is no tenable and convincing estimate of future Russian delivery systems" and furthermore that "current estimates do not reflect the possibility that the Russians may have overtaken the U.S. in advanced guided missile research and development." The memorandum then describes the activities of the Special Study Group in this regard and includes a statement which shows that saucer sightings were definitely not ignored:

> The Special Study Group has undertaken a comprehensive study of Russian capabilities in the field of advanced delivery systems. This study is expected to determine the nature of such systems, their strategic implications and probable time tables as to development and operational availability. As an important side product, it is hoped that some much needed light can be shed on the vexing 'flying saucer' problem.

Obviously this memorandum justifies the trip by appealing to the "Soviet menace" in a manner similar to the previously discussed memorandum written by General Garland about four months earlier. This memorandum is unique, however, because it contains an argument against the ET hypothesis in order to make the Soviet Hypothesis seem reasonable. In essence it says that saucers could not originate from nearby planets or be from far outer space because astronomers would see them coming. However, this document also points out the difficulty with the Soviet Hypothesis:

> Nothing in this argument is designed to brush over the improbability that the Russians have such a considerable lead over the U.S. In order to fly saucers over the U.S. the Soviets would have to be at least 20 years ahead of us. They would have attained such superiority by keeping a large scale development in complete isolation, even during the last war.

In other words, the memorandum provides reasons to reject both hypotheses.

The following statement from the memorandum is the most interesting, since it reflects the thinking at the top of the Air Force:

In connection with flying saucers the Group is attempting to develop a proper framework for fruitful analysis. The Air Force cannot assume that flying saucers are of non-terrestrial origin, and hence they could be Soviet.

Whoa, there! Let's look at that last sentence again and rewrite it a bit: The (high level) Air Force (officers) cannot (simply) assume that flying saucers are of non-terrestrial (i.e., of extraterrestrial) origin and (ignore them because there still is a slight possibility that) they could be Soviet (aircraft). The fact that Possony and Sterling included this statement in their memorandum means that the "impossible" may have been true: *top Air Force officers assumed that saucers were interplanetary and therefore disregarded the Soviet secret weapon hypothesis.*

In order to justify his trip to Europe for saucer investigations, Possony first argued against the ET hypothesis and then he made it seem plausible that the Soviets had in some unimaginable way achieved a twenty-year lead on the U.S. in the development of advanced delivery systems. This "reverse" argument worked. He got his trip, probably because the most important person he had to convince was none other than General Garland.[*]

By the end of the April, the sighting report rate on a daily basis had picked up. Ruppelt and the Blue Book staff attributed this to the *LIFE* article and the resulting press interest. What Ruppelt didn't know was that the onslaught that would make this the year of the UFO was just beginning.

It is instructive to list the number of objects reported per month to see how this sighting flap developed.[**] According to the final report of the Air Force sponsored UFO study at the University of Colorado in 1967-1968,[***] the monthly numbers starting with

---

[*] Ruppelt characterized Possony as a "believer" who had a direct "channel" to General Samford and who traveled around the USA and Europe studying advanced weapon systems and collecting UFO reports.

[**] This is the number of objects reported by witnesses. Some of these objects were subsequently identified, so they are not all UFOs.

[***] *Scientific Study of Unidentified Flying Objects* (Bantam Books, NY; January, 1969), page 514.

September, 1951 and going through through June, 1952 are:

September: 16	April: 82
October: 24	May: 79
November: 16	June: 148
December: 12	
January: 15	
February: 17	
March: 23	

The sudden upsurge in April, May and June is obvious. What was happening? Were people going crazy? Did a magazine article and the associated publicity cause ordinary people to report any unfamiliar objects they might see in the sky? That's what ATIC and Captain Ruppelt thought, or at least that's what they said they thought, but it was clearly not the whole story.

On May 12, the FBI received another jolt: the UFOs were seen at yet another "vital installation," the Savannah River atomic bomb fuel processing plant:

FBI, Savannah URGENT 7:58 PM 5 - 12 - 52
Savannah River Plant, Atomic Energy Commission, Flying Disc. At approximately 10:45 PM, May 10, four employees of Dupont Co., employed on the Savannah River plant near Ellington, S.C., saw 4 disc shaped objects approaching the 400 area from the south, disappearing in a northerly direction. At approximately 11:05 PM, above mentioned employees saw two similar objects approach from south and disappear in northerly direction. At approximately 11:10 PM one similar object approached from the northeast and disappeared in southwesterly direction. One more object sighted about 11:15 PM traveling from south to north. Employees described objects as being about 15 inches in diameter having yellow to gold color. All of these other objects were traveling at high rate of speed at high altitude without any noise. The . . . object which approached the 400 area from the (northeast) was traveling at altitude so low it had to rise to pass over some tall tanks in 400 area. This object was also flying at a high rate of speed and noiseless. Witnesses stated observed objects weaving from left to (right) but seemed to hold general

course. Also stated due to speed and altitude they were only visible for few seconds. Savannah office is not actively conducting investigation in this matter and is furnishing this info to bureau for whatever action they deem advisable.

FBI headquarters immediately reported this to the head of the AFOSI. Project Blue Book lists this sighting as unidentified.

In early July an article in *LOOK* Magazine partially reversed its stance of a year and a half before. Recall that in the January 1951 issue, Robert Considine had trashed the subject, claiming that the Air Force had explained everything and that witnesses were essentially kooks and nuts, deluded or publicity seekers. The author of the new *LOOK* article, J. Robert Moskin, took a more positive attitude. He visited Project Blue Book two weeks after the publication of the *LIFE* article. He received full cooperation from the Blue Book staff. He quoted General Hoyt Vandenberg, the Chief of Staff of the Air Force as saying that as long as there were any unexplained sightings the Air Force would continue to study the problem. Moskin went on to summarize the Project Blue Book plans to obtain better scientific data. He pointed out that many atomic installations had been "visited" by UFOs but that there was no evidence that anyone, meaning the Russians, was spying on our country, even though "this fear still lies deeply in some responsible minds."

He also pointed out that the Air Force had given up trying to explain sightings as cold war jitters, as a result of societal tension, as a response to publicity about saucers or as mass hysteria. Instead, the Air Force was sure that the answer would be found as misinterpretations of conventional objects, optical phenomena, manmade objects or extraterrestrial objects. Regardless of what the final answer might be, it was clear from Moskin's article that the Air Force was actively investigating, verifying the claim made in the *LIFE* article two months earlier.

Although Project Blue Book, after months of organizational work, was now prepared to handle the typical flow of sightings, it was "whelmed many times over" (i.e., over-overwhelmed) by what happened in July. During previous months the sightings had been coming in at a rate of one every two days or so. In the latter half of April this increased to a rate of several per day and stayed that way until the latter half of June. Then the sighting rate increased to four per day, then five, and then ten.

During the latter half of July, however, UFO sightings were running at more than twenty per day. These were from all over the USA, as well as some from foreign countries.

The locations of the sightings read like a geography lesson. Consider, for example, the sighting activity during just two days. Between early morning July 20 and midnight July 22 there were sightings in New Jersey (7), Colorado (2), Illinois (2), Michigan (2), Pennsylvania (1), Kentucky (1), California (3), Texas (5), North Carolina (1), Florida (2), Georgia (1), Missouri (1), Massachusetts (5), Maine (1), Indiana (1), New Mexico (1), Alabama (1), Oregon (1), New Hampshire (1), South Dakota (1), New York (1), Maryland (2), Virginia (1), and Washington, D.C. (3). There were also two reports from Germany and single reports from Mexico and Morocco.

Fourteen of these fifty-one sightings were from military observers, six of whom were at Air Force Bases. From Project Blue Book's point of view the whole flying saucer mess was getting far out of hand. Figures 24A and 24B provide some examples of the frenetic press reporting of the sightings.

As if this weren't bad enough, the pot really began to boil when flying saucers were reported over the nation's Capitol! (See Figure 25.)

At least, that's the way it appeared to the experienced radar controllers at National Airport the night of Saturday, July 19 and again a week later. Several times targets were detected by two independent radars, one at National Airport (now Reagan National Airport) and one at Andrews Air Force Base. These targets appeared as strong point returns rather than as diffuse blobby images that characterize the effects of "anomalous propagations" or "radar angels."

During the sightings F-94 jets were scrambled from Newcastle Air Force Base in Delaware. Usually the scrambled aircraft did not see lights associated with the targets, but there were at least two visual confirmations. On the other hand, civilian aircraft flying in the area at the time reported several visual sightings of unusual moving lights, as did ground observers.

Figure 24A: Newspaper stories in July

The events began at about 11:40 p.m. on Saturday, July 19 when the Washington Air Route Traffic Control Center

(WARTCC) radar at National Airport detected targets which moved toward Andrews AFB (AAFB). Then at 5 minutes past midnight a phone call was received at AAFB control tower advising that there was an orange lighted object to the south. A control tower operator, while talking to the person on the phone, looked south and saw the:

> . . . orange ball of fire, trailing a tail . . . it was very bright and definite and unlike anything I had ever seen before. . . . It made a kind of circular movement . . . [then] took off at an unbelievable speed. It disappeared in a split second.

The person on the phone saw the same thing. A few seconds later the tower operator "saw another one, same description. As the one before, it made an arc-like pattern and then disappeared." During the next 25 minutes, 5 AAFB personnel saw two more lights, reddish-orange in color, moving erratically on a generally southeastward track through the eastern sky. They were seen from 5 to 30 seconds on 3 occasions. At 1:20 and again at 1:25 fast moving lights with an orange hue and a tail were seen by AAFB tower personnel. At 2:35 WARTCC received a call from an airline pilot who said he had seen 3 objects near Herndon, Virginia, west of Washington, and reported that "they were like nothing he had ever seen."

Figure 24B: Newspaper stories

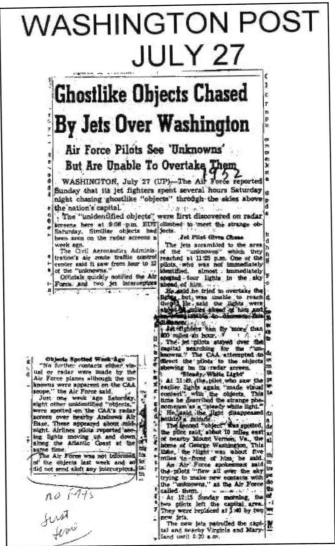

Figure 25: Saucers Over Washington

A week later, on July 25 at 9:15 p.m., WARTCC again detected from 4 to 8 anomalous targets "described by radar operators as 'good sharp targets." According to the AFOSI report, at 11:20 p.m., two F-94s were scrambled from Delaware, whereupon one of the jets:

... reportedly made visual contact with one of the objects and at first appeared to be gaining on it, but the object and the F-94 were observed on the radar scope and appeared to be traveling at the same approximate speed. However, when it attempted to overtake the object, the object disappeared both from the pursuant aircraft and the radar scope. The pilot of the F-94 remarked of the 'incredible speed of the object.'

The next night was a repeat. At 8:15 p.m., July 26, the pilot and stewardess of a National Airlines plane flying at 1,700 feet and 200 mph saw a lighted object which appeared similar to the glow of a lighted cigarette (dull red) and which passed "directly over the airliner." They estimated the object speed to be 100 mph.

At 8:54 p.m., AAFB radar began detecting 10 to 12 unidentified radar targets in the Washington area. An hour and a half later, at 10:23, WARTCC detected 4 targets at various locations in the suburbs of Washington. According to a document not released until 1985, a Civil Aeronautics Administration official flying at an altitude of 2,200 feet at 10:46 p.m. saw "5 objects giving off a light glow ranging from orange to white." The same document says, "Some commercial pilots reported visuals ranging from 'cigarette glow' (red yellow) to 'a light' (as recorded from their conversations with ARTC controllers)." At 10:38 p.m. the USAF Command post was notified of unidentified targets, and at 11:00 p.m. two F-94s were scrambled. The document says that "one pilot mentioned seeing 4 lights at one time and a second time as seeing a single light ahead but unable to close whereupon the light 'went out.'"

During the sightings on July 26 two members of the Project Blue Book staff, one of whom was a radar expert, were in the Washington area. They were notified quickly of the radar sightings and arrived at AAFB shortly after midnight. When they arrived they could see "7 good, solid targets." The radar expert checked with the airport radar and determined that there was a slight temperature inversion. The expert believed that the inversion was too weak to cause targets such as these so a second intercept flight was requested. By the time it arrived the strong

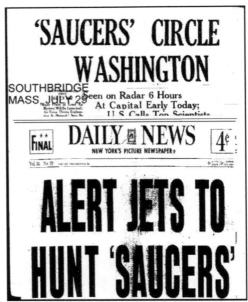

Figure 26A: More Reports and "Shoot down" orders

targets had departed. That ended the Washington, D.C. sightings but the Air Force response was only beginning.

As far as the general public was concerned the first hint of something unusual happening during the month of July was the increase in local and national press reports of saucers. Then on July 19 the national press reported the Air Force admission that people were really seeing something unusual, that the numbers of reports had doubled over what had occurred years ago and that the Air Force couldn't track all the saucers. Some details of the Saturday and Sunday, July 19-20, sightings in Washington, D.C. were leaked to the press and were reported the following Tuesday. Captain Ruppelt, who was in Dayton, Ohio, at the time, was not told about these sightings. When he arrived in Washington, D.C., on routine business on Monday, July 21, he still did not know about them. He read about them in the Tuesday morning paper and immediately began phoning people to find out what had happened because he was responsible for supplying the

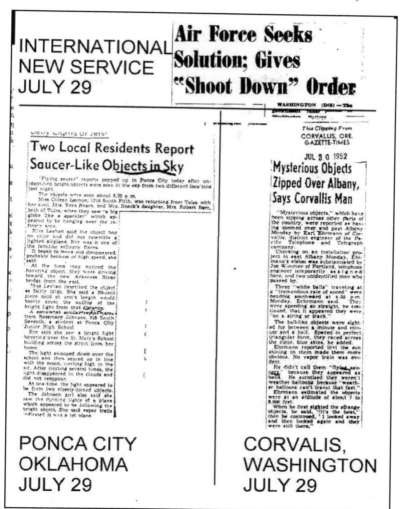

Figure 26B: More Reports and Shoot-Down Orders

technical backup for whatever the Air Force would tell the press. Unfortunately he had no answers, only questions. His predicament was not helped when a general told him that President Truman wanted to know what was going on. Apparently, some of the radar targets had been over the White House restricted area. By late in the afternoon Ruppelt had an "answer" for the press: the Air Force would have "no comment" on the sightings because investigation was ongoing. The next day the newspapers interpreted this as meaning that the Air Force "won't talk."

The press activity related to saucer sightings and Air Force investigations increased on a daily basis. Local papers throughout the country were loaded with the reports of local sightings. As just one example, the *Indianapolis News* carried the following front page headline on July 28: "Hundreds in state see 'flying saucers." The story reported that military personnel and police officers "kept a running check on saucers for more than 4 hours." See Figure 24B.

The reports of the Washington, D.C., sightings of July 25 and 26 - 27 only added to the furor. And then on July 28 newspapers across the nation carried a startling story, from the International News Service, which said that . . .

> . . . jet pilots have been placed on 24-hour 'alert' against 'flying saucers' with orders to 'shoot them down' if they refuse to land. It was learned that pilots have gone aloft on several occasions in an effort to shoot the mysterious objects to the ground but never came close enough to use their guns.

It was nearly a panic situation. What on Earth—or off the Earth—was causing all the sightings? The press and the public wanted answers, not soon, but *now*. The Air Force was about to give them some.

Several days earlier, on July 24, Lt. Colonel W. K. Smith in the Policy and Management Group of the Directorate of Intelligence had written a memorandum summarizing the situation. This memorandum was written at the request of Major General John Samford and was sent to General White, the Deputy Chief of Staff for Air Force Operations. According to this memorandum there had been "between 1000 and 1050 [reports] since 1947" and the recent influx of reports was a result of the April *LIFE* magazine article and the subsequent press coverage. The memorandum stated that "there is no significance attached to the location of these sightings other than that they are random in nature." According to Colonel Smith's notes, used in preparation of the memorandum, there were 180 unexplained sightings, only 53 of which "came from what are considered reliable sources." In other words, the fraction of unexplained sightings was nearly 20% and the "hard core" unexplained was about 5% of the total.

At the bottom of the memorandum General Samford had written a note to General White which said that a briefing by ATIC officers had been scheduled for July 29 "at such time as you may desire." As it turned out, General Samford was fortunate that he had prepared a briefing because he did give one on that date, but not to General White.

During this time, UFO reports were coming like snow in a blizzard. On July 28, ATIC received about 50 reports, of which 43 occurred on that day. The remainder were older reports that had been delayed for various reasons. Months later, the Project Blue Book staff discovered that this day had the largest daily sighting rate ever recorded by the Air Force. During the following week, the sighting rate dropped back to less than 10 per day, which was still very large. However, on July 28 Captain Ruppelt, the Project Blue Book staff and AFI didn't know the sighting rate was about to decrease; they didn't know what to expect. It may well have seemed to them that a landing or a shootdown would soon occur. What would happen after that? A war of the worlds?

July 29 began with more sightings, including one which provided further proof that radar could detect UFOs. A fighter-interceptor was flying on a routine training mission from Selfridge AFB in Michigan when ground control asked the fighter to check on an object picked up by the ground radar. This object was moving southward over Saginaw, Michigan, at a speed of about 625 mph, which was within the capability of jet fighter. Was it simply an intruding Canadian military jet?

The pilot began a right turn and the copilot picked up a radar target at 60 degrees to the right. The plane kept turning until the target was straight ahead and the radar locked on to the object. The lock-on lasted for about 30 seconds as the plane flew at high speed toward the object. The copilot determined that the object was four miles ahead and at the altitude of the plane, about

20,000 feet. The copilot later said he saw:

> . . . the target . . . putting off what seemed like a changing light in definite sequences of white, red and bluish-green. That is the only means of identification we had. From a bombardier, radar observer, navigator, I have never experienced any sighting like this before.

During this time, ground control announced that it had both the jet and the unidentified target on the radar screen. Then suddenly the object broke the airplane's radar lock. Before the jet could react, the object reversed its course. Ground radar, which had been tracking both the jet and the unidentified target, was startled to see the unidentified target make a 180 degree turn and head northward toward Canada. The F-94 gave chase but could not catch up as the unknown increased and decreased its speed in an erratic manner. The top speed of the unidentified was unknown because the radar only determined its location once every 10 seconds (the radar rotation rate). However, typically it would travel about 4 miles during that time (4 miles/10 seconds = 1,440 mph). This was about twice the top speed of the jet.

The jet followed the object for about 20 minutes, then radioed that it was running low on fuel and would have to break off the chase. The jet turned home, at which point the ground control saw the speed of the unknown suddenly drop back to its original value. Months later Blue Book would leave this as an unexplained case. Two of the other sightings on the morning of July 29 occurred near Roswell, New Mexico and at Los Alamos. The Los Alamos sighting resulted in a scramble from Kirtland, AFB.

Meanwhile back in Washington, the press was in an uproar because of the July 28 announcement that the Air Force had directed pilots to shoot if necessary. Did the Air Force really mean it? Were things out of control? Had any saucer been shot down? What would the Air Force do if one were shot down?

Everyone wanted answers and General Nathan Twining was about to give some. Twining, the head of AMC in 1947, had left that post in January 1948 (General Benjamin Chidlaw replaced him) and was now the Chief of Staff of the Air Force, having replaced General Vandenberg. Twining ordered Samford to hold

Figure 27: The Air Force Explains. General
John Samford.

a press conference to outline the official Air Force position
regarding Unidentified Flying Objects.

During the morning of July 29, General Samford's press
officer announced that a flying saucer conference would be held
at the Pentagon late that afternoon. General Samford was about
to give to the assembled press part of the briefing that had been
prepared for General White. He was also about to accomplish in
public what Vandenberg had accomplished in private four years
earlier: General Samford would put a major damper on interest
in UFO sightings by telling the press that, in his opinion, none of
the reported saucers was an interplanetary vehicle. What he
didn't say was what Air Force Intelligence, his office, told the
FBI on this same day.

At 4 p.m. the longest post-WWII press conference to that date
began. It lasted 80 minutes. General Samford brought with him
several military experts in radar, Captain Ruppelt, and Major

General Roger Ramey—mentioned in the first chapter of this book. Ramey had been the head of the Eighth Air Force when he invented and publicized the weather balloon explanation for the Roswell crash debris. Now he was in charge of Operations of the Air Defense Command.

General Samford told the assembled press that because American secret weapons did not cause the sightings the Air Force was obligated to investigate them. He further said:

> We have received and analyzed between 1,000 and 2,000 reports that have come to us from all kinds of sources. Of this great mass of reports we have been able adequately to explain the great bulk of them, explain them to our own satisfaction. However there have been a certain percentage of this volume of reports that have been made by credible observers of relatively incredible things. It is this group of observations that we are now attempting to resolve. We have, as of this date, come to only one firm conclusion with respect to this remaining percentage, and that is that it does not contain any pattern of purpose or of consistency that we can relate to any conceivable threat to the United States.

General Samford gave few explicit answers to the questions from the press. The discussion concentrated on the Washington sightings even though the General and his support team did not have all the information needed to decide what caused them. General Ramey provided some information about the jet scrambles and General Samford advanced the opinion, ostensibly based on the work of Air Force radar experts, that an atmospheric "inversion" had caused the radar targets. Various members of the press pushed hard to get a definite answer as opposed to an opinion, but he would not give a definite answer. He did say the Air Force was giving all reports "adequate but not frantic checks."

General Samford rejected the interplanetary theory, implying that all the unexplained sightings were the results of natural phenomena. However, he could not be pinned down as to which natural phenomena. Whenever he was questioned about specific sightings, he would plead a lack of information. There were no actual witnesses at the conference, not even the Blue Book staff members who were in the control tower at AAFB during the July 26-27 sightings.* Because of this, members of the press could not directly confront the General with witness testimony. Some of the reporters were aware of sightings by military personnel and of sightings near the "vital installations." They asked the General about these, but he pleaded a lack of information. The most they could do was get him to admit that about 20 percent of the sightings were unknown, an admission which was, by itself, quite startling.

The next day, the national press (in front page headlines) distilled the whole conference down to the simple answer which the Air Force wanted the public to believe about the Washington, D.C. sightings: summer heat had warmed the air above the earth's surface and caused temperature inversions which, in turn, caused the unidentified radar targets. And that was it.

Most members of the press, being skeptical of saucer sightings and not being radar experts, accepted this simple answer, albeit with reservations. A few news articles expressed a minority viewpoint that the Air Force was trying to debunk the whole phenomenon. Drew Pearson, a famous columnist, pointed out that the Air Force had now admitted for the first time that radar detections had occurred at the same time as visual observations. Pearson went so far as to suggest the objects might be from another planet. Other dissenting press organizations did not go that far, but did criticize the Air Force for boasting about scientific advances when it was clear the Air Force did not completely understand the saucer phenomenon.

During the following days and weeks, there were scientists and radar experts who publicly disputed the General's explanation of the Washington sightings. However, their arguments did not carry the weight of the pronouncements of General Samford and his staff. No one outside the Air Force had all the information, so

---

* Those staff members had indicated that the radar targets were like strong aircraft returns and not like diffuse "anomalous propagation" targets.

Figure 28: It's All Hot Air!

his explanation could not be carefully examined for accuracy. When interviewed many years later, the air traffic controllers who were involved at the time still rejected the official explanation, saying that they were thoroughly familiar with the types of radar images which appear during periods of anomalous propagation, and the images seen that night emphatically were not anomalous propagation images.

Perhaps the Air Force felt that General Samford's conference was not enough to dampen the saucer frenzy. General Vandenberg was interviewed a day later and expressed his dismay at the continued "mass hysteria about flying saucers." Vandenberg told the press that the objects were not extraterrestrial craft nor secret weapons. He said that the Air Force had been investigating reports for several years and had found no convincing evidence. Then General Ramey appeared on television. He repeated what Samford had said at the big press conference and admitted the Air Force had been forced to come up with some quick answers to prevent a public panic. And sightings continued (see Figures 29, 30 and 31.)

To the outside world it may have seemed that the Air Force had everything under control. Not so, to the inside world. If the press had known what General Samford's staff was telling other "insiders" on the same day as the press conference the lid would have blown off the UFO cover-up.

Figure 29: More Saucer Stories

Jenner Assails Demos On Flying Saucer Bungling

Aerial "Mystery" Will Now Become Political Issue

French Lick, Ind., Aug. 1 (INS)—America's flying saucer mystery has become a political issue in the 1952 campaign, with charges that the Truman administration either has been unprepared to learn the origin of the saucers of that it has deceived the public.

The charges were made last night by Senator William E. Jenner in an address before the Indiana Trailer Coach Association at French Lick.

Jenner said:

"THE AMERICAN people don't know anything positive about the so-called flying saucers except that —once again—the Truman administration appears to have been caught flat-footed. For many months now, there have been reports that seemed to be much more than mere rumors regarding the saucers. But what has the administration, with all of its multi-billion-dollar facilities for military preparedness and research done about them?

"Not until now, it seems, has Washington taken the saucers seriously. Not until they were reported right over the White House itself has the little man with the world's biggest expense account chosen to bestir himself. Now—at long last—we get reports of frenzied activity by the pentagon to look into the matter. Washington is in such a dither that we have around-the-clock radar and jet interceptor watches set up to learn something about the illusive lights.

"IT IS ENTIRELY possible, of course, that some branch of our military service has been secretly experimenting with the saucers, and that they are devices of our own. But if that is so, then the administration has gone to great lengths to delude the people, to confuse the people, and now to drive many of them toward a state of near-panic."

Jenner then said:

"We have, then, either unpreparedness or deceit, both of which are typical of the Truman ˙ ˙ ˙ ˙d of bad government."

Figure 30:
Saucers a Political Issue

Figure 31: More Press Reports

Chapter 20
Ships from Another Planet

On July 29, several hours before General Samford's press conference, Gilbert Levy, Chief of the Counter Intelligence Division of the Office of the Inspector General of the AFOSI, decided to contact AFI to find out how the press had learned so much about the Washington, D.C. sightings. He may have wondered if someone had broken security and leaked the information. He reported the result of his investigation to General Carroll, the Director of AFOSI. His report is contained in the AFOSI section of the Blue Book file that was released in 1975:

1) In light of recent wide publicity concerning the [radar sightings at National Airport] I caused a check to be made for the purpose of determining the basis of recent releases to news media.

2) We were advised by the Current Intelligence Branch, Estimates Division, AFOIN, [i.e., General Samford's office], which has staff responsibility with respect to these reports, that much of the publicity of the past few days is the result of a radar sighting of unidentified aerial objects by the Civil Aeronautics Administration at National Airport at 2115 hours, 25 July 1952. These sightings continued from 2115 hours, 25 July until 0010 hours on 26 July, and were described by radar operators as "good sharp targets." They were observed in numbers from four to eight.

3) At 2320 hours, 25 July 1952, two (2) Air Force F-94s were dispatched from New Castle AFB, Delaware, for the purpose of intercepting objects which have been sighted by radar. One of the F-94s reportedly made visual contact with one of the objects and at first appeared to be gaining on it, but the object and the F-94 were observed on the radar scope and appeared to be traveling at the same approximate speed. However, when it attempted to overtake the object, the object disappeared both from the pursuant aircraft and the radar scope. The pilot of the F-94 remarked of (sic) the 'incredible speed of the object.'

4) The Director of Intelligence advises that no theory exists at the

present time as to the origin of the objects and they are considered to be unexplained. Much of the publicity has been based on authorized news releases by the Air Force.

Oops! Now the cat is out of the bag. Reread paragraph 4: the Director of Intelligence said that no theory exists to explain the sightings which are considered to be unexplained. That's not what he told the press only a few hours later.

In the absence of any other information, one might assume that this is a mistake. Perhaps Mr. Levy misunderstood what the General had told him. However, there is other information which is consistent with what Mr. Levy wrote. In fact, much more information was withheld from the American people until it was released in the FBI *X File*.

On the same day, and perhaps even at about the same time, as Mr. Levy's contact with AFI, the FBI also asked AFI for information about the sightings. Mr. N. W. Philcox, the FBI liaison with the Air Force, arranged through General Samford's office to be briefed by "Commander Randall Boyd of the Current Intelligence Branch, Estimates Division, Air Intelligence, regarding research into the numerous reports regarding flying saucers and flying discs."* This is what Mr. Philcox was told.

> Commander Boyd advised that Air Intelligence has set up at Wright-Patterson Air Force Base, Ohio, the Air Technical Intelligence Center which has been established for the purpose of coordinating, correlating and making research into all reports regarding flying saucers and flying discs. He advised that Air Force research has indicated that the sightings of flying saucers goes back several centuries and that the number of sightings reported varies with the amount of publicity. He advised that immediately if publicity appears in newspapers, the number of sightings reported increases considerably and that citizens immediately call in reporting sightings which occurred several months previously.

Commander Boyd erred in his statement that ATIC was set up to investigate saucer sightings. ATIC was set up at Wright

---

* This is exactly the same branch that provided the above information to Mr. Levy!

Patterson Air Force Base with the mission to investigate all foreign aviation technology, particularly Russian aircraft. Blue Book was a project involving some of the ATIC personnel. Commander Boyd's claim that the number of sighting reports was correlated to press reporting on the subject was a statement of belief on the part of the Blue Book staff, but it had not been proven true. In fact, important evidence to the contrary would occur within days of this statement as the press kept up a barrage of sighting stories while the sighting rate actually dropped precipitously.

Continuing with Agent Philcox's report:

> Commander Boyd stated that these reported sightings of flying saucers are placed into three classifications by Air Intelligence:
>
> 1) Those sightings which are reported by citizens who claim that they have seen flying saucers from the ground. These sightings vary in description, color and speeds. Very little credence is given to these sightings inasmuch as in most instances they are believed to be imaginative or some explainable object which actually crossed through the sky.
>
> 2) Sightings reported by commercial or military pilots. These sightings are considered more credible by the Air Force inasmuch as commercial or military pilots are experienced in the air and are not expected to see objects which are entirely imaginative. In each of these instances, the individual who reports the sighting is thoroughly interviewed by a representatve of Air Intelligence so that a complete description of the object sighted can be obtained.
>
> 3) Those sightings which are reported by pilots and for which there is additional corroboration, such as recording by radar or sighting from the ground. Commander Boyd advised that this latter classification constitutes two or three per cent of the total number of sightings, but that they were the most difficult to explain. Some of these sightings are originally reported from the ground, then are picked up by radar instruments. He stated that in these instances there is no doubt that these individuals reporting the sightings actually did see something in the sky. However, he explained that these objects could still be natural phenomena and still could be recorded on radar if there was some electrical disturbance in the sky.

Commander Boyd stated that about 3% of sightings constitute

the "hard core" of the phenomenon. This percentage agrees closely with the approximately 5% (53 sightings out of about 1,000) which Colonel W. Smith said on July 24 came from "reliable sources" (see last chapter).

Although not a large percentage, these were the sightings, a few of which have already been presented in this book, which absolutely could not be explained without resort to such bizarre hypotheses as the idea that several witnesses could all go insane or hallucinate the same vision at the same time, perhaps even at the same time that instruments (e.g. radar, theodolite telescopes) malfunction, and then immediately after the sighting the witnesses and instruments would be normal again.

Commander Boyd did not tell the FBI that at that time the fraction of unexplained sightings was about 20%, which included the 3% "hard core" sightings. Presumably the other 17% unexplained sightings had elements or features which would allow them to be possibly explained if enough reasonable assumptions about erroneous reporting were made. The hard core 3%, on the other hand, required unreasonable assumptions before any explanation could be offered (see Figure 32).

Agent Philcox's report continued:

> He stated that the flying saucers are most frequently observed in areas where there is heavy air traffic, such as Washington, D.C. and New York City. He advised however, that some reports are received from other parts of the country covering the United States and that sightings have also recently been reported as far distant as Acapulco, Mexico; Korea and French Morocco.

It is amusing to note Commander Boyd's claim that saucers were most often seen in areas of high air traffic, which typically are areas of dense population, because one of the reasons offered against the reality of flying saucers was this: "If saucers are real, why are they only seen by the unsophisticated witnesses in the countryside and not over cities?" The Battelle Memorial Institute study, which was going on even as Commander Boyd spoke, discovered many months later that there was a degree of correlation between the number of sightings and areas with military and

233

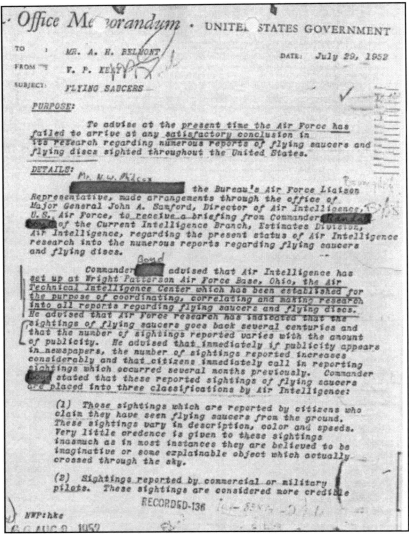

Figure 32A: FBI Report on AFI Opinion

civilian airports. However, this does not mean that there were more misidentified aircraft reported as saucers in the vicinity of airports. Instead, the correlation may have resulted from a greater tendency of people living near airports to look upward and see the saucers.

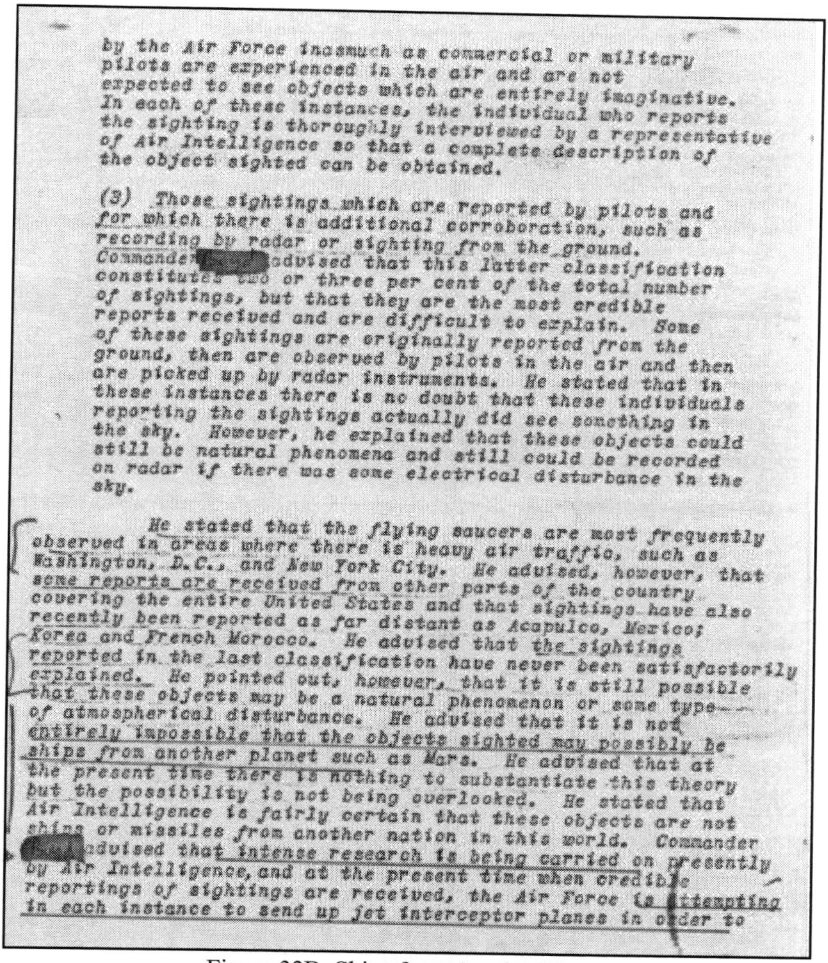

by the Air Force inasmuch as commercial or military
pilots are experienced in the air and are not
expected to see objects which are entirely imaginative.
In each of these instances, the individual who reports
the sighting is thoroughly interviewed by a representative
of Air Intelligence so that a complete description of
the object sighted can be obtained.

(3) Those sightings which are reported by pilots and
for which there is additional corroboration, such as
recording by radar or sighting from the ground.
Commande███████advised that this latter classification
constitut██ two or three per cent of the total number
of sightings, but that they are the most credible
reports received and are difficult to explain. Some
of these sightings are originally reported from the
ground, then are observed by pilots in the air and then
are picked up by radar instruments. He stated that in
these instances there is no doubt that these individuals
reporting the sightings actually did see something in
the sky. However, he explained that these objects could
still be natural phenomena and still could be recorded
on radar if there was some electrical disturbance in the
sky.

He stated that the flying saucers are most frequently
observed in areas where there is heavy air traffic, such as
Washington, D.C., and New York City. He advised, however, that
some reports are received from other parts of the country
covering the entire United States and that sightings have also
recently been reported as far distant as Acapulco, Mexico;
Korea and French Morocco. He advised that the sightings
reported in the last classification have never been satisfactorily
explained. He pointed out, however, that it is still possible
that these objects may be a natural phenomenon or some type
of atmospherical disturbance. He advised that it is not
entirely impossible that the objects sighted may possibly be
ships from another planet such as Mars. He advised that at
the present time there is nothing to substantiate this theory
but the possibility is not being overlooked. He stated that
Air Intelligence is fairly certain that these objects are not
ships or missiles from another nation in this world. Commander
████████advised that intense research is being carried on presently
by Air Intelligence, and at the present time when credible
reportings of sightings are received, the Air Force is attempting
in each instance to send up jet interceptor planes in order to

Figure 32B: Ships from Another Planet

When, in 1973, I decided to make a graph of the number of
sightings in an area as a function of the population in the same
area I discovered, using data from the Battelle Memorial Institute, that there was little or no correlation. That is, an area with
several hundred thousand people could have the same number of
sightings over the years as an area with millions of people. That
is not what would be expected if the skeptics were correct in
saying that many sighting reports were "people generated," that
is from psychopathological people who reported hallucinations

or other mental aberrations. The number of reports such as these would be correlated with the population.

Continuing with Agent Philcox's report:

He advised that the sightings in the last category (category 3 above) have never been satisfactorily explained. He pointed out, however, that it is still possible that these objects may be a natural phenomenon or some type of atmospheric disturbance. He advised that it is not entirely impossible that the objects sighted *may possibly be ships from another planet such as Mars*. [emphasis added] He advised that at the present time there is nothing to substantiate this theory but the possibility is not being overlooked. He stated that Air Intelligence is fairly certain that these objects are not ships or missiles from another nation in this world. Commander Boyd advised that intense research is being carried on presently by Air Intelligence, and at the present time when credible reportings of sightings are received, the Air Force is attempting in each instance to send up jet interceptor planes in order to obtain a better view of these objects. However, recent attempts in this regard have indicated that when the pilot in the jet approaches the object it invariably fades from view.

Oops, again! Another cat out of the bag? Ships from another planet? If the press had found out what General Samford's staff had told the FBI there would have been an explosion at the press conference.

In retrospect, it appears that the good General was not being totally truthful when he implied that there was no evidence for the interplanetary hypothesis and then stated that the Washington sightings could be explained as temperature inversions and implied that all sightings would be explained as natural phenomena. There is no theory to explain these, Mr. Levy was told. Surely Samford knew what his staff knew. Did he publicly reject the interplanetary hypothesis to calm down the saucer hysteria? Or did he reject it because the Top Brass didn't want the American public to know that some Unidentified Flying Objects were identifiable . . . as ET craft?

By early August the UFO flap was tapering off. The sighting rate generally exceeded ten per day from July 19 through August 3. After that it dropped to five to ten per day through the rest of

August. By the end of September it was below five per day even though the publicity about the sightings continued at a high level. Months later the Project Blue Book staff determined that the sighting rate had in fact peaked about the time of the order to shoot and just before the press conference. Could it be that the saucers reacted to the fact that jet aircraft were now pursuing them whenever possible?

Although the sighting rate was diminishing, Air Force investigative activity continued at a high rate. At ATIC there were 8 full time people working on the sightings and the Battelle Memorial Institute had assigned 2 full time employees. There was also a panel of experts to be called upon as needed. The FBI officially learned of the high level of activity on August 15 when the AFOSI told the FBI it would accept reports and transmit them to Wright Patterson Air Force Base. A few days later the AFOSI liaison at Bolling Air Force Base contacted FBI headquarters and requested that any information be telephoned to him immediately. According to a memorandum dated August 18:

> . . . the Air Force is greatly concerned about (flying saucers) and would appreciate the Bureau's cooperation in immediately advising of details received concerning such complaints.

A few days after that, a review of communications from the field offices showed that the local FBI agents were not following the instructions issued in 1947 and 1949 to report sightings to the local AFOSI offices, so a new SAC letter, #83, was issued on August 29 to reiterate the instructions. The same letter pointed out the FBI should do no more than collect the basic sighting information to forward to the AFOSI because the investigation of such reports was the responsibility of the Air Force, not the FBI.

On August 26, the Air Force contacted the FBI with a rather strange request: please analyze a hat that was burned by a flying saucer!

The burning occurred after dark on August 19 in Florida. A scoutmaster named "Sonny" Desvergers and three boy scouts were driving a car near West Palm Beach when they saw a lighted object descend quickly into some woods across a field.

Sonny felt that he had to stop in the event that it was a crashed airplane. Before he left the boys to walk into the woods, he told them if he didn't return in ten minutes they should walk to the nearest phone and alert the police. As Desvergers approached the edge of the woods, the boys could see the light from his flashlight. Then another light appeared and reddish ball of fire moved downward and seemed to knock Desvergers down. Then a reddish thing like a disc moved upward and disappeared. The boys panicked and ran to a farm where the farmer phoned the police. The deputy sheriff and another officer arrived about half an hour later, in time to see Sonny stumbling out of the woods. He said he had been knocked unconscious by a flying saucer. The deputy sheriff said that Desvergers looked terrified. As they rode to the sheriff's office, Desvergers noted that his arms and face and the cap he had on his head were all burned. It was this cap which showed up at the FBI testing laboratory.

The FBI found no residue on the cap and no way to explain the burning. They did not think it had been burned by a flame. The boy scouts testified that the cap seemed to be in perfect condition before the event. Captain Ruppelt investigated this case and sent soil samples to the Battelle Memorial Instititute for analysis. It was found that the grass above water in this marshy area seemed healthy but the roots had been burned.

Ruppelt and the Project Blue Book staff discovered that people who knew Desvergers did not trust him. Many people thought he had made up the sighting. The Air Force investigators decided that the scouts probably had misidentified aircraft lights or something else and had not really seen a flying disc in the woods. Consequently they decided that the sighting was probably a hoax. However, they never did explain the burned cap and the burned roots!

The FBI did not want the public to know about its minimal involvement with the saucer phenomenon. Therefore, when an article appeared in the *New Yorker* magazine on September 6 stating that the FBI conducted certain inquiries for the Air Force, the FBI contacted several of the AFOSI offices and the office of

General Samford to find out who had leaked the information. No one knew where the reporter might have gotten the impression that the FBI investigated sightings. The FBI contacted ATIC. Captain Ruppelt responded that ATIC did not in any way implicate the FBI and he offered his opinion that the reporter had made it up. He also said that, so far as he knew, the FBI had never been called upon to furnish saucer information.* Finally the FBI contacted the Air Force public affairs officer. He, too, denied giving the reporter any information about the FBI. The FBI never did learn where the reporter got his information or whether Ruppelt was correct is assuming that the reporter simply made it up.

While the FBI was trying to get its field agents straightened out on how to handle the saucer business and, at the same time, not reveal its minimal but secret involvement, the sighting rate slowed. It did not stop, however. To get an overview of what had happened, consider the number of sighted objects for every month from April through December:

April: 82   September: 124
May: 79   October: 61
June: 148   November: 50
July: 536   December: 42
August: 326

Clearly something strange had happened, with the maximum strangeness occurring in July and August. Adding all the sightings of 1952 together gave a total of 1,501 objects sighted for the year—the year of the UFO.

Needless to say, the Blue Book and Battelle analysts were kept busy. The time lag between a sighting and its analysis could be months. Such was the case with a very famous photographic sighting that occurred on July 2, 1952, a sighting which had a major impact on the insiders.

---

* His incorrect belief that the FBI had never investigated was published in the book he wrote three years later.

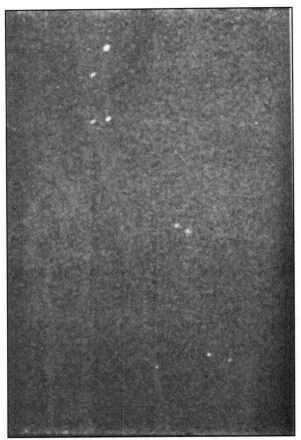

Figure 33: One frame from the film of Delbert
Newhouse, July 2, 1952.

Navy Warrant Officer and Chief Photographer Delbert
Newhouse and his wife were driving through Utah on their way
to California. They were were about seven miles west of
Tremonton when Mrs. Newhouse saw some strange looking
objects moving erratically through the sky. She pointed them out
to her husband. After 21 years in the Navy and 2,000 hours as an
aerial photographer he knew what ordinary objects in the sky
looked like, and these weren't ordinary. According to Newhouse,
they were circular and looked like two pie pans, one inverted on
top of the lower one. He hurried to get his movie camera out of

the trunk of his car. During this time, the objects were moving away from him and by the time he got the camera going they were quite far away. They made small images on the film, with no particular features. [See Figure 33]

Newhouse turned his film over to the Navy for evaluation right away. The Air Force photo lab at Wright-Patterson AFB also studied the film. After several weeks of work they ruled out birds, balloons and other aircraft. No one knew what they were. Word of this extraordinary evidence worked its way up through the ranks and finally showed up in the *X File*. An FBI memorandum, shown in Figure 34, written on October 27 reads as follows:

Air Intelligence advised of another creditable and unexplainable sighting of flying saucers. Air Intelligence still feels flying saucers are optical illusions or other atmospheric phenomena but some military officials are seriously considering the possibility of interplanetary ships.

You will recall that Air Intelligence has previously kept the Bureau advised regarding developments pertaining to Air Intelligence research on the flying saucer problem. Air Intelligence has previously advised that all research pertaining to this problem is handled by the Air Technical Intelligence Center located at Wright-Patterson Air Force Base, Dayton, Ohio; that approximately 90 per cent of the reported sightings of flying saucers can be discounted as products of the imagination and as explainable objects such as weather balloons, etc., but that a small percentage of extremely creditable sightings have been unexplainable.

Colonel C. M. Young, Executive Officer to Major General John A. Samford, Director of Intelligence, Air Force, advised on October 23, 1952, that another recent extremely creditable sighting had been reported to Air Intelligence. A Navy photographer, while traveling across the United States in his own car, saw a number of objects in the sky which appeared to be flying saucers. He took approximately thirty-five feet of motion picture film of these objects. He voluntarily submitted the film to Air Intelligence who had it studied by the Air Technical Intelligence Center. Experts at the Air Technical Intelligence Center have advised that, after careful study, there were as many as twelve to sixteen flying objects recorded on this film; that the possibility of weather balloons, clouds or other explainable objects has been completely ruled out; and that they are at a complete

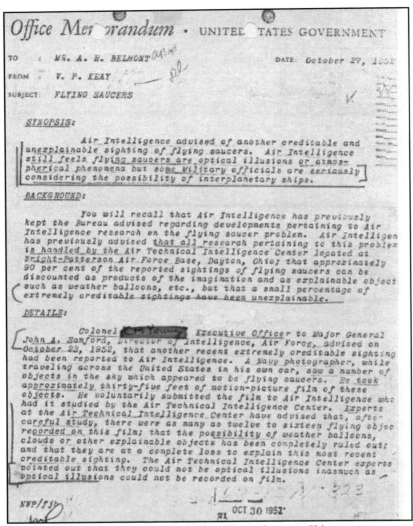

Figure 34A: A Possibility of Interplanetary Ships

loss to explain this most recent creditable sighting. The Air Technical Intelligence Center experts pointed out that they could not be optical illusions inasmuch as optical illusions could not be recorded on film.

Colonel Young advised that Air Intelligence still feels that the so-called flying saucers are either optical illusions or atmospheric phenomena. He pointed out, however, that some Military officials are seriously considering the possibility of interplanetary ships.

Memo to Mr. A. H. Belmont
from V. P. Keay   RE: FLYING SAUCERS

                    Young,
        Colonel ▓▓▓▓▓ advised that Air Intelligence still feels
that the so-called flying saucers are either optical illusions or
atmospherical phenomena. He pointed out, however, that some
Military officials are seriously considering the possibility of
interplanetary ships.

ACTION:

        None. This is for your information.

Figure 34B: A Possibility of Interplanetary Ships

Oops, again! Military officials are seriously considering interplanetary ships? Had this been published in the newspapers in 1952, the history of the UFO subject would have been quite different.

This FBI report clearly indicates the confusion within the middle ranks of the Air Force as to what was really going on. Experts in film analysis had ruled out optical illusions or atmospheric phenomena as an explanation for this film, and subsequent analysis has proven that optical illusions and atmospheric phenomena could not have explained this sighting. Nevertheless, the Air Force was holding out the hope—that's the only way one can explain it, hope—that saucer sightings could be explained as optical illusions and atmospheric phenomena.

However, at times it must have appeared there was little hope. Things looked bleak for the explainers. At a January 23, 1953 briefing for the Air Defense Command (ADC) on the status of UFO investigations, the Project Blue Book personnel admitted in private what they would never say publicly. Based on a statistical breakdown of about 1,000 sightings received through military channels in 1952 the Blue Book staff concluded that—incredibly— only 11% of the reports could be positively identified. These reports fell into the categories astronomical, balloons, aircraft, other and hoaxes. Most of the remaining sightings were labeled probably identified (17%), possibly identified (29%) and unknown (20%). There was also a separate category for sightings which were indeterminate. That is, they couldn't make a definite decision as to whether or not these sightings were identifiable because of "insufficient information" (23%). Considering that a large proportion of these sightings had been generated by ADC personnel (pilots, air traffic controllers, etc.) on duty at the times of their sightings, the ADC officials, who were in charge of protecting the USA from a Soviet attack, must have been sorely dismayed to learn how many sightings were not immediately identifiable.

It is to be noted, by the way, that the low percentage of positive identifications was not public knowledge. Whenever public statements were issued regarding the percentages of unknowns and knowns, the possible, probable and insufficient information cases were all added to the positively identified cases, thereby creating a statistic which showed the largest portion of sightings (roughly 80%) as identified, and the public was given the impression that these were "positive" identifications. The Air Force, appealing to the "logic" of the situation (based on the assumption that there was no evidence to show saucers were real), would then claim that the unknown sightings could have been explained, too, if there had been more information about them. In other words, they essentially reclassified the unknowns as insufficient information even though there was a separate category for indeterminate cases and the unknowns could have been placed into that category initially, if the analysts had thought there was not enough information for a clear decision for or against identification.

After learning what happened in 1952, one wonders just how many times the saucers would have to beat the Air Force over the head before it would admit they were real. Could it be that the people having delusions were not the witnesses but the Air Force intelligence experts who so desperately wanted to disbelieve the information which was pouring in from all over the United States—the evidence that was right in front of their noses?

Or was this denial of evidence effectively orchestrated from above, from the top of the military and government command structure in order to cover up something about flying saucers that certain government officials didn't want people to know?

Another secret government agency decided it was time to find out just what was going on. Too bad this agency contacted the Air Force first, before doing its own independent investigation.

Chapter 21
FBI Employee Sighting

Over the next few years the FBI received one or two reports per year (while the Air Force was still receiving hundreds per year). Two of these are worthy of mention. The first of these was reported to the FBI about a year later by one of the bureau's employees.

...........(name censored) on 4/9/56 reported the following rather unusual occurrence which is in the 'flying saucer' category. On 4/5/56 (......) left Washington by car with her fiance (.....) (employee of the National Security Agency), to go to Morven, North Carolina to meet the (.....) family. Around 5 a.m. on 4/6/56 as dawn was breaking and while driving on Route 1 north of Henderson, North Carolina, the pair was startled by what appeared to be a round low-flying object coming directly toward the car. The object appeared to pass over the car and (....) turned to see it appear to speed up and then veer off out of sight. She and (....) both felt they had seen something unusual which was difficut to explain and certainly did not appear to be an optical illusion. (...) stated that the object as she saw it appeared round, was spinning and was bright as though containing a series of lights in a zig-zag pattern. The object appeared to be flying very low as it came toward them, moving at a great speed and gave off no particular sound. The object, to the best of her belief, was at least as wide as the highway and appeared no more than two to four feet in thickness. (....) who is one of our best employees, stated heretofore she has placed little credence in 'flying saucer' stories and felt that had she and her boyfriend not seen the same object she would be inclined to think she had imagined something. She appreciates that what they saw may have been some kind of optical illusion; however, at the time, the object appeared very real to them.

The FBI decided that she should be interviewed again before passing the information on to the Air Force. On April 12 she reviewed the information from the April 9 interview and then added the following information:

> She advised she had seen the object for only a few seconds, that it
> was still dark when she observed it, although it was near daylight on
> April 6, 1956. She stated when daylight came she observed the sky
> to be cloudy and it started raining approximately 30 minutes after she
> had observed the object. She recalled the object had approached their
> car on the driver's side from straight ahead at a height which she
> thought to be less than 25 feet. She was unable to estimate the speed
> of the object. She described it as being oval shaped, being very bright
> and having a light blue color. It made no sound that she could hear.
> She advised her fiance would be able to state exactly where they had
> observed the object in North Carolina, inasmuch as he was familiar
> with that area. She was unable to recall any additional pertinent
> information.

On August 16 the FBI wrote a letter based on the above
information to Air Force intelligence. However, this appears to
be yet another credible sighting that fell through the cracks. It
does not appear in the Project Blue Book sighting file.

During the late 1950s and 1960s the FBI typically received
between zero and two "complaints" a year. Meanwhile, as
pointed out before, Project Blue Book received hundreds of
sightings, except in 1957, 1965, 1966 and 1967 when the totals
were even greater (around 1,000 each of those years). Although
the FBI was not very active in collecting sighting reports, it did
receive and respond to letters from the general public, it did
investigate a few cases, and it did keep track of some of the
prominent UFO groups and personalities.

The last case investigated by an FBI agent is worthy of mention
because it became one of the most important sightings in the
history of the UFO phenomenon. This case was the "last straw"
for Dr. J. Allen Hynek, who was the astronomy consultant to
Projects Sign and Blue Book from 1948 through 1969. Until this
case he had remained very skeptical of the idea that flying
saucers and UFOs were evidence of ET visitations. This case
shook his confidence. Although he still doubted that saucers were
craft from other planets, he was now certain that the UFO
problem deserved a better investigation than the Air Force was

giving it. One effect of this case was that after Project Blue Book closed in 1969, Dr. Hynek decided to start a research group of his own, the Center for UFO Studies, which he founded in 1973. It exists today as the J. Allen Hynek Center for UFO Studies. Hynek died in 1986.

Hynek was not the only person who was intrigued by this sighting. Major Hector Quintanilla, Jr., the Director of Project Blue Book at the time, was so impressed that he wrote about it in a 1967 issue of the classified version of the CIA journal, *Studies in Intelligence*. The fact that an FBI agent was almost immediately on the scene and conducted an in-depth interview, even though "unofficial," was an important factor in establishing the credibility of this case.

Chapter 22
The Policeman's Sighting

It had been several years since the FBI received a sighting of any importance when suddenly on April 25, 1964, the teletype machine at the Washington headquarters began to chatter out an urgent message [see Figure 35]:

5:37 PM MOUNTAIN STANDARD TIME 4 - 25 - 64 URGENT
TO: DIRECTOR, FBI
FROM SAC, ALBUQUERQUE 62 - NEW MEXICO
UNIDENTIFIED FLYING OBJECT. SOCORRO, N.M. APR TWENTY FOUR, NINETEEN SIXTY FOUR
INFORMATION CONCERNING
    INFORMATION RECEIVED APR TWENTY FOUR AND TWENTY FIVE, FROM (police officer) LONNIE ZAMORA, CONSIDERED SOBER, DEPENDABLE, MATURE, NOT OF FANTASY, (Zamora's address) SOCORRO, THAT AT ABOUT FIVE FIFTY PM MST, WHILE IN SOUTH AREA OF SOCORRO NOTED FLAME IN SKY TO SOUTHWEST, WHICH HE DECIDED TO CHECK OUT IN BELIEF DYNAMITE SHACK IN AREA HAD BLOWN UP.
    WHILE TRAVELING IN ISOLATED AREA APPROXI-MATELY ONE MILE SOUTH AREA OF SOCORRO, NOTED IN DEPRESSION ABOUT EIGHT HUNDRED FEET AWAY WHITISH OBJECT WHICH, UPON GLANCING AT SAME, APPEARED TO BE OVERTURNED AUTOMOBILE. TWO PERSONS IN APPARENT WHITE COVERALLS WERE ADJA-CENT TO OBJECT.
    THEN TRAVELED OVER ROUGH ROAD TO SPOT ABOUT ONE HUNDRED THREE FEET FROM OBJECT AND ABOUT TWENTY TO TWENTY FIVE FEET HIGHER. NO PERSONS VISIBLE. HEARD TWO OR THREE LOUD THUMPS, LESS THAN A SECOND APART, THEN WITH A ROAR AND BLUISH AND ORANGE FLAMES, OBJECT SLOWLY VERTI-CALLY ROSE TO ABOUT CAR HEIGHT, THEN NOISE AND FLAME STOPPED AND OBJECT TOOK OFF AT HIGH SPEED

> IN STRAIGHT LINE AND ALMOST HORIZONTALLY TO DISAPPEAR OVER DISTANT MOUNTAIN.
>
> ZAMORA GREATLY FRIGHTENED, RADIOED HIS OBSERVATIONS AND OFFICER CHAVEZ AND FBI AGENT BYRNES QUICKLY ON SCENE, NOTED FOUR SMALL IRREGULARLY SHAPED SMOULDERING AREAS AND FOUR REGULAR DEPRESSED AREAS APPROXIMATELY SIXTEEN BY SIX INCHES IN RECTANGULAR PATTERN AVERAGING ABOUT TWELVE FEET APART.
>
> ZAMORA STATES OBJECT WAS OVAL SHAPED, SIMILAR TO FOOTBALL, POSSIBLY TWENTY FEET LONG, AND HAD A RED INSIGNIA ABOUT THIRTY INCHES HIGH AND TWO FEET WIDE, CENTERED ON OBJECT. NO OTHER WITNESSES KNOWN TO NOISE, FLAME OR OBJECT.

The teletype message also reported that Mr. Byrnes had immediately notified Army Captain Richard Holder, Commander of the Stallion Range Center, a White Sands Missile Range tracking station south of Socorro. Mr. Byrnes also mentioned that by the time of the teletype message the press was already showing considerable interest. Mr. Byrnes concluded by pointing out that the FBI was "conducting no investigation," but that he would advise headquarters of pertinent developments.

It may be that the FBI agent was conducting no official investigation but it is clear from the record that he was a key factor in it. Within half an hour after Officer Zamora radioed a message to police headquarters for help, Mr. Byrnes was on the scene.

On May 8 he wrote a summary of his activities related to the sighting:

> Special Agent D. Arthur Byrnes, Federal Bureau of Investigations, stationed at Albuquerque, New Mexico, was at Socorro, New Mexico, and at the State Police Office there on business late afternoon of April 24, 1964.
>
> At approximately 5:45 to 5:50 P.M. Nep Lopez, radio operator in the Socorro County Sheriff's office, located about thirty feet down the hall from the State Police Office, came into the State Police Office.
>
> Mr. Lopez advised Sergeant Sam Chavez, New Mexico State

Police, that he had just received a radio call from Officer Lonnie Zamora to come to an area about one mile southwest of Socorro. The call was in relation to some unknown object which had 'landed and has taken off.' Agent Byrnes finished his work in the State Police Office at Socorro at approximately 6:00 P.M., April 24, 1964, and thereafter proceeded to the site where Officer Zamora, Socorro County Undersheriff Jim Luckie, Sergeant Chavez and Officer Ted Jordan, New Mexico State Police, were assembled.

It may be noted that it has been the observation of Agent Byrnes that Officer Zamora, known intimately for approximately five years, is well regarded as a sober, industrious and conscientious officer and not given to fantasy.

Officer Zamora was noted to be perfectly sober and somewhat agitated over his experience.

Special Agent Byrnes noted four indentations in the rough ground at the 'site' of the object described by Officer Zamora. These depressions appeared regular in shape, approximately sixteen by six inches rectangular. Each depression seemed to have been made by an object going into the earth at an angle from a center line. Each depression was approximately two inches deep and pushed some earth to the far side.

Inside the four depressions were three burned patches of clumps of grass. Other clumps of grass in the same area appeared not to be disturbed. One burned area was outside the four depressions.

There were three circular marks in the earth which were smooth, approximately four inches in diameter and penetrated in the sandy earth approximately one-eighth of an inch as if a jar lid had gently been pushed into the sand.

No other person was noted in the area the night of April 24, 1964. No other objects were noted in the area possibly connected with the incident related by Officer Zamora.

So far as could be noted, there were no houses or inhabited dwellings in the area or in sight of the area.

In a message dated April 30, Agent Byrnes wrote that Officer Zamora was "a well regarded and capable officer who was noted to be perfectly sober and thoroughly frightened." Agent Byrnes said that he visited the site and saw the indentations and immediately contacted Captain Holder. When Captain Holder arrived later that evening he and Agent Byrnes made measurements of the burned areas. They then interviewed Officer Zamora "at length" and learned that the sighting had begun when Officer Zamora was chasing a speeder in Socorro. He happened to see a bright flash and hear a noise which made him think that a dynamite shack on the other side of a hill had blown up. He broke off the chase of the speeder and turned onto a dirt road toward the shack. He got a first glimpse of the object as he came up the hill. It appeared to be an overturned car with two children next to it. He lost sight of it for a few seconds as he continued traveling over the rough land. At the same time he radioed that he was going to check on an overturned car.

When he got to the top of the hill he could see it again below him in a depression (arroyo). It was oval shaped and seemed to have two legs and a red design or insignia on the side. As he was getting out of the car to call to the two "children," who were no longer visible, he dropped the microphone and turned to pick it up. At that moment he heard a "roaring noise" from the object, a noise that started at a low pitch and then increased in frequency. He turned and saw what appeared to be a bluish and orange flame that seemed to be beneath it. Thinking it was going to explode he dashed around the car, losing his glasses as he ran, in order to put the car and the hill between himself and the object. As he ran he turned his head to watch.

After several seconds the oval shaped object rose straight up. He ran for about 50 feet and dropped onto the ground while covering his eyes. Then he realized that the noise had stopped. He looked back in time to see the object moving away from him. He quickly got up and ran back to the car, picking up his glasses as he ran, to call Nep Lopez. He asked Lopez to look out the window but didn't think, in the heat of the moment to tell Lopez to look out a west window. (The window in Lopez' office faced north.)

Zamora asked Lopez to send Sergeant Chavez immediately. The other officers who arrived at the scene shortly after (Luckie, Jordan) heard the radio message and also went there. When Chavez arrived a few minutes later he found a pale and sweating Zamora, as well as slightly smoldering grass and brush where the

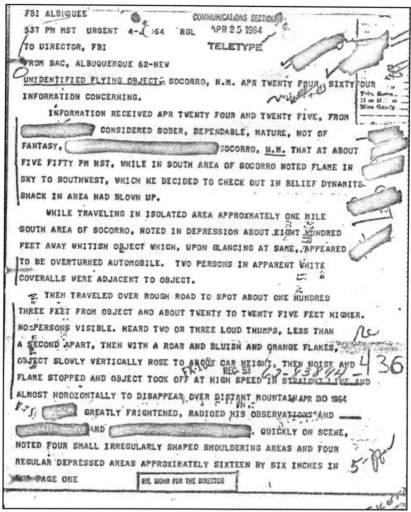

Figure 35A: Zamora Sighting in Socorro

object had been.

By 1 a.m. the next morning Agent Byrnes and Captain Holder had typed up the interview. In the following days, the Army and Air Force checked every known project in the area and could not find an explanation. Project Blue Book was contacted quickly and Dr. Hynek traveled to Socorro for his first visit five days later. He interviewed all the people involved and was not able to

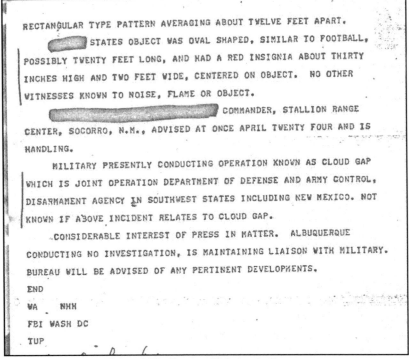

RECTANGULAR TYPE PATTERN AVERAGING ABOUT TWELVE FEET APART.

███████ STATES OBJECT WAS OVAL SHAPED, SIMILAR TO FOOTBALL, POSSIBLY TWENTY FEET LONG, AND HAD A RED INSIGNIA ABOUT THIRTY INCHES HIGH AND TWO FEET WIDE, CENTERED ON OBJECT. NO OTHER WITNESSES KNOWN TO NOISE, FLAME OR OBJECT.

████████████████████ COMMANDER, STALLION RANGE CENTER, SOCORRO, N.M., ADVISED AT ONCE APRIL TWENTY FOUR AND IS HANDLING.

MILITARY PRESENTLY CONDUCTING OPERATION KNOWN AS CLOUD GAP WHICH IS JOINT OPERATION DEPARTMENT OF DEFENSE AND ARMY CONTROL, DISARMAMENT AGENCY IN SOUTHWEST STATES INCLUDING NEW MEXICO. NOT KNOWN IF ABOVE INCIDENT RELATES TO CLOUD GAP.

CONSIDERABLE INTEREST OF PRESS IN MATTER. ALBUQUERQUE CONDUCTING NO INVESTIGATION, IS MAINTAINING LIAISON WITH MILITARY. BUREAU WILL BE ADVISED OF ANY PERTINENT DEVELOPMENTS.

END

WA   NHH

FBI WASH DC

TUP

Figure 35B: Zamora Sighting in Socorro

arrive at a conclusion. About five months later he visited again. Still no answers. Some people believed that Officer Zamora had seen a top secret military vehicle or perhaps the NASA moon lander that was being discussed in the press at the time. A very few people thought it was a hoax, perhaps to draw tourists to Socorro. However, no evidence of a hoax ever turned up and Officer Zamora's credibility remained high.

Major Hector Quintanilla, Jr., Project Blue Book Director, took a special interest in this case. He was convinced that Zamora had told the truth about what he had seen and that it was not a hoax. Writing in the classified CIA journal, *Studies in Intelligence*, in 1967, Quintanilla summarized the sighting and then wrote:

Diagnosis: Unsolved

There is no doubt that Lonnie Zamora saw an object which left quite an impression on him. There is also no question about

Zamora's reliability. He is a serious police officer, a pillar of his church, and a man well versed in recognizing airborne vehicles in his area. He is puzzled by what he saw, and frankly, so are we. This is the best documented case on record, and still we have been unable, in spite of thorough investigation, to find the vehicle or other stimulus that scared Zamora to the point of panic.

During the course of the investigation and immediately thereafter, everything that was humanly possible to verify was checked. Radiation in the landing area was checked with Geiger Counters from Kirtland AFB. The Holloman AFB Balloon Control Center was checked for balloon activity. All local stations and Air Force bases were checked for release of weather balloons. Helicopter activity was checked throughout the state of New Mexico. Government and private aircraft were checked. The reconnaissance division in the Pentagon was checked. The White House Command Post was checked. The Commander at Holloman AFB was interviewed at length about special activities from his base. Down range controllers at the White Sands Missile Range were interviewed. Letters were written to industrial companies engaged in lunar vehicle research activity. The companies were extremely cooperative, but to no avail. The Air Force Materials Laboratory analyzed soil samples from the landing area.

The findings were altogether negative. No other witnesses could be located. There were no unidentified helicopters or aircraft in the area. Radar installations at Holloman AFB and at Albuquerque observed no unusual blips; but the down-range Holloman MTI radar, closest to Socorro, had been closed down for the day at 1600 hours (4 p.m.). There was no unusual meteorological activity, no thunderstorms; the weather was windy but clear. There were no markings of any sort in the area except the shallow 'tracks' Chaves and Zamora found. The soil analysis disclosed no foreign material. Radiation was normal for the 'tracks' and surrounding area. Laboratory analysis of the burned brush showed no chemicals that could have been propellant residue.

The object was traveling at approximately 120 miles per hour when it disappeared over the mountain, according to Zamora's best guess of the time it took. Not an interplanetary speed, at any rate; and the findings are also negative for any indication that the Socorro UFO was of extraterrestrial origin or that it presented a threat to the security of the United States.

Here is an example of a well reported, well researched sighting with more than sufficient information for identification, yet identification was impossible. Even Major Quintanilla admitted defeat: there was no explanation for Officer Zamora's sighting. Yet, according to Quintanilla, it was not evidence of an extraterrestrial device and it was not a threat to the United States. One can certainly ask how he arrived at that conclusion, considering that he had failed to identify it. Apparently the speed, "not interplanetary," was evidence that the object was not interplanetary.

Major Quintanilla, being consistent with the official Air Force position on Unidentified Flying Objects, was skeptical of the ETH, and his skepticism kept him from admitting that Zamora might actually have seen an ET craft. There have been numerous civilian investigations of this case since Quintanilla's article. A couple of people have proposed that Quintanilla saw a new type (at that time) of hot air balloon with the flame from the heater causing the noise and the burned plants on the ground. To accept this explanation would require rejecting major portions of Zamora's testimony and certainly raise lots of questions such as, why didn't Zamora recognize a large balloon? This shows how desperate some people are to avoid admitting that there are unexplained objects/craft flying around. The investigations since Quintanilla's article have ruled out every other manmade or natural phenomenon. What remains?

There were physical effects caused by this object—burned grass and depressions in the ground. One odd aspect of the physical evidence was the nature of the burned material. Officer Chavez found it cold to the touch only minutes after the event. Therefore the burns were not made by an ordinary rocket-type blast of fire, which would have consumed whatever it contacted and would have started hot fires in nearby brush. Perhaps it was more like flash burning from an intense radiation source or extremely hot air (or a plasma?) that doesn't last long enough to heat the internal part of an object, but only long enough to "fry" the outer surface.

Another odd effect, not mentioned in the official reports, was noted by Officer Ted Jordan. He had a camera with him and took 35 mm pictures of the site within half an hour of the event. The next day one of the Air Force investigators asked him for the film with the promise to provide Jordan with duplicate copies of the pictures. Many weeks later Jordan asked about his film and was told that his film didn't turn out; it had been ruined by radiation. Sergeant Chavez took Polaroid pictures the next day which came out all right. Also, a Geiger counter was brought to the site almost 48 hours later. It registered no excessive radiation. Could it be that some intense form of radiation was present at the site for a short time afterward but then had decayed away by the next day?

It certainly appeared to Zamora that he saw a real, solid, structured, manufactured device, a large oval-shaped flying craft that made no noise as it traveled after the initial take off. It did not look like any man-made flying craft or balloon. But if it we didn't make it, then who did? And, what was it doing near Socorro on that fateful day?

Chapter 23
The FBI Files Today

After the Zamora case the FBI received only a few sighting reports from citizens over the next thirty years. These were immediately passed to the Air Force, except for one which is discussed below. The FBI did receive letters asking for information to which the FBI often replied that the investigation of UFO/saucer sightings is "not a matter within the investigative jurisdiction of the FBI" or that the investigation of sightings "is not and never has been a matter within the investigative jurisdiction of the FBI."

One more sighting report is worthy of mention because it provides an answer to a question raised in recent years: considering that abduction of a human being is a federal offense, what would the FBI do if a person reported being abducted by aliens?

JANUARY 18, 1967 UNIDENTIFIED FLYING OBJECT
ALLEGEDLY SIGHTING (sic), JANUARY 17, 1967
At 4:10 A.M., January 18, 1967, Mr. ... (name and address censored) advised that he desired to report that he had observed a large oblong-shaped object which alighted in the street in front of him when he was on his way home from his television repair shop, the (name censored), Chesapeake, Virginia. He believes that he was taken into this craft which he recalls as being made of a glass like substance and being transparent. It was manned by several individuals who appeared to be undersized creatures similar to members of the human race, probably not more than 4 feet tall. They were allegedly wearing regular trouser pants and T-shirts. Mr.... believes that he was transported by this craft for an undetermined distance and returned to his point of take-off approximately one hour later.

Mr. ... spoke in a coherent manner although he appeared to be under certain emotional strain. He claimed he had not been drinking any intoxicants but he was unable to account for the time between 8:00 p.m. and 4:00 a.m. He stated he was telephoning from his workshop but had no recollection of being elsewhere between 8:00 p.m. and 4:00 a.m.

The above is being furnished for your information.

Below the above message is a slightly "ominous" addition:

NOTE: Mr. ... furnished information to night supervisor Special Agent (name censored), Special Investigative Division. A check of Bureau indices did not disclose any information which could be identified with Mr. ....

So, if you contact the FBI to report being abducted, they may check their files to see if you have a record, but don't expect them to investigate.

Clearly the witness took this event seriously. He didn't wait until daytime to make his report. Instead, he called the FBI shortly after his "return" at 4:10 in the morning. The FBI, however, did not take this report seriously, as there is no indication that it was sent to the Air Force, although numerous other sighting reports do contain appended statements which say the reports were sent to the Air Force.

During the 1976 Presidential campaign, then-Governor Jimmy Carter reported that he had seen a UFO in Georgia in 1973. Aware of the continuing arguments over the subject, he promised to release all the government files if he were elected.* He was elected and in June, 1977, Jody Powell of the President's Staff, initiated a search within the Executive Branch to find out if there were any group coordinating the flow of information on the UFO subject. As result of Mr. Powell's request, Stanley Schneider of the Office of Science and Technology of the White House contacted the FBI. The FBI told him that:

... as far as the FBI is concerned there appears to be no conceivable jurisdiction for us to conduct any inquiries upon receipt of information relating to a UFO sighting and, in the absence of some investigative jurisdiction based upon the information furnished, that information would be referred to the Department of the Air Force without

---

* Apparently he did not realize that the Project Blue Book file had already been released in 1975.

any action being taken by the Bureau.

That is the present policy. Hence, if you contact the FBI to report a sighting, the local agent may accept your report and then he will turn it over to the Air Force. He may also send a copy to headquarters where it will join the real X File.

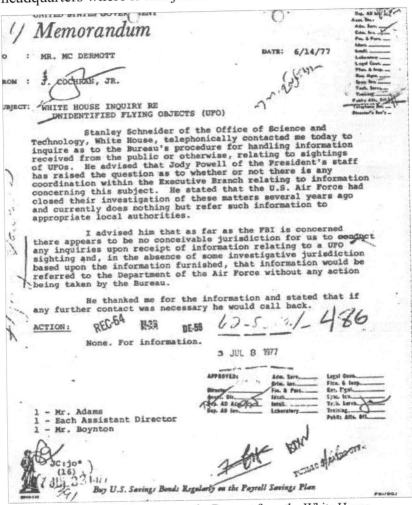

Figure 36. FBI Response to the Request from the White House.

Finis Part the First

Part II
The UFO-CIA Connection

CIA Headquarters, Langley, Virginia.

Chapter 24
The X File, CIA Version

T he Central Intelligence Agency also had files of documents on the uneXplained. A large portion of that file is related to psychic phenomena—a subject for another book. This chapter is based on UFO-related documents that were released by the CIA in December, 1978. These documents were released as a result of a successful lawsuit by the organization Ground Saucer Watch (Peter Gersten, attorney for the plaintiff; Brad Sparks consultant). The judge in charge of this case directed the Agency to search itself for all documents related to UFOs and to release all the information that was no longer classified. The Agency had initially admitted to having only about two dozen pages related to the Robertson Panel (see below) but, during the search they found about 900 pages, many of which were copies of pages, copies of foreign newspaper articles and reports on internal discussions. It is the latter which forms the basis for this chapter.

One very important effect of the 1952 flap is not what happened in the press, but what happened behind closed doors. Recall that in July, ATIC received 536 reports. Apparently this tremendous flow of reports combined with the sightings over Washington, D.C. were too much for the Director of Central Intelligence (DCI), Walter Bedell Smith. He decided that it was time to find out what was really going on out there.

The CIA had been monitoring the flying saucer sightings worldwide on a very casual basis since 1947. A memorandum written on March 15, 1949 indicates that at least one CIA employee was unimpressed by sightings he had studied. The memo mentions some of the usual explanations (meteorological balloons, meteors, psychological effects) and rules out the possibility that secret aircraft or guided missiles by either the USA or the Soviet Union could account for the sightings.

Another memorandum, dated March 31, 1949, mentions the official (post-Estimate) conclusion of Project Sign, that sightings can be categorized generally as explained (misidentifications of conventional aircraft , balloons, natural phenomena or hoax) or as unexplained, and goes on to offer the following possibilities for the unexplained sightings:

a). Natural terrestrial phenomena
   (1) Meteorological (ball lightning)
   (2) Some type of animal
   (3) Hallucinatory or psychological phenomena
b). Man-made terrestrial phenomena:
   (1) Advanced type of aircraft
c). Extra-terrestrial objects:
   (1) Meteors
   (2) Animals
   (3) Space ships

The memorandum concludes by mentioning the scientists involved in the investigation and their conclusions regarding the unexplained cases:

Studies on the various possibilities have been made by Dr. Langmuir of GE (General Electric Corporation), Dr. Valley of the MIT (Massachusetts Institute of Technology), Dr. Lipp of Project Rand, Dr. Hynek of Ohio State and (by the) Aero Medical Laboratory.

That the objects are from outer space or are an advanced aircraft of a foreign power is a possibility, but the above group have (sic) concluded that it is highly improbable.

Following the date of this memorandum the CIA maintained a continuous review of sighting data. Evidently there was nothing found of interest to the CIA because there are no further entries in the CIA's "X" File until 1952. The 1952 concentration was, however, just too much to ignore.

On July 29, the same day as General Samford's press conference (and the day that the FBI was told that some Air Force officials were seriously considering interplanetary ships), Acting Assistant Director for Scientific Intelligence of the CIA, Ralph

Clark, wrote a memorandum for the Deputy Director of Intelligence that stated as follows:

In the past several weeks a number of radar and visual sightings of unidentified aerial objects have been reported. Although this office has been maintaining a continuing review of such reported sightings for the last three years, a special study group has been formed to review this subject . . .

Three days later, a member of the study group, Edward Tauss, the Chief of the Weapons and Equipment Division of the Office of Scientific Intelligence, responded to Mr. Clark's request "for an overall evaluation" of the saucer situation. He said, "of 1000 to 2000 such reports received by ATIC, a large percentage are clearly 'phoney'" and an "equally large percentage can be satisfactorily explained" as known phenomena. However, about a hundred "reasonably credible reports" had not been explained. He pointed out that there was no discernible pattern to the unexplained reports and offered his opinion: "it is probable that if complete information were available for presently 'unexplainable' reports, they, too, could be (explained)." If his opinion were correct, there would be no need for CIA involvement. However, he added a cautionary note which formed the basis for continued CIA involvement:

Notwithstanding the foregoing tentative facts, so long as a series of reports remains 'unexplainable' (interplanetary aspects and alien origin not being thoroughly excluded from consideration) caution requires that intelligence continue coverage of the subject.

He recommended continued "CIA surveillance of subject matter" in coordination with AMC/ATIC and said that he had arranged for a briefing by ATIC personnel on August 8. He recommended that:

. . . no indication of CIA interest or concern reach the press or public, in view of their probable alarmist tendencies to accept such interest as 'confirmatory' of the soundness of 'unpublished facts' in the hands of the U.S. Government.

At the August 11 meeting of the special group, members were

assigned various duties to contribute to the study of the saucer sightings. CIA memoranda written by several study group members dated August 14, 15, and 19 provide details on what the CIA learned from ATIC and from the CIA's own study of sightings.

According to the August 14, memorandum the CIA made its own check on the "U.S. secret project" explanation. The Chairman of the Research and Development Board denied, at the Top Secret level, that any U.S. development could account for saucer sightings. Not satisfied with this top level denial, the author of the memorandum pointed out:

> . . . two factors which tend to confirm the denials—first, the official action of alerting all Air Force commands to intercept [author note: this refers to the shoot-down order issued in the latter part of July], and second, the unbelievable risk of such flights in established airlanes.

On August 20 the Director of Central Intelligence (DCI), Walter Bedell Smith, was briefed on the flying saucer situation. He directed his staff to prepare a memorandum for the National Security Council which would state the need for an investigation and direct various agencies to cooperate in the investigation.

A document entitled "The Air Force Stand on 'Flying Saucers,'" as stated by CIA, in a briefing on 22 August 1952" contains the following information based on the CIA visit to ATIC:

> I. The Air Force has primary responsibility for investigating the 'flying saucers.' The unit concerned with these investigations is a part of the AIr Technical Intelligence Center at Dayton, Ohio, and consists of three officers (a Captain in charge) and two civilians. They receive reports of sightings, analyze and attempt to explain them. A standard reporting form has been prepared which is used on a world-wide basis. The Air Force Office of Special Investigations checks into each sighting attempting to determine its authenticity and the reliability of the observer.
>
> II. (A) The Air Force officially denies that 'flying saucers' are:
> (1) U.S. secret weapons
> (2) Soviet secret weapons
> (3) Extra-terrestrial visitors

II. (B) It is believed that all sightings of 'flying saucers' are:

(1)Well known objects such as balloons, aircraft, meteors, clouds, etc. not recognized by the observer

(2) Phenomena of the atmosphere which are at present poorly understood, e.g., refractions and reflections caused by temperature inversion, ionization phenomena, ball lightning, etc.

III. Not a shred of evidence exists to substantiate the belief that 'flying saucers' are material objects not falling into category II B(1), above.

IV. A study of 'flying saucer' sightings on a geographical basis showed them to be more frequent in the vicinity of atomic energy installations (which is explained by the greater security consciousness of persons in those areas). That by-products of atomic fission may in some way act catalytically to produce 'flying saucers' has not been disproved. The greatest number of sightings has been made at or near Dayton, Ohio, where the investigations are going on.

V. Of the thousands of 'flying saucers' sighted of which there are records, the Air Force says that 78% have been explained by either II B(1) or II B(2) above, 2% have been exposed as hoaxes and the remaining 20% have not been explained, primarily because of the vague descriptions given by observers.

VI. The Air Force is mostly interested in the 'saucer' problem because of its psychological warfare implications. In reviewing publications designed for Soviet consumption, there has not been a single reference to 'flying saucers.' On the other hand, several 'saucer' societies in the United States have been investigated. Key members of some of these societies which have been instrumental in keeping the 'flying saucer' craze before the public have been exposed as being of doubtful loyalty. Furthermore the societies, in some cases, are financed by an unknown source. The Air Force realizes that a public made jumpy by the 'flying saucer' scare would be a serious liability in the event of air attacks by an enemy. Air defense could not operate effectively if the Air Force were constantly called upon to intercept mirages which persons had mistaken for enemy aircraft.

Evidently the ATIC/Blue Book opinion of the "saucer craze," as understood by the staff of the CIA study group, was considerably different from the opinion expressed by AFI personnel in the Pentagon to the AFOSI and to the FBI (see Chapter 20). The AFI personnel admitted to the FBI that there was a "hard core" amounting to about 3% of the sightings, such as many reported by commercial and Air Force pilots, which could not be explained and this led some top level officials to believe that saucers could be interplanetary vehicles.

However, because the Project Blue Book personnel were very skeptical, even cynical, about UFO sightings, they did not tell the CIA study group about the "hard core" cases. Instead, the CIA representatives were told that ". . . 20 % have not been explained, primarily because of the vague descriptions . . ." This was misinformation provided (perhaps intentionally) to the CIA by the Blue Book personnel. The fact is that the hard core 3% of the total number of sightings (15% of the unexplained sightings) had well reported, explicitly described details which prevented identification as known phenomena.

Instead of being told that saucers were most often reported in the vicinity of airports, as Commander Boyd had correctly told the FBI, the CIA was told, incorrectly, that saucers were most frequently seen near Dayton, Ohio. The Blue Book personnel did not tell the CIA representative that whenever a pursuing jet tried to get close to a saucer it invariably would fade from view, nor did they tell the CIA that the extraterrestrial hypothesis (ETH) was not being overlooked. Instead, as the CIA perceived it, the Air Force had officially taken a rigid stand against the ETH: Anything But ET.

Why would the Blue Book personnel do such a thing? We know from the FBI documents that the Top Brass at the Pentagon did not flatly deny that flying saucers could be extraterrestrial visitors. We also know that there was a considerable amount of highly credible testimonial evidence available to the ATIC personnel to show that saucers could not be explained as II (B) above. We also know that the hard core unexplained cases did not have "vague descriptions" which prevented identification. In fact, the Battelle Memorial Institute study was finding the opposite: the unexplained cases had lots of details that prevented identification as mundane objects. Furthermore, Battelle discovered that, on a statistical basis, the better the sighting, with more details and more credible observers, the more difficult it was to explain.* Several examples of such cases have been presented in previous chapters.

So, the question is, why did Project Blue Book misinform the CIA? Was it because the Blue Book staff really believed there was no ET evidence at all, or was to it to prevent the CIA from looking more deeply into the saucer problem and perhaps discovering something the Air Force wanted to keep secret?

Although the document contains some incorrect information, it also provides some information not found elsewhere. It states that a geographical study showed that saucer sightings occurred more often at nuclear installations. This contradicts General Samford's statement to the press that there seemed to be no threatening pattern to saucer sightings.

The comment about the "publications designed for Soviet consumption" (the Soviet press) not having any saucer reports, while the U.S. press was full of them, was intended to indicate a disparity that could work to the advantage of the Soviets if there were an attack. The importance of this disparity is clarified in the last sentence which indicates that public reporting of saucers during an attack on the USA could be a "serious liability," whereas the Soviets would have no such liability.

In future months this would develop into three fundamental worries of the CIA: (a) a large flux of saucer sightings, whether saucers were "real" or not, during a time of national emergency could have a negative psychological impact on the American people, (b) saucer reports could act as "decoy unknowns," diverting the limited number of defensive aircraft from protecting against attacking aircraft, which would initially also appear on radar sensors as "unknowns," and (c) a large flux of saucer reports could clog defense communications channels.

One more thing to note in the CIA document is the statement that individuals and groups that promoted saucer studies had

---

* A year or so later the Battelle study would discover that nearly 33% of the best sightings by military witnesses who were on duty at the time of the sighting were not explainable!

been investigated to check on the possibility of subversive activity. The reference to groups being funded by an unknown source indicates that the CIA suspected that some saucer groups might actually be funded by the Soviets or communist sympathizers. Evidently the CIA did not know that the FBI had already looked for subversion and hadn't found any in 1947. However, in the 1950s both the CIA and the FBI did keep track of some saucer enthusiasts and groups. (Yes, Big Brother was watching.)

By early September, the CIA staff had collected enough information to make an informal report to the DCI. Dr. H. Marshall Chadwell, the Assistant Director for Scientific Intelligence, reported that the study had been undertaken to determine "whether or not adequate study and research is currently being directed to this problem in its relation to national security implications" and what further work should be carried out. He reported that the only work on the problem was that being done by the Air Technical Intelligence Center under the authority of the Air Force Directorate of Intelligence. Chadwell wrote:

> OSI (Office of Scientific Intelligence within the CIA) entered into its inquiry fully aware that it was coming into a field already charged with partisanship, one in which objectivity had been overridden by numerous sensational writers, and one in which there are pressures for extravagant explanation as well as for oversimplification. The OSI Team consulted with a representative of the Air Force Special Studies Group (Stephen Possony: see Chapter 19); discussed the problem with those in charge of the Air Force Project at Wright Field (Blue Book); reviewed a considerable volume of intelligence reports; checked the Soviet press and broadcast indices; and conferred with three OSI consultant, all leaders in their scientific fields, who were chosen because of their broad knowledge of the technical areas concerned.

> OSI found that the ATIC study is probably valid if the purpose is limited to a case-by-case explanation. However, the study makes no attempt to solve the more fundamental aspect of the problem which is to determine definitely the nature of the various phenomena which are causing these sightings, or to discover means by which these causes and their visual or electronic effects may be immediately identified. Our consultant panel stated that these solutions would

probably be found on the margins or just beyond the frontiers of our present knowledge in the fields of atmospheric, ionospheric, and extraterrestrial phenomena, with the added possibility that our present dispersal of nuclear waste products might also be a factor.

The consultant panel recommended the formation of a study group to analyze the fundamental sighting information, determine what fundamental sciences would be involved and make recommendations for further study.

Dr. Chadwell then got to the heart of the problem from the national security point of view. First there was the psychological aspect. The CIA could find no mention of saucers in the Soviet media, so the Russians were not being "conditioned" to believe in saucers by the Russian press. In the USA, on the other hand, the recent continual press interest and "pressure of inquiry on the Air Force" indicated that a fair proportion of the population had been "mentally conditioned to the acceptance of the incredible. In this fact lies the potential for touching-off of mass hysteria and panic." In other words, if a nefarious group of individuals bent on destroying the United States were to start publicizing UFO reports, the U.S. citizens might panic.

The second national security aspect was air vulnerability. There was the possibility that a flux of saucer sightings at a time of air attack could cause the Air Force to divert precious hardware (airplanes) to check out spurious unidentified saucers when they should be flying toward the unidentified conventional aircraft, presumably Soviet. Dr. Chadwell suggested immediate steps should be taken to improve the methods of quickly identifying unknown objects or phenomena. He also suggested that U.S. intelligence agencies should determine the level of Soviet knowledge about the phenomenon so we could defend ourselves against attempts by the Soviets to use their knowledge to our detriment, while at the same time using our knowledge of saucers to our advantage. By this he meant using saucer sightings as part of psychological warfare against the Soviets. Finally, he recommended the National Security Council direct the CIA to begin a study along the lines he outlined.

Dr. Chadwell's memorandum to the Director apparently met with some favor because in early October the recommendations were formalized and sent to the DCI. Chadwell recommended:

(a) That the Director of Central Intelligence advise the National Security Council of the implications of the 'flying saucer' problem and request that research be initiated.

(b) That the DCI discuss this subject with the Psychological Strategy Board.

(c) That the CIA, with the cooperation of the Psychological Strategy Board and other interested departments and agencies, develop and recommend for adoption by the NSC a policy of public information which will minimize concern and possible panic resulting from the numerous sightings of unidentified objects.

A draft proposal was written for presentation to the Intelligence Advisory Committee (IAC) and Secretary of Defense, Robert Lovett.[*] On December 2, Dr. Chadwell summarized the situation regarding the NSC directive and included in his memorandum to the DCI the following statement which indicates a level of concern that goes beyond what the Air Force had conveyed to the CIA months earlier:

Recent reports reaching the CIA indicated that further action was desirable and another briefing by the cognizant A-2 (air intelligence) and ATIC personnel was held on 25 November. At this time, the reports of incidents convince us that there is something going on that must have immediate attention. The details of some of these incidents have been discussed by AD/SI (Assistant Director of the Scientific Intelligence Division) with DDCI (Deputy Director of the CIA). Sightings of unexplained objects at great altitudes and traveling at high speeds in the vicinity of major U.S. defense installations are of such nature that they are not attributable to natural phenomena or known types of aerial vehicles.

Note that Dr. Chadwell did not say that the sightings are or might be attributable to natural or manmade phenomena; he said they are not attributable to natural or manmade phenomena.

---

[*] Recall that he had been an Undersecetary of Defense during the December 6, 1950 alert.

Could it be that he was convinced?

He went on to say that OSI was about to establish a "consulting group of sufficient competence and stature to review this matter and convince the responsible authorities in the community that immediate research and development on this subject must be undertaken." Notice that he expected the "consulting group" would be able to convince the "responsible authorities" to immediately undertake research on "this subject." This statement gives the impression that Chadwell was quite certain the consulting group would conclude, as he apparently had, that saucers were real, non-conventional objects flying around U.S. defense installations and other locations.

Chadwell's proposal was accepted and on December 4 the IAC was briefed on the problem. Present at the meeting were representatives of the Air Force, the Army, the Navy, the Department of State and six representatives from the CIA, including Dr. Chadwell. General Samford, representing Air Force Intelligence, offered complete cooperation. Also present was Mr. Meffert Kuhrtz, acting for the Assistant to the Director, FBI.

The CIA version of the minutes of the IAC meeting shows only that the IAC approved having the CIA set up a review of the available evidence and scientific theories. Any further work would depend upon the the result of the scientific study. Mr. Kuhrtz' report to the FBI, written December 5, provides a bit more information. It says that Dr. Chadwell talked about a theory of saucers that had been suggested by a German atomic scientist (name censored from the released document). He also said that a "recent" saucer sighting in Africa "presents some evidence that the 'saucers' are not a meteorological phenomena, which theory has been held to date by the Air Force." Mr. Kuhrtz said that details of the African report were not given but that he would try to get the details from the Air Force.

According to Khurtz's report, the IAC approved the idea of having a group of scientists study the sightings and try to identify the saucers. This would be carried out under CIA direction. The IAC would not get involved unless the scientists determined that the saucers were devices "under control of our enemy." (Presumably, then, if ET's controlled the saucers and if ET's were not our enemy, then the IAC would not become involved.) On December 23 Mr. Kuhrtz reported the CIA had information about an explosion in Africa that had been picked up on seismographs. There were reports "of unknown reliability" that associated the explosion with a flying saucer.

During December, Dr. Chadwell wrote several memoranda which show that he was impressed by the Tremonton, Utah (Newhouse) film and by the Florida scoutmaster (Sonny Desvergers) landing case (both discussed in Chapter 20). He also met with several scientists to brief them and get their opinions. Most of them agreed that the subject should be studied, but Chadwell's memoranda do not indicate they were enthusiastic about studying saucer sightings.

Also during December and January, the CIA and ATIC (under Captain Ruppelt) prepared for the big meeting that would decide the fate of the CIA study of UFOs. The CIA asked Dr. H. P. Robertson, a distinguished scientist, formerly of Princeton and the California Institute of Technology, and a consultant to the CIA, to establish a panel of "top scientists and engineers in the fields of astrophysics, nuclear energy, electronics, etc., to review this situation." AFI and ATIC offered full support and Captain Ruppelt and the Project Blue Book staff prepared a briefing for the scientists. Unfortunately, the Battelle study was nowhere near completion (it wouldn't be finished for about a year), so the complete statistical analyses of several thousand sighting reports were not available.

The meeting convened on Wednesday, January 14. Attending were Dr. Robertson, Dr. Samuel Goudsmit (co-discoverer of electron spin), Dr. Luiz Alvarez (professor of physics; Nobel prize winner many years later) and Dr. Thornton Page (professor of astronomy). Two days later Dr. Lloyd Berkner (physicist; radar engineer) arrived in time for the closing sessions. The ATIC representatives (E. Ruppelt and D. Fournet) had spent weeks preparing for this meeting but because of time limitations were only able to present in detail about two dozen of the seventy-five sightings which they considered to be their best evidence. Green fireball sightings and the results of Project Twinkle were presented with, no doubt, the conclusion that "no information was gained." Two of the best sightings were the Newhouse film and the Washington, D.C. sightings discussed in previous chapters.

The panel of scientists, after a few days of presentations by ATIC study, concluded that "reasonable explanations could be suggested for most sightings and 'by deduction and scientific method it could be induced (given additional data) that other cases might be explained in similar manner.'" One particularly egregious example of their explanations was that "birds" explained Delbert Newhouse's film, which the expert photoanalysts of the National Photographic Interpretation Center (NPIC) had said couldn't be explained. The claim by the photographic analysts that the images were too bright to be reflections from birds was discounted. And Newhouse's visual sighting of pie-pan like objects before he started filming was not even mentioned.

Obviously these expert scientists did not get the full picture in their several day review of the five year phenomenon that had generated thousands of reports. Hence their conclusions were based on a lack of information and a lack of understanding combined with a natural bias against anything unusual that wouldn't fit their scientific world view. Another example of a scientist who reached a faulty conclusion based on insufficient information is that of Dr. Thornton Page. He argued that saucers couldn't be ET craft because such craft wouldn't appear in only one country, the USA. Of course he was correct: they would show up all over the world. What he didn't know, and apparently no one told him, was that saucers *had* been seen all over the world.

The panel concluded that, even though they were not "real," the saucers were a danger for the reasons already cited above. An enemy could use an existing saucer flap or create one with balloons or some other devices in order to swamp the communications channels with sighting reports while using the objects as decoys for the actual attacking aircraft. To reduce the danger, the panel recommended stripping the saucers of their special status and starting a program of education and "debunking" or explaining so the general public would be better able to identify normal aerial objects and phenomena. Once the subject had been sufficiently debunked, the general public would believe that all the sightings had been explained and so there would be less interest in reporting.

Although the debunking recommendation of the panel was not widely disseminated it did have an effect. Over the next 12 months, after Ruppelt left the project (and retired), Project Blue Book went from being an active analytical organization to mere shadow of its former self, with investigations carried out by another organization (the 4602 Air Intelligence Service Squadron). The activities of Project Blue Book were centered on categorizing sightings into two classes, those which they could explain and those which they could not explain, and then filing these sightings away, with no further study of the unexplained sightings. The other major Blue Book activity was handling the publicity surrounding UFO sightings. Whenever the press asked the Air Force about sightings Blue Book provided an answer.

During the following year, the Air Force issued two new regulations which virtually guaranteed secrecy about saucer sightings by military people. These documents restricted information release to those sightings which had been explained and threatened a fine and prison term for military people who intentionally released information about unexplained UFO reports without proper authorization.

In the months and years following the Robertson panel the number of sighted objects fluctuated from roughly 500 to roughly 1,000 per year. Project Blue Book claimed that all but about 3% could be explained and, without supporting evidence, claimed that even those could have been explained if more information had been available. Not only was there no supporting evidence for this claim, the Battelle scientists, many months after the Robertson panel, discovered evidence to contradict it. They discovered that the highest quality sightings with the most information were the least likely to be explainable. The most obvious example of well reported sightings came from on-duty military witnesses between 1947 and 1952: about 33% of these sightings were unexplained.

Chapter 25
After the Robertson Panel

Insofar as could be determined from the released CIA documents, after the Robertson Panel the agency had only an
ongoing low level interest in "maintaining current knowledge" of
UFO reports, according to a document dated July 3, 1953. A
review of the situation showed that since there was no apparent
"serious direct treat to national security" the UFO project would
be:

> . . . considered as inactive . . . incoming material will be reviewed
> periodically to segregate reference to recognizable and explainable
> phenomena from those which come under the definition of unidenti-
> fied flying objects [and] . . . all material on unidentified flying
> objects will be deposited in the files for future reference unless it
> raises an immediately recognizable problem of concern to national
> security.

The Agency did collect sightings from around the world and
occasionally reviewed the situation, but never again did the
agency officially take the same level of interest that was shown
in the summer of 1952.

A document dated December 8, 1953 is a short review and
discussion of the book *Flying Saucers from Outer Space*,* which
was the second such book by retired Marine aviator and investigative reporter Donald Keyhoe. Apparently the CIA was interested in the book because the author "built up a case for saucers
being interplanetary (and) insists that the Air Force (and CIA)
know the 'truth' and are refusing to give the public the facts."
Keyhoe had apparently learned through the grapevine that there
had been a secret CIA meeting that recommended debunking

---

* Henry Holt, NY, 1953.

sightings, and the CIA wondered if there had been a security breach.* The author of this document also mentioned a person who has been mentioned previously, Stephan Possony, who was Chief of the USAFOIN Special Study Group, and who said he was "not aware of any concern in the Pentagon over Keyhoe's assertions." **

A document dated December 17, 1953 says that the CIA's project to monitor what it called the "saucer scene," was "confined to maintaining awareness of the activities of other agencies (notably the Air Force) in the unidentified flying objects business and the maintenance of files." The document then summarized the activities of the various branches of the department of defense. According to this document, the Air Force maintained its UFO investigative activities but with "decreasing emphasis," and Blue Book was no longer conducting field investigations. These were being done by other organizations. Of particular note was the fact the Blue Book was being transferred to the Air Defense Command because ADC had been doing most of the investigative work of the project and:

> If it turns out that these things are space ships or long range aircraft from another country, the ADC is the command that would have to take action.

The document also says that the Navy was devoting only part of the time of a single analyst in the Office of Naval Intelligence and the Army was not interested in doing any more than cooperating with the Air Force in investigations that involved Army witnesses.

A document dated February 9, 1956 provides even more evidence of CIA disinterest in the UFO sightings that weren't directly relatable to technological developments of foreign nations such as the Soviet Union. The document says that the

---

* It is to be noted that in later years Keyhoe accused the CIA of controlling the cover-up of proof that "UFOs are real."

** Recall that it was Possony who wrote that the Air Force could not simply assume that UFOs were interplanetary.

group responsible for "Non-conventional Types of Air Vehicles" would maintain files on raw reports "where in our judgement, the subject matter may provide information bearing on foreign weapons system research or development." Reports that did not seem to relate to foreign weapon systems or science develop- ments would be destroyed. Existing finished reports, correspon- dence, and documents related to the "United States U.F.O. program" would be maintained. The document recommended the destruction of all raw intelligence and obsolete finished reports to avoid accumulation of reports.

The documents released as a result of the lawsuit and FOIPA request show that from 1953 onward into the 1970s the CIA's main UFO-related activity was collecting reports, generally newspaper reports, of UFO sightings and trying to prevent its activities from becoming public knowledge. From 1947 through the late 1970s the Agency collected nearly 200 sighting reports from around the world. In the early 1990s, the Foreign Broadcast Intelligence Service (FBIS) collected reports and discussions that appeared in the Russian and former Soviet bloc countries.

The CIA UFO-related activities in the 1980s and 1990s are the subject of Part III of this book. But before proceeding to those activities, consider this foreign report that united the FBI and the CIA as they tried to find a logical explanation for a sighting by a famous "unimpeachable" American witness.

Chapter 26
Unimpeachable Witnesses

Richard Russell saw two flying saucers while he was riding on a train. Now, by itself this wouldn't seem very important. There have been other reports by people on trains. However, those other people were not in charge of the Senate Armed Services Committee. Richard Russell was. Moreover, those other people were not riding through Russia when they had their sightings. Senator Russell was. And when those other people told their stories few people paid any attention. But when Senator Russell told his story the FBI and the CIA sat right up and listened closely. According to the records of the Air Force, CIA, and FBI this is what happened.

It occurred on October 4, 1955, at dusk. The Senator, Colonel E.U. Hathaway (a U.S. Army Staff officer assigned to the Senate Armed Services Committee), Reuben Efron (a committee consultant who was keeping records and acting as interpreter), and another business man (possibly a covert CIA agent) were riding on a train through the Baku area of the Soviet Union near the Caspian Sea. Senator Russell, who was not feeling well at the time, was alone in one compartment with the lights off while the others were in the next compartment talking with the lights on.

Senator Russell happened to be looking outside when he saw a yellow-green light rise vertically upward from a location some distance south of the train. It moved upward at a moderate speed from some initial altitude to a higher altitude. Then it accelerated and traveled northward, passing directly over the moving train. He ran into the next compartment and yelled "Did you see that out there? I just saw a flying saucer." The three men in the compartment had not been looking outside. They turned out the lights and all four looked out the window. "I saw it coming up from over there," he said. "Here it is coming up again." Suddenly a second one repeated the performance.

After the second one had disappeared over the train, Senator Russell said "We saw a flying saucer. .... I wanted you boys to see it so I would have witnesses." The verbal descriptions and the illustration presented by Colonel Hathaway and Mr. Efron to the Air Attache at the Embassy in Prague ten days later indicate that they saw a rotating, circular craft with two stationary lights. The Air Attache wrote a report on what he was told and sent it to the Air Force. His report begins with the following statement by Colonel Hathaway:

> I doubt if you're going to believe this but we all saw it. Senator Russell was the first to see this flying saucer and he called us to the window and we both (Hathaway and Efron) saw the second one. We've been told for years that there isn't such a thing but all of us saw it. There were two lights towards the inside of the disc which remained stationary as the outer surface went around. The lights sat near the top of the disc. The aircraft was circular (and) resembled a flying saucer. (It was) revolving clockwise or to the right. There was no noticeable color. The disc rose in the same position as it was in when it sped away. Some sparking or flame came out of the bottom as the craft rose.

The report contains an illustration showing an object that was flat on the bottom with a raised portion or dome on the top. The witnesses saw no protrusions or anything like wings.

The Air Attache's report also included conventional intelligence information on Soviet aircraft, radar installations, and railroads which had been observed by Senator Russell's party during their trip. The report was classified Top Secret until 1959 when it was downgraded to Secret. It was not released until 1985.

Shortly after Senator Russell returned to the United States, the CIA got into the act. Over the next month or so the CIA agents interviewed the witnesses. Herbert Scoville, Assistant Director for Scientific Intelligence, tried to make some sense out of the four somewhat divergent descriptions of what happened. One gets the impression that even before he interviewed all the witnesses, Dr. Scoville had more or less concluded they had not seen a flying saucer. He suggested they had seen helicopters or jets taking off. He even mentioned the remote possibility they had seen a Soviet version of something like the Air Force's circular aircraft referred to as "Project Y" which at that time was being researched by the AVRO company in Canada under a USAF contract. The Chief of the CIA's Applied Science section pointed out that if the Soviets had, in fact, flown a circular "Y-type" craft then they had jumped far ahead of our own work. However, he doubted that possibility since there had been no other reports to indicate such progress by the Soviets.*

The FBI first learned of this sighting during the IAC meeting of October 18. At that meeting CIA Director Allen Dulles reported the very basic details of the sighting by Senator Russell and the others. FBI Liaison Khurtz wrote that the IAC members thought it could have been a helicopter or something else, but that more information was necessary. Several weeks later, on November 8, an FBI agent summarized the information received from the CIA, which had by now interviewed all the witnesses. The CIA had concluded that the only testimony which "would support the existence of flying saucer or radically unconventional aircraft is that of Colonel Hathaway." The CIA claimed that:

> All other observations can probably be explained as (a) steep-climbing aircraft or missile or (the) exhaust of (a) normal jet aircraft in a dive, followed by a sharp pull-up in such a way (that) nothing could be seen until (the) exhaust (became) visible to observers on (the) train, but (it is) possible (the) aircraft was indeed of the short or almost vertical take-off variety.

The implication was, of course, that if the other descriptions could be explained away, then probably Colonel Hathaway's could be, too, in spite of the fact that he was probably the most qualified of the observers.

A comparison of the November 1955 assessment with the

---

* Note the similarity here between the 1948-1949 period when the Air Force considered the possibility that the green fireballs and saucers might be Soviet developments of atomic powered aircraft and then rejected this possibility because the Air Force did not believe the Soviets had gotten that far ahead.

initial interview a month earlier shows how much the information had been watered down, with various important elements of the description being rejected one after another as necessary to arrive at an explanation. Perhaps the most surprising part of the description was the rotation of the outer surface while the two lights, like "eyes," stayed constant. Obviously any man-made craft with wing lights or whatever that went into rotation would cause the lights to also rotate. This portion of the description was ignored.

There probably was no liklihood that Dr. Scoville would have arrived at any conclusion other than "identified" considering what he had written in a memorandum to the DCI on this sighting before he had interviewed all the witnesses:

> Two years ago Dr. Robertson headed a group which investigated U.S. sightings of flying saucers. This group was able to explain almost all the sightings and reached the conclusion that these phenomena represented no threat to the security of the U.S. Even if the present sightings by Russell are confirmed, it should not be inferred that these unconventional aircraft have actually been flying around the U.S. and were the source of U.S. speculation.

Such was the stature of the Robertson panel that Dr. Scoville willingly believed that the panel had explained "almost all sightings," which, of course, it had not done. Furthermore, Dr. Scoville was willing to believe that, even if by some chance Senator Russell's sighting turned out to be a real flying saucer, that would not mean that saucers had actually been seen over the USA. Fortunately civilization persists even in the face of "logic" like this.

PART III
I Investigate the CIA

Prologue

Starting during the 1950s, the CIA was accused by some ufologists of hiding the really important UFO information, such as military sightings. In later years, after the Roswell crash case became known, many ufologists accused the CIA, along with the Air Force and other intelligence agencies, of covering up the hard evidence, the efforts to understand by "reverse engineering" the technology behind Alien Flying Craft (AFC), and the efforts to learn about the aliens piloting the craft.

Of course, the CIA and other agencies denied any such activities and denied withholding the hard evidence. But ufologists knew from their own studies of the sightings and physical evidence (e.g., radar, photos, landing traces) that something unusual really was happening, and they could not believe that the agencies like the CIA, with access to the best military and surveillance data, didn't know that too. When the CIA, to comply with a court order, searched its own files for UFO related documents, they found many hundreds of pages that they had only recently denied existed. Ufologists wondered, what more might they be covering up? Were they really running the show, ufologically speaking, or were they really as much in the dark as the rest of us?

As fate would have it, I had the opportunity to find out whether or not the CIA had any UFO programs as a result of meetings and discussion with employees of the agency over a period of 25 years or so. What you are about to read are some of my experiences with the CIA which lead to a conclusion regarding the activities of the CIA relative to the UFO cover up.

Chapter 27
A Top Level Briefing

The date was April 13, 1993, and I was at home, taking time off from work to do some necessary chores during the pleasant Tuesday afternoon, when the call came. It was a call that I certainly didn't expect and hardly believed when I heard it. The caller was Dr. Ronald Pandolfi, a scientist and CIA employee whom I had known for about 9 years. He explained the reason for his call: he wanted me to write a UFO briefing for the President's Science Advisor, Dr. John Gibbons!

"*What?* You must be kidding!"

Something like that was my initial response. First of all, I was surprised that the science advisor would want a UFO briefing and second, I was stunned by the request for me to write it. At the same time, I was excited. Few people get a chance to present such a high level briefing on this subject.

Immediately, while still talking, I began planning what I would write and how I would write it. I envisioned a standard briefing format, done in person, with visuals (slides/vuegraphs). Naturally I expected I would have a week or more, or several days at least, to get a briefing ready, assuming Ron wasn't pulling my leg. After all, I had to collect information, write the briefing document and create the visual aides. For the White House Science Advisor, it had to be a real production.

"When will the briefing be, sometime next week?" I asked.

Apparently one shock was not enough.

He continued, "The briefing is to take place tomorrow morning."

"What? You *must* be kidding!" was my mental response.

My train of thought was suddenly switched on to a faster track, a track I had not previously considered. I now assumed they had placed the briefing late in the morning. After all, I was more than an hour driving time from Washington. If I had to visit the Science Advisor, I should have time to travel to D.C.

But then Ron derailed my new train of thought.

"He needs the written briefing by 8 a.m."

"What? . . . (you know the rest.)

My immediate response was a cross between excitement and dismay. How could I prepare a Presidential-level UFO briefing in less than a day?

Ron explained that the basic requirement was that I had to fax whatever I wrote to the CIA representative who worked in the Science Advisor's office by 8 a.m. the next day, and the CIA representative would give it to the Science Advisor. Ron left it to me to decide on the briefing document format and the content. He did not even want to see it before Gibbons.

Of course, anything I wrote could not be based on classified information because I didn't know any classified information about UFOs. Knowing this, I asked Ron why he didn't give it himself. After all, he was aware of the hundreds of documents that had been declassified and released in previous years and he was generally aware of the "UFO scene" and what I had told him about various sightings over the years. Moreover, he—unlike I—would have access to any documents that were still classified, if there were any.

His response, as I recall was somewhat diffuse and unclear, but basically he didn't want to do it because he did not consider himself to be an expert in the subject. I speculate that it may also be that he (or his superiors) didn't want Gibbons to think that the CIA itself had any expertise or interest in UFO phenomena. Whatever the reason, he pointed out that in the past he had acted as an aid to the Science Advisor, so he wanted to help John Gibbons in an unofficial way, as a friend. He could do this because John had not formally asked or tasked the CIA to provide a briefing. Ron merely acted as a link between me as a source of information, and the Science Advisor who needed the information.

The fact that he went outside the Agency for help indicates to me that he knew of no employee within the Agency who was sufficiently familiar with the UFO subject to be able to give a briefing. He had worked there as a high level scientist for more than nine years and was, in fact, in charge of the "weird desk" (see below). One would think that he would have known if there had been an ongoing Top Secret UFO project, just as both he (and his predecessor at the weird desk—see below) were aware of Top Secret paranormal research projects that had been carried in previous years.

One might also ask why a top scientist like Dr. Gibbons wanted a briefing on such a supposedly ridiculous subject. The answer is based on what Ron had told me eight days earlier. It appears that multi-millionaire Laurence Rockefeller, and C.B. Scott Jones of the Human Potential Foundation, were trying to get recognition of UFOs and aliens or even some sort of "Disclosure" by the then-new Clinton administration. They told Gibbons that they wanted thirty minutes with President Clinton to brief him on "advanced technology." Rockefeller, as a large contributor to Clinton's presidential campaign, could get time with Clinton, but he had to go through the Science Advisor first.

Gibbons' response to Rockefeller was that it could be arranged, but he required more specific details than just "advanced technology." Rockefeller then indicated that he wanted to brief Clinton on what was known about UFOs and aliens. According to Ron, Gibbons was "petrified." He was afraid he'd make a total fool of himself by asking for a half hour of the President's time to discuss UFOs and aliens. He wanted Ron to help him get out of this meeting.

Ron never explained what, if anything, he or Gibbons did to try to squash the meeting. Whatever it may have been, it was not successful, because eight days later Ron asked me to provide Dr. Gibbons with UFO information so he would have some background in the subject at the time of the meeting.

I worked into the evening on the briefing and faxed it to Dr. Gibbons' office shortly after 8 a.m.. Unfortunately, the meeting was finished by that time—it had started at 7:30 a.m.!*

You may well wonder why Dr. Pandolfi asked me, and not someone else outside the Agency, to give the briefing. I think it was because we had been acquainted for about nine years, and he knew that I knew a lot about UFO history and phenomena, probably more than he did, because I had been studying the phenomenon for about 25 years. Furthermore, he knew that I was capable of providing a good briefing because he had heard my previous briefings to the CIA (see below). So it was logical for him to ask me.

But then the question is, how did I meet Pandolfi in the first place. That's a long story.

---

* The briefing document is in Appendix 2.

Chapter 28
First Contact

Just as my "connection" with the FBI's X-file was a result of my investigation of a UFO sighting (the Trent photo case of 1950), my investigation of sightings in New Zealand was the cause of my connection with the CIA.

By 1978, I was known to the National Investigations Committee on Aerial Phenomena (NICAP) as a photoanalyst who lived in the Washington, D.C. area near the headquarters of NICAP, and who was willing to analyze photos of alleged UFOs.* I had investigated several cases of interest to NICAP so, Jack Acuff, Director of NICAP at the time, called on me quite often to provide quick analyses of photographic sightings.

Meanwhile, a world away, internationally reported UFO sightings were taking place in the summer and fall of 1978. The most widely reported was the October 1978 disappearance of Frederick Valentich while flying over the Bass Strait, south of Melbourne, Australia, under "UFO conditions." Valentich reported to the control tower at Melbourne that a strange object, not an airplane, was flying near his plane. The conversation about this strange object ended abruptly and the air traffic controller heard a metallic crashing noise and then nothing. A several day search failed to find any evidence of a wreck or any other explanation for his disappearance.

The disappearance of Valentich is an interesting UFO event by itself, but its importance here is that it provided something of a set up for TV media interest in sightings that occurred several months later in New Zealand. A senior TV station reporter,

---

* This refers to the original NICAP, founded in 1957 and closed in 1980. There is a new NICAP that exists on the internet only.

Leonard Lee, who worked for Channel 0 (now Channel 10) in Melbourne noticed the great public interest in the Valentich story. Therefore, when sightings were reported in New Zealand during the night of December 20-21, Lee was intrigued and thought this would make an interesting story to be shown during the holiday period.

These night time sightings were made by aircrews flying freighter aircraft off the eastern coast of the South Island of New Zealand. Besides visual sightings from the air and ground, there were also radar targets picked up by air traffic control. Lee convinced his editor to ask fellow reporter, Quentin Fogarty, who was on vacation in New Zealand, to file an extended news story about the sightings.

Fogarty arranged for himself and a camera crew to interview the radar controllers and then to fly in the same airplane along the same flight route as he filmed and recorded brief descriptions of the previous sightings. To everyone's surprise, there were sightings that night, and the TV crew recorded the events on audio tape as well as 16 mm color movie film. After the plane landed, Fogarty took the film to Melbourne. There it was developed and incorporated into a half hour documentary that was shown around the world as the "world's first film of UFOs."

Of importance here is the fact that skeptics immediately proposed explanations for the sightings ranging from Venus and Jupiter, to squid boat lights, to light reflected from the breasts of mating mutton birds!* The TV station was dismayed by these supposed explanations, but most stinging was the accusation of outright hoax: the TV station was accused of creating these sightings in order to increase the number of viewers during New Years Eve. The TV station officials denied the charge of hoax, but admitted that they had not submitted the film for any independent review. They decided to meet the hoax accusation head on: they announced that they would support an investigation of the sightings and announce the results, whatever they were.

---

* The investigation subsequently showed it was none of these.

Then they had the problem of locating some person or organization that would undertake the investigation with a high level of credibility.

Paul Norman was an American who emigrated to Australia in the 1960s. He lived in a town about a hundred miles southwest of Melbourne and was well known for investigating sightings on behalf of VUFORS, the Victorian UFO Research Society. Channel O contacted Norman to find out if he could recommend someone or group that could do a thorough investigation. Norman recommended contacting NICAP in Washington, DC.

Of course, I was unaware of all this except that I had heard about the sightings and had seen them discussed during Walter Cronkite's CBS network evening news show the night of January 1. The news show presented a jumble of information and my thought after the show was over was that there probably was no true UFO, no alien craft, but some lucky person on the other side of the world would get to investigate and maybe find something interesting. I promptly put the sightings out of my head and went on to other things, like practicing for a major piano concert I planned to perform in two weeks.

That was Monday night. Three days later, I was sitting at my office desk when the phone rang. It was Jack Acuff. He got right down to business. "Have you heard about the New Zealand sightings?" I said, "Yes, of course." Then the shock:"They're bringing the film here to NICAP. Want to see it?" It probably took me about 4 microseconds to respond, "Yes, of course."

A couple of days later, I had the original film and began the analysis, an analysis that was intense for the first few months and then went on for several years, the result of which can be seen at my web site.*

---

* The story of these sightings and my analysis of the verbal testimony, the radar-visual events and the film images can be found at: www.brumac.8k.com . Scroll down to NEW ZEALAND SIGHTINGS, and download the WORD document; also scroll down to NEW ZEALAND RADAR SIGHTING, also a WORD document; also see
http://www.brumac.8k.com/NEW_ZEALAND/NZFlashingLight/NZFlashingLight.html and http://www.brumac.8k.com/NEW_ZEALAND/NZSB.html

Figure 37. The author in 1979, preparing to analyze the film

By late February 1979, I had determined that there had been some interesting "targets" (radar signal reflections) detected by the Wellington ground control radar that monitored the airplane. I understood radar, but I decided I needed some consultation with radar experts to confirm or deny my conclusions. Acuff knew that there were experts at the MITRE Corporation, so he suggested I contact Dr. Gordon MacDonald, geophysicist and environmental scientist at the MITRE Corporation in McLean, Virginia. Acuff knew MacDonald because MacDonald had contacted NICAP several years earlier when MacDonald was investigating loud sonic booms that had been heard along the east coast. MacDonald wondered if NICAP had received any reports of booms occurring at the time of UFO sightings.[*]

I presented a three-hour discussion to MacDonald and several

---

[*] The booms were eventually attributed to flights of the Concorde and other supersonic aircraft.

other MITRE employees in early March. As far as I could determine from their reaction, they seemed to agree with my conclusions regarding at least some of the radar targets (conclusion: unexplained) but they suggested I get a further opinion. MacDonald suggested I ask a man he knew at the CIA.

I was shocked. Talk about UFOs to someone from the CIA? I never would have thought to talk to the CIA. After all, the general feeling among UFO investigators was that the CIA and Air Force intelligence were responsible for the government cover-up of information and evidence that would prove UFOs are real. It was thought (and still is thought by many investigators) that these organizations controlled access to proof that some UFOs were actually alien spacecraft (such as Roswell crash material and bodies).

The CIA was believed to be a major bad boy in all this. After all, several months before, in December 1978, the CIA had released almost 1,000 pages of documents related to UFO phenomena as a result of a FOIPA lawsuit. This, after stating (read as "lying") before a judge that the agency had no more than a couple dozen pages related to the Robertson Panel of January 1953.

As you may imagine, my initial reaction was entirely negative. But as I thought about this suggestion, I realized that this was a chance to learn something about the CIA from direct interaction with employees, a chance to investigate the CIA while at the same time getting some useful comments on the radar sightings. So, after thinking about it, I told MacDonald I would do it under the condition that I get some feedback on the radar sightings.

About the middle of March, as I was working in my office, I got a call from a man who said he worked at the CIA. He said he had heard from MacDonald about my presentation at MITRE and offered me the opportunity to get some technical help if I would present my work to the CIA.

Thus it was that about a week later I went to the famous CIA headquarters in Langley, Virginia. There, in a small conference room, I presented to seven employees the result thus far of my in-depth investigation into the rather complicated series of New Zealand sightings.

When I ended my presentation there was, of course, a discussion and the employees proposed typical explanations such as Venus, Jupiter, bright stars, ground lights and so on, including hoax by the TV station. I gave reasons why none of the conventional explanations was satisfactory. As for the hoax hypothesis, I pointed out that the sightings were made by people who were strangers to each other: the pilot and copilot knew each other but no one else; the cameraman and sound recordist, residents of New Zealand, had been hired for the job by the reporter, a resident of Australia, who previously had known neither of them; and, of course, no one on the airplane was acquainted with the air traffic controller who reported the ground radar targets. This information squelched the hoax theory.

Then several of the employees discussed the possibility that flying at night could have had some physiological effects on the passengers (the news crew). Could there have been disorientation and hallucinations? One man raised, then questioned, the possibility: granted that the news crew, first time passengers on this very noisy freighter aircraft, might have become disoriented, would the air crew, thoroughly familiar with flying in one of these planes, have suffered a similar disorientation? And even if one allows that possibility, how does one account for the filmed lights and the radar targets? The man decided that it wasn't physiological effects.

The discussion ended and, unfortunately, I had not gotten the hoped for radar consultation. However, I did meet the man who, five years later, would make the connection between me and Ron Pandolfi. That man was Christopher "Kit" Green, a neurophysiologist and medical doctor. All the other attendees departed, but Green stayed and we talked a bit. Before he escorted me to the door, he invited me to return in a week or so for a more general discussion of the UFO subject. He seemed genuinely interested in the subject, so I agreed. Unfortunately, the radar expert had not been able to attend the briefing so another visit to CIA headquarters was arranged to meet him.

When I returned to the CIA headquarters about a week later, I met with Kit and two other interested employees. Kit portrayed his interest in the subject, and that of the others, as more of a personal than an agency interest. He had been involved in the judge-ordered search of the CIA files that led to the release of the nearly 1,000 pages discussed previously. He pointed to the bottom drawer of a filing cabinet and indicated that it contained copies and originals of all the released documents.

One of the questions raised by ufologists after the December 1978 release of the nearly 1,000 pages was whether or not there were other documents that hadn't been released or at least identified as releasable in part or not at all. Therefore, I asked Kit if he knew of any other documents. He pointed out that, because of security rules, information about a particular subject can only be accessed by employees who have a "need to know" in order to do their job. This meant there could have been lots of documents, even as many as (he threw out a random number to illustrate) 15,000 documents, in other branches of the Agency that he didn't know about. All he could account for were the ones in his office.

We then discussed more general sightings and other topics (I don't recall) and then I left. A week or so later, I returned and visited the radar expert. He gave me some useful information, but was non-committal on whether any of the radar targets were unexplainable.

Thus ended my visits to the CIA, or so I thought.

Many years later, I learned why Kit was interested in the New Zealand sightings: he chaired the "weird desk" at the Agency. In particular, he had an interest in psychic phenomena and had been instrumental in carrying out a program of remote viewing during the 1970s.*

Remote viewing isn't directly related to UFOs, but sometimes a remote viewer would "see" a UFO, and so the people who ran

---

* A search of the internet will locate several web sites which discuss his paranormal interests.

the remote viewing study decided they had to know if UFOs, as alien spacecraft or whatever, were real. The New Zealand case provided evidence at least some unexplainable UFOs could be alien devices.

After my visits to the CIA, I told researcher Todd Zechel, one of the ufologists who had been instrumental in bringing the CIA lawsuit to fruition, about Kit's statement that there could be more documents at the Agency that he knew nothing about, perhaps even 15,000. This caused a bit of a flap that lasted for weeks as Zechel tried to get me to tell him who had been the source of this information so that they could use him (Kit) as a witness in a continuation of the lawsuit. I called up Kit and asked if he would be willing to talk to Zechel and he refused. He also explained more fully what he had meant and that he knew of no other documents. I told Zechel about Kit's refusal, which angered Zechel who accused me of covering up my source—which in fact I was doing, because I didn't want to get Kit in trouble if he had actually revealed to me some secret information.

After several months or so, this blew over and these adventures with the CIA faded into history. The outcome of my visit was that I had given a lot of information about the New Zealand sightings but I had not learned much about what the CIA might know about UFOs. They gave me a small amount of technical help, and that was it.

Now jump ahead about five years. A lot of water had flowed over the dam and under the bridge, a lot of UFO reports had been made, and the world famous New Zealand sightings had faded into the oblivion known as history—only to be replaced by the new kid on the block, the Roswell crash.*

It was now 1984, and I was still a research scientist working at

---

* The Roswell crash case had died an unnatural death in 1947 when General Roger Ramey said the material came from a weather balloon. The case was resurrected in 1978 when Jesse Marcel, the Roswell base intelligence officer at the time, told researchers Bill Moore and Stanton Friedman that it wasn't a weather balloon but rather something "unearthly." The 1980 book *The Roswell Incident* (Charles Berlitz and William Moore, Grosset and Dunlap, NY, 1980) provided the results of the investigation as of early 1980.

a large Navy laboratory, then known as the Naval Surface Weapons Center (NSWC), in Silver Spring, Maryland, where I had been working since 1972.* Beginning in 1973, I became involved with what turned out to be a long duration (over 20 years) effort to understand and utilize the phenomenon of laser generated underwater sound (LGUS) created by the impingement of microsecond-long pulses of radiation from a high power (megawatts) carbon dioxide "TEA" laser on the water surface. (We often referred to this as "laser zapping" the water.)

LGUS was being studied for its possible use in various phases of antisubmarine warfare (ASW). LGUS could be used in tracking and localization of enemy submarines from the air when used with an array of passive sonobuoys (underwater microphones attached to floating radio transmitters) to detect pulse echoes. LGUS could also be used for one-way covert communication from an airplane to a submarine. It also could be used for detection of surface and underwater mines. By 1984, several reports had been written on the subject by myself and several other NSWC scientists. LGUS was the reason for the call from an organization I thought had been relegated to my past.

It was the morning of the first of August 1984, and I was working at my desk when the totally unexpected call came. It was from Dr. Ronald Pandolfi, a scientist and intelligence analyst in the Scientific Intelligence branch of the CIA. He wanted me to tell him what I knew about LGUS. He had discovered what seemed to be a "laser zap gap" between USA research into LGUS and the similar work by the Soviets. Specifically, he had noted that the Soviets had published numerous papers on the subject in the open literature, and open literature publications by the Soviets often indicated that even more classified research was being done at government laboratories. The "free world" literature on LGUS was, by comparison, miniscule, so there was a sizeable gap between the numbers of USSR publications and the number of

---

* This was formerly the Naval Ordnance Laboratory. In 1996, it was replaced by the Naval Surface Warfare Center in Dahlgren, Virginia.

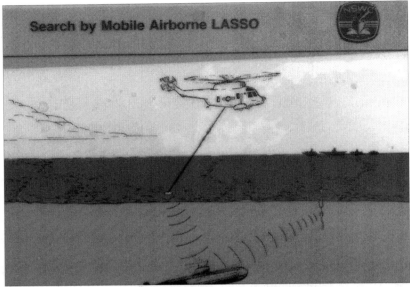

Figure 38: LASSO Used in ASW

USA publications. Hence Ron wanted to know if we were behind the Soviets in this potentially valuable research.

Naturally I was surprised to receive this phone call and relieved that there was no mention of "Topic A" (UFOs). Ron wanted me to visit the CIA headquarters the next day and brief him on our experimental and theoretical research and also what we knew about the Soviet research. This was fine with me. It was a legitimate reason to visit the CIA and I was gratified by Ron's interest in our research. I had already briefed many Navy people on our work, so it didn't take me long to get the presentation ready. Then, late in the afternoon, came the dreaded phone call.

It was Ron again. We talked a bit about the next day's LGUS presentation, but then he changed to a topic definitely not related to LGUS. "I understand that you were here before, several years ago," he said. I cautiously admitted that I had been there. Then he indicated that he knew about my involvement with Topic A.

I was dismayed. I never would have mentioned my side interest in ufology, but he had discovered it so I had to admit it. There goes my credibility, I thought. I asked how he found out, and Ron said that one of his coworkers had heard him talking about me coming to provide a briefing on LGUS research and had recognized my name. That coworker was none other than Kit Green who was, by this time, a top level CIA scientist who briefed high level government officials and Presidents. Thus began a more than fifteen-year association with Ron based on the official CIA interest in LGUS—and on an unofficial interest of Ron and other agency employees in the subject of UFOs and the status of UFO research.

That there would be some agency employees interested in UFOs was not surprising to me. Over the years, I visited many armed forces and government laboratories and found that at most of them there were employees who were interested in the subject. What was surprising to me was that none of the CIA employees seemed to know more about the UFO subject than I did. One would think that if the CIA had an official interest in UFO phenomenology and related subjects (UFO history, sightings, physical effects, alien physiology and communications, etc.) there would be at least several employees who had studied the subject and would know at least as much as I did. If there were such employees, one would think that, considering the number of visits I made to CIA headquarters over the years (and several visits were publicized within the agency—see below), I would have met at least one of them, but I didn't. Instead, I got the impression that, if there was an institutional interest in the subject, it was based on the curiosity of the employees who wanted an answer to the age-old question, are UFOs real? You, dear reader, can decide for yourself, after reading the following anecdotes, whether or not the CIA as an institution was covering up the answer to that question.

Incidentally, I have often been asked how the Navy reacted to my UFO activities. Did anyone complain or try to curtail my activities? I respond that I never ran into any interference, even when it was impossible to maintain low profile.

Consider what happened as a result of my investigation of the New Zealand case. In January 1979, when I requested leave without pay so I could travel to New Zealand and Australia, the manager of my branch did not criticize me for investigating such a "ridiculous" subject as UFOs. Instead, he asked that I present what I knew at that time to everyone in the branch. Hardly a low profile.

After the initial investigation was finished in the middle of March, the Channel 0 TV station in Melbourne which had supported the investigation held a press conference in New York City to publicize the results. A few hours before the conference, I appeared with one of the witnesses in a short news segment on ABC's *Good Morning America* (not exactly low profile). The editor of the NSWC laboratory newspaper saw me on TV and decided that would be a great story for the laboratory newspaper. So I ended up being the "centerfold" of the April 13, 1979 edition of *On The Surface*, the laboratory newspaper! The editor later told me that the Captain in charge of the lab congratulated her on the high quality of the newspaper. Another employee of the lab told me of his sighting many years earlier.

Then I was called into the office of one of the lab directors. I admit that I was a bit apprehensive, but he didn't threaten me with expulsion or reprimand for my UFO activities. Instead, he said "We don't care what you do on your own time, just leave the lab out of it," by which he meant I could do what I wanted on my time but don't mention that I work for the Naval Surface Weapons Center.

Chapter 29
Searching for the Cover-Up

A lthough I had established a "UFO Connection" inside the agency, the continued association between Ron and myself was mostly based on our mutual interest in exploring the phenomenology and utility of LGUS. My interest (Navy interest) was to determine, through laboratory and field experiments and theoretical analysis, the feasibility of making an operational LGUS-based ASW or anti-mine system. Ron's interest (CIA interest) was based on his desire to learn what we at NSWC knew so that he could compare the state of the art in the USA with that of the adversaries (USSR/Soviet Bloc Countries).

We had meetings every several months as needed to discuss the various phases of the program. Ron became a valuable asset as part of the LGUS briefing team as we visited various Navy commands to promote the program and seek support ($$) for the research. Ron was able to provide classified information that indicated the nature of the "Russian Threat." His assessment of the Russian work provided another reason for our continued research: if we didn't continue our research, we might miss something the Russians discovered and then we would be behind them in making LGUS operational.

At the time of our "first contact," NSWC was in a year long process of promoting LGUS, a process that was planned eventually to lead to a review at the Admiral level which, it was hoped, would result in an increase in funding for field tests. Through the latter part of 1984 and during the spring of 1985, briefings were given at higher and higher levels of command. Ron's information about the Soviet version of LGUS complemented what we knew and when, in July 1985, the NSWC LGUS team briefed five Admirals in the same day(!), Ron was there. Unfortunately, this effort did not result in an escalation of funding, but the program did continue at a low level for another ten years. During that time, it was determined that the Russians were experimenting with another type of laser, and the CIA contracted with the LGUS team to do experiments with a similar laser to determine whether or not the underwater sound thus generated would be more useful in some way than the sound generated by our TEA laser. It wasn't.*

During the last fifteen or so years of the LGUS program, while Ron and I were in contact, there were of course numerous developments related to ufology. Many UFO sightings occurred and some of these were discussed after the LGUS meetings. There were also developments related to investigating the assumed government cover-up. Through the first half of the eighties, before Ron was involved, Bill Moore, Jaime Shandera, and others continued to investigate the Roswell crash story.**

As Moore stated publicly, soon after his Roswell book was published in 1980, he was contacted by a high level employee of a government agency who offered to help in his research. This man was given the code name Falcon. Soon after that, Moore and Shandera were also recipients of supposedly leaked documents that referred to "Project Aquarius," "MJ-12" and other allegedly highly classified projects related to locating and retrieving downed Alien Flying Craft (AFC), alien bodies, and even the capture of a living alien. At the end of 1984, Moore and Shandera received the "Eisenhower Briefing Document" (EBD; see below). They investigated it, but kept it generally secret until the early summer of 1987.

Ever since the 1950s, civilian ufologists have suspected that the government was covering up proof that there was some organization, perhaps the Central Intelligence Agency, the Defense Intelligence Agency (DIA), or the National Security Agency (NSA), as well as the Air Force, that was controlling the information about or evidence of the reality of flying saucers.

---

* This was the closest I ever came to "being employed by" the CIA.

** Investigations started in 1979 and continue as of this writing.

This suspicion was greatly increased when Jesse Marcel, the intelligence officer who picked up the crash debris, testified in 1979 that the Roswell crash was not a weather balloon, as claimed by the Air Force in 1947.

Civilian researchers were not the only people interested in determining whether or not some section of the government controlled the hard evidence. Many military and defense department personnel had their own personal interests. One of these was army Colonel John Alexander, who had Top Secret code word clearance for numerous Army programs. John called me up on August 27, 1984 to introduce himself and discuss his effort to locate the assumed control group. At this time, very few people, only friends of Bill Moore, knew about the Aquarius document with its reference to MJ-12 (which we assumed was the name of the control group). I knew about the Aquarius document, but I didn't tell anyone since Bill and Jaime wanted their investigation to remain secret. So, when John said he hadn't located any group yet, I wasn't surprised. However, he said that he and some other interested people would keep trying.

He called again on May 6, 1985, for a further discussion of his attempts to locate the assumed control group. What he didn't tell me was that he was, according to one of author Richard Dolan's information sources, about to form a panel of interested people.[*] According to Dolan's source, Alexander's panel was called the "Advanced Theoretical Physics Group" (ATP) and its first meeting took place about two weeks after our conversation.

The next time I heard from John was over a year later, when he indicated that he wanted to talk face to face at NSWC, a lunchtime meeting, when he would reveal interesting information based on his attempts to locate the control group. So, on August 4, 1986, I met him at the security office and, since this was an unclassified discussion, I escorted him directly to the dining hall and we got our food and sat down to eat and chat. He began by

---

[*] See *UFOs and the National Security State: 1973-1991* (Keyhole Publishing Co. Rochester, NY, 2009); page 382.

saying that he had spent several years trying to discover what government organization, either civilian or military, was in charge of, or controlled, UFO-related information and research. And, as I expected, he wanted to know if I had any evidence that the Navy studied UFOs.

At this point I probably looked at him with a blank stare because I knew that many people previously had tried to find out what the government was doing and had come up empty handed. So, I answered his question: I was not aware of any Navy project that studied UFOs. All the UFO research work that I had done was not at all related to my Navy research. I also probably pointed out that the Navy had not interfered with my UFO research.

Then Colonel Alexander got to the main point. "There is good news and there is bad news," he said, "and they are the same!"

"What is this news?" I asked.

"The bad news is that there is no government organization in charge of UFOs. The good news is the same."

He went on to explain that the lack of a government agency with responsibility for UFO research was bad news because it meant that no one was officially "minding the store" by paying attention to UFO phenomenology. On the other hand, it was good news because that left it up to the civilian sector, i.e., UFO researchers outside (and inside) the government, to do the research. In other words, there would be no government interference with ufologists and the government, so far as his investigation had determined, was not officially interested in the subject and wasn't covering up anything.

My two-part immediate mental response was something like this: (a) not impressed with this claim and (b) this guy doesn't know what he is talking about.

I assumed that he had not looked in the right place (i.e., the right organization) or high up enough in secret defense and intelligence organizations. Even if he were to find the right place there is no guarantee that he would be told anything significant unless he were read into the project, in which case he wouldn't be talking to me.

That was my response because, as the reader of this book knows, I had read many of the case files of Project Blue Book, the files of the Air Force Office of Special Investigations, the FBI Flying Disc File, the CIA UFO files, files of the National Security Agency and on and on, government files that had been released under the Freedom of Information Act during the 1970s, '80s and '90s. I knew there were unexplained sightings described in these files. I also knew that the files proved there had been at least some interest on the part of these government agencies. Moreover, I knew there were other first-class sightings that weren't in these files, sightings that proved there really was something strange going on, i.e., some UFO sightings couldn't be explained as mundane phenomena. I knew from reading certain documents in the FBI "X" File that by the latter half of 1952, some top people in the Air Force had concluded that at least some UFOs were "interplanetary craft" or that "these objects are not ships or missiles from another nation in this world."

I therefore found it hard to believe that the government could ignore the positive evidence contained in these files and have no research project going. I, like most UFO investigators, including Colonel Alexander, assumed that someone or some organization was covering up first class sightings, in particular those by on-duty military personnel and equivalent sightings by technically trained civilians, especially instrumented sightings.

Of particular interest to me at the time of this discussion with Alexander was the testimony of Colonel Ernie Kellerstrauss, a.k.a. "Hawk." Kellerstrauss had been head of an advanced research branch of the Foreign Technology Division at Wright-Patterson Air Force Base. His testimony alone—if it could be proven true—which I learned about eight or so months before talking to Colonel Alexander, was enough to blow the lid off of UFO secrecy.* Having this all in my mind, I wasn't convinced by

---

* See the only complete report of Hawk's testimony at
http://www.brumac.8k.com/HAWKTALES/

Alexander.

Before he left, Alexander made reference to a "panel of experts" that would study the subject. He didn't say the panel had already met three times.* From what he said, I got the impression that I might be invited to be part of it. Then he left. More than a year later, in November 1987, I learned that the panel already existed. I learned that from a "spy" within that panel: Ronald Pandolfi. (Ron told me he only attended the meeting in 1987 and that he wasn't impressed.)**

During the first half of the 1980s, secret investigations to find out if there was a government cover-up were carried out by a few civilians, notably Moore, Shandera, Stanton Friedman, and others, (including myself), who had no access to highly classified government secrets. There also were secret investigations by people like John Alexander and associates who did have access to (some) highly classified government secrets. These investigations were independent. However, they merged somewhat during the early summer of 1987 in reaction to documents received and revealed to the general public by Moore and Shandera: the Eisenhower Briefing Document (EBD), the associated Truman letter establishing "Operation Majestic Twelve," and the Cutler-Twining memorandum that mentions a meeting of the "NSC/MJ-12 SSP," generally interpreted as the "National Security Council/MJ-12 Special Studies Project.***

These documents had been leaked to Moore and Shandera at the end of 1984, so when they released the documents in late

---

* According to Dolan's source: May 21, 1985, August 6, 1985, and April 24, 1986.

** In 2011 Dr. Alexander published his book, *UFOs, Myths, Conspiracies and Realities* (Thomas Dunne Books, St.. Martins Press, NY, 2011), in which he discussed his 25-year effort to locate any defense department organization responsible for UFO studies. He also described the activities of the "Advanced Theoretical Physics" group. A requirement for membership was a Top Secret clearance, which explains why I wasn't invited: I had only a lowly Secret clearance.

*** The EBD and the Truman letter can be seen at http://www.majesticdocuments.com/pdf/eisenhower_briefing.pdf and the Cutler-Twining Memorandum can be seen at http://brumac.8k.com/CutlerTwiningMemo/CutlerTwining.html

May 1987, they could say that they had investigated the validity of the documents for several years. They claimed that, although they could not prove the documents were real, because they could not locate the originating agency (no one admitted to owning the documents), they also could not prove they were faked. Therefore they presented the results of their investigation and let the public decide for itself.

The release of these documents led to a greatly increased interest in UFOs on the part of the press and the general public. The public had already been stirred up by the publication in February of Whitley Streiber's book about his abductions by alien creatures, followed a month later by Budd Hopkins' book, also on the topic of UFO abductions.* But the increased public interest in UFOs didn't begin with the documents released in June, nor with the books released in February and March. Instead, it began in January with the publicity surrounding what would eventually become one of the most famous UFO sightings of all time. And, for me, investigation of this sighting began with a phone call from Ronald Pandolfi.

---

* Whitley Strieber, *Communion* (Wilson and Neff, New York, 1987) and Budd Hopkins, *Intruders* (Random House, New York, 1987).

Chapter 30
The Fantastic Flight of JAL 1628

During the late evening of November 17, 1986, a 747 Jumbo Jet, designated as Japan Air Lines 1628 (JAL 1628 or JL1628), was traveling at about 600 mph over the northern expanse of Alaska and heading toward a landing at Anchorage with a crew of three and a cargo hold full of wine. There was a dim sliver of light toward the west, broken high clouds below and a bright moon behind. The captain saw a couple of lights moving around the left side of the plane and below. Since they were less than 1,000 miles from the Bering Strait and the border with Soviet Russia, the captain assumed he was seeing U.S. Air Force jets patrolling the area. Had the sightings ended there, there would never have been a report. But that wasn't the end. It was only the beginning of what became The Fantastic Flight of JAL1628. What follows is a brief summary.[*]

Several minutes after the assumed jet lights had disappeared from view, two "spaceships" (to use the captain's terminology) suddenly appeared a few thousand feet ahead of the jumbo jet, one above the other. Each "ship" consisted of a rectangular array of yellow and white lights and each array rocked side to side in synchronism with the other as in formation flying. Each light gave off bursts of brightness like rocket exhaust—except these weren't rockets.

After about two minutes they suddenly reoriented to become side by side. They remained in front of the plane for about ten more minutes. The captain said he felt heat on his face. He tried to take a picture but his camera failed to operate. The plane called

---

* The complete history and analysis of the sightings are reported on the web at http://www.brumac.8k.com/JAL1628/JL1628.html

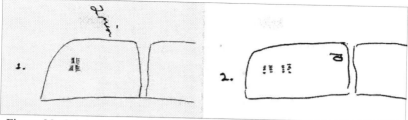

Figure 39. Original drawings by Captain Terauchi of the initial orientation of the objects (1) in which they were situated on top of each other for two minutes, and then the second relative orientation (2) in which they appeared side by side for ten minutes.

the Anchorage Air Route Traffic Control Center (AARTCC) and asked if there were any aircraft in their vicinity (besides them) on radar. AARTCC said no.

Suddenly the objects disappeared. As the crew scanned the sky looking for them, the captain spotted two dim elongated white lights to his left (to the southeast, as they were now flying nearly southwest). The captain turned on his weather radar and found a target in the direction of the lights at the 10 o'clock position (60 degrees to the left of straight ahead) at about ten miles.

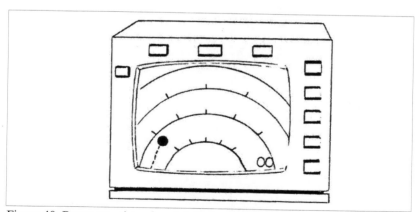

Figure 40. Reconstruction of captain's sketch of how object appeared on radar.

As he continued southwestward toward Fairbanks he suddenly saw, behind and to the left, what he called "the silhouette of a gigantic spaceship." He requested permission to decrease altitude to get away from the spaceship. AARTCC gave him permission to deviate from the planned flight route. During the flight to this point both AARTCC and Elmendorf Air Force Base radar indicated sporadic detections (primary radar returns) that appeared to be from a non-transponding object near the plane.

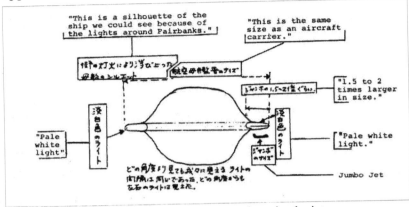

Figure 41. Spaceship compared to a jumbo jet.

A few minutes later, AARTCC requested that he make a turn near Fairbanks to see what was behind his plane. As he made this turn he was told that radar had detected something following behind the plane: there was a "flight of two." As he completed the turn and headed toward Anchorage he again saw the "gigantic ship" but it soon disappeared, as another passenger jet that had left Anchorage and was flying north approached JAL 1628.

JAL 1628 landed soon afterward. The UFO sightings had taken about half an hour. Because JAL 1628 had reported unknown aircraft, and because there seemed to have been some radar confirmation, two Federal Aviation Administration (FAA) investigators immediately interviewed the captain with the help of a translator. They filed brief reports. One job of the FAA is to investigate aircraft that are flying illegally, and the job of the Air Force is to protect the USA from foreign aircraft, in this case Soviet jets.

Since the objects seen were clearly not Soviet jets or any

known type of aircraft, the investigation would have ended there if it hadn't been for the fact that the air crew told friends in Japan that they had seen UFOs that had been detected by radar. The Japanese press learned about the sighting and the supposed radar confirmation. On December 24, a Japanese news agency called the Public Information Officer (PIO) at Anchorage Airport, Paul Steucke, and confirmed the story. It was published in Japan and the American press learned of the story from the Japanese newswires. The story first appeared in the American press on December 29, and on January 1 the *Washington Post* reported that the FAA would investigate.

It was Tuesday, December 30, 1986, when I first learned from Ron about the sighting. He didn't have much information on it, so he suggested I get as much of the story as I could from the press and general media. Over the next few days, I read what appeared in the newspapers and so on, but I couldn't make much out of the mishmash of information in the press reports. The FAA announced that it would investigate so, on January 5, 1987, I, like several dozen news organizations and interested investigators, called the PIO at Anchorage and asked him what he knew about the sighting. He gave me some further information, and added that the radar tape still existed and that the voice tape was being transcribed.

The media reports included illustrations made by the captain showing objects or groups of lights that were decidedly non-aircraft-like. It seemed to me that they might have actually seen an unexplainable object, a "true UFO," and I was worried that the FAA might try to make it go away by doing a poor investigation that ignored the visual sightings and much of the related information. I doubted that the FAA had any employees who had experience investigating UFOs and I expected them to propose any explanation that would make the sighting go away. I told Ron about my concern and boldly asserted that I could do a better investigation than the FAA. The only thing that prevented me from carrying out an independent investigation was that I had no access to the sighting information, the data, both instrumental (radar) and testimonial.

Ron took me at my word and decided to do me a favor. He contacted the director of the FAA, Admiral Donald Engen, to set up a meeting with the individual who was in charge of the investigation, John Callahan. Callahan was Division Chief of the Accidents and Investigations Branch of the FAA, whose office was in Leesburg, Virginia, not far west of Washington, D.C.

It took about a month for this meeting to be set up. In the meantime, the FAA investigated. This involved getting written testimony from the captain, the copilot, the flight engineer and the radar controllers, transcribing the AARTCC voice tape, and analyzing

Figure 42. John Callahan.

the radar data. Callahan had directed that the radar tape be sent to the tech center in Atlantic City, New Jersey. This organization had equipment that could play the radar tape and regenerate the radar screen as seen by the air traffic controllers during the flight. Callahan had further directed that the Branch arrange to play both the radar tape and the voice tape at the same time and have them synchronized.

Callahan and his boss drove to the Atlantic City facility and watched the viewgraph presentation, dated January 12, 1987, that the National Terminal Field Support/ Maintenance Branch, ATR-240, had written. The series of viewgraphs presented the salient details related to the radar, including the opinion that there was at least one actual unknown target when NORAD "advised and confirmed a flight of two." Supplementary maps at a large scale and drawings based on the captain's testimony presented further details. Then the synchronized radar and voice tapes were played, and Callahan used his new video camera to record the computer monitor screen and the voice.

Years later, when I interviewed him in June 2001, Callahan said that he was back at the FAA in Leesburg the next day where he briefed Admiral Engen. Engen then set up a meeting to brief President Reagan's science team. Exactly when this meeting occurred I do not know, but it was the meeting at which, according to Callahan, there were three FBI, three CIA and three science team representatives, as well as FAA radar experts. These people were briefed on the flight details and characteristics of the hardware and software and, lastly, they were shown Callahan's combination video. At the end of the meeting, according to Callahan, a CIA agent said, "You are all now sworn to secrecy." Callahan was surprised at this and wondered why. His first thought was that it was related to Stealth aircraft. Then the CIA guy said it would panic the public so it had to be kept secret. Of course, the public already knew about the sighting, so it couldn't be secret. What could be secret was the meeting itself, which could be interpreted by the news media and general public as evidence of governmental interest in true UFOs, perhaps alien spacecraft, which the government officially claims doesn't exist.

After this meeting, the FAA continued its investigation and analysis of the data. There also were discussions about how to present a credible explanation to the general public. In the meantime, on January 22, the skeptics publicized their first explanation, proposed by Philip J. Klass: the captain and crew had failed to identify Mars and Jupiter, which were quite bright at this time. The press picked up on this but it didn't convince those ufologists who had been following the case through press stories. The problem for ufologists was that without the hard data it was impossible to be sure that Mars and Jupiter did not play some role in the sighting.

Then, on February 5, Ron's effort to get me the needed data paid off. I drove to CIA headquarters where I met Ron and another CIA employee and we all drove to the FAA facility in Leesburg. We were given name tags. Mine read "No Escort" and, even though I was presented as a CIA employee, it gave my actual employer, "USN" (U.S. Navy). We were led to a small office where we were greeted by John Callahan and a couple of other people who answered questions I had regarding the radar detections. Ron and I also watched Callahan's video of the radar being replayed while synchronized with the voice recording of the communications between the plane and the AARTCC. I watched carefully to see if there were any radar targets near the JAL jet. I did see an occasional blip that appeared close to the blip that represented the jet, but the anomalous blips were sporadic and didn't form any consistent track.

I told Ron that the FAA would say there was no ground radar evidence of an unknown object near the jet and no ground radar support for the sightings. (Ron later told me he was impressed with my prediction.) Then, as we left, Ron surprised me with a gift: a box containing radar printouts, transcripts of interviews, a copy of the AARTCC voice tape and numerous other valuable documents. I didn't ask how he got all the stuff. I just walked out with it acting as if this were a normal occurrence, to be carrying a box of documents out of FAA headquarters. From the point of view of ufologists, I walked out with a goldmine.*

Now I had the ammunition with which to do battle with the skeptics, and battle I did—but it was too late. After several months of intense effort, I published the most complete analysis of the radar and testimonial data, in June 1987 (see the web link given above). It was published in the *International UFO Reporter*, the publication of the Center for UFO Studies (CUFOS), so it was read by maybe a thousand subscribers. The FAA, on the other hand, announced its radar-only analysis in a press release on March 5, several months before I had finished my analysis. The FAA also offered to sell the public a data package consisting of testimonies of the air crew and radar controllers and the radar printout and some other documents. This was almost identical to what I had gotten a month before. However, I also got several original analysis documents that weren't in the data package.

---

* Rhetorical Question: if the CIA had a Top Secret group studying UFOs, and if the group was interested in studying the JAL case, wouldn't they have been the recipient of that box of goodies?

As I predicted, the FAA said there was no radar evidence of an unknown object near the jet and the anomalous targets were "split returns." The FAA did not discuss the visual sightings. The FAA press release was publicized by the news media, and millions of people heard or read that there was no radar support for the claims by the Japanese air crew. This effectively squashed the case.

Several months later, the press paid no attention to my analysis which showed that the visual sightings by themselves were strong evidence that anomalous objects had been flying around the jet. So, the FAA won the battle, but not the war. About ten years later, long after he had retired, none other than John Callahan reentered the field of battle on the side of the UFO. He soon became an important member of several disclosure efforts that have taken place since the year 2000.

* * *

Amusing Postscript One: As part of the press's standard adversarial approach to the UFO subject, I was asked to appear on March 6 on WRC TV, the Washington, D.C. local NBC station, to discuss the March 5 FAA press release and report. My "adversary" was Dr. John Pike of the Federation of American Scientists, representing the skeptical point of view. When we got to the "Green Room" in preparation for the discussion, Dr. Pike started asking me questions about the case. It was clear to me that he knew next to nothing about it. Therefore I took special pains to tell him that the skeptics had already published what they called the most likely explanation for the lights, Mars and Jupiter. (I set him up. Nasty me.) I described to him some of the events of the sighting, such as the first appearance of the "spaceships" in a one-above-the-other orientation, followed by a quick reorientation to side-by-side. Then we went before the cameras and, sure enough, Dr. Pike said that the lights were probably Mars and Jupiter. I responded that this was highly unlikely because Mars and Jupiter could not reorient their positions in the sky from one above the other to side-by-side in a matter of seconds. The planets do not appear as arrays of yellow and white lights and they do not produce a feeling of heat. Furthermore, the planets were still in the sky when the plane landed, long after the UFO had disappeared.

Amusing Postscript Two: The publication of my research by CUFOS caused the skeptics to revise their proposed explanation. They now proposed that the air crew had seen moonlight reflect from clouds. As discussed in my article,* this explanation fails to account for bright lights in rectangular arrays, heat on the captain's face, and the colors of the lights.

Amusing Postscript Three: While I was explaining the JAL sighting to Dr. Pike, in walked Dr. Christaan Barnard, the South African surgeon who was the first to accomplish a human-to-human heart transplant about 20 years before this, accompanied by three lovely ladies. He overheard me describing the JAL sightings to Dr. Pike and I guess he decided that it was OK to discuss weird stuff with us. He proceeded to tell us of a paranormal experience he had while lying in a hospital bed many years before. There were, of course, nurses coming in and going out of his hospital room and he recognized them. Then he suddenly became aware of a female figure that entered his room, even though he hadn't seen the door open. He thought it was a nurse he didn't recognize. He then realized that this "nurse" had left the room and so he called for one of the nurses to ask who had just been in his room. When one of the regular nurses entered the room, through the door, Barnard asked who was the nurse that was just in here? The nurse said there had been no nurse in his room. All of the nurses had been assisting in an attempt to save the life of the female patient in the room next door. Then the nurse told him that their efforts had been unsuccessful and she had died. Barnard made it clear to me and Dr. Pike that, in his opinion, the woman that had passed through his room a few minutes before, without opening the door, was the spirit or ghost

---

* http://www.brumac.8k.com/JAL1628/JL1628.html

of the woman next door.

Amusing Postscript Four: at the time of my investigation I wondered whether or not Ron would get into trouble for supplying me with the information I needed to analyze the sighting. After all, UFO investigation was not supposed to be a task of the CIA. Despite my slight concern I didn't discuss this with him. Many years later (2008) he told me that there was an official concern but it was not that the UFOs might have been ET craft. Rather, it was that they might have been Soviet jets trying to use a large commercial jet aircraft as a sort of cover for clandestine flights over Alaska.

Chapter 31
Creating Spies Inside the Agency

As I have already pointed out, the public and general media interest increased through the spring of 1987 with the controversy over the widely publicized JAL sighting and the publication of two widely read books that discussed UFO abductions, *Communion* (Strieber) and *Intruders* (Hopkins). Radio and TV stations were avidly interviewing these authors and just about anyone with "UFO credentials." For example, on Sunday, May 31, Budd Hopkins and I appeared together on WUSA, the CBS network station in Washington, D.C. Then, on June 1, Bill Moore and Jaime Shandera held a press briefing on the just-released Eisenhower Briefing document and associated documents with the clear implication that they thought the documents were real. They gave copies to various news services and the documents got national attention on June 4 when Paul Harvey, a well known radio commentator, featured them in his nationally syndicated *Paul Harvey News*.

That same day I was interviewed by a Phoenix radio station, by *New York Times* science journalist William J Broad and by Nat Sheppard of the *Chicago Tribune*. On June 15 a reporter from *Nightline* called to set up an interview which took place two days later. The interview was aired on June 24 on the ABC network.

The next day, June 25, began an event which had been building for a year, ever since the Executive Committee of the Fund for UFO Research (FUFOR) had volunteered to put on the 1987 Symposium of the Mutual UFO Network (MUFON) in the Washington, D.C. area. FUFOR was not an organization that investigated UFO sightings. Instead, as a 501(c)(3) charity, it acted somewhat like the National Science Foundation in the sense that it would raise money from those people interested in the subject and would use this money to support various UFO-related research and education projects. MUFON, on the other hand is an organization that investigates sightings, publishes a monthly journal and, every year since about 1970, has held large conferences at various cities in the USA. The conferences are put on by local MUFON members or MUFON-affiliated local groups such as FUFOR.

During the summer of 1986, FUFOR announced that it would hold the 1987 conference at The American University within a couple of days of the "Fortieth Anniversary of UFOs" that is, the Kenneth Arnold sighting which initiated public attention to the subject on June 24, 1947. The motto of the conference was "Forty Years is Long Enough," an oblique reference to the presumed government cover-up. (Too bad the motto was rather premature.) It was also to be the first MUFON conference to feature speakers from many countries, a truly international symposium, providing that sufficient money could be raised from interested donors to pay the transportation costs. During the ensuing year money was raised and speakers from a dozen countries, as far away as Australia, Italy, Argentina, and Japan, and as close as Canada were brought to Washington, D.C. to speak about UFO sightings and research in their respective countries.

The MUFON conference officially got underway on June 27, but there were two events which preceded the conference: a briefing at the National Press Club, June 25, for the foreign press, and a briefing for Congress, held June 26 at the Rayburn Building, arranged through a member of the House Science and Astronautics Committee. At the press briefing the various speakers gave short summaries of UFO-related activities in their own countries and made themselves available for interviews. In this way, the conference made international news. At the House briefing I and others, for several hours, discussed UFO sightings and related phenomena, the history of Air Force investigation, the documents from the FBI, CIA, NSA, and other governmental organizations that had produced UFO documents. Of course the then-recent EBD and related documents were also discussed.

Although no congressman attended, numerous congressional aides did attend.

The conference itself was spectacular. About 500 registered attendees filled the Ward II lecture hall at The American University as the international speakers took the stage during the day. Saturday evening in particular was packed (standing room only and spillover into the hallways) as half a dozen UFO witnesses who believed they had been abducted, appeared in public for the first time to discuss their experiences. On the stage were Whitley Strieber, who challenged skeptic Philip Klass to interview the abductees who were present, several of which were featured in Budd Hopkins' two books, the then-recent *Intruders* and his 1981 book, *Missing Time*.

During Sunday afternoon, there was a special session on the government cover-up as it appeared in various countries and, of course, discussions of the various documents that had been officially released by agencies such as the FBI, CIA, Air Force, and NSA, as well as the latest on research into the Roswell case and "leaked" documents such as the EBD.

Needless to say, but I'll say it anyway, the news media picked up on various aspects of the conference and so it was well publicized. Of course Ron knew about it and he could see the large level of public interest, which apparently extended to the CIA. He did something unprecedented: he invited me to speak about the UFO subject at CIA headquarters!

It was to be an unclassified lecture of the type that featured a speaker giving a lecture on a popular topic of interest to CIA employees, such as they had had numerous times in the past. For example, in February 1986, Ron invited me to a lunchtime lecture by Tom Clancy, author of *The Hunt for Red October*, a story about a very quiet Russian submarine that was stolen by a Russian captain and brought to the USA. In that book Clancy had written about technology used in anti-submarine warfare (ASW) with such accuracy that he had been asked by the Navy to remove about 100 pages of his manuscript. Whereas the submarine story was fiction, the ASW technology was real and classified. The

CIA employees were surprised at the amount of ASW knowledge he had been able to acquire from the unclassified literature.

The day of my lecture was a hot Tuesday, July 7, 1987 and my day began at work at the Naval Surface Warfare Center (NSWC). A little after noon I drove around the west side of Washington to CIA headquarters across the Potomac River. I parked and entered the building and was standing in the spacious lobby when Ron appeared. He escorted me to what, if I recall correctly, was the director's conference room. There was a long table in the center of this room with perhaps two dozen people, some sitting at the table and others standing along the wall. Evidently this lecture had been publicized. There was a slide projector and screen and everything was ready for a "historic" lecture.

At about 1:00 p.m. I began and you'll never guess what I told them, so I won't keep you waiting. I told them about their own documents.

Yes, that's right. Most CIA employees did not know that the agency had released hundreds of pages of UFO-related material about eight and a half years before. I discussed the history of CIA involvement with the UFO subject and some of the interesting cases contained in the document collection. Of course, I also discussed some of the FBI documents and the Eisenhower Briefing Document.

At the end of my formal lecture, about 3 p.m., there were questions. No one fell asleep and no one said their time had been wasted. Apparently I had made quite an impact because sometime later Ron told me that my lecture had created a lot of "spies" within the agency, that is, employees who were using their Top Secret clearance levels to nose around and try to find Top Secret UFO-related information and projects. Whether anyone found such projects, I do not know. At least no one told me, which is not surprising. I wouldn't have been told even if someone had found something. The government, meaning mostly the Air Force but including the CIA, officially denied the existence of any cover up by any secret group controlling access to the hard evidence. This meant that the CIA employees had to be careful as they did their own investigations into the supposed cover up. What if a CIA agent suddenly learned of the existence of MJ-12 (or whatever it may have been called) and the UFO proof? All he could do would be to not tell anyone, and of what value is that?

After the MUFON conference and the CIA lecture, UFO related activities decreased, but LGUS research continued and so did meetings at the CIA headquarters where "Topic A" continued to be a subject of discussion. Late in the year, Ron told me of a CIA employee who had started a search on his own for UFO-related documents or activities and "got stomped on." I guess he tried to gain access to some information for which he was not cleared or had no legitimate "need to know." On November 18, 1987, Ron told me that a CIA archivist had spent some amount of time searching but had not found MJ-12 in the CIA files. He thought that MJ-12 might have been a real organization, but not part of the CIA and unrelated to UFOs. In his opinion the Eisenhower Briefing Document was a hoax, but he couldn't prove it.

The same day, November 18, according to Richard Dolan's previously mentioned source, was the date of the last meeting of John Alexander's Advanced Theoretical Physics group, the meeting that was held in the "tank," the vault in the Pentagon in which Top Secret meetings were held. On the same day Ron told me he had attended the meeting and he told me the names of some of the attendees, several of whom I knew. Ron said he had suggested that they invite me, but they decided against it because "I might talk."* On the last day of the year I visited Ron at CIA headquarters and John Alexander was there. I don't recall him telling me about the ATP meeting and I also don't recall telling him that I knew about the meeting, anyway.

After the MUFON conference and the CIA lecture, my CIA interactions continued with a concentration on LGUS experiments. A CIA programmer helped me develop a computer

---

* As I've already pointed out, Alexander wanted every attendee to have a TS security clearance and my clearance level was only S.

program in Fortran to calculate the amplitude and waveshape of LGUS. But a storm was brewing, a storm that started in November in a small town in Florida, a storm that would lead to another lecture at . . . you know where!

Chapter 32
Gulf Storm

I will never forget Wednesday, November 11, 1987. Veteran's Day. A day off for "non-essential" government workers . . . like me. It's a good thing, too. The previous several days had been quite mild with 70 degree weather, but during the morning of the 11th it began to snow. It looked like no more than an annoyance at first, only a couple of inches. Yet that was already a record for the earliest snow for the Washington, D.C. area. Then the storm intensified to white-out level, a blizzard, and before it stopped at night it dropped nearly a foot of snow, an amount that was far beyond what the weather forecasters had expected. School was cancelled and only the essential federal employees reported for work. So I had another day off, which was fine with me since I couldn't drive anywhere anyway, the road was blocked by snow.

Meanwhile, in a tiny town in Florida, another type of storm was brewing, a storm that would impact my life and keep me busy for months and even years. But I didn't know about this gathering storm for more than a month after it began, and when I did learn of it in early January 1988, it seemed to me to be like the first two inches of snow in the D.C. area on November 11—a mere annoyance!

The town is called Gulf Breeze and the storm was a large number of UFO sightings. Gulf Breeze is in the panhandle of Florida, sandwiched between the large city of Pensacola and the small town of Pensacola Beach which borders the Gulf of Mexico. Not an area where one might expect to find numerous UFO sightings. Yet, for about six years, starting in late 1987, Gulf Breeze was UFO central for the world.

What people remember most about the Gulf Breeze sightings are the sightings by Ed Walters and the controversy over his many photos. In fact, most people probably think that Ed's sighting reports and pictures constitute the totality of the Gulf Breeze phenomenon. But Ed wasn't the only one to see a UFO in the vicinity of Gulf Breeze; there were several hundred other witnesses over the roughly six year period. And he wasn't the first, which is why what happened during November 11 is so important.

Sam was the first witness.

It was about 2:30 a.m. when he awakened his owner, Billie Zammit, and indicated that he wanted to go outside by growling and nuzzling her cheek. Sam, the normally placid Labrador Retriever that sleeps next to her bed, was being bothered by something outdoors. Billie got out of bed and held the restless dog by the back of its neck while she led it to the back door. Evidently the dog wanted to go outside. She assumed it was for the usual reason, so she opened the door expecting him to run out into the back yard.

To her surprise the dog didn't go running out as she expected. Instead, it looked up and started to bark. It was barking at something in the sky. She looked up and was startled to see something that she had never seen before. She described it in a letter that was published about two weeks later by the *Gulf Breeze Sentinel,* a weekly Gulf Breeze newspaper published every Thursday. She wrote:

> I looked up and *this same object* [author's emphasis, referring to the object/UFO shown Ed's photos, which were published in the Sentinel a week after Zammit's sighting] was in the sky, about one mile high, 15 degrees to the northwest and there was a stream of light that came down into our canal.

After watching this object for several minutes she became so frightened that she grabbed the dog and ran into the house. "I thought that maybe the object was here to get my dog," she told MUFON investigators during interviews on November 25 and December 3.

She reported to MUFON that the UFO was circular with a bright pastel yellow or orange light at the bottom, that it appeared to be brighter than Venus and that it was two to three times larger than the apparent size of the moon, which was also in the sky at the time.* She added the information that the "stream of light" was blue in color and that it made about an 8" diameter spot on the dock in the canal behind her house.**

In her letter to the *Sentinal*, Billie wrote that the next morning she "wanted to call the Air Force, but chose not to." Therefore, her sighting probably would have never been reported if it hadn't been for the publication of Ed's photos a week after the sighting.

The next reported sighting occurred only six hours later at a location less than a mile from Mrs. Zammit's house. At 8:15 a.m., November 11, Jeff Thompson was driving his truck north on Orliola Beach Road when he saw a large object moving slowly just above the trees. He drove a bit further while watching it. Then it stopped moving and he noticed two Air Force jets flying eastward toward the object. The jets were also at low altitude. He stopped his truck and stood on the ground where he watched as the object, perhaps less than 500 feet away, suddenly increased its altitude and hovered while tilted at about 45 degrees. After about 45 seconds the object seemed to zoom upward with a flash that caused "dark spots" in Jeff's eyes. The two jets then turned northward.

In his letter to the *Sentinel* (published about two weeks later in response to the publication of Ed's photos) Jeff said that the object had "window type formations" similar to the dark rectangular areas in the published photos, but he didn't see any lights. (Perhaps lights were not obvious in daylight.) When interviewed about six months later, Jeff provided further details. "I saw this big object that I had never seen before heading from east to west

---

* The moon was in its last quarter phase at the time. The full moon had been about six days earlier.

** Her report of the pastel yellow or orange color at the bottom of the object and of the blue beam of light are consistent with what Ed reported to the MUFON investigators over a month later, in January 1988. However, at the time of her letter to the newspaper or her report to the MUFON investigators, she did not know the colors that Ed reported, because those details had not been published.

at just treetop level. And it crept along super slow." Jeff stopped his truck at Highway 98 and got out to look at the object.

It was 30 by 15 feet I would say. And then it suddenly shot up at an angle and stayed there. I looked to the right and saw two jets coming side by side about 200 feet above the trees, maybe a little higher. The object just sat there waiting for them to come closer ...and then there was a glaring flash and it shot straight up in the air and it was gone.

He estimated that he had seen it for perhaps three minutes. He said he could see the "porthole windows . . . door looking objects." Jeff said that he got angry when, many weeks later, he read of the criticisms of Ed's photos.

The next sighting occurred at about 5 to 5:30 p.m. Charles Somerby, former editor of the *Sentinel*, and his wife, Dori, were walking near their house when they saw an object that was grey with white "portholes." It had lights on the bottom and a light on the top, and it seemed to drift like a balloon. It appeared larger in angular size than the full moon and was last seen drifting southwestward. Charley has publicly stated that, based on his Naval wartime (World War Two) experience as an aircraft spotter, he is certain that "what I saw on Veteran's Day night (i.e., Nov. 11) was exactly what was depicted in the pictures published in the Sentinel." The Somerbys watched the object move slowly southwestward out of sight. As with the previous witnesses, and as with the witnesses to be mentioned, the Somerbys' report was a response to the publication of Ed's pictures.

At sometime between 5:30 and 6:30 p.m., Linda Lube saw "a type of light moving very slowly across the sky southeast toward Gulf Breeze" as she was cooking outside her home. At about 5:30 p.m., a 38 year old mother and her 15 year old son (witnesses wished anonymity) were driving along Highway 98 in Gulf Breeze when they saw a "crown-shaped" object which she subsequently described as looking exactly like what Ed photographed. It seemed to float along at tree top level while keeping pace with her car.

About ten miles southwest of the Somerbys, Ed Walters, a

custom home design and construction contractor, was working at his desk which faced a large window looking toward the west. At about 6 p.m., he happened to look out the window and see a strangely lighted object moving from left to right, i.e., northward, some distance away over the houses across the road.

At first he thought it was a helicopter, but then he realized it didn't look like a helicopter. The lighting and shape weren't like a helicopter. He was puzzled at not being able to recognize it, so he got up and walked the few steps from his office to the front door where he walked outside and stood just outside the door. Now, looking more closely, he realized that he was looking at something he truly couldn't identify—a UFO. His first thought was to call the police, but then he realized that it was moving and would be gone by the time the police arrived. Then he thought, "Quick, get a photograph."

And take a photo he did, with a Polaroid camera that was immediately available (see Figure 43). Figure 44 is a blowup of the UFO image. Notice that the nearby tree blocked the view of part of the left side of the object.

The above picture was the first of five photos he took during that first sighting. He took many more photos over the next five months. "Hoax," said the skeptics but they couldn't prove it. Through the winter, spring and summer of 1988, the controversy over Ed's photos raged in the private conversations of ufologists and in the publications of the press and TV media. At the same time, the number of witnesses increased to over a hundred.

My investigation began in February with the initial assumption that it was all a hoax. But then Ed began producing photos that would be difficult to fake, and I was most impressed with his stereo photos which were capable of measuring the distance to the UFO. In particular, stereo photos taken on May 1 showed two UFOs hundreds of feet away and high over the water of the Santa Rosa Sound on the southern shore of Gulf Breeze.

The whole "Gulf Breeze Complex" of sightings from November 1987 to July 1988 is extremely complicated. More information about the sightings and controversy, pro and con, can be

Figure 43. First photo by Ed Walters.

found on the internet using a search for "Gulf Breeze UFO." However, for the purposes of this book about my interactions with the CIA, it is only necessary to know that, in spite of the controversy and claims of the skeptics, I had concluded that Ed's sightings, and those of the many other witnesses, were *real*, that is, of an actual "alien" craft (without any assumptions about where it came from, how it got here or what it was doing).

My conclusion was based on hard evidence, namely the technical difficulty—verging on impossibility in the case of the May 1 stereo photos—in producing all of his photos as compared to Ed's evident lack of knowledge of photography. I also took into account his lifestyle, which had no "need" for UFO sightings, the fact that his family members were also witnesses, the fact that he passed two polygraph tests administered by a skeptical polygrapher and, of course, the fact there were numerous other witnesses who reported the same object.

Ron and I had a series of LGUS meetings in preparation for a test series at a Florida laboratory that occurred at the end of

Figure 44. Blow-up of the first photo.

August 1988. Then we had further meetings to discuss the report that would be written. At our meetings I kept Ron apprised about my Gulf Breeze research and conclusions. Because of the high level of publicity of these sightings during the spring and summer of 1988, he was of course familiar with the controversy over the photos, and if I understood him correctly, believed them to be a hoax.

Nevertheless, there apparently was a considerable level of interest on the part of CIA employees. About the middle of September, I showed some of Ed's pictures to several employees and was invited to discuss this and other UFO subjects with a branch chief. Then, a few weeks later, Ron arranged for me to give a lecture about my research into the Gulf Breeze sightings. This lecture occurred near the end of October. I did not have time to present the complete sighting history and technical analysis during the allotted time, so I was invited to return and finish the discussion, which I did about two weeks later, in November 1988.

Chapter 33
UFO Cover-Up? Yes!

October 14, 1988 is a date that has gone down in history as the day the UFO cover up went public. That is the date of the TV show called *UFO Cover Up? Live!* This was a unique show in that it was, as the title said, live. This showed some bravery on the part of the producer, Michael Seligman, because all the various portions of the show had to work correctly the first time—no chance to go back and edit or make corrections if something went wrong. Of course, the show was scripted, but there was minimal rehearsing so no one knew exactly what the interviewees would say.

Hosted by actor Mike Farrell of the *M*A*S*H* TV show, the show filled two hours (including advertisements). It consisted of sighting testimony from a number of witnesses and testimony from researchers about the possibility that there was (is) a government cover up. The quality of the show was degraded, in my opinion, by the use of 1950s flying saucer film clips to illustrate various types of sightings, but there was also a lot of good information.

One segment of the show, which is pertinent to this discussion, featured the appearance of about 100 Gulf Breeze witnesses who believed that they had seen the same object that Ed Walters photographed. That segment also included me as I defended Ed's photos against an attack by an unconvinced government photoanalyst, Dr. Robert Nathan of the Jet Propulsion Laboratory. I pointed out that he had examined only a few of Walters' three dozen photos whereas I had studied all of them, including those taken with Ed's stereo cameras. I also pointed out that it would be illogical to claim that Ed's photos were all hoaxes while, at the same time acknowledging that all or even just one of the sightings of the same object by the other witnesses were real. The appearance of all these witnesses increased the credibility of Ed's sightings and probably played a role in Ron's decision to invite me to lecture on the Gulf Breeze sightings about two weeks later, as mentioned in the previous chapter.

The *Cover Up? Live!* TV show could trace its beginnings to the investigation of the EBD, MJ-12, and related documents, and to the early 1986 investigation of testimony of Ernie "Hawk" Kellerstraus, mentioned above. Bill Moore told me in 1986 that he was working on a script for a show, but it really didn't get underway until 1987. Robert "Condor" Collins in his book, *Exempt from Disclosure, The Disturbing Case About the UFO Cover Up** has described the "spook-like" secret meetings that occurred as the show was developed.

Of particular interest were the segments of the show that presented evidence of a government cover up. One particular segment featured an air force pilot, William Coleman, who had a very convincing multiple witness sighting while flying in the mid-1950s. He recalled that he and the other witnesses were interviewed and reports were written. Years later he was the press officer for Project Blue Book. While at the Blue Book office he decided to look for his sighting report and the reports by the other witnesses. The reports were not there, nor was there any evidence that they had ever been in the Blue Book file. So, where did they go? Coleman didn't know.**

The most shocking segments of the show involved the testimony of two secret agents known only as Falcon and Condor and seen only as silhouettes with their voices modified to be unrecognizable. These were code names assigned by Bill Moore and Jaime Shandera to two government employees who claimed to have inside knowledge of interactions between the government and UFO aliens. Moore told me soon after the show what years

---

* Available from Robert Collins, Peregrine Communications, Vandelia, OH 45377 and Amazon.

** This was not the only sighting that wasn't in the Blue Book file. As I have pointed out before, several reports in the FBI file were not in the Blue Book file.

later became general knowledge in the UFO community—namely that the real Falcon, who had contacted Moore soon after the Roswell book was published, was not part of the show.

Instead, Richard Doty, who knew the information provided by Falcon, substituted for the real Falcon. Doty was a retired Air Force officer who had been assigned to the AFOSI at Kirtland Air Force Base. Doty had also contacted Moore after the Roswell book and provided some documents that mentioned sightings near Kirtland Air Force Base. Condor was retired Captain Robert Collins, who had been working at an advanced science branch at Wright-Patterson AFB. I had interviewed Doty several years earlier about a report of UFO landings near KAFB* and it was Collins who introduced me to Ernie Kellerstraus, mentioned above.

Some of the information presented by Falcon (e.g. Doty) was rather bizarre: there was a crashed saucer and bodies, and one living alien had been a "guest" of the U.S. government for several years. Perhaps the most memorable comment by Falcon/Doty, a comment that most people remember and which was guaranteed to reduce the credibility of the show to near zero, was that aliens prefer Tibetan music and strawberry ice cream. The show also presented an organizational chart or "wiring diagram" that indicated that the CIA and other government intelligence organizations had the responsibility for controlling access to hardware and bodies from UFO crashes and the MJ-12 organization had responsibility for developing policy related to how to handle the information.

It seems that the CIA did not appreciate this accusation. The day after the show, two Colonels who were Doty's superiors, either of whom could potentially have been the real Falcon, were interviewed by Ron in an effort to determine whether or not some classified information had been released and what they knew of Falcon. The questions that were crying for answers were, where did Falcon get this information and was the information (and

---

* See http://www.brumac.8k.com/kirtland1.html

documents) accurate and truthful, or were they bogus. Thus began the hunt for the Falcon and the hunt for proof of a government cover-up, a hunt that would last for years.

Chapter 34
The Helpful CIA

I t should be apparent from the preceding discussion that there was considerable interest by CIA employees in the various aspects of UFO studies, including sightings themselves and the history of sightings. An example of being helpful has already been described, namely, the JAL 1628 investigation. Here are a few more examples.

Several weeks after Yasuhiko Hamazaki of Kanazawa, Japan, took a home video of a UFO, on July 7, 1989, I was asked by MUFON to evaluate the sighting and analyze the images he obtained. I decided to do more than that, I would write a journal article about it because of the rare coincidence between the shape of his UFO and the shapes of the three images captured by Michael Lindstrom using a 35 mm camera while on vacation in Hawaii in January 1975, more than 14 years earlier. During early 1990 (these investigations take *time!*), as I was completing my article, I needed a copy of a single frame of the video to publish. I could do a lot of analysis with the equipment I had, but I did not have the equipment to print out on paper a copy of a single frame. A friend of Ron's who worked at Photon Research Corporation (a CIA contractor) arranged to have some frames of the video digitized and printed with different contrast and brightness levels. I chose a couple of these to use in the publication.*

During the late spring and summer of 1989, a rash of UFO

---

* See "A Rare Photo Coincidence" published in the *International UFO Reporter* (IUR) 15, 3 pg. 6. Oddly enough, two years after the Hamazaki video there was yet another coincidence: a chance occurrence of an image of the same basic shape was photographed by a tourist in Medjugorje in western Bosnia who took a picture of the St. James Church. She did not notice the UFO, the image of which appears in the sky almost over the church. I am not aware of any other photos with images of a similar shape (see IUR 17, 2 pg. 12).

sightings broke out in the Soviet Union. Western ufologists learned of the sightings through Russian newspaper stories but the language barrier prevented the ufologists from realizing the magnitude of the flap.

The CIA, through the language translators who worked for the Foreign Broadcast Information Service (FBIS), overcame the language barrier. The CIA had collected UFO sighting reports published in Soviet newspapers since the late 1940s, but there were not many published UFO reports to collect because from the 1950s up to the mid-1980s the reporting of UFO sightings was discouraged in the Soviet Union. The official policy, set in the 1950s, was that flying saucer reports were mere tricks of the decadent capitalist nations to deceive the peace loving peoples of the Soviet Union into thinking that the western countries had developed some new weapon systems. However, with the onset of *glasnost* (openness, transparency) in the mid-1980s under the leadership of Mikhail Gorbachev, restrictions on UFO stories were lifted. So, when the flap, began the Russian language newspapers were suddenly full of reports, both new and those that were previously unreported.

In August 1989, I pointed out to Ron that we could not keep up with the Russian flap because of the language problem, so he arranged to have newspaper articles translated for agency use and for me to receive copies of FBIS translations. From then on and for about two years afterward I was well informed about Soviet UFO sightings and events. For example, I received information about the famous Voronezh sighting on September 27, 1989, when multiple witnesses reported seeing a UFO landing and "creature."* Another major sighting found in the FBIS translations was made by multiple military witnesses near Moscow Military District (actually Pereslavl-Zalesskiy) on March 21, 1990. Soon afterward, numerous Soviet newspapers published the report on the March 21 sightings written by Air Defense

---

* According to the staid, conservative newspaper *Tass*. See http://www.ufocasebook.com/Voronezh.html.

General Igor Maltsev.[*]

About two months later, in June, Ron told me that the fact that Maltsev had made a serious official report about the March 21 sighting had caused quite a stir at upper CIA levels. Apparently there was also a stir at the top levels of the Soviet government because, according to a report published on May 4, 1990, Gorbachev, while giving a speech to workers in the Ural Mountain area, said that the UFO phenomenon exists and should be studied.

Another news story that caught the interest of the CIA was based on a November 1990, interview of Air Force General Ivan Tretyak, the Commander of all the Soviet Air Defense Forces. Tretyak essentially confirmed what Maltsev had reported about eight months before and went on to say that Soviet military research into devices (such as advanced radar) that could detect American Stealth aircraft "will simultaneously promote the solution to the UFO riddle."

Older sightings were also discussed in the news reports, one of the most interesting being the crash of some object near Dalnegorsk on January 29, 1986. Analysis of the crashed material showed that part of it had an unusual composition that included tiny (17 micron) fibers of quartz twisted around tiny gold wires. Kit Green was interested in this report because, as he told me, he was aware of three similar cases of debris with tiny fibers that occurred years before. I sent him copies of the information I had but he didn't tell me the dates or locations of the other cases.[**]

In return for the translations, I helped the FBIS. The translator asked if I would be willing to provide a briefing to the FBIS on the subject of UFOs and I said I would. Shortly thereafter, I received a formal invitation from the Chief of the Soviet Sciences branch of the FBIS and so, on October 19, 1990, I drove to the

---

[*] See http://ufo-blogg.blogspot.com/2012/04/russian-jets-chase-ufo-over-moscow.html and http://www.ufoera.com/articles/mufon-russian-jets-scramble-for-ufo_1190311164.html.

[**] For more information on the Dalnegorsk case see http://en.wikipedia.org/wiki/Height_611_UFO_Incident.

FBIS headquarters and presented a lecture on UFOs with an emphasis on Soviet sightings. I pointed out that in the previous several years there had been growing interest in the subject and that all of the major newspapers had carried one or more UFO-related stories. I presented a brief comparison history, what was happening in the USA compared to what was happening in the USSR, that started in 1947 and ran to 1990. The audience, about 30 FBIS employees, gave my lecture "rave reviews."

On July 14, 1990, six Army intelligence analysts, from an Army listening post in Augsburg, Germany, were arrested in Gulf Breeze, Florida, for leaving their duty station without permission. They had been stopped by police because of a broken tail light and the police had run a standard check of files for any charges against the driver. The police had found that the driver was AWOL and reported to higher authorities including the FBI, the CIA, and the National Security Agency (NSA). Several days later, the newspaper reported that this group of six people (five men and one woman) were part of the "End of the World" cult intending to locate and kill the anti-Christ and then wait for the rapture, which they predicted would occur at Pensacola Beach in October 1990.

News stories also indicated that they had an interest in UFOs, and so the connection was made between them and the Gulf Breeze sightings and the annual meeting of the Mutual UFO Network (MUFON) that had taken place in Pensacola during July 6-8 of that year. Naturally, I and others in MUFON were afraid that this would degrade the Gulf Breeze sightings and ufology in general, i.e., the general public might view the actions of the six as typical of "those nutty UFO believers."

Then Ron provided me with information that showed that their appearance in Gulf Breeze had nothing to do with the sightings or the conference, but rather was a sort of accident of fate: they wanted to visit a friend who lived in Gulf Breeze. He also told me that, although the newspapers had said that they had Top Secret clearances they actually had only Secret clearances and apparently had scared themselves by downloading UFO and religious information from highly questionable sources on the Internet. He said that the NSA computer analysts had found nothing that was classified on their computers, nor any classified documents, so they were ultimately released as deserters.

One might ask, why no more than a slap on the wrist? Because to go to trial would have been an embarrassment to the intelligence services that screen personnel for work in highly sensitive posts: they would have to explain why they missed the "cult" connection.

Chapter 35
UFO or U2?

On December 13, 1993, Robert James Woolsey, then the Director of Central Intelligence under President Clinton, was interviewed by Dianne Rehm, a well known National Public Radio talk show host. His appearance on the show, which originated at The American University in Washington, D.C., had been announced in advance. When Elaine Douglass, a ufologist who lived in the D.C. area at that time, learned of his appearance she decided to call into the show in the hope that she could ask him what the CIA knew about the flying saucers/UFOs and a possible cover-up of information. As fate would have it, she was one of the callers selected and Woolsey answered her question with something like "I don't know."

Although she didn't get a straight answer, her phone call had a lasting impact because, combined with requests for UFO information from other people, it caused Woolsey to ask agency employees if there was or had been any project related to UFOs. Sometime after this, he asked a historian who worked at the National Reconnaissance Office, Gerald K. Haines, to review all the records on the subject and write what would be the official history of the CIA involvement with the subject of UFOs. This Haines did over the next several years, ultimately resulting in an unclassified report.[*]

Haines began his research in early 1994 with an agency-wide search for programs and documents, and in late 1995 completed the first version, which was classified Secret. The article covered the history from 1947 through 1990 and was based largely on the documents that formed the FOIPA release some 16 years earlier,

---

[*] Gerald K. Haines, "CIA's Role in the Study of UFOs, 1947-90," from the CIA journal *Studies in Intelligence* (Spring, 1997).

in 1978.

I learned about the history project in the summer of 1994. In November 1994, he told me the first draft of the article was almost finished and that he wanted me to review it for accuracy, especially regarding the Air Force UFO investigation activities referred to in the article. In February 1995, he told me it was undergoing review for classification. I eagerly awaited a copy so I could compare what he wrote with what I was writing for use in the first version of my book, *The UFO-FBI Connection*, which included a section on the history of CIA activities related to UFO investigations (essentially Part II of this book).

I thought I would see it soon but I didn't hold my breath. It was a good thing I didn't, because it was almost a year later, in 1996, that the review was finished and he gave me a copy. Because the document was classified Secret, I thought I might learn something about saucers/UFOs that I didn't already know.

No such luck. His history mostly described the initial flurry of CIA activities during the latter half of 1952, the Robertson Panel in early 1953 and the subsequent efforts of the Agency, during the latter 1950's through the 1970s, to prevent the general population from learning that the Agency had ever had any interest in the subject. This was not new to me, but imbedded in the general history was something new, something that was the reason for the Secret classification: his discussion of the early U-2 flights and their impact on Project Blue Book sighting statistics. This discussion was later declassified and appeared in the published version mentioned above in May 1997.

Soon after I read the article, I told him his claims about the U-2 would be criticized by ufologists and I would be the first critic. Having foreknowledge of what he claimed, I wrote a rebuttal for publication the day after his article became available. My article, with the title, "CIA Explanation is Preposterous," is summarized in the next few paragraphs.

According to Haines, the CIA agents who ran the U-2 spy plane project thought that they could use the UFO phenomenon as a cover for U-2 flights. These agents believed that when the U-

2 high altitude spy plane began flying in early August 1955, "commercial pilots and air traffic controllers began reporting a large increase in UFO sightings."

The U-2 is the high altitude spy plane made famous by the 1960 shootdown of Gary Powers as he flew over the Soviet Union and by photos of Russian missile sites in Cuba during the 1961 Cuban Missile Crisis.

Haines wrote:

> According to later estimates from CIA officials who worked on the U-2 project and the OXCART (SR-71 or Blackbird) project, over half of all UFO reports from the late 1950s through the 1960s were accounted for by manned reconnaissance flights (namely the U-2) over the United States. This led the Air Force to make misleading and deceptive statements to the public in order to allay public fears and to protect an extraordinarily sensitive national security project. While perhaps justified, this deception added fuel to the later conspiracy theories and the coverup controversy of the 1970s. The percentage of what the Air Force considered unexplained UFO sightings fell to 5.9 percent in 1955 and to 4 percent in 1956.

This explanation for many ("over half of all") UFO reports was new to the general public and ufologists in particular because it had been classified information (Secret level) until it was declassified for use in this article by Haines. There was no mention of it within the documents that have already been discussed that were released by the CIA in December 1978 (see Part II).

According to Haines, the U-2 was reported as a UFO because:

> . . . the early U-2s were silver (they were later painted black) and reflected the rays of the sun, especially at sunrise and sunset. They often appeared as fiery objects to observers below. Air Force BLUE BOOK investigators, aware of the secret U-2 flights, tried to explain away such sightings by linking them to natural phenomena such as ice crystals and temperature inversions. By checking with the Agency's U-2 Project Staff in Washington, BLUE BOOK investigators were able to attribute many UFO sightings to U-2 flights. They were careful, however, not to reveal the true cause of the sighting to the public.

The claim that the U-2 caused "over half of all UFO reports from the late 1950s through the 1960s" is, to put it gently, preposterous. The U-2, with its wingspan 80 feet long by 6 feet wide (front to back) flew at 60-70,000 feet, at which altitude it was essentially invisible during the day. It created no contrail because of the lack of moisture at that altitude. It was, after all, intended to be invisible. During the hour before sunrise and the hour following sunset it would be possible for an unpainted aircraft to reflect the sun enough to be visible, perhaps with a reddish glow resulting from the reddening of sunlight.* High altitude balloons (e.g., Project Skyhook) did cause some UFO reports during these times of day and were so identified by the Air Force and civilian investigators. However, only a small fraction of sightings occur during these times. The largest fraction of sightings is at night, when the U-2 can't be seen, and the next largest fraction is during the daytime.

If the CIA officials had been correct, there should have been a noticeable increase in the number of reports per month received by Project Blue Book when the U-2 started flying. One can find the monthly Project Blue Book sighting numbers in the *Scientific Study of Unidentified Flying Objects* a.k.a. *The Condon Report.***
The numbers include reports by pilots and air traffic controllers as well as by military personnel and civilians.

Consider, for example, the numbers of reports starting ten months before and continuing to ten months after the August 1955 start of U-2 flights.

During 1954: October (51), November (46), December (30).

During 1955: January (30), February (34), March (41), April (33), May (54), June (48), July (63), August (68), September (57), October (55), November (32), December (25).

During 1956: January (43), February (46), March (44), April (39), May (46), June (43).

---

* Caused by passage of the sunlight through the atmosphere, which acts like a filter that removes blue and green relative to red.

** E. Gilmor, Ed., Bantam Books, NY, 1968, pg. 514.

Looking through this list of numbers of reports per month one sees a jump from 63 in July 1955 to 68 in August, and then a decrease to 57 reports in September. Even if all of the increase of five reports was a result of reports of the U-2, it would be nowhere near "half of all reports." Adding all the reports for ten months earlier yields a total of 430, or an average of 43 reports per month. Doing the same for 10 months after also yields 430 (an unexpected coincidence!). If flights of the U-2 were to add to the basic average sighting rate before the U-2 started flying, 43 per month, surely there would be a noticeable increase in the sighting rate after the U-2 started flying, but there is no indication of an increase during the 10 months after the start of U-2 flights! The sighting rate fluctuated considerably during the years before and after the U-2 started flying but these fluctuations had little or nothing to do with U-2 (and SR-71) flights.

In the early 1960s, many of the U-2s were painted black or other camouflage colors, thus reducing the number of flights when U-2s could potentially be seen by glint reflection from the sun. Aside from the statistics, it should be pointed out that many unexplained sightings involved relatively nearby, structured objects, not nearly invisible distant points of reflected light. These unexplained objects were reported to move rapidly at (angular) speeds that would exceed the apparent (angular) speed of the U-2, which flew at about 500 mph (730 ft/sec) at 70,000 feet altitude, if seen at all.

Chapter 36
UFO with a Magnetic Personality

The subject of my last UFO lecture at the CIA was a UFO that had a "magnetic personality." I had been working on this case for about half a year and had told Ron and some other CIA employees about it. They were very interested because this was a unique type of physical trace case. That is, after the sighting was over, there were permanent or temporary effects—physical traces—on the environment.

In this instance, the most unusual physical trace was a magnetic field that conventional physics would consider to be impossible. I formally presented my analysis and conclusions at the spring meeting of the American Physical Society (APS) on April 15, 1993.* Ron suggested that I give my APS lecture at the CIA, which I did on May 28, 1993. Here is a shortened version of my discussion.

On Friday, September 11, 1992, at approximately 6:20 PM Mrs. A (name confidential) was entering the driveway at her home in Gulf Breeze, Florida, when she saw to the northeast, over the roof of her house, an unusual round object. She saw the object rise upward, move to the right a short distance while flipping over and disappearing in the clear sky.

It appeared brownish-grey at the top and bottom with a pinkish-red line around its circumference. The center of the bottom seemed to be glowing. The object was at some distance

---

* "Strong Magnetic Field Detected following a Sighting of an Unidentified Flying Object," *Bulletin of the American Physical Society*, Vol. 38, p. 1041, 1993. Note: so far as I know, I am the only ufologist to have presented a number of UFO papers at the annual APS meetings over the years.

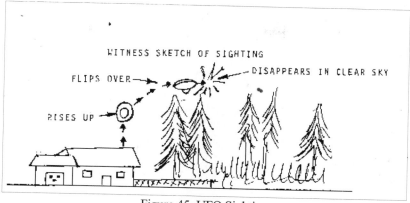

Figure 45: UFO Sighting

and apparently had risen upwards from behind her house where there was a lawn, a pond and trees. The total duration of the sighting was several seconds. Within an hour or so, the witness told her husband, John, (who also wanted anonymity) about the sighting. Several hours later, he contacted two local UFO investigators, Bland Pugh and Bruce Morrison, both members of the Mutual UFO Network.* They agreed to visit the site during the afternoon of the next day.

There were thunderstorms in the area and it rained for a while late Friday night. The next morning, John used a transit to determine Mrs. A's sighting line direction from her observation point in the driveway. He then searched the area behind the house to determine whether or not there was any trace of magnetism left by the UFO. He decided to do this because about 19 years before, he had had a UFO sighting during which a UFO had passed over his car and the gauges in his car were affected. It was his opinion, whether right or wrong, that the gauges had been affected by a strong magnetic field associated with the UFO.

Back then, he had no instrument to confirm that there was a magnetic field. But in 1992, he had a very sensitive device, a flux gradient magnetometer or "gradiometer" (model GA-52, manu-

---

* Note: the MUFON investigators were well known in the area of Gulf Breeze and Pensacola because of the numerous newspaper, radio, and TV stories about the Gulf Breeze Sightings.

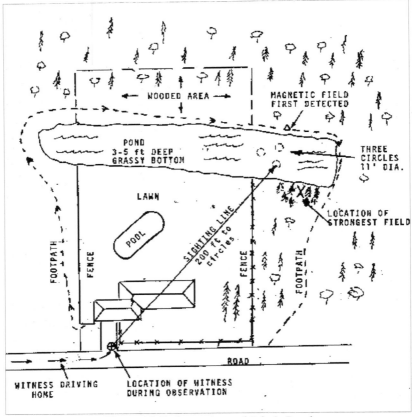

Figure 46: Pathway Around John's Pond

factured by the Schoenstedt Instrument Corporation) which he had used during the previous ten years to search for buried oil well casings (iron pipes) as part of his work.

John began his search by following a footpath that leads around the west (left) end of the pond and then eastward on the north side the pond. He was continually waving his gradiometer rod in various directions to the left and right while pointing it toward the ground and also upward.

The gradiometer generates an audible tone in the presence of a magnetic field. The frequency of the tone increases as the field gradient increases. As he approached the east end of the pond,

Figure 47: John Holding the Gradiometer Rod

approximately at the location of the triangle (see Figure 46), he began to notice an increase in frequency. He subsequently determined that the frequency was highest when he stood on the shore of the pond and pointed his instrument upward and over the pond. He believed that either he was detecting a "magnetic cloud" in the air over the pond or else his instrument was not operating correctly.

He checked the operation of his instrument at a location a considerable distance away from the magnetic field and convinced himself that there was nothing wrong with the gradiometer. He then continued his search around the pond and discovered an area where he obtained the highest frequency when he pointed the wand straight upward or nearly so. This area, which seemed to him to be beneath the source of the field, was under some pine trees on the south side of the pond (see the X in Figure 46), about 60 feet (18 meters) from where he first detected the field. His impression was that the source was actually at or above the tops of the trees.

He also noticed, while looking over the 4 to 5 foot deep pond, that there were three circular areas of depressed pond grass at the bottom (Figure 46; the circles are not to scale). He had been fishing there several days earlier and had not seen any circles. Subsequently, after plotting the locations of the circles and the strong magnetic field on a map of the area, he found that they were roughly in the direction of the his wife's sighting line to the UFO and about 200 feet (60 meters) from her location in the driveway (Figure 46).

Several hours later the two MUFON investigators arrived with a video camera and a Geiger counter. Mr. Pugh made an area search with the Geiger counter and found no clearly elevated readings. John showed them the circles at the bottom of the pond and demonstrated the operation of the gradiometer. Mr. Morrison used a video camera to record the way John operated the gradiometer as he searched the area for the presence of magnetic field sources. The video camera also recorded the audio pitch of the gradiometer as John waved it around at various locations. I subsequently determined from the videotape and from my own experiments with a nearly identical gradiometer that John operated it in a completely normal manner. A simple experiment carried out later by John at my request provided a calibration of the gradiometer and proved that it was operating normally.

Mr. Morrison first recorded John operating the gradiometer on the north side of the pond (triangle location, Figure 40) looking southward toward the clump of pine trees. As John moved the gradiometer from side to side the audio pitch was maximum when the wand was pointed somewhat upward (20-30 degrees of elevation) and generally in the direction of the trees which were about 60 feet (18 m) away across the pond. This suggested to John and the investigators that the source of the field was above the lake or perhaps at or above the treetops on the other side. As the gradiometer rod was turned away from the direction of maximum frequency (maximum gradient), i.e., rotated to the left, right, upward or downward, the frequency decreased considerably. The maximum pitch was at such a high frequency that John offered his opinion, based on using the gradiometer under many conditions for about ten years, that the response of the gradiometer was comparable to what one would get by putting the gradiometer very close to a large piece of iron or steel.

The investigators then walked to the clump of pines. There the videotape shows that the highest frequency recorded, higher than at the location (triangle) across the pond, was obtained when the gradiometer was vertical or nearly vertical under the trees. As John walked away from the clump of trees in various directions, the maximum frequency diminished, indicating that he was moving away from the field source. A search of the area failed to turn up any source of field other than the source which seemed to be at or above the treetops.*

When John was across the pond from the trees and pointing the gradiometer toward the direction of maximum frequency the audio pitch of the gradiometer was not perfectly steady. Instead, it fluctuated rapidly by small amount in pitch ("warbled") at a roughly constant rate of about 8-12 Hz in a manner similar to a lightly modulated FM signal.** This warbling was also apparent when the gradiometer was under the trees, where John called the attention of the investigators to this unusual effect. Subsequent experiments with a magnet (see below) created greater gradients and higher frequencies than were obtained under the trees, yet there was no warbling of the audio tone during the experiments. The warbling suggests that the magnetic field was pulsating slightly (changing in amplitude and/or direction) at a rate around 10 Hz.

While the investigators were under the trees, Mr. Morrison pointed his camera upward and videotaped the treetops and the clear blue sky. Nothing unusual was seen in the sky or on the trees.***

---

* There was no boat available at the time, so a search was not made over the water.

** FM stands for frequency modulation in which a "carrier wave" of relatively high frequency is caused to change frequency slightly, usually a few percent, at a rate determined by a much lower modulating frequency.

*** Recorded on the videotape is a discussion by investigators in which they speculate as to whether or not the source of the field, assumed to be the UFO, was still there but "cloaked" so as to be invisible.

John repeated the area search the next day. He reported that the gradiometer had a slight response only under the trees, indicating a considerable decrease in the magnetic field gradient. Unfortunately there was no one to record these measurements of the magnetic field.

On September 14, three days after the sighting, the MUFON investigators returned to the area and videotaped John with his gradiometer standing under the same trees where, two days before, the audio tone was very high. Now the pitch was at a value that corresponded to "no detectable gradient."

On that same day, the grass circles were measured and found to be about 11 feet (3.3 meters) in diameter. A week or so later, the investigators thought of checking the magnetic field in the area with compasses at several locations. All the compasses pointed north, indicating that there was no large magnetic anomaly in the area. (It is unfortunate that they didn't think to use compasses on the day after sighting!)

John did a simple experiment with a calibrated magnet that I sent to him. Using the experimental results, I was able to calibrate the gradiometer for frequency vs. gradient. I then measured the gradiometer frequencies on Morrison's videotape. When he was at the triangle location looking southward toward the clump of pine trees and swinging the gradiometer back and forth, the gradiometer gave a clear indication of a strong field when it pointed in the direction of the trees, which were about sixty feet away at the time. Furthermore, the maximum frequency, corresponding to about 0.18 Gauss per meter, was obtained when the gradiometer was tilted upward by an angle in the range 20°-30°—suggesting that the source of the field was above the treetops on the other side of the pond! As the gradiometer rod was turned away from the direction of the treetops, the frequency decreased.

To confirm that the source was at the tops of the pine trees, they all walked to the clump of pines. There the videotape shows that the highest frequency, corresponding to about 0.25 Gauss per meter, was obtained when the gradiometer was pointed upward toward the treetops.

A search of the area failed to turn up any source of field other than the source which seemed to be at or above the treetops. The field gradient near the trees was so strong that, according to a magnetic expert at NSWC where I worked, it was roughly equivalent to the distortion in the earth's field caused by the presence of a destroyer battleship at a distance of eighteen meters!*

To understand the significance of the strength of the magnetic field gradient consider the following facts:

1. Wood is not ferromagnetic (it cannot be magnetized as iron can).

2. While John was standing under the trees with his gradiometer pointed upward and generating a high pitch on September 12, Morrison was videotaping the tops of the trees, which were silhouetted against a clear blue sky—they could see nothing up there that could cause such a field gradient.

3. If, somehow, the wood had been made ferromagnetic by a UFO (an impossibility, according to the physics of magnetic materials), or if the UFO had deposited a massive amount of some ferrous (i.e., containing iron) magnetic material on the trees, then the strength of the magnetic field should have been the same on the second day of the investigation because ferrous materials do not lose their magnetism at environmental temperatures (they do lose it at temperatures of many hundreds of degrees).

4. There had been rain off and on during the days following the sighting, yet there was no magnetic field near the ground, so no magnetic residue had washed off the trees. Hence we are left with a double mystery: how did the field get there in the first place, and, once there, why did it disappear?**

---

* Alternately, the field gradient could have been created by a one-meter-diameter coil of wire at a distance of eighteen meters and with an ampere-turns product of about three million.

** For further details and magnetic field calculations see http://www.brumac.8k.com/MagneticUFO/MagneticUFO.html.

The CIA employees were as puzzled as I by this "magnetic sighting." No one has yet provided an explanation based on conventional physics.

Chapter 37
CIA Cover Up?

From the time I first visited the CIA, I wanted the answers to two main questions, sort of the UFO counterpart of "what did they know and when did they know it." I wanted to know (a) if they had Top Secret information about UFOs and (b) if they were in control of the assumed cover up. Furthermore, if (a) were true, I wanted to know what the secret information was and if (b) were not true, who was in control of the cover up. In other words, I wanted to know everything the CIA knew.

Of course I wasn't so naïve as to think they would actually tell me anything that was classified above Secret level, and that would mean that the really good stuff would remain out of reach. But I didn't need to have access to actual Top Secret UFO information in order to deduce, from the way the employees themselves treated the subject, that they did or did not have information that they couldn't tell me.

My first knowledge of UFO-related activities of the CIA came from the documents released in 1978. According to those documents, as I have described in Part II, the CIA interviewed the Air Force's Project Blue Book after the Washington D.C. sightings of July, 1952. The Air Force told the CIA that there was no convincing evidence that UFOs were devices with advanced technology. Evidently, the Air Force was covering up the real situation, as described to the FBI, that several percent of the sightings could be not be explained, and this caused some high level Air Force personnel seriously to consider the possibility of interplanetary ships!

It appears that in the early 1950s the CIA accepted the Air Force explanation for sighting reports: mostly misidentifications or failure to correctly identify phenomena, a few hoaxes and a few caused by delusional witnesses plus sightings with "insufficient information to decide." After the Robertson Panel conclusion in early 1953 that there was no unknown technology involved in UFO reports but that such reports themselves could be a threat during a military emergency by clogging up communications channels, the CIA treated the UFO problem as more of an irritant than something to pay close attention to. In the released documents, there was scant evidence of a continuing interest into the latter 1970s, when the documents were released.

The professed innocence of the CIA and other government agencies including the Air Force relative to withholding convincing evidence was not accepted by ufologists. However, at the time of the CIA document release (December 1978) they could not point to any withheld information that would be absolute proof that some UFOs might be Alien Flying Craft (AFC). Then, starting in late 1978, came the beginning of revelations relative to the Roswell crash case—and the whole scene changed. Ufologists could now accuse the government of covering up hard (literally, hard) evidence. The question then became, what organization was in charge?

Once again the CIA was under the gun, so to speak, as a logical place to put a Top Secret UFO project dedicated to studying all aspects of a crashed AFC. This presumed project would have started in 1947 and, if it were within the Agency, would have been deeply buried by the 1980s. Most Agency employees wouldn't know of it. But what of those few employees (e.g., Kit, Ron) whose job involved keeping track of the UFO scene? Even if they did not have access to the project itself, they may have known of its existence. And if they knew of its existence they would have acted as if there was something going on in the Agency. They would have treated the subject seriously.

In my opinion, however, the way they actually treated the subject was rather different. Kit seemed to treat the subject as something of medium importance, not *very* important but also not something to laugh about. Coming from his background in paranormal research (remote viewing), this is not surprising. Ron, on the other hand, seemed to treat it as a joke or an amusement, at least initially.

During the first decade of my interactions with the Agency, I often wondered why the Agency, through the activities of first Kit and then Ron, was taking such a continued interest in UFO investigations and the activities of people pursuing UFO studies. There was, of course, the intrinsic interest on the part of many agency employees in the UFO subject itself, but there didn't seem to be an official reason for the CIA to pay any attention to UFO research.

Then, in 1990, Ron told me the official reason: the possibility of espionage! He said that in the 1970s, the CIA had obtained "firm evidence" that the KGB had devised a plan to use U.S. citizens, including ufologists, to penetrate U.S. defense programs. This reason was echoed in Haines' history wherein he wrote, "Agency analysts from the Life Sciences Division of OSI (i.e., Kit) and OSWR (i.e., Ron, in the Office of Science and Weapons Research) officially devoted a small amount of their time to issues related to UFOs. These included counterintelligence concerns that the Soviets and the KGB were using U.S. citizens and UFO groups to obtain information on sensitive U.S. weapons development programs (such as the Stealth aircraft), the vulnerability of the U.S. defense network to penetration by foreign missiles mimicking UFOs, and evidence of Soviet advanced technology associated with UFOs."

I presume that the Soviets developed this plan because ufologists, while trying to penetrate through the walls of secrecy in order to locate government information about UFOs, might discover and publicize secret information about (legitimately) classified defense programs. Thus, they would become unwitting agents of the KGB. Since the KGB had everything to gain and little to lose by tracking the efforts of ufologists to uncover secret UFO programs, the KGB could actually go so far as to support UFO research. Furthermore, this research could be of value to the KGB whether or not some UFOs were AFCs.

Of course, I knew nothing of the Soviet plan during the 1970s, but I certainly was aware of the possibility that the efforts of ufologists could produce information of value to the USSR. Furthermore, I knew of an event that proved the Soviet interest in American ufology. Sometime in the latter 1970s, when I visited the NICAP office for some long forgotten reason, Jack Acuff (recall that he was the director of NICAP) told me he had had a visitor. A man had walked into the NICAP office and introduced himself as an employee of the Russian embassy. (This automatically meant that there was a "good chance" (99%?) that he was a KGB agent or reported to one.) He began discussing UFOs and the voluminous files of UFO cases in the NICAP office (over 10,000). According to Acuff, the man made it clear that his (meaning the KGB!) interest in UFOs extended to a quid-pro-quo sort of monetary support of NICAP: you send me UFO reports and related information and I'll make continuing contributions to NICAP. He then departed. Acuff told me he immediately called the FBI to report the visit. He never heard from the man again.

This possibility of unintentional espionage by ufologists is the basic reason why Ron called two Air Force Colonels to the CIA to testify regarding the claims made by "Falcon" during the *UFO Cover-Up? Live!* TV show mentioned before. Ron wanted to know if either of them was Bill Moore's secret source, Falcon. If not, he wanted to know what they knew about Falcon and about AFOSI officer Richard Doty, who had acted as a go-between for Falcon and Moore and had substituted for Falcon in the video-taped testimony during the show. Ron wanted to know where Falcon had gotten his information and if any information about classified defense programs, such as Stealth, had been contained within Falcon's televised testimony.

Two years later, in November, 1990, Ron told me why he was so interested in Falcon and another person who was presumed to exist that was known only as "Number 1." He said that "top people (in the Agency) are assuming that #1 is a KGB spy who leaks names of real defense programs as (if they were clandestine) UFO programs." This would be done in the hope that ufologists would try to penetrate these legitimately classified programs, as they looked for the hidden UFO programs, and publicize the secret technology.

The need to protect classified programs from espionage resulted in a continual pursuit of the Falcon and a continual search for the source of the leaked documents that might contain legitimately classified defense information. For years Ron suspected Doty was the source but he was not able to prove it. Then, in the summer of 2012, Bill Moore released the name of Falcon. According to Moore, Falcon was Harry A. Rositzky, a retired CIA counterintelligence agent who died in 2002.

While he was searching for Falcon and the source of the documents, Ron told me the answer to one of the questions I had at the time of our first contact, about fifteen years earlier. The question was, is there a hidden organization within the CIA that studied or "controlled" the UFO evidence? He told me in March, 1994, "The Director of Central Intelligence and the Deputy Director come to me when they want to know what is going on in UFOs." He admitted that there might be a liaison person, a sort of "mole" in the CIA, working with a UFO group in another agency, but he was "not aware of any group effort in the CIA."

This essentially answered the question of whether or not the CIA was in charge of the UFO evidence but this information didn't answer another key question: was the information in the documents true, bogus or "half-truths" and disinformation? It also didn't answer the question of whether or not there might be some super secret project in another agency or outside the government. Kit, during a conversation in 2008, provided a partial answer to this question. He told me that he had questioned 18 top level people over the years, ranging from CIA officers to cabinet members and high level military and even a President. Most didn't know anything about the subject but some did. This led him to conclude that there was something going on, but not in the government. I then mentioned Colonel Alexander's conclusion after years of searching that there was no secret project and Kit responded that he had discussed this with Alexander and had concluded that Alexander hadn't "knocked on the right doors" or hadn't looked "high" enough.

From the preceding discussion one might conclude that if there is a secret project to study UFOs/flying saucers/AFCs it is carried on outside the CIA and few, if any, employees are aware of it. This is not surprising since, if there is such a project, it was most likely started by the Air Force as a contractor program outside the government back in the early 50's and is now buried so deeply "no one" can find it. That's not to say that there is no CIA employee who knows about a project or important UFO evidence.

In the summer of 2012, about the same time as the announcement that Harry Rositzky was the Falcon, another CIA employee, Chase Brandon told interviewers that he had once seen, some years before, a "Roswell box" inside a Top Secret vault that contained part of the Historical Intelligence Collection of the CIA. According to Brandon, he saw in that file box "proof" that confirmed his opinion that the Roswell crash was of an Alien Flying Craft (although he didn't use that terminology). Unfortunately he would not be specific regarding the nature of the proof. Soon after Brandon's claim was publicized a CIA historian searched the vault and failed to find the Roswell box, but it could have been removed days to years before the search. So, if Brandon did see this proof (if it isn't just a fabrication to promote his book), then there was, at least at one time, important UFO evidence within the CIA which few knew about.

Chapter 38
None Dare Call it Conspiracy

The FBI-CIA-UFO connection and the "X-Files" of Air Force intelligence show that as far back as the early 1950s some Air Force, FBI, and CIA personnel knew, or strongly suspected, that "UFOs are real," or, more accurately, some UFOs were tangible objects with capabilities far exceeding our own aircraft. Not only that, but, as early as 1948 Project Sign personnel had concluded that the saucers had an interplanetary origin, i.e., some UFOs were Alien Flying Craft. In 1952 Dr. Stephen Possony indicated in a travel request memorandum that the Air Force "assumed" saucers were interplanetary (Chapter 19) and Captain Ruppelt indicated in his personal memoranda that some top officials accepted the interplanetary explanation. This was confirmed in August and October 1952 when Air Force intelligence told the FBI that top officials were seriously considering the interplanetary explanation (Chapter 20).

However, in public the Air Force presented a unified front, consistently claiming that all saucer sightings could be explained as misidentified natural phenomena or man made objects, with some being hoaxes or delusions. The Air Force consistently denied any evidence of a threat from or interplanetary origin of the saucers.

This raises a major question: why did the Air Force publicly deny what at least some top officials knew to be true? Was it because there was no universally accepted absolute proof—that is, no hard evidence? Was it because the very top generals really were not convinced and so they set forth a policy of denying the evidence? Or did they know the saucers were real and orchestrated a cover-up—a conspiracy to withhold the evidence—because they believed the information too dangerous to be released?

These questions cannot be answered directly. There are no documents of unquestioned authenticity that are presently available which indicate the specific reasons why the Air Force consistently denied the evidence. All that can be demonstrated is that the Air Force *did* withhold the evidence by classifying the sightings and the internal discussions about the sightings and, through public statements, by giving the American people the impression that a good investigation was ongoing but that nothing new had been discovered.

It is very likely that the failure of the Air Force to level with the American People can be traced to General Vandenberg's rejection of the Estimate in late September or early October 1948. This rejection had a lasting impact by forcing the intelligence analysts to classify each unexplainable sighting as either an unknown (to them) domestic project, a foreign (Soviet) advanced aircraft, a misidentification of natural or manmade phenomena, a hoax, or a delusion.

We know that the analysts rejected the first explanation because no one, not even the top military and government officials, was aware of any domestic aircraft project with the capabilities attributed to the flying saucers (and none has been discovered as a result of recent investigations into the state of aeronautical research in the late 1940s and 1950s). We now know that for several years the analysts clung to the foreign aircraft explanation, using it to justify the expenditure of funds for further research. However, this explanation was not really believed even as early as 1948, and it was not used after the big flap of 1952. The inadmissibility of the ET explanation, combined with the essential impossibility of the domestic and foreign project explanations, forced the analysts to invent explanations based on misidentification, hoax, or delusion.

One might say that Vandenberg's rejection was the triumph of policy and politics over logic. Within half a year of Vandenberg's rejection, the ATIC personnel who had worked on Sign and the Estimate had been transferred to other projects. The remaining low level personnel and the new hires who joined the project in later years realized that there was no glory and no promotion for those who went against the official policy. The Grudge investigators therefore simply treated the sightings as trivial wastes of time, to be studied only because of orders from above. The final Grudge report was a travesty of science, proposing unlikely or impossible explanations for sightings just so they could claim to have explained each sighting.

Yet, in spite of the Air Force public attitude that saucer sightings signified nothing, by the early 1950s, as we now know, some top officials admitted to leaning toward, if not fully accepting, the interplanetary hypothesis. Yet, the public admission of this never happened. The Vandenberg Policy carried the day. When, at the peak of the sighting fervor, when flying saucers seemed to be very real and appearing everywhere, General Samford publicly stated that all unexplained sightings were natural phenomena, even though privately his intelligence office told the AFOSI that there was no theory for the unexplained sightings, and even told the FBI that the interplanetary explanation was under serious consideration.

It would appear that the real intent of the Air Force generals who made public statements in July and August 1952 (Samford, Vandenberg, and Ramey) was not to provide the public with real information about flying saucers, but rather to damp down the public near-hysteria over the sightings. To do this, all they had to do was appeal to the previous public Air Force statements that all sightings could be explained, and those which weren't explained probably could have been if there had been more information (an outright lie, as we now know).

In 1953, the CIA proposed a defense-based reason to deny saucer reality: if people thought saucers were real they might report more of them and the reports could clog communication channels, especially if the Soviet Union were to generate spurious saucer reports at the time of an attack. Furthermore, spurious saucer reports could cause fighter aircraft to be diverted from attacking the real Soviet aircraft. However, these reasons no longer applied in the 1960s (and afterward), so one might think that the Air Force could have admitted to the saucer reality at least by the time of the Colorado University study in 1967-1968. But no, this study, even though leaving about one third of its cases unexplained, claimed that there was nothing threatening or new about saucer reports which were made, according to the project director, Dr. Edward Condon, by "poor observers."

So the question arises, did the top Air Force officials orchestrate an effort to withhold information and downplay (debunk) saucer sightings? And, if so, was it because the Air Force officials didn't want egg on their faces for suggesting something that seemed ridiculous (ET visitation)? Or was there another reason?

Consider, again the early history of Air Force involvement. Within a couple of weeks after the first publicized sightings, and only a couple of days after the Roswell Army Air Base reported finding a flying saucer, the Air Force (General Schulgen) asked the FBI for help. It is at this point that the history of the Air Force involvement could be interpreted in either of two ways.

The first way, "Interpretation A," is based on the available documents from the Blue Book file, from the FBI, CIA, State Department, Army, etc. These documents do not say there was hard evidence.* Therefore Interpretation A is based on the assumption that the Air Force never got hard evidence, i.e., that the Roswell debris was not from an ET vehicle and there was no evidence of a saucer crash at any other time.

Interpretation B of the Air Force UFO history is based on the assumption, as yet not documented in an indisputable way, that the Roswell object was, in fact, an alien craft, probably with bodies. This latter interpretation is based upon the wealth of witness testimony collected since the 1970s by a number of researchers, as well as upon testimony from individuals such as Dr. Robert Sarbacher, Wilbert Smith, and others.

Let us first consider Interpretation A.

---

* In fact, some of them at the Secret level of classification, and one at the Top Secret level, indicate that there was no hard evidence.

A. The Air Force Had No Hard Evidence

If there never was hard evidence, then the policy to withhold information might be interpreted as follows: the Air Force investigators and the Top Brass, being as puzzled as everyone else, were trying honestly to find the explanation and never were able to because the sighting data were never good enough. There was no conspiracy to withhold the ultimate secret of saucer reality because the sightings were unimportant and no one was sure the objects were real. Nevertheless, the Air Force withheld information to minimize public interest in the subject.

A more realistic interpretation of the Air Force involvement is based on the idea that the Top Brass knew there was convincing evidence, it was just not "hard." The idea that the Top Brass knew of convincing evidence is based, in part, upon the 1952 FBI "X-File" documents that say the interplanetary explanation was given serious consideration; upon the April 1952 memorandum by Dr. Stephen Possony, wherein he indicated that some top Air Force generals assumed saucers were interplanetary; and upon the private notes of Captain Edward Ruppelt. One may speculate that the top Air Force officials were afraid of the consequences of publicly admitting saucer reality because they would at the same time have to admit that the Air Force and the government didn't know what was going on and couldn't do anything about the saucers. Therefore, they covered up their belief in UFO reality and directed the lower ranking officers to make it appear as if there were no convincing evidence. If this were the case, then there was a plan for withholding evidence, which in turn would require the acquiescence of the AFI personnel and those at ATIC where the sighting information was stored. This could be called a conspiracy to convince the American people, and the world, that there was nothing to flying saucer sightings.

B. The Air Force Had Hard Evidence from the Start

This one is a no-brainer, a slam dunk: if Roswell (or any other crash report) is true, if an alien craft did crash and the material and perhaps bodies were retrieved by the Army Air Forces, then we have collusion on a grand scale to prevent the American public from knowing the truth.

But, some might say, the open record as presently available shows that there was no hard evidence because no "evidence of the hard evidence" ever showed up in Air Force documents. In Secret level classified documents, the Air Force repeatedly denied having hard evidence.

However, recall the conversation that Wilbert Smith had with Dr. Sarbacher (Chapter 17). Smith's Top Secret memorandum about that conversation said that flying saucers are real. Dr. Sarbacher told me directly that he had been told of debris and alien bodies (built somewhat like insects) at Wright Patterson AFB. This information is direct evidence that at the Top Secret/Special Access level people were saying things they didn't say at the Secret level of classification.

Just because a Secret level document says something doesn't mean it is true! Subject matter, material, information, whatever you want to call it, which is very highly classified is not mentioned, and sometimes cannot even be alluded to in documents of lower classification. Statements can be made at the Secret level which tend to draw the reader away from the Top Secret truth.

Hence General Twining could put into a Secret level letter to General Schulgen a statement that there is no hard evidence. Then at another time, by directly communicating through Top Secret channels with Schulgen, he could have told him that there *was* hard evidence but it should never be mentioned in correspondence at the Secret level or discussed with people who did not have special access to the information.

Why wouldn't it be mentioned at the Secret level? Because many more people had Secret clearances than Top Secret and the more people who know, the better the chance that the information would leak out. Furthermore, people working at the Secret level, and even most of the people working at the Top Secret level, had no "need-to-know" about the existence of hard evidence. They could do their jobs perfectly well in response to a direct order without being told why the order was given.

In the realm of further speculation, assume that the Top Brass knew that saucers were real because of the hard evidence. They would not know merely from the debris (and bodies?) what saucers were doing or where they were doing it. To find out this information, they could order the Lower Brass to create an information collection and analysis project. A simple collection project would not be good enough, however, because there would be a lot of "noise," i.e., false sightings. These false sightings would obscure the "signal," namely the true saucer sightings, and only the true sightings could provide information about what the ETs were doing.

Therefore an analysis project would also be needed. It wouldn't be necessary for such a project to do any more than separate the signal from the noise. In fact, if it went beyond that—for instance, trying to determine the nature of the signal—there could be a problem for the Top Brass. Indeed, actually discovering the true nature of the signal would be the worst thing for the analysis project. For then, the "cat would be out of the bag" and the cover-up would be much more difficult to maintain. Hence, if the analysis project proposed to identify the signal as Alien Flying Craft, then the analysis leading to that identification would have to be rejected for lack of convincing proof, no matter how good the sighting information might appear to be.

Something like this is what happened when General Vandenberg rejected the Estimate of the Situation for lack of proof. The question we cannot answer based on the available documentation is, did he reject it (a) to prevent the project from finding out the truth and thereby jeopardizing the top level cover-up, (b) because he knew there was convincing sighting evidence but he didn't want the Air Force to face political consequences of admission (like "what are you doing about these saucers, sir?"), or (c) because he really was not convinced by the available evidence?

These questions cannot yet be answered. However, the important thing to understand from this discussion is that, although the publicly known history of the UFO activities of the Air Force does not prove there was a crashed ET saucer and an orchestrated effort to withhold that information, the publicly known history is also not incompatible with that possibility. That is, the history of Air Force activities could appear just as it does even if an alien spacecraft crashed at Roswell.

* * *

But enough of speculation about crashed saucers. The fundamental questions of overriding importance are these: does the information in the available files of the Air Force, the FBI and the CIA contain evidence which proves (a) that flying saucers/UFOs are real and (b) that top Air Force officials knew it but withheld that information from the public?

My answer to both questions is . . . *yes.*

As for myself, if sometime in the future a government or military official admits that there really was a crashed flying saucer near Roswell or that there were alien bodies stored in "Hanger 18" at Wright-Patterson Air Force Base in Dayton, Ohio, or that there really was an alien flying disc tested at Area 51 north of Las Vegas in Nevada . . .

I won't be a bit surprised.

Appendix 1
The Trent Photo Case

Numerous UFO sightings occurred in the late 1940s and early 1950s throughout the great northwest of the United States. Perhaps the most famous sighting of that time period occurred in the farmland some miles south of McMinnville, Oregon, (hence it is often referred to as the McMinnville Sighting).

It was just about sunset on May 11, 1950, when Evelyn Trent saw a strange object traveling roughly southwestward through the slightly hazy evening sky. At first, she thought it was a parachute drifting sideways and falling, but then she realized there was no one hanging beneath it. As it got closer she realized it was really strange and called for her husband, Paul, to get the camera. As the object slowed its flight for a minute or so he took two of the most famous UFO photos from his back yard before the object zipped away to the west.

Afterward, they didn't think too much about the sighting and their photos. Indeed, they waited a week or so to finish the roll of film before having it developed. Another week or so later, a friend took the pictures to the local banker who put them in his bank window. The photo editor of the local paper saw them, thought they were interesting, and went to the Trent house where he found the negatives—under the sofa (!). He studied the negatives and, taking into consideration the good character of the Trents, published them in early June 1950. They were an immediate national sensation, being the best UFO photos to that date. Since then, they have appeared in hundreds of UFO books and magazine articles.

Unlike most UFO photos which show distant (or small), indistinct objects in the sky, or lights at night, the image of the UFO in these photos is relatively large and sharply outlined. It is clearly not a manmade flying machine of that era (not a balloon or blimp, not an airplane or glider, not a helicopter, and not a parachute). What makes the Trent photos important for study is that they are so clear that they must be either a hoax or the real thing—an Alien Flying Craft (AFC).

Over the years, skeptics have tried to explain the Trent case as a hoax. They know the Trents did not use fancy photo manipulation such as is sometimes used to make modern UFO photo and video hoaxes and, since there is no evidence of image blur caused by rapid rotation, as one would expect if it were a thrown model like a Frisbee, the skeptics claim that the Trents used a string or thread to hang a small UFO model under the power wires that appear at the top of the picture. That would mean it was a bit more than a dozen feet away from the camera.

An astronomer, William Hartmann, who worked for the 1967-1968 University of Colorado UFO study,* examined the photos. He found no indication of a supporting thread. He then used photographic and atmospheric theory along with measurements made on the original negatives to estimate the distance to the object. He calculated that the UFO could have been thousands of feet away and therefore large, perhaps thirty feet in diameter and obviously not a model. He also interviewed the Trents and concluded that they were probably telling the truth.

The skeptic response to Hartmann's conclusion was to point out that he hadn't taken into account a particular photographic phenomenon (veiling glare) that made the calculated distance shrink to zero. I reanalyzed the original negatives and found that both Hartmann and the skeptics had forgotten a surface reflection brightness correction factor which, when included in the calculation, once again led to a distant object. Thus, the photographic and optical physics of the sighting supports the Trents' claim that it was a large object at some considerable distance.

I studied the whole McMinnville case, combining the most complete photo analysis ever done with the life history and character of the Trents. Besides talking directly to Evelyn many times in the 1970s, I interviewed others who had known the Trents for years. Everyone referred to the Trents as honest people who would never hoax anything. I concluded that the Trents told the

---

* Published by the Air Force in 1968 as the *Scientific Investigation of Unidentified Flying Objects*, mentioned in the main text.

truth and therefore the object was an AFC.*

   The Trents died in the middle 1990s. During their last interview in the early 1990s, they affirmed once again the truth of the story they had told more than forty years earlier.

---

* For the complete analysis see www.brumac.8k.com/trent1.html and www.brumac.8k.com/trent2.html.

Appendix 2

Briefing Document
for
Dr. John Gibbons,
Science Advisor to President Clinton

Ihave described how the briefing document came about. I will now discuss the format, which may seem peculiar, and the choice of information.

I knew that the typical government format for briefing high level officials was to write a document with the basic important information, the summary or "bottom line" information, right "up front." This is because the "briefee" is assumed to have very little time to read the document. On the other hand, the briefing document must be substantive, with a discussion that justifies the statements made in the first page or two. Since I didn't have time to write a complete document with a long discussion I chose the "tab" format in which the summary information (the "bottom line") was in the the first page or two and there were references to "Tabulated Information" or "Tabs" that contained the explanations of the statements in the first page.

Thus you will read a statement followed by "See Tab ....". In a real briefing book (which I did not have time to prepare) the tabs would actually be small protruding "tabs" that are attached to the first pages of each of the explanatory sections. In this case, I simply labeled the explanatory paragraphs as "Tab A" "Tab B," etc.

I tried to compress the important information, the "whole story," into one page, but was not able to do so. It actually ran about 1 1/3 pages. In the presentation below I have numbered the pages so you can see the way it was presented to Dr. Gibbons.

It was not pleasant to write because I did not have time to write the tabs as I wrote the first page summary statements. Instead, I had to guess what I would write in a Tab statement. More typically one would write each Tab explanation along with the front page reference to the Tab, so there would be a good correlation between the summary statements on the first page and the explanatory statements within the Tabs.

It took several hours to write the summary pages because at each step of the way, for each statement of fact, I had to look up information that would support the statement so I could refer to it in a Tab. This included information that I thought would indicate there were U.S. government activities, information about UFO related activities of other governments and some information that would show that UFOs are real based on government, hence "official," information. But because of the time constraint combined with the knowledge that whatever I wrote had to be supportable, I could not throw in everything including the ufological kitchen sink. I had to be selective and accurate. I could imagine the science advisor asking me to justify something I had written: "You wrote this. Prove it!"

The toughest part was, of course, the conjecture about the possibility of a crashed disc at Roswell. I could hardly ignore the information that had been accumulated in the decade before this briefing, yet I could not point to any guaranteed government documents. Therefore I had to take a tentative approach, beginning with the title which says "the Government approach to the UFO problem *as determined* by civilian UFO investigators during the last twenty years." In other words, this was based on information obtained by civilians, information that was outside of government classification channels. This was not a case of the government (a government employee) itself preparing an official briefing based on knowledge of everything that the government might be doing about UFOs.*

Anyway, what you will read below is what I came up with in less than a day. I completed the summary pages (page one and page two) and faxed it to the office of the President's Science Advisor at 7:59 a.m. on Wednesday. Note that Ron Pandolfi had exactly no input to what I wrote and, in fact, didn't find out what I had written

---

* It was two and a half years after this briefing, in 1995, that the Air Force released its "Mogul balloon" explanation of the reports of a crashed saucer near Roswell and about 2 years after that, the "dummy drop theory," to explain the reports of alien bodies.

until some time later that day after I faxed a copy to him. It took me another day to complete the section on "Tab" data, which I faxed on Thursday morning

Now comes the disappointment, so characteristic of government programs (e.g, just as a program becomes successful it is cancelled). I learned from Ron later that day that the Jones/Rockefeller/Gibbons meeting had taken place at 7:30 a.m. That is, a half hour before I faxed the briefing!

Apparently, because of Gibbons' schedule of meetings on other (more important!) topics, the UFO meeting time had been changed late Tuesday afternoon. Ron didn't know about the time switch, and I certainly didn't. Thus Gibbons had not read my briefing document by the time of the UFO meeting.

Whether or not it would have had an impact on the outcome of that meeting is now a moot point. I was told subsequently that Gibbons did eventually read what I had written, at least the first page and a half. I never had any direct correspondence with him, however, and never got any expression of interest in the topic.

* * *

Briefing on the U.S. Government Approach To the UFO Problem as Determined by Civilian Researchers During the Last Twenty Years
Sent to Dr. John Gibbons, Presidential Science Advisor during the Clinton Administration, at 0800 on April 14, 1993.

During the early summer of 1947 hundreds or thousands of people including military saw shiny circular objects flying through the sky. Civilian researchers over the last 15 years have learned from several former Air Force officers that during this time the Air Force retrieved, from the desert near Roswell, New Mexico, debris with unusual physical properties, which evidently came from a non-man made device that crashed.

Based on the testimony of numerous witnesses and government documents some civilian researchers now believe that the government, with top level authorization, took a two pronged approach to the problem. On the one hand the Air Force set up an intelligence collection program at the Secret Restricted level run by the Air Material Command (AMC) at Wright-Patterson Air Force Base in Ohio. (TAB A, TAB B) On the other hand, the government at the compartmented level carried out analysis of the retrieved material and attempted to correlate this with sighting information collected through official channels. The compartmented project was completely independent of the collection effort.

Subsequently the Air Force set up three consecutive publicly-known projects to collect and analyze civilian and military sightings which did not involve debris (Project Sign, 1948-49; Project-Grudge, 1949-1951; Project Blue Book, 1952-1969). In 1952 the Battelle Memorial Institute, under Air Force contract, began a statistical study of over 3,000 sightings between 1947 and 1952. (TAB C) The statistics showed that on the average about 20 % were not explained and that of the best sightings (best witnesses, most complete reporting) over 30% were unexplained. The report included several examples of unexplainable sightings.. (TAB D)

In 1967 the Air Force, at Congress' direction, supported an independent investigation at the University of Colorado. (TAB E) After about a year and a half the Director of the investigation concluded that "nothing had been learned" and that the Air Force should end its involvement. However, the Colorado investigators couldn't explain about 30 of the about 90 sightings it investigated. The American Institute of Aeronautics and Astronautics pointed out that the large percentage of unexplained was justification for continuing the investigation. (TAB F)

In 1969 the Air Force closed Project Blue Book and has not maintained a publicly known investigation since. However, the Air Force does admit to investigating sightings over Air Force Bases. (TAB G)

Since 1969 there have been thousands of sightings worldwide. Some have involved the U.S. military. (TAB H). One sighting was investigated by the Federal Aeronautics Administration. (TAB I)

Other governments have taken a more open attitude toward the subject and some have set up official investigating groups. (TAB J) The recent (1989-1990) sighting flap in Russia and Belgium involved military Russian and Belgian jet "chases" of UFOS. General Igor Maltsev, in charge of the Air Defense of the Moscow Area, reported publicly that he had "more than 100 visual observations" compiled by military commanders concerning a UFO that was flying near Moscow and was detected on radar (TAB K). Later, General Ivan Tretyak, Chief of all the Russian Air Forces, confirmed Maltsev's report and hinted that Soviet developments to counter Stealth might provide further information about UFOS. (TAB L) Gorbachev, during a speech to workers in the Urals in the spring of 1990 said that UFO reports should be studied. (TAB M)

Serious investigators of this subject have concluded that some unusual phenomena have, in fact, been observed visually and on instruments (TAB N). Furthermore, combining the early history of the Air Force approach to the subject with numerous documents and "leaked information" some investigators have concluded that there has been a compartmented study of debris and bodies from at least one crash of an alien craft.

* * *

Summaries of Tab-Referenced Information

TAB A:

A letter of 23 September, 1947, was sent from Lt. General Nathan Twining, Commander of the Air Materiel Command (AMC) at Wright Field (later Wright-Patterson AFB) to Brig. General George Schulgen, Chief, Air Intelligence Requirements Div., USAF. The letter describes certain characteristics of "flying saucers" as reported by military and qualified civilian witnesses and states that, after conferring with several laboratories at Wright Field, it is the opinion of AMC that "the phenomenon reported is something real and not visionary or fictitious." The letter recommends that Headquarters, Army Air Forces "issue a directive assigning a priority, security classification and Code Name for a detailed study of this matter" by the Army Air Force along with the Navy, the Atomic Energy Commission, the Joint Research and Development Board, the Air Force Scientific Advisory Group, the National Advisory Committee on Aeronautics (predecessor of NASA), the RAND Project (Research Applied to National Needs) and the NEPA Project (Nuclear Energy for the Propulsion of Aircraft).

TAB B:

A document entitled "Intelligence Requirements on Flying Saucer Type Aircraft" issued by General George Schulgen on 30

October, 1947. This was circulated to continental intelligence agencies and to military attaches throughout the world. It requested any and all information on craft that resembled flying saucers and which had unusual characteristics such as "absence of sound when operating under high performance conditions, a plan form approximating that of an oval or disc with a dome shape on the top surface, the ability to disappear by high speed or complete disintegration, the ability to appear without warning as if from extreme altitude (and) the ability to clear a path through clouds." The agents were requested to supply information on craft that had the above characteristics and which were constructed of lightweight, strong material like composite or sandwich construction utilizing various combinations of metals, metallic foils, plastics and perhaps balsa wood or similar material." (Note: "metallic foil" and "like balsa wood" were terms used by former Air Force officers to describe debris found near Roswell, New Mexico in July, 1947.) The agents were also instructed to provide information on propulsion of special design including nuclear powered craft "which would be characterized by lack of fuel systems and fuel storage space" and craft in which "the power plant would ... be an integral part of the aircraft and could possibly not be distinguished as a separate item."

TAB C:

Project Blue Book Special Report # 14, Project 10073 (Project Stork); text - 94 pages; tabulated statistical data.- 170 pages. (see page TAB C -1)

The classified version was completed in late 1953; a declassified version was published for government use only in 1955 by the Air Technical Intelligence Center. Although the unclassified report does not name the contractor, other documents in the Blue Book file make it clear that the contractor was the Battelle Memorial Institute, probably because of its proximity to Wright-Patterson Air Force Base ("home" of the Air Technical Intelligence Center, the parent organization of Project Blue Book) and because of its uniquely large (at that time) computing facility. The project carefully analyzed 3,201 sightings that occurred between June, 1947 and December, 1952. Numerous characteristics of these sightings were converted to IBM card format and statistically processed by the computer. Of these 3,201, 21.5%, were listed as "unknown." The sightings were ranked according to credibility of the observer and quality of the information supplied. Four classifications were used: Excellent, Good, Fair, Poor. Of the 213 Excellent sightings, 33% were "unknown" whereas for the 435 Poor sightings only 17% were "unknown." (see TAB C -2)

(Note: this contradicts expectation, which is based on the idea that flying saucers or UFOs are not truly extraordinary phenomena but are conventional phenomena which were misperceived by the witness(es). If UFOs are explainable, then the Excellent sightings, made by better witnesses who supply, on the average, better descriptions of the phenomena than the Poor sighting witnesses, should have a lower percentage of unexplainable sightings ("unknowns") as compared to the Poor sightings. The actual statistical result reported by Battelle shows that the unexplainable fraction of the Excellent sightings is larger than that of the Poor sightings, the opposite of what was expected. This indicates that the witnesses have, in fact, seen extraordinary phenomena.)

TAB D:
The Battelle study found 12 sightings which were so detailed that they could not be explained by any amount of rationalization. One of these, Case 10 (Rogue River, Oregon; May 24, 1949) was reported by five witnesses, two of whom reported it to the Security Office at the Ames Research Laboratory where they worked (see page TAB D - 1).

TAB E:
Scientific Study of Unidentified Flying Objects, Dr. Edward Condon, Director; E. Gilmour, Editor under contract F44620-67-C-0035 from the Air Force Office of Scientific Research. (Jan. 8, 1969)
Dr. Condon stated his opinion that "nothing has come from the study of UFOs in the past 21 years that has added to scientific knowledge. . . . (we) conclude that further extensive study of UFOs probably cannot be justified in the expectation that science will be

advanced thereby." However, the study left unexplained approximately one third of the sightings it investigated.

TAB F:

"UFO: An Appraisal of the Problem," written by the UFO Subcommittee of the American Institute of Aeronautics and Astronautics, *Astronautics and Aeronautics Magazine*, November, 1970, pp. 49-51.

The UFO subcommittee found no "basis for his (Condon's) prediction that nothing of scientific value will come of further studies." The subcommittee pointed out that "it is difficult to ignore the small residue of well-documented but unexplainable cases which form the hard core of the UFO controversy" and that, furthermore, "a phenomenon with such a high ratio of unexplained cases (about 30%) should arouse sufficient scientific curiosity to continue its study."

TAB G:

Document entitled "Alleged Sightings of Unidentified Aerial Lights in the Restricted Test Range," filed by Special Agent Richard Doty at the Air Force Office of Special Investigations, Kirtland AFB, Albuquerque, N.M., 9 September, 1980.

This document reports several sightings of lighted objects between 8 August and 9 September, including a "round disc shaped object" with a bright light which landed in a secured area at night and subsequently, as a security guard approached, took off in a vertical direction at a high rate of speed" with no sound. This document also reports that "the USAF no longer investigates such sightings unless they occur on a USAF base." (see Tab H)

TAB H:

Military reports of UFOs include:

Hunter Army Airfield, Georgia, 8 September 1973, 0220 hours; a UFO was sighted by military policemen was traveling at a high rate but subsequently stopped and hovered for about 15 minutes in front of them while flashing brilliant blue, white and amber lights. It then flew off.

Near Mansfield, Ohio, 18 October, 1973, 2305 hours: a UFO

approached an Army helicopter at some speed causing the captain to put the helicopter into a dive, The UFO appeared to stop over the helicopter before traveling on. After it departed the captain found that the helicopter was at a greater altitude than when he began the dive.

NORAD documents indicate penetrations by unidentified craft over several Strategic Air Command Bases, including Loring AFB (Maine), Wurtsmith AFB (Michigan), Minot AFB (North Dakota), Malmstrom AFB (Montana) and Falconbridge Radar Site (Ontario) during late October and early November, 1975. The NORAD Command Directors Log and the 24th NORAD Region Senior Director's Log (Malmstrom AFB) show that on 8 November 1975 at 0635Z a Sabotage Alert Team (SAT) reported a UFO with white lights and a red light 50 yards behind the white lights. Ten minutes later height finder radar detected objects at 10-13,000 feet. At 0753Z two F- 106's were scrambled out of Great Falls to check on an object tracked on radar at 12,000 feet which was seen by ground Sabotage Alert Teams (SAT). Over the next hour and a half jets were scrambled several times but never made visual contact because, according to the SAT, the object decreased its altitude to about 300 feet and turned off its lights whenever the jets approached over the mountains. (Note: the object was hovering near a missile launch site.) Similar sightings occurred on the next night and also on the 10th of November. Also on the 10th, Minot Air Force Station reported a bright object "about the size of a car" that passed slowly over the station at an altitude less than 2,000 feet. No noise was heard.

Tehran, Iran, 19 September, 1976, 0130 local: Iranian Air Force General Yousefi was alerted by Mehrebad Airport Tower that a UFO was hovering over Tehran. Youssefi spotted it himself and launched an F-4 from Shaharoki AFB at 0130 local. As the jet approached the bright light over Tehran and reached a radar distance of 25 nm it lost all communications (UHF and intercom). It turned and headed back to base. Youssefi ordered a second jet to be launched at 0140. The second jet approached on afterburner and the radar determined a rate of closure (VC) of 150 nautical miles per hour. However, as the range approached 25 nm the VC decreased to zero. The object was giving off rapidly flashing colors of blue, green, red and orange. The jet and the light were headed toward the Iranian border when the light released a smaller light, which the pilot took as a threatening move and commenced to arm an AIM-9 missile. At that time he lost all communication (UHF and intercom) and turned away from the chase.

Fort Ritchie, MD, 30 July 1976, 0345 EDT: Ft. Ritchie called the National Military Command Center to report that they had received reports of UFOs from civilians near Mt. Airy, MD at "0130, from two separate patrols from Site R" at 0255, from a Desk Sergeant at Site R at 0300 and from an Army police Sergeant at 0345. The 0255 sighting was of "3 oblong objects with a reddish tint moving east to west." The 0300 sighting was of "a UFO over the ammo storage area at 100 to 200 yards altitude."

Mariano Melgar Air Force Base, La Joya, Peru, 9 May 1980 (morning): a group of Air Force Officers saw a round UFO hovering near the airfield. The air commander scrambled an SU-22 aircraft to intercept, but the UFO outran it. A second sighting occurred at night, 10 May. Again a jet was scrambled but the UFO outran it.

Kirtland Air Force Base, Albuquerque, NM; August, 1980: security guards at the Manzano Weapons Storage Area (nuclear weapons storage) east of Kirtland AFB reported that they saw a lighted object performing odd maneuvers over the Coyote Canyon area of the Department of Defense Restricted Range at 2350 hours, August 8, 1980. This lighted object descended behind some small hills, from their point of view. A Sandia Security guard on routine patrol observed the light behind an alarmed structure on Coyote Canyon Road and went to investigate at 0020 hours, August 9, 1980 (i.e., 30 minutes later). As he approached he thought it was a helicopter but then he saw it was a "round disk shaped object." He attempted to radio for help but the radio did not work. As he approached the object armed with a shotgun it accelerated upward at a great rate of speed. The Manzano guards saw the light proceed straight upward and disappear.

Lake Erie, east of Cleveland, Ohio, 4 March 1988, 2035 local: civilians reported to the Coast Guard a large, lighted object hovering over lake. Two Coast Guard unit members went to the viewing site and confirmed the object. The civilians reported that 3 to 5 smaller lighted objects had come from the larger ones and these "were zipping around rather quickly. These objects had red, green, white and yellow lights on them that strobed intermittently. They also had the ability to stop and hover in mid-flight." The two members of the unit reported the same activity and watched for approximately 1 hour before reporting that the large object was almost on the ice. They reported that the ice was cracking and moving abnormal amounts as the object came closer to it." After a period of time and numerous "activities" by the object, the unit members reported that "1 object was moving toward them at a high speed and low to the ice. Mobile 02 backed down the hill they had been on and when they went back to the hill, the object was gone." The Coast Guard reports that "the unit was unable to identify any of the objects using binoculars and after contacting local police and airports this unit was unable to identify the objects." (Note: a civilian took a photograph of one of the small objects flying by. It shows a glowing triangular shaped object.)

TAB I:

The Federal Aviation Administration investigated sightings by a Japanese air crew flying a jumbo jet over Alaska in November, 1986. The FAA could not explain the visual sightings by the crew of two very unusual lighted objects which held station ahead of the jet for many minutes before moving to the left and then behind. Occasionally Elmendorf AFB radar detected a non-identifiable target in the vicinity of the jet. The weather radar on the jet also detected a large target.

TAB J:

In 1977 France set up a special investigating group (GEPAN) under the auspices of the French National Space Agency (CNES). (GEPAN has published reports of investigations, including an investigation of ground effects (after a UFO was seen to land and take off) which could not be explained. In 1985 the Commission for the Investigation of Anomalous Atmospheric Phenomena was established under the Academy of Sciences of the Soviet Union with Cosmonaut Pavel Popovich as its director. More recently UFO investigation has been carried out by the SOYUZUFOTSENTR (Unified UFO Center) under the Academy of Sciences. Rather high level contacts have been established between American and Russian investigators in recent years. The Chinese government announced the founding of the Chinese Society of UFO Research as a branch of the Chinese Academy of Social Sciences in 1980.

TAB K:

General Igor Maltsev reported in RABOCHAYA TRIBUNE (Workers Tribune newspaper), 19 April, 1990, that he had reports of "more than 100 visual observations" compiled by commanders of several air defense units of the Moscow Military District of a UFO (or UFOs) which was seen in the area of Pereslavl-Zalesskiy (northeast of Moscow) on 21 March, 1990. Maltsev included with his report to the newspaper 5 testimonials, including a report by a pilot who flew over the object and a report from a ground radar tracking station. The pilot saw only two lights and a dimly perceived silhouette of the object against city lights. The radar post reported a visual sighting of a rapidly moving, shining object with red lights and another with white lights that followed the first. The report included times, azimuths and distances of the reported objects.

TAB L:

General Ivan Tretyak was interviewed by a writer for LITERATURNAYA GAZETA (Literary Gazette magazine) in November, 1990. Tretyak was the Soviet Deputy Minister of Defense as well as being the Commander in Chief of the Air Defense Forces and General of the Army. He said that during the events reported by Maltsev one UFO had been photographed and optical and thermal signals had been detected by the aircraft pilot. However, the aircraft radar did not detect the object.

TAB M:

Optical, magnetic and acoustic devices and instruments have recorded or have been affected by the presence of UFOs. Optical devices include simple cameras, movie cameras, cinetheodolites, videocameras and even cameras fitted with diffraction gratings. Magnetic sensors include simple compasses and magnetometers. Acoustic sensors (microphones) have, occasionally, detected sounds associated with the presence of UFOs, although most often no sound is heard. In 1947 a witness reported that his compass rotated as several flying saucers passed overhead. Years later another witness noticed that a saucer seen in the daytime near the horizon appeared to have dark rings around it when viewed through polarized glasses, but not when viewed directly, possibly a result of Faraday rotation in the atmosphere caused by an extremely large magnetic field. A scientist working for the French National Space Agency in the early 1970s determined that there was a inverse relationship between the vertical component of the geomagnetic field measured at field stations scattered throughout France and distance to a reported UFO. Self-propelled machines such as automobiles have been affected in the presence of UFOs. One incident involved two combines operating in a field of grain at night. During the passage of a glowing UFO the gasoline powered combine stopped, whereas a diesel type continued to operate. In April, 1949 at the White Sands proving ground high flying (estimate 150,000 feet) UFOs were tracked and filmed with cinetheodolite cameras. The size was estimated from the image size and the triangulated altitude to be about 30 feet. Electronic devices have been affected, including gyrocompasses (TAB H - Mansfield, Ohio, 1973; the gyrocompass had to be repaired after the incident) and radios (TAB H - Tehran, Iran, 1976; Kirtland AFB, 1980). Plants have been affected by UFOs. An incident in 1980 in France was investigated by GEPAN (see TAB J). The GEPAN report shows that after a circular UFO landed on a lawn (as reported by the witness) the chlorophyll in the grass was affected by an amount which diminished as $1/r$ where r is the distance from the center of the landing spot. Plant scientists could not explain how the chlorophyll change had been caused. UFOs have been detected on radar coincident with visual sightings (TAB H - NORAD documents regarding Malmstrom AFB, 1975; Tehran, Iran, 1976; TAB I - Jumbo Jet over Alaska, 1986; TAB K - Moscow area, 1990).

Epilogue

Several years later, I learned that some UFO researchers had obtained, through the Freedom of Information Act, documents held by the White House Office of Science and Technology Policy (OSTP) that referred to the Gibbons meeting.

In August 1996, I requested the documents (addressing the Executive Office of the President, Office of Science and Technology Policy, Washington, DC 20502). I received a letter indicating that they had found 44 documents related to Rockefeller's attempts to get John Gibbons or President Clinton (or Mrs. Clinton) or someone to do something about UFOs. I was amused to find that, although many letters to Gibbons on the subject of UFOs were included in the document release, my briefing document was not included.

Index

About the Author

Dr. Bruce Maccabee has a Ph.D. in physics and was employed for thirty-six years at the Naval Surface Warfare Center doing research on numerous projects, including generation of underwater sound with lasers, high power beam control systems for use in the Strategic Defense Initiative and defense against chemical/biological attacks.

He became seriously interested in the UFO phenomenon in the late 1960s, while working for his Ph. D. at The American University. During the 1970s, he joined the National Investigations Committee on Aerial Phenomena (NICAP) and the Mutual UFO Network (MUFON) and helped to found the Fund for UFO Research (FUFOR). He analyzed sighting reports and found reasonable explanations for many sightings, but not all.

Over the years, he has investigated and reported on numerous sightings, including the Gemini 11 and Skylab 3 astronauts sightings, the famous McMinnville UFO photos of 1950, the 1978 New Zealand sightings, the 1986 Japan Airlines sighting, the Gulf Breeze sightings from 1987 to 1996, and the Mexican Air Force sighting of 2004. He also studied the history of sightings and the U.S. Air Force response as presented in the files of Projects Sign, Grudge, and Blue Book. He was the first to obtain the secret FBI file on "flying discs," wherein he found indisputable evidence that the Air Force withheld—some might say covered up—important UFO evidence from the American people.

By chance, during the 1980s, his Navy work allowed him to establish a decade-long investigation of the CIA. The story of this investigation is published here for the first time.

A more complete biography/resume of Bruce Maccabee is available at www.brumac.8k.com, wherein there are reports on numerous case investigations and analyses of historical information.

Also by Richard Dolan Press

Grant Cameron and T. Scott Crain, Jr. *UFOs, Area 51, and Government Informants: A Report on Government Involvement in UFO Crash Retrievals*.

Richard M. Dolan, *UFOs for the 21ˢᵗ Century Mind: A Fresh Guide to an Ancient Mystery*.

Richard M. Dolan, *UFOs and the National Security State: The Cover-Up Exposed, 1973-1991*.

Chase Kloetkze with Richard M. Dolan. *Admissible: The Field Manual for Investigating UFOs, Paranormal Activity, and Strange Creatures*.

Eve Lorgen. *The Dark Side of Cupid: Love Affairs, the Supernatural and Energy Vampirism*.

Philip Mantle. *Once Upon A Missing Time: A Novel of Abduction*.

David Marler. *Triangular UFOs: An Estimate of the Situation*.

Richard Sauder, Ph.D. *Hidden in Plain Sight: Beyond the X-Files*.

Robert M. Wood, Ph.D. *Alien Viruses: Crashed UFOs, MJ-12, & Biowarfare*.

http://richarddolanpress.com

Made in the USA
Coppell, TX
07 March 2021